Leonardo da Vinci and the Italian High Renaissance

George R. Bent, Ph.D.

PUBLISHED BY:

THE GREAT COURSES
Corporate Headquarters
4840 Westfields Boulevard, Suite 500
Chantilly, Virginia 20151-2299
Phone: 1-800-832-2412
Fax: 703-378-3819
www.thegreatcourses.com

Printed in the United States of America

George R. Bent, Ph.D.

Sidney Gause Childress Professor in the Arts
Washington and Lee University

Professor George R. Bent has taught in the Department of Art and Art History at Washington and Lee University since 1993. The holder of the Sidney Gause Childress Professorship in the Arts, Professor Bent offers courses on the art and architecture of Northern and Southern Europe from the fall of the Roman Empire to the end of the Renaissance—including lecture courses on medieval art in Byzantium and Italy, Italian Renaissance art, and Northern Renaissance art as well as seminars on the art of Venice, the High Renaissance in Italy, and Gothic art in France.

A two-time holder of Fulbright Scholarships to Italy, Professor Bent received his B.A. from Oberlin College in 1985 and his Ph.D. in Art History from Stanford University in 1993. He cofounded Washington and Lee's interdisciplinary program in Medieval and Renaissance Studies in 1995, chaired it from 2000 to 2003, served as Associate Dean of the College from 2003 to 2006, and currently serves as chair of the Department of Art and Art History.

Professor Bent's early scholarly work focused on issues of artistic production, the function of liturgical images, and institutional patronage in early Renaissance Florence. He is the author of *Monastic Art in Lorenzo Monaco's Florence*, a book that addresses these subjects through an examination of panel paintings, manuscript illuminations, and religious rituals performed in the monastery of Santa Maria degli Angeli from 1300 to 1415.

Professor Bent's current research interests revolve around paintings produced for public spaces in Florence between 1250 and 1450, which have caused him to consider works such as Madonnas in street-corner tabernacles, frescoes of virtuous heroes in guildhalls, cult images that worked miracles for common people, and images of political propaganda that decorated offices of state bureaucrats.

Professor Bent and his wife, Lorriann Olan, have three children, each of whom tolerates their father's obsession with the art and culture of the Italian Renaissance. ■

Table of Contents

INTRODUCTION

LECTURE GUIDES

Table of Contents

Leonardo da Vinci and the Italian High Renaissance

Scope:

Leonardo da Vinci is one of the most recognized figures in history: a master of art, science, and engineering, the consummate "Renaissance man" who excelled in a wide array of fields. He was regarded as one of his day's most insightful mathematicians. He could cast figures in bronze. He understood warfare so well that rulers periodically sought his views on military strategy. He knew more about the physics of motion, energy, and flight than anyone else of his age. And he possessed a vision of the distant future that was just as prescient as it was daring.

Yet while he worked on projects ranging from new bridges to the diversion of rivers to war machines, Leonardo da Vinci also produced some of the most important—and most famous—artistic images of all time. Visitors flock to the Louvre to swarm around the small portrait of the *Mona Lisa.* Leonardo's mural of *The Last Supper* was understood during his lifetime to be the pinnacle of contemporary painting. And his drawing of the *Vitruvian Man* has been reproduced in a variety of contexts to symbolize human potential and accomplishments, most recently on the Euro coin minted by the Italian government in celebration of its cultural patrimony.

This course examines the life and work of Leonardo da Vinci from all of these perspectives, and more. But the course also considers the context in which Leonardo da Vinci lived, the period from 1452 to 1519—dates that also can be said to bracket the period commonly known as the High Renaissance. This was a great age of intellectual advancement, as thinkers began to seek solutions that went beyond traditional wisdom passed down from the Middle Ages, or even from antiquity. This was an age of geographic exploration, as navigators boldly set out to test their hypotheses about the dimensions of our globe. This was an age of tremendous political instability and rapid consolidation, as European statesmen collected armies and then turned them loose against the vulnerable city-states of Italy. And it was an age of tremendous political intrigue, a time when the papacy managed to transform Rome from a decaying city into one of the world's most magnificent—and, in the process, nearly realized the day's ultimate dream of reviving the Roman Empire of antiquity. This was the world that shaped Leonardo's thinking and actions—a world that was, in turn, also directly and profoundly influenced by Leonardo.

In this course, we will examine the 19 paintings that comprise Leonardo's surviving output as a painter—paintings we are certain are his, thanks to archival evidence and art-historical consensus based on stylistic grounds. In our analysis of paintings like *The Last Supper*, *The Adoration of the Magi*, and the *Mona Lisa*, we address the issues and ideas that Leonardo wished to convey in his art. Thanks to drawings by Leonardo and by others, we can also consider lost pictures—like *Leda and the Swan* and the *Battle of Anghiari*—which demonstrate Leonardo's desire to experiment with both subject matter and artistic technique, sometimes with disastrous consequences. We will also look at several paintings by followers that have at various times been attributed to Leonardo himself.

Leonardo's truly exceptional output as a draftsman will be a common thread throughout this course. Leonardo was a member of the first generation of early modern artists to use paper as a tool for exploration and experimentation, and the sheer volume of his drawings and notations can overwhelm when considered in their entirety. While considering only a small subset of his entire output, we will focus on understanding his drawings both as independent works of art and as thought pieces used to work out scientific and technical problems. The drawings subjects' range across many fields, including physics, engineering, architecture, and anatomy—all of them produced by one of the world's first truly modern scientists.

Leonardo's unpublished writings will also receive our consideration at important moments in this course. We will hear his words of self-promotion to the ruler of Milan; his musings about mechanics, aviation, and hydraulics; and his extraordinary observations of the human body. And we will hear Leonardo celebrate the underappreciated glories of the painterly profession, as well as his profoundly felt belief that painters should be considered intellectuals—superior even to poets or sculptors.

The course moves chronologically through Leonardo's career, beginning with an overview of his life and work, following him from the village of Vinci

to Florence to Milan—all the way to his last years in Franc
also stop periodically to consider his interests and innovations
We will meet the power brokers whose decisions affected his
and his actions, and we will examine the events of the late 15
16th centuries that, directly or indirectly, shaped Leonardo's own
and visions of what the future might hold. For Leonardo da Vinc
his fame not only because of his truly exceptional gifts as an artist, t
because of his ability to foresee the things that people would value and
and how they might live their lives, hundreds of years in the future. ■

Colossus—The Sculpture for Ludovico Sforza

Lecture 19

Leonardo was not trained as a sculptor, but he was trained by a sculptor, and that was good enough for Ludovico Sforza, who wanted a bronze equestrian monument erected in Milan to help legitimize his family's rule. Leonardo's design was incredibly ambitious and, unsurprisingly, went through numerous iterations, but in the end, it was not Leonardo's perfectionism but political upheaval that doomed the project to failure.

Ludovico's Dream of a Monument

- The letter Leonardo wrote to Ludovico Sforza to promote his own skills ended with a boast about his skills as a sculptor in "marble, bronze, and clay." He added, "Moreover, a bronze horse could be made that will be to the immortal glory and eternal honor of the lord your father of blessed memory and of the illustrious house of Sforza."

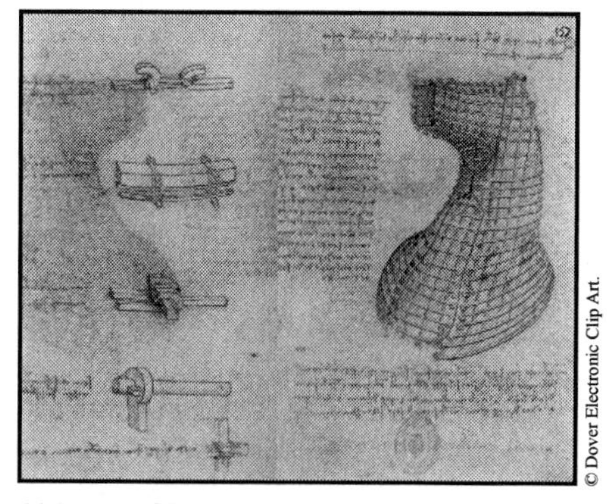

Although Sforza's monument never came to pass, the sketches survive.

- Most scholars believe the letter we currently have is a copy, since the handwriting is not Leonardo's. Some believe it was written well after Leonardo's arrival at court, maybe as late as 1485, and was more like a contract between Leonardo and Ludovico crafted to spell out the tasks that Leonardo was expected to execute in return for his stipend.

- The fact that the letter ends with a reference to sculpture in general, and to a large bronze horse in particular, should signal to us the importance of these aspects of Leonardo's job. This statue may have been the single most important thing that Ludovico wanted Leonardo to do.

- Ludovico was anxious to create an **equestrian monument** even before Leonardo arrived on the scene. He appears to have inherited the idea from his brother, Galeazzo, who in 1472 had made inquiries about the availability of a local sculptor to create the likeness of his father, Francesco, astride a horse.

- Ludovico revived the idea almost as soon as he took control of Milan. The monument was the sort of thing that could help legitimize the Sforza reign. Indeed, Ludovico believed it was a symbol he quite literally could not live without.

- Leonardo was not a complete neophyte when it came to three-dimensional art, thanks to his experience in Verrocchio's workshop. But it was more than a bit presumptuous for Leonardo to claim that this work had prepared him to cast a monument that would make all others before it pale by comparison.

- In the 1480s, Ludovico still held the official title of Regent of Milan. He believed that the monument, as a symbol, would confirm his hold on the city, yet he understood that a monument to himself would be unacceptable self-aggrandizement. Ludovico also could not feature his violent brother Galeazzo for obvious reasons.

- Thus, Ludovico settled on featuring his father, Francesco, who had earned the respect of his peers and enemies during his reign. Most people acknowledged that Francesco had stabilized the city-state after a period of crisis.

- Even after hiring Leonardo, Ludovico was not confident that he was up to the challenge. A letter written in 1489 by the Florentine ambassador to Lorenzo the Magnificent tells us that the Milanese court was filled with concern over Leonardo's ability to complete the project as designed.

- Lorenzo the Magnificent appears to have suggested **Antonio Pollaiuolo**, a Florentine sculptor of note, as an alternative to Leonardo. In 1489, Pollaiuolo submitted his vision to Ludovico.

- Leonardo was in jeopardy of losing this commission, but by this time, he had some significant connections at court, and he managed to outmaneuver Pollaiuolo. By 1490, Ludovico approved Leonardo's plans to move ahead with the project.

The Technical Challenge

- Casting a life-size horse and rider in bronze was spectacularly complicated. Just because Donatello had managed to do it once in the 15th century did not mean it was included in every apprentice's training.

- Among the artistic concerns Leonardo had to address were the size and appearance of the figures; who would see the figures, from what distance, and from what angles; and how could the figures' weight be distributed evenly, yet still show movement and vibrancy?

- Leonardo also faced many technical challenges, such as how to obtain the expensive and precious bronze; how many pieces to cast the piece in and how to assemble them; whether to cast them as solid or hollow figures and, if hollow, how to fill the mold properly; where to find the space, equipment, and assistants to cast such a large piece; and how to move such a large but delicate piece from the foundry to its final destination.

- In this age of innovation, Leonardo also knew that he would not be able to get away with copying what sculptors had done before him. Donatello's *Gattamelata* had set a standard; Verrocchio was set on surpassing Donatello. Leonardo's task was to outshine them both.

- His first idea was to approximate Verrocchio's idea of a man and beast; the earliest drawings show a sophisticated composition that emphasizes motion, action, and violent energy. The rider—Francesco Sforza—struggles with his horse in much the same way that Man battles Nature, implying that the Sforza family has the skill to tame it.

- Leonardo realized that to outdo his master, he had to go beyond mere compositional ingenuity. He decided to make his statue both bigger and more lifelike than his predecessors' and tripled its size. The 8-foot-tall horse would now be a 24-foot-tall horse.

- This decision forced Leonardo to compromise elsewhere: He would have to eliminate the rider altogether because it would require too much bronze. The horse alone would weigh about 60 tons.

- Leonardo planned to make the most life-like, naturalistically faithful horse ever sculpted. He bought and studied books about horses and their anatomy, about the history of the horse from antiquity to the present, and about the characteristics and qualities of various kinds of horses.

- He spent the better part of a year in these studies. Following this, he ventured into Ludovico's stables to draw stallions from life. In the end, Leonardo settled on a traditional posture for the horse, striding forward on three legs with the front left hoof elevated.

- Leonardo was faced with the most daunting part of the project—how to cast it. This time-honored but complicated process, known as **cire perdu** (or lost wax), required

    - caking an actual size, fully detailed clay model of the sculpture;

    - creating separate molds for each piece to be cast;

    - caking a consistent layer of wax, roughly an inch thick, all the way around the clay model;

- adding a second clay layer on top of the hardened wax and carving channels into it;

- burying the whole model and pouring tons of molten bronze into it, liquefying the wax, which flows away;

- unearthing the model, chipping off the outer clay shell, and digging out the inner clay shell;

- finally, pulling the bronze pieces out of the earth, smoothing and polishing it, and loading it onto a cart to be taken to its final destination.

- Cire perdu had never been attempted on this scale before, but Ludovico approved Leonardo's project, and Leonardo began the inner model in 1492 or early 1493. Ludovico ordered the purchase of 75 tons of bronze for the project.

What Became of Leonardo's Colossus?

- The clay model was finished and installed in 1493 in time for the marriage of Ludovico's niece to the Holy Roman Emperor. Leonardo had the horse erected inside the Milan Cathedral, where the wedding took place.

- Through this marriage, Ludovico secured the emperor's support as the legitimate ruler of Milan, and the sculpture symbolized that triumph. It was, in many ways, the very apex of his reign. And then, everything fell apart.

- Recall that Ludovico had invited the French army into Italy to destroy the Kingdom of Naples, only to have the French king turn on him. He had to divert the 75 tons of bronze designated for the equestrian monument to make cannons to fight the French. The monument would never be cast.

- The French were expelled from Italy in 1495, but they returned in 1499 under the command of a new king. They quickly seized Milan and held it. Leonardo was there to witness it all. He may also have been there to witness the destruction of his clay colossus at the hands of the French army, who used it for target practice, but of his reaction, we have no record whatsoever.

Important Terms

cire perdue: In French, literally "lost wax"; a technique used to cast figures in bronze. A clay mold is covered with wax, which is in turn encased in a shell. Molten bronze is poured between the shell and the mold, replacing the wax, which melts and drips out from between the two surfaces. The shell is then chipped away and the mold dug out from the hardened bronze encasement.

equestrian monument: A large-scale sculpture of a horse and rider.

Name to Know

Pollaiuolo, Antonio (1433–1498): Prominent sculptor, painter, draftsman, and printmaker, Pollaiuolo and his brother Piero operated one of Florence's largest artistic workshops. He designed the sculptural tomb monument for Pope Sixtus IV and painted the influential altarpiece of *The Martyrdom of Saint Sebastian*, now in London.

Suggested Reading

Ahl, *Leonardo a Vinci's Sforza Monumental Horse.*

Brugnoli, "The Sculptor."

Radke, *Leonardo da Vinci and the Art of Sculpture.*

Colossus—The Sculpture for Ludovico Sforza
Lecture 19—Transcript

In the remarkable letter that Leonardo da Vinci wrote to Ludovico Sforza to promote his own skills, the painter from Florence billed himself not only as an engineer and inventor. Let's recall that Leonardo ended his letter with the following lines:

> I can carry out sculpture in marble, bronze, and clay; and in painting can do any kind of work as well as any man, whoever he may be. Moreover, a bronze horse could be made that will be to the immortal glory and eternal honor of the lord your father of blessed memory and of the illustrious house of Sforza.

Now most scholars believe that the letter we currently have is a copy of the original, based largely on the fact that the handwriting is not Leonardo's. The letter is widely considered to have been, basically, a job application, with the writer alerting a potential employer of his skills and his talents.

But some believe the letter we now have was actually written well after Leonardo's arrival at court—maybe as late as 1485. Maybe what we have instead is a job description that's more like a contract between Leonardo and Ludovico. In this scenario, the items in the document were crafted to spell out clearly the tasks that Leonardo was expected to execute, in return for which Leonardo would be entitled to the stipend that Ludovico offered to pay him.

These are intriguing possibilities, and I must say that I rather like the idea that the letter we have from Leonardo was written after he had started working at court, and that the letter reflects something of an itemized list of the artist's responsibilities. Now, there's no smoking gun to prove or disprove this theory, but if it was a contract, that might explain why someone went to the trouble to make a copy of Leonardo's original letter.

Anyway, the fact that the letter ends with a reference to sculpture in general, and to a large bronze horse in particular, should signal to us the importance of these aspects of Leonardo's job, as well as the emphasis placed on them by Ludovico Sforza. The horse obviously mattered to him.

In fact, this statue may have been the single most important thing that Ludovico Sforza wanted Leonardo to do as a member of his court in Milan.

Ludovico, it turns out, was anxious to create an equestrian monument even before Leonardo arrived on the scene in Milan in the early 1480s. He appears to have inherited the idea from his brother, Galeazzo, who in 1472 had made inquiries about the availability of a local sculptor to create the likeness of his father, Francesco, astride a horse. But that project had never gotten very far, and the idea appeared to have died with Galeazzo when he was assassinated in 1476.

But Ludovico revived the idea almost as soon as he wrestled control of Milan away from Galeazzo's wife and son in 1480. There was something noble and important about a bronze equestrian monument: It was the sort of thing that could help legitimize the Sforza position in Milan. Indeed, Ludovico believed it was a symbol that he quite literally couldn't live without. He made inquiries to Lorenzo the Magnificent in Florence about finding someone experienced in the art of bronze sculpture, and we've always presumed that the target he had in mind was a familiar character in our story—Andrea del Verrocchio.

Verrocchio, of course, was the most gifted bronze sculptor in Italy at the time, and maybe in all of Europe. The Venetians, you might recall, had identified him as the artist they wanted to design and produce the enormous equestrian monument to Bartolomeo Colleoni right around 1480, at the time that Leonardo was beginning to consider his own future in Florence. Verrocchio accepted their offer, and he moved his studio to Venice in order to focus his energies entirely on the equestrian monument in Venice. Given this level of involvement, Verrocchio was unavailable to help Ludovico in Milan, which caused Il Moro to look elsewhere for assistance.

Now Ludovico was a product of his times, and in these times it was not at all uncommon for patrons who could not secure the services of a particular master to instead approach that master's most gifted student with an offer for a commission. Pedigree matters, after all, and in the Renaissance it mattered even more than it does today—and that's where Leonardo stepped in. Now although Leonardo had been largely responsible for painterly projects during his partnership with Verrocchio, he wasn't a complete neophyte when it came to three-dimensional art.

Leonardo had been a member of Verrocchio's workshop when the bronze Putto with Dolphin had been cast. He had been on hand, and had maybe even posed, for Verrocchio's David, for the Medici villa in Careggi. And Leonardo, we now believe, had participated in the decorative elements adorning the tomb of Piero de'Medici in the Old Sacristy of the Florentine Church of San Lorenzo. You remember the vines and the turtles that make that casket so unusual.

While Leonardo's participation in those projects is largely speculative, we do have written confirmation that Leonardo helped Verrocchio with one very important project dealing with metal work. In the early 16th century, when trying to work out a problem in one of his notes, Leonardo urged himself to remember the way Verrocchio and his fellow workshop assistants had soldered the bronze orb on the lantern of the Florence cathedral back in the early 1470s.

Although Verrocchio led the sculptural part of that workshop, Leonardo had received enough training in the medium to be more than just proficient in his abilities. We think that Verrocchio trained Leonardo well in metal working, and when he petitioned Ludovico Sforza for the post of court engineer and sculptor, he did so with confidence that he could handle the tasks that his new patron had in mind for him.

Still, it was more than just a bit presumptuous for Leonardo to claim that his periodic work with Verrocchio on works of modest size had prepared him to make a horse that by all accounts was intended to make all others before it pale by comparison. This was more than just a matter of scaling up early works to fit the proportions desired by the patron. It was much more than that. For Ludovico Sforza didn't want just any old statue. He needed something that would do no less than symbolize the very legitimacy of his reign.

Remember that Ludovico's entire regime was always quite literally one famine or one diplomatic crisis away from total collapse. The status of his father, Francesco, as a mercenary soldier and his grab of power in 1451 had always called into question the legitimacy of the Sforza legacy.

The outrageous cruelty, the brutality, and the abuse of power by Ludovico's brother, Galeazzo, only intensified the sentiments of those who opposed Sforza rule. And in the 1480s, Ludovico still held the official title of "Regent of Milan," for his little nephew Giangaleazzo was the rightful heir to Galeazzo's inheritance. Everyone knew, of course, that Giangaleazzo wouldn't get near the throne of Milan as long as his uncle stood in his way, and that meant that Giangaleazzo's supporters weren't at all supportive of Ludovico's role as regent. His position in Milan was tenuous at best, and Ludovico knew it.

The bronze monument, he hoped, would help convince his subjects that Ludovico was the legitimate ruler of Milan: And because he believed that this symbol would confirm his hold on a city that was still, technically, under the rule of his little nephew, the bronze horse came to represent the very core of Ludovico's artistic and cultural program for the city that he governed.

Wisely, though, the ruler of Milan recognized that the identity of the rider atop the horse would matter greatly: Placing himself there would be an unacceptable statement of self-aggrandizement that even a 15th-century Italian prince wouldn't dare risk—it was a much wiser policy to feign humility than to trumpet one's own success, for mobs in that period didn't take kindly to usurpers gloating over their victories. The last thing Ludovico wanted to witness was a mob pulling a set of ropes attached to his effigy, toppling his equestrian monument to the ground in the center of town.

And Ludovico couldn't feature his violent brother Galeazzo there, either, for obvious reasons. Thus, Ludovico settled on focusing the project on the power and virtues of his father, Francesco, who had initiated the Sforza line only 30 years earlier after the Visconti lineage had crashed and burned in 1447. Francesco, although not noble born, had earned the respect of his peers and enemies during his reign, and most people acknowledged that Francesco had stabilized the city-state after a period of crisis. The father was the best person to commemorate in a public monument, and even Galeazzo had understood this when he initiated his short-lived equestrian project in 1472.

Equestrian monuments were only gradually becoming images of prestige in Italy at this time. Only one example in bronze had been made in Italy in the 15th century as Ludovico considered his options in the early 1480s: That one was in Padua, about 100 miles east of Milan, just outside of Venice, and had been designed and cast in 1453 by the Florentine sculptor Donatello.

In this bronze horse Donatello chose to create a frontally composed sculpture that allows us to see the horse and rider facing one direction pretty much irrespective of where we stand in relationship to the sculpture. For example, if we stand to the side, both horse and rider take on a profile position where we can see the armor that Gattamelata wears, but also we can pay attention to the way that a diagonal has been created by Donatello through the use of the scepter and also the sword at Gattamelata's side.

More pressing for Ludovico, though, was the fact that Andrea del Verrocchio had already begun to work on a similar commission offered to him by the city of Venice that would place in a public piazza a vibrant and triumphant bronze equestrian monument of the local condottiere named Bartolomeo Colleoni.

Now, Verrocchio is intentionally, we think, trying to play off what Donatello had already done. Although now, Verrocchio lifts one of the hooves of that horse up off the ground. Both the rider and that beast twist their heads, turn their bodies, and give us a sense of genuine anger, power, and victory, I would argue.

Verrocchio was surely Ludovico's first choice to sculpt his equestrian monument for he knew that the Colleoni design was going to top Donatello. But Verrocchio was obviously already spoken for. With no other bronze caster readily available, the next best option was Verrocchio's protégé: And when word came to the Sforza court—perhaps from Lorenzo the Magnificent himself—that Leonardo was interested in full-time employment at his court, Ludovico snapped him up, and rather quickly at that. Indeed, there's a good chance that Ludovico remembered Leonardo's diplomatic mission to

Milan that reputedly featured the painter playing the silver lyre before the assembled court—so maybe we shouldn't be so surprised that Leonardo got this job.

Still, even after hiring on Leonardo as his court engineer with the assumption that he'd complete the equestrian monument, Ludovico Sforza was not completely confident that Leonardo was up to the challenge. We're told in a letter, written in 1489 by the Florentine ambassador sent to Lorenzo the Magnificent, that the Milanese court was filled with concern over Leonardo's ability to complete the project as designed. The Ambassador reported that:

> Prince Ludovico is planning to erect a worthy monument to his father, and in accordance with his orders Leonardo has been asked to make a model in the form of a large horse ridden by Duke Francesco in full armor. As his Highness has in mind something wonderful, the likes of which has never been seen, he has directed me to write to you and ask if you would kindly send him one or two Florentine artists who specialize in this kind of work. Moreover, although he has given the commission to Leonardo it seems that he is not confident that Leonardo will succeed.

From this note, four things come clear: First, Ludovico was seeking help from the Florentines, who had the best sculptors in Italy; second, as late as 1489 the plan was still to have Francesco astride his horse; third, that Ludovico was the one driving both the size and the subject matter of the commission; and fourth, that Leonardo da Vinci was struggling mightily to impress Ludovico Sforza with this endeavor.

Now this appeal to Lorenzo the Magnificent appears to have sparked him to contact Antonio Pollaiuolo, a Florentine sculptor of note, and in 1489 Pollaiuolo submitted to Ludovico his vision for the equestrian monument of Francesco Sforza, complete with the old man seated astride the horse, directing imaginary subordinates at his feet. Leonardo was surely in jeopardy of losing this commission.

But let's remember that by 1489 Leonardo had established some pretty significant connections at court, and he managed to outmaneuver Pollaiuolo to secure his place at the head of this commission. By 1490 Ludovico had approved Leonardo's plans to move ahead with the project.

Now we must remember that casting a life-size horse and rider in bronze was spectacularly complicated. This kind of thing just wasn't done in 15th century in Italy, and just because Donatello had managed to do it once didn't mean that it was automatically included in every apprentice's training in workshops across the continent. Making such an image required tackling a wide array of problems that artists just weren't accustomed to dealing with then.

Leonardo was immediately struck with a whole set of really good questions that never really left him throughout the entire equestrian project. Among the things gnawing at him were these: 1) What would the figures look like? 2) Who would see them? 3) How big would the figures be, and from which vantage point would viewers encounter them? 4) How could the weight of the bronze be both distributed equally across the pedestal and at the same time show some kind of movement or vibrancy? 5) How could you get all that precious and wildly expensive bronze for your sculpture? Where would the money come from? 6) How could you cast such a large figure? Would you do it in one piece? Two pieces? Ten pieces pegged together? 7) Should the figures be hollow or solid? If hollow, how could you get the bronze to swirl around an entire mold without cooling halfway down the body? 8) How much room would you need to cast such a big figure? How big must the pit be? How many furnaces would you need? How many laborers would you need to run the furnaces? 9) When you break the molding off the cooled sculpture, how would you ensure that the bronze would be thick enough not to crack, but thin enough to be able to be moved to its destination? 10) How could something that would weigh in the thousands of pounds be moved from the foundry to the artist's workshop for finishing touches, and from the workshop to its final location? How could you get something that heavy and that delicate up on a pedestal that's another 10 feet off the ground?

This was no game. The costs were astronomical, as the bronze used for such an object would be hard to find, expensive to buy, and lusted after by defense ministers desirous of making cannons and swords and shields with which to defend the state. Failure could mean Leonardo's ruin.

The problems facing Leonardo were daunting right from the start. In this age of innovation, where the use of paper promoted artistic ingenuity and raised the bar of expectations among patrons who were quickly coming to value originality over tradition, the artist knew that he would not be able to get away with merely copying what earlier sculptors had done before him.

Donatello's Gattamelata had set a modern standard that surpassed even the ancient monuments, like the one of Marcus Aurelius. But Verrocchio was obviously set on blowing that up with his remarkable equestrian sculpture of Bartolomeo Colleoni. How could Leonardo outshine them both?

Leonardo began experimenting with a number of different sketches and drafts for the monument. His first idea, predictably, was to approximate Verrocchio's idea of a man and a beast. But Leonardo pretty quickly realized that the distinctions between Verrocchio's Colleoni and the design that he was working on were really quite small. He wouldn't be able to call attention to the Sforza figure by bettering the one done by Verrocchio. It soon became apparent to Leonardo that if he were to outdo his master, he'd have to go beyond mere compositional ingenuity.

Martin Kemp has made a good argument about Leonardo's final decision about this. Kemp believes that the artist ultimately recognized that there were two things that could be improved upon in the Gattamelata and the still-unfinished Colleoni—Leonardo decided to best his predecessors by making his statue both bigger and more lifelike than theirs.

First of all, Leonardo knew that successful public monuments all contained a sense of grandeur as well as elegance. People want to see their leaders writ large. So Leonardo proposed to Ludovico that the equestrian statue be the largest sculpture of a horse ever made, that would tower over the people of Milan as a symbol of Sforza power and dominance.

The original design, which called for an eight-foot tall horse and a rider of similar proportions, was now to be tripled in size—almost overnight. The horse would now stand a full 24 feet from top to bottom, a spectacularly intimidating sculpture if ever there was one.

But in making the decision to go big, Leonardo was forced to compromise on his original plan: He now realized that he would have to eliminate the rider altogether, erasing Francesco Sforza from the equation. Why?

Once he decided that size alone would be its calling card, Leonardo realized that it would require too much bronze to make both a 24-foot high horse and a 12-foot high man. The horse alone would weigh somewhere around 60 tons, and adding another 30 would be cost prohibitive. Second, adding a rider to the composition would make it too heavy to do anything energetically innovative on par with the Colleoni. The horse would need to stand on all four feet in order to balance it. Although he would be able to best Verrocchio with size alone, the static quality of the rider would knock it down a peg in people's eyes when they compared it to Verrocchio's Colleoni. Third, just getting it up on the pedestal would be a logistical nightmare. With a rider attached, it would be too delicate to move at all. And finally, Leonardo realized that no one had ever made a single object in bronze this large. The horse alone would be considered a technical marvel and adding a rider wouldn't be necessary to acquire the desired shock value. In retrospect, this was an appropriate goal and solution for Leonardo, what with him being an engineer and all: He was setting up for himself a scientific problem that he was confident he was smart enough to solve it. So the rider was jettisoned from the plan early on.

Now that the rider was gone, and the horse was bigger, Leonardo set his sights firmly on the second element of this sculpture that would distinguish it from its predecessors: quality.

This is not to say that Leonardo didn't respect the quality of the equestrians sculptures of Marcus Aurelius and Gattamelata, or that he thought the Colleoni would be poorly executed: just the opposite was true, for Leonardo appreciated the excellence of his predecessors just as much as anyone else did, if not more so.

Rather, Leonardo determined that he would make the most life-like, naturalistically faithful horse ever sculpted in human history, from the hooves to the mane, and that no one would be able to look at this sculpture without marveling at the detailed perfection of the beast he had created.

When he arrived at this conclusion, Leonardo set out to make the mother of all equestrian sculptures.

Ever the academic, Leonardo bought books about horses and their anatomy—an inventory of his personal library of over 100 books, written in 1503, indicates that he owned about a half dozen manuscripts dedicated to the subject alone. He read about the history of the horse from antiquity to the present. He read about the characteristics and qualities of various kinds of horses. He studied the shape and appearance of the different parts of the horse's body, the average distances between the various joints of the legs, the lengths and widths of its limbs—inch by inch—up and down its legs and torso and neck. Leonardo wanted to know every single millimeter of his subject, and he spent the better part of a year focusing his energies on doing just that.

These intensive studies surely helped him when he began venturing into the Milanese stables of Ludovico Sforza to draw from life the stallions there. He meticulously rendered areas large and small as closely as he possibly could, adding details to his studies that he knew would help him produce a sculpted beast that would stun his viewers with its microscopic accuracy.

In the end, Leonardo settled on a fairly traditional approach to the horse. Realizing that pose and posture weren't the important things in the work, Leonardo chose a more subtle positioning of the beast, showing it striding forward on three legs, with the front left hoof elevated. If Verrocchio had been the master Leonardo wanted to outdo, it was Donatello whose horse Leonardo borrowed.

But once he had decided on the features of his sculpture that would make it original, and the actual form his horse would take, Leonardo was faced with the most daunting part of the entire project—how to cast the bloody thing.

For Leonardo had determined a complicated project that required him to do a number of things, including the following: First, he'd have to make a big clay model of actual size that included every single detail. He'd need to create separate molds for different parts of the horse. He'd have to prepare to cast the legs in solid bronze, but the body he conceived of as a hollow shell. Around the torso and the head, he'd have to cake onto a clay model a layer of wax of absolutely consistent dimensions, roughly an inch thick all the way around. He'd have to add another clay layer pressed up against the hardened wax surface. Then he'd need to send down into that overcoat layer of clay, hollow rods leading to the wax coating inside. He'd then have to bury the whole object underneath the ground and cover it with dirt.

With huge furnaces working to heat and liquefy the bronze, he'd then pour the mixture through the rods at various points so that the molten bronze—literally tons of it—would flow in between the inner and the outer shells of clay and strike the wax layer. This in turn would allow the wax to melt away and flow out of holes at the bottom of the clay model.

It would also allow the molten bronze to fill the space vacated by that fleeing wax, but Leonardo would have to make sure that the earth was packed snugly against that shell so that the bronze wouldn't also escape with the wax. Once it was filled and Leonardo created censors there to be installed inside the model to indicate when the bronze had seeped all the way around it. Then Leonardo would stop the pouring and allow the liquid bronze to cool.

Once it was cool, Leonardo would then unearth the model slowly. He'd chip off the outer shell, and dig out the inner shell very carefully, using some holes that were intentionally placed in the shell to do so. Using cranes and pulleys, he'd then lift that enormous bronze object out of the earth and onto a cart. It would be put on wheels and then pulled over to the workshop, where it would be smoothed over so that every imperfection could be roughed out and made perfect.

The object would then be placed back onto a cart and beasts would pull it to its final resting place—presumably a pedestal inside or in front of the Castello Sforzesco. Again he'd have to use pulleys and cranes for this and lift it from the cart and onto that pedestal, and secure it into place.

That's an awfully complicated way of going about doing these things but it's actually, this is the ancient way of casting bronze figures, and it had been known to the ancients as they cast their figures, big and small, in Greece and

Rome some 1500 years earlier. It's now known in French as "Cire Perdue," or the Lost Wax method.

But it had never been done on this scale before. After coming up with the process I've just reviewed with you, which again took roughly two years to conceive and prepare, Leonardo got the go ahead to begin work on the actual image—which probably occurred in 1492 and early 1493.

According to plan, Leonardo started this project by carving and then painting an enormous plaster model of what would soon be called the Colossus of Milan. The clay model was made completely to scale, 24-feet high, and in this work Leonardo demonstrated his close attention to the anatomy of horses, which intrigued him until his death some 30 years later. As he worked, Ludovico ordered the purchase and preservation of, get this, 75 tons of bronze for this singular project alone.

I'm showing you here two modern reconstructions of what Leonardo's clay model might have looked like. They have both been produced to scale, so they're utterly enormous as we stand next to them. We can see how the artists in this modern reconstruction emphasized the muscles, the joints, and the poses that Leonardo appears to have wanted this horse to strike. The clay model was finished and installed in 1493, just in time for the marriage of Ludovico's niece, Bianca Maria Sforza, to the Holy Roman Emperor. Leonardo had the horse erected on a pedestal underneath an archway inside the Milan Cathedral, where the wedding was to take place.

What a wonderful way for Ludovico Sforza to show off to the Emperor Maximilian I, who was about to become a member of his extended family. And what a wonderful feeling it must have been for him when Maximilian bestowed upon him the title of duke of Milan that he had craved above all other things for almost 15 years.

Ludovico was now the legitimate ruler of Milan. It was, in many ways, the very apex of his reign in Lombardy. And then everything got screwed up. We recall that Ludovico had a rather strange view of his own place in European geo-politics at precisely this time. In 1494, in an act of rash shortsightedness, Ludovico invited into Italy the army led by the French king, Charles VIII, whose portrait I show here. The idea was for Charles to destroy the Kingdom of Naples, which was becoming bothersome to Ludovico diplomatically, and Charles happily marched his soldiers south through Italy, essentially whipping everyone in his path.

When Ludovico realized that he had allowed a fox into the henhouse, he scrambled to repair the damage he had done. He entered an alliance with other Italian principalities, and in an effort to participate fully in their campaign to push Charles back across the Alps, Ludovico diverted those 75 tons of bronze that he had designated for the equestrian monument to Ercole d'Este of Ferrara in order to make cannons that they'd need to pound the French into submission.

The casting of the bronze equestrian monument wouldn't happen, and Leonardo knew it. He had to remain content with the clay model he had carved and installed in the Milanese cathedral. As we'll see next time, Leonardo was engaged in a new project soon after the French were expelled from Italian soil in 1495. But meanwhile, the story of the Colossus of Milan didn't end, it was merely put on hold.

In 1499, the French made a return to Italy, this time under the command of their new king, Louis XII. And this time the French crossed the Alps not as friendly guests of Ludovico Sforza, but as his enemies. They took the city quickly and held it, and in the fall of 1499 it was clear that the French were there to stay. Leonardo was there to witness it all. He may also have been there to witness the destruction of his clay colossus at the hands of the new governors of Milan. We are told by a number of contemporary chroniclers that, out of either spite, boredom, or whimsy, French troops detached their bows from their backs and arrows from their quivers, and practiced their archery skills by using Leonardo's clay Colossus of Milan as a target. It disintegrated in very short order and was never seen again. Of Leonardo's reactions we have no record whatsoever.

The colossus of Milan was probably not the first sculptural project that Leonardo participated in, and we know it was not the last. But the equestrian monument for Ludovico Sforza was by far the most impressive, the most ambitious, and the most famous of them all. It was also the most disappointing artistic project of his entire career.

And yet the years between the time when Leonardo was forced to set the colossus aside for want of bronze in 1495, and the final destruction of his model in 1499, would also be the period when Leonardo conceived and completed his single greatest work of art and his most magnificent triumph: *The Last Supper*.

The Making of *The Last Supper*

Lecture 20

The Last Supper is not only one of Leonardo's most famous works; in many ways, it is the epitome of Italian High Renaissance painting. Leonardo took a traditional theme, combined it with the best techniques of the day, and added his own unique innovations to create a work that astounded his peers and continues to awe viewers today. Unfortunately, Leonardo's choice of medium is the painting's single flaw, leading to its rapid deterioration.

The Greatest Painting of the Italian Renaissance

- Leonardo's *The Last Supper* was the culminating artistic achievement of the entire 15th century. It simultaneously summarized every innovative principle of the period and added new elements that Leonardo realized all quality works of art must contain. It is fair to call it the most coherent expression of the High Renaissance as a cultural period.

- In this lecture, we will address how the picture came to be—why and how it was made, which directly affected both the audience's viewing experience when it was finished in 1498 and the way we see it today.

- One reason for its importance lies in Leonardo's perfect compositional choices. It is naturally balanced, bordering on symmetrical. The focal point is the figure of Christ, who extends his arms to the sides, forming the triangle of a classical composition.

- To Christ's left are six disciples, who sit and rise in two groups of three, each with features and poses that distinguish him from his counterparts. A similar approach has been taken to those on the other side of the table.

- The figures are seated in a long, rectangular room with three windows on the back wall that look out over a distant, mountainous landscape. The image's orthogonal lines converge on a vanishing point on the forehead of Christ.

The Last Supper Tradition

- The painting began with the ambitions of Ludovico Sforza and his quest to establish the legitimacy of his rule. One of his projects in the 1490s was the renovation of a Dominican monastic complex called Santa Maria della Grazie, which had been built under his father's patronage a few decades before.

- Ludovico chose Donato Bramante to lead the renovation. Leonardo and Bramante had already developed a close working relationship, and most believe the two were collaborating unofficially on this project.

- As a monastic institution, Santa Maria della Grazie was a large and expansive complex. Part of Bramante's charge was to repair and alter not only the church, which was to house the Sforza family tombs, but portions of the monastic cloister and dependencies.

- The monastery's decorations needed to be updated along with its architecture. So in 1494 or 1495, Ludovico commissioned Leonardo to paint at least two of the walls in the monks' **refectory**.

- The Last Supper was a tried and true image for such settings at that time, although not all Last Suppers looked alike. Medieval and early Renaissance representations generally replicated the dining habits of the viewers for whom they were produced.

- By Leonardo's day, refectory Last Suppers had developed a particular tradition. **Taddeo Gaddi**, who painted his version for Santa Croce around 1355, established the template: a linear structure, with figures stretched out behind the table like actors on a stage. The figures are individuated and face the viewer.

- The scene depicts the specific moment when Judas takes his bread and reveals himself as a traitor. Judas is also placed on the other side of the table from the disciples to emphasize his otherness.

- About 100 years later, **Andrea del Castagno** painted a Last Supper for the refectory of the Florentine nunnery of Sant'Apollonia. In many ways, it follows Gaddi's lead, but armed with a knowledge of linear perspective, the painter also created the illusion that this image was another room, adjacent to the refectory.

- Domenico Ghirlandaio understood the sense of intimacy Andrea del Castagno had created and employed the same kind of composition in his 1480 version of the Last Supper for the Dominicans at the Florentine convent of San Marco. He also cuts the table back toward us at the ends, added windows at the back, and placed natural elements in the background to expand the illusion.

- All of this was meant to make communal dining more engaging from a spiritual perspective by merging the Last Supper's setting with the real setting of the refectory. Therefore, to use this formula effectively, Leonardo had to consider the setting in which his painting would appear.

Leonardo's Choices

- Leonardo's first decision was to elevate his picture so that it could be seen over the monks' heads, even from the back of the refectory. He also chose to pare his composition down to bare essentials and to paint his figures as large as possible for the benefit of those at the back. Building on the precedents, Leonardo also planned on an illusionistic extension of the refectory.

- Per his usual practice, he created a slew of preparatory drawings. If we include the life drawings Leonardo drew in Milan's streets and later used in this work, we can safely estimate that the number of sketches he produced for this single painting was well into the hundreds by the time it was done.

- Even in the earliest drawings, Leonardo's composition placed Christ at the heart of the group, surrounded by apostles who were easily distinguished from one another, both by physical appearance and by posture and gesture, which reveal each man's psychological state.

- Leonardo's perspectival system did not create the illusion of a second room; rather, it created the illusion that the painting was part of the same room. Leonardo extended the stringcourse, or horizontal roofline of thc refectory's cornice, along the side walls that lead toward his picture.

© Dover Electronic Clip Art.

Many intricate early sketches for *The Last Supper* have survived.

- A number of his early designs for the project have survived and often appear alongside or even embedded in drawings and notes about completely unrelated works. This reminds us that, although he was engaged in producing this complicated painting, Leonardo was simultaneously working on all sorts of other projects, too.

- Studies of human physiognomy come into play; the figures' faces have proportions and properties that follow Leonardo's idealized concept of the human head. The furrowed brow, deep frown, and right hand of the disciple thought to be Saint Peter convey enormous psychological depth.

- When he settled on the features of each of his figures, Leonardo worked up his drawings into nearly finished form so that he knew exactly what he wanted them to look like in the final painting. His final drawing for Jesus, which Vasari tells us he struggled with, is a magnificent and unprecedented experiment in the human psychology of Christ and is one of the most beautiful drawings Leonardo ever produced.

- One of the things Leonardo had to think about was how his picture would look inside a darkened refectory, illuminated only by natural sunlight—which varied according to season and the time of day—and by candles, which flickered continuously. Leonardo knew that the best way to paint a dramatic scene was to employ tenebrism.

- It should come as no surprise that Leonardo yearned to employ oil paints in this picture. But the traditional method for **mural** painting was **fresco**, which employed **egg tempera** on wet plaster to make the color a permanent part of the wall. This required a painter to work quickly, and there was no going back to rework an area once it dried.

- Leonardo had never worked in egg tempera, and he hated to be rushed, so ironically, he was ill-suited for this project. But this also explains why Leonardo chose to experiment with a different painting technique.

- Leonardo's idea was to combine a layer of tempera with layers of oil pigment applied to dry plaster. He believed that the oils would replace the sealing quality of the wet plaster, and that his two sets of pigments would allow him to paint at his preferred pace while retaining the appearance of a true fresco. This experiment was destined to go wrong, as we shall see.

- Leonardo began painting sometime in 1496 and worked through all of 1497. The painting was finished by early 1498. Word got out about Leonardo's achievement almost as soon as the scaffolding came down. The fame of the image soon spread throughout Italy.

- Word quickly spread from there to Northern Europe, and then all the way to the Middle East, where the Sultans of Turkey learned of it and referred to it by name in documents written in 1502. *The Last Supper* became a standard, iconic image almost as soon as it was finished, and its popularity and power have never waned since.

Important Terms

egg tempera: Water-based painting medium in which ground colors are suspended in egg yolk. It is characterized by a gleaming surface, decorative flatness, and durability. The principal paint medium before the Cinquecento.

fresco: Italian for "fresh," the technique of painting in wet plaster on a wall. If the color becomes part of the plaster wall, the painting is a true fresco (*buon fresco*).

mural: A generic term for a painting on a wall. The term often used to distinguish the image from a true fresco painting.

refectory: The dining hall in a convent or monastery.

Names to Know

Castagno, Andrea del (c. 1419–1457): Florentine fresco painter who worked for a variety of patrons, including the nuns in the convent of Sant'Apollonia, where his *Last Supper* demonstrated how linear perspective could be employed on a horizontal surface to great effect.

Gaddi, Taddeo (c. 1300–1366): A disciple of Giotto, Taddeo Gaddi painted frescoes and altarpieces primarily in Florence from 1328 until 1360. Among his best-known works are the cycle called *The Life of the Virgin* in the Baroncelli Chapel of Santa Croce (1328–1330) and the *Tree of Life and Last Supper* in the refectory of the same complex (c. 1355).

Suggested Reading

Barcilon and Marani, *Leonardo: The Last Supper.*

Kemp, *Leonardo da Vinci: The Marvellous Works of Nature and Man*, chap. 3.

Ladwein, *Leonardo da Vinci, The Last Supper: A Cosmic Drama and an Act of Redemption.*

The Making of *The Last Supper*
Lecture 20—Transcript

Leonardo da Vinci's *Last Supper* was the culminating artistic achievement of the entire 15th century. In this truly exceptional painting, the artist and inventor simultaneously summarized literally every innovative principle of the Italian Renaissance and added new elements that he realized all quality works of art had to have. The painting might not be considered the first image of the High Renaissance, but I think it's fair to say that it is the most coherent expression of the High Renaissance as a cultural period.

Because of its importance, we'll devote two full lectures to *The Last Supper* in this course, back to back. In the next lecture, we'll discuss the content of the image—its meaning: We'll see both how Leonardo and his viewers would have understood the image as it was being created, but also the overall significance of the work as an icon of Western Civilization.

But first, we'll use this lecture to understand how this picture came in to being in the first place. For, in this particular instance, the way the painting was made—and the reasons why it was made that way—directly affected his audience's viewing experience when it was finished in 1498, and it directly affects the way we see it, today.

One of the reasons for its importance lies in the seemingly perfect compositional choices made by the artist. Leonardo creates a naturally balanced—even a symmetrical—design in this painting. The focal point is the figure of Christ, who sits at the center of a lengthy table, covered with a white cloth, upon which have been placed cups, plates, and cutlery.

Christ extends his arms to his sides, thus forming that internal triangle that we have come to expect from a classically composed painting by Leonardo da Vinci. He nods his head slightly to his left, acknowledging the six figures who sit and rise in two groups of three, each disciple striking an individualistic pose that distinguishes him from his counterparts. A similar approach has been taken to those disciples on the other side of the table, where we see men whispering into each other's ears, raising their hands in response to the central action and literally recoiling from Christ in their midst.

They're seated inside a long, rectangular room with three windows on the back wall that look out over a distant landscape that ends with blue mountains dissolving in the background. And on either side of the picture, two side walls appear that slope down in our visual field, with diagonal lines converging on a vanishing point that's fixed on the forehead of Jesus Christ.

Everything is in perfect alignment here: figures, setting, and action all coalesce in a painting that has come to represent for many the ideal picture of the entire Italian Renaissance.

The making of *The Last Supper* really begins where we've already been: in the ambitious brain of Ludovico Sforza. By the early 1490s, Ludovico had come to realize that he was well ensconced in his position as de facto leader of Milan, but that he needed to establish public expressions of legitimacy and legacy in his city.

In 1463, Ludovico's father, Francesco Sforza, had instigated the building of a Dominican monastic complex called (or, Holy Mary of the Graces). The church was well-appointed, but modest, and because of his father's patronage, Ludovico felt a familial connection to it.

Right around 1490, Ludovico decided to alter the facility that his father had built, and the architect he chose for the project was Donato Bramante, who had already made a name for himself in Milan with some of his earlier architectural designs. Now, we might recall that Leonardo and Bramante had, by now, developed a working relationship—and maybe even a friendship—while they were both working in Ludovico's court, and most of us believe that the two were collaborating unofficially on this project. Leonardo's drawings of centrally planned churches, like this one, appear to have influenced Bramante's thinking as he laid out the square crossing and transept of Santa Maria della Grazie that would serve as the family burial ground for the Sforza family.

But Santa Maria della Grazie was more than just a church. As a monastic institution, it was a large and expansive complex of buildings and rooms. It held a number of cells for the Dominican friars who lived there, a chapterhouse where they met to discuss policies, and support structures where they could cook, clean, and eat. It was a self-sufficient community, where all facets of life were accounted for, and where lay donors like Ludovico Sforza could demonstrate their own piety by donating the funds for their continued maintenance and survival. And part of Bramante's charge in his refurbishing of Santa Maria della Grazie was to repair and alter portions of the cloister and dependencies next to the church. By 1494, Bramante had made excellent progress.

As work continued, it came time to think about how the monastery's decorations could be similarly updated in ways that would be consistent with this new kind of modern architecture. Interestingly, this included the support buildings where the friars ate and worked and slept.

Sometime around 1494, and maybe as late as 1495, the transept of the church—those perpendicular arms that extended out from the nave at the crossing—was nearing completion and the cloister was being remodeled. At that time, the duke of Milan commissioned Leonardo da Vinci to paint not one, but at least two of the walls in their refectory, the dining hall, where the Dominican friars who resided there ate their meals, three times each day.

We know this because in June of 1497, before *The Last Supper* had been completed, the duke of Milan wrote in a directive to one of his lieutenants that he wanted Leonardo, "to bring the work begun in the refectory of Santa Maria delle Grazie to a conclusion so that he may begin work on the other wall of the dining hall," which makes it quite clear that Leonardo's painting formed only one portion of the intended decorations of that space.

Ludovico doesn't describe the subject of this second mural that he envisioned for the Refectory, and no other documents echo this desire to add a partner for *The Last Supper*. But if I were to take a guess as to what that picture was supposed to be, I'd say that Ludovico probably had in mind a Crucifixion scene, like those sometimes seen in refectory halls in Renaissance monasteries. Andrea di Cione had painted one of these for the great Florentine convent of Santo Spirito in the early 1360s, which featured Christ on the cross, flanked by swooning followers and severe-looking Roman centurions.

Taddeo Gaddi had done the same with his large fresco of the *Tree of Life* in the Franciscan church of San Croce, although here Taddeo combined the crucifixion with a genealogical *Family Tree of Christ* that was bordered at the base with a lengthy depiction of *The Last Supper*. As crucifixions were appropriate subjects for dining halls, it stands to reason that Ludovico might have wanted one for the Refectory of Santa Maria delle Grazie. It would've worked nicely with the scene of *The Last Supper* that preceded the execution of Christ in the Passion narrative.

In any case, we're pretty confident that one of the easiest issues addressed in this project was the choice of subject matter for the wall that was actually painted—the scene of *The Last Supper*. It was, after all, a tried and true image that had long been popular among the general public, who had opportunities to see images of them in a variety of venues. There were a lot of them decorating the walls and chapels of churches all across Italy by 1495.

Now, that said, not all *Last Supper*s looked alike. Depending on the setting, Medieval and early Renaissance representations could show Jesus in the middle of a throng of disciples, Christ on one end of a group, or some combination of the two.

This mosaic from the nave of the 6th century church of Sant'Apollinare Nuovo in Ravenna, shows Christ at one end of a circular table, with the apostles winding around behind it. They recline around this oval table, reflective of the way Romans ate their meals in antiquity: from the very beginning, *Last Supper*s were intended to replicate the eating habits of the viewers for whom they were produced.

Giotto's fresco from the private burial chapel for Enrico Scrovegni in Padua, called the Arena Chapel, also shows the disciples ringing the table, now with Christ at the head. In this painting from 1305, we see the fleshy bodies of the disciples seated in a circle, with the beardless figure of John the Evangelist sleeping on Christ's chest, conforming to the lines in the Bible that indicate that one of the apostles dozed during the meal.

Neither of these examples were created for dining halls, though. Refectory *Last Supper*s were painted in a different manner, and by the time we get to Leonardo's time a certain tradition had been formed for dining hall pictures. Among the most important was the large fresco that we just saw by Taddeo Gaddi, who painted his version of *The Last Supper* for Santa Croce sometime around 1355, that helped establish something of a template for scenes of this subject in monastic Refectories.

Gaddi's composition depends on a linear structure, with his figures stretched out behind the table as though actors on a stage: These actors now all face out toward us, and with the individual characteristics of each disciple displayed in plain view. There's a specific moment in the fresco that he chooses to represent, as the figure of Judas accepts the bread—which designates him as the traitor responsible for Christ's arrest and execution. We can see him to the right of Jesus, intentionally placed on the other side of the table to emphasize his otherness, and his conscious act of separation from Christ and the Apostles.

This formula for *Last Supper*s in monastic settings resonated with viewers, patrons, and painters, and it became something of a standard that would remain in favor for centuries. But the change in stylistic interests and approaches of artists during the Renaissance ushered in some important changes that affected the way *Last Supper*s were painted and interpreted by their cloistered audiences.

About 100 years after Taddeo Gaddi's *Last Supper* in Santa Croce, the artist Andrea del Castagno painted this *Last Supper* for the Refectory in the Florentine nunnery of Sant'Apollonia. In many ways, Andrea follows Gaddi's lead, like the way in which each figure has his own identity, and how Judas has been separated from everyone else.

But in this image from the 1440s, Andrea del Castagno added a feature that made his version of *The Last Supper* more personal and more immediate for his audience. Armed with the knowledge of linear perspective,

Andrea extended the room in which his picture was situated. Through the employment of multiple orthogonal lines that converge at a vanishing point on a horizon line, Andrea was able to extend the space of this image so that it appeared to be a new room adjacent to the refectory in which it was located.

It's a brilliant employment of linear perspective that helped the nuns conceive of themselves as being more than just viewers: they could imagine themselves being actually present in the setting, and could picture this scene transpiring inside their own refectory because the representation of depth made it look like it was.

Domenico Ghirlandaio understood what Andrea del Castagno had done, and in 1480 employed the same kind of composition in his *Last Supper* for the Dominicans at the Florentine convent of San Marco.

Much of the composition and story line are familiar to us, with the disciples seated behind the table and with Christ in the middle of the picture. Now, though, Ghirlandaio has cut the table back toward us at the ends, added windows in the back, and placed natural elements in the background to expand the illusion of additional space beyond the painted wall.

All of this was an attempt by painters to make the experience of communal dining more engaging from a spiritual perspective, and to make the theatrical setting of *The Last Supper* merge into the real setting of the refectory. By 1495, it was something of a standard operating procedure to employ this kind of optical illusion, and this kind of theatrical setting, in dining hall *Last Supper*s.

Now in order to abide by this formula, Leonardo had to take into consideration the setting in which his painting would appear. The refectory was a long, rectangular room that contained lots of tables and chairs for the friars to use. Leonardo knew they'd be sitting in front of the wall that would bear his picture, and he knew that there would be many, many people in this room all at the same time. Thus he chose to elevate his picture enough so that it could be seen over their heads as they processed into the space, took their seats, and ate their meals.

He also knew that roughly half of his audience would only be able to see his picture from the back end of the refectory; and so he chose to pare down his composition to the bare essentials and to paint his figures as large as he possibly could so that they could be seen from the back of the room.

And building on the precedents set by Andrea del Castagno and Domenico Ghirlandaio, Leonardo elected to create an illusionistic extension of the dining hall so as to enhance the immediacy and intimacy of the scene for his cloistered audience. Now Leonardo clearly had all of these things fixed firmly in his mind when he began to focus his attention on this project, probably in 1495.

As was his custom by now, Leonardo began by roughing out his composition through a slew of preparatory drawings he'd need to do in order to map out the general composition and craft the individual figures within it. He knew he would need to pull the entire thing apart to work on sections of it, and then concentrate on even smaller subsections to build up the details that then could be inserted back into the complete, thorough, large-scale composition. If we add in the number of life-drawings of different characters that Leonardo reputedly drew in Milan's city streets, we can safely estimate that the number of sketches he produced for this single painting was well into the hundreds by the time it was done.

In this early drawing, Leonardo roughs out a preliminary, possible composition, whereby he shows Christ at the heart of the group, surrounded by apostles. Quite clearly, Leonardo, doesn't think of these apostles collectively as a group of indistinguishable or interchangeable human beings, for he actually has identified each of them by writing their names by each figure.

Bartholomew has his own physical appearance—he's the tall one with the receding hairline in the lower left. Andrew, next to him, is taller, hairier, but also more nervous—you can see him rubbing his hands with a furrowed brow. And Philip, further down the line, is younger, clean-shaven, and deferential as he nods toward the older disciple next to him. In the same vein, the psychological state of each of these characters is equally distinctive, one from the other. They bend, they interact, and they have a physical presence that reveals an emotional condition that they feel on the inside.

The one whose features we can't really see very well in this early sketch is the apostle John the Evangelist, the one who had the temerity to fall asleep during *The Last Supper*.

And that's because, here, John's not just resting gently against Jesus's chest, as he did in Giotto's version—now he's passed out completely, with his long hair flowing across the table in a sign of total exhaustion. Leonardo is playing just little bit here, just the way he does in his caricatures: He knows that this drawing won't be seen by anyone else, and it becomes a place where he can work out even his most extreme ideas with impunity.

But Leonardo also knew that these figures would need to be placed within an illusionistic spatial extension that he wanted to create inside the monastic refectory, for he knew that one of the most successful features of Renaissance *Last Supper*s was their appeal as intimate connectors to the lives of the people who saw them.

As he worked up his basic designs for the overall composition of *The Last Supper*, Leonardo set about employing a perspectival system that would extend the appearance of the dining hall into the imaginary annex that he was creating. Leonardo didn't want to just paint a new room up there, sitting above the one used by the friars, like Andrea del Castagno had done: He wanted it instead to be a continuation of the one they were actually using.

Leonardo the mathematician began to play with the organization of this space and the way orthogonals—those diagonal lines perpendicular to the picture plane—might enhance the experience that he was trying to create.

As he had done in his early drawing for the Adoration of the Magi, which I show here, Leonardo worked out a perspectival system that allowed him to construct his three-dimensional space as a naturalistic progression from the reality of the actual room to the fiction of the imaginary room he was painting. Leonardo extended the stringcourse, or the horizontal roofline of the refectory's cornice, along the side walls that lead toward his picture. He then proceeded logically from them, taking into consideration the vantage point of his audience seated below the painting and at the far end of the refectory. The painting became an extension of the room, which implied that those friars dining in the refectory were actually a part of the scene, too.

A number of his early designs for the project have survived and often appear alongside or even embedded in drawings and notes about completely unrelated things. It reminds us that, even though he was engaged in producing this very complicated painting, Leonardo was simultaneously working on all sorts of other projects too.

The disciple in this drawing, probably that of Saint James, has been beautifully rendered to reveal an expressive response to the dramatic core of Leonardo's *Last Supper*—his eyes, his mouth, even the tilt of head suggest a certain sense of shock.

Studies of human physiognomy come into play here, as facial features have proportions and properties embedded in Leonardo's idealized concept of the human head. The furrowed brow and deep frown of this disciple, thought to be Saint Peter, convey, physically, the psychological content of his figure, while the finger of the right hand, caught in mid-flight, tells us almost as much about his state of mind as his face does.

And when he finally settled on the features of each of his figures, Leonardo worked up his drawings to an even higher state of finish so that he knew exactly what he wanted them to look like in the final painting.

This beautifully rendered drawing provided all the details that he needed in order to work up the central figure of Christ, which Vasari tells us was difficult for him to do. There's a quiet elegance about these features that conveys to us the resignation of a man who knows his fate, who has come to terms with it, and who now must share the bad news with the people he loves. Leonardo employs lights and shades brilliantly, literally illuminating the thoughts of this heroic figure by clouding a portion of his face in red and grey shadows. The eyelids have been composed to indicate that Jesus is looking down at the table before him, lost in thought, unable to meet the eyes of his comrades directly. It is a magnificent and unprecedented experiment in the human psychology of Christ, and it's one of the most beautiful drawings Leonardo da Vinci ever produced.

By about 1496, Leonardo had come up with what he wanted compositionally. But now he turned to a consideration of how to capture the overall atmosphere and energy of this most dramatic moment in the Passion sequence.

One of the things that Leonardo had to think about was how his picture would look inside a darkened refectory that had only a few windows located above his image. Without electricity to generate light through incandescent bulbs, Leonardo's painting could be illuminated only by natural sunlight—which varied according to season and the time of day—and by candles, which flickered continuously in ways that would create interesting, but uneven, effects across the surface of his painting.

Leonardo knew that this particular moment from Christian history was one of its most dramatic ever, and Leonardo knew that the best way to paint a dramatic scene like *The Last Supper* was to employ the tenebristic technique that he had used previously in his portraits of Ludovico's mistresses and courtiers, like Cecilia Gallerani. Allowing his figures to emerge out of darkness and then retreat back into it had gained him fame and notoriety from patrons, sitters, and critics alike. It should come as no surprise that Leonardo yearned to employ oil paints.

This, in and of itself, was a major problem. The traditional method used to produce wall paintings was the ancient technique of fresco painting, which had been practiced by Leonardo's peers and predecessors for centuries. In fresco painting, the painter must create a smooth skin on bumpy walls by smearing at least two thin coats of plaster across an uneven brick surface. When everything was ready, the artist would select a section of the wall to work for that day, and he lays down a third and final coat of plaster, but now only enough that he could paint on while it was still wet. Timing was essential in fresco painting, because the master now had to race against the clock as that plaster dried; he needed to apply his wet, egg tempera pigments to the wet, plaster wall, and as both substances dried together they became bound, one in the other. It is one of the most durable forms of painting ever created, and even today you can see frescoes from the 1st century B.C. that still retain their brilliance and their beauty even after 2000 years.

There are no good shortcuts to achieve this same result. If, for example, a painter attempts to simplify this process by placing the egg tempera pigments directly on a dry wall with no wet plaster, the he runs the risk of seeing his work crumble before his eyes. The wet plaster in a fresco technique provides a protective sealant, and if the pigments are no longer bound inside the plaster, then the paint tends to discolor or flake away. So Leonardo was searching for a way out.

First, Leonardo had never really done a fresco painting before. The only other instance of Leonardo producing a mural picture up to this time was the decoration for the Sala delle Asse in Ludovico's ducal palace. But that project was executed really about the same time that Leonardo was busy painting the *Last Supper*, and there's been much speculation that the master only provided the designs for that other project to his assistants did all the work.

The second problem was that Leonardo had never worked in the medium of egg tempera before. Every painting that he had produced since his earliest days as a member of Verrocchio's workshop had been executed in oil.

And the third big problem was that Leonardo hated to be rushed—he loved to mull over his paintings, rework troubling areas, and lay down his glazes thinly, one on top of the other, over a long period of time. Fresco painting, with wet plaster drying and the sands of the hourglass sliding through the jar so quickly, just didn't allow for this.

So ironically, Leonardo was actually quite ill-suited for this project. But it also helps explain why Leonardo, ever the experimental scientist and inventor, chose to experiment with it.

The experiment he had in mind was to combine the two types of pigments that artists of the 1490s had available to them. Rather than being hemmed in by the limitations of either, Leonardo would employ both. His idea was to combine a layer of tempera pigment with layers of oil pigment. For this purpose, he decided to wait until the skim coat of plaster had already dried before applying his tempera, which (as we've just seen) was a poor way to paint a mural picture. But then he planned to layer onto that tempera undercoat all those glazes of oil paint that he was so fond of using. He believed that the oils he added onto the egg tempera paint would be able to replace the sealing quality of the wet plaster, and that his two sets of pigments, together, would allow him to paint at his preferred pace and retain its appearance with the same kind of resiliency as a true fresco painting.

If we think back to the very first breakout moment of Leonardo's career, 20 years earlier, we remember that Leonardo had painted his angel in the Baptism of Christ in oils, while the rest of the picture was painted by his colleagues in the workshop in tempera. The two had worked together then, and it stands to reason that Leonardo believed the two could be employed again on the surface of the dining hall.

Also, Leonardo had layered different media on top of each other in some of his drawings, like this drapery study from the 1470s that I show here. Leonardo would prepare and tint the surface of the paper; then use some black chalk as an underdrawing; then build up that section with metal point; then draw on top of that with pen and ink; and then finish it off with white chalk highlights. When artists use this kind of combination of materials, we call it a "mixed media" image, and what Leonardo aimed to do with *The Last Supper*, in effect, was extend his mastery of mixed media in drawings to the format of a large mural painting.

But from our perspective today, it's an experiment that sounds destined to go wrong. "Oil and water don't mix," as the saying goes, and most of us who have painted our own homes know that you don't layer oil-based paint over water-based latex; those who defy this basic principle come to regret it within months.

But Leonardo believed that his approach would work. After spending about 18 months mapping out the overall composition, the individual figures in it, and then the overall composition again (with more detail this time), Leonardo began applying his layers of plaster, egg tempera paint, and oil pigments, probably in 1496 and through all of 1497.

Despite, or maybe because of, the complaints of Santa Maria della Grazie's prior to Ludovico Sforza about Leonardo's slow working method, the painting was finished by early 1498.

Word got out about Leonardo's *Last Supper* almost as soon as the scaffolding came down, and maybe even before that—all of Milan was abuzz. The fame of the image within the city soon extended beyond its walls to other regions of Italy. People ventured to Milan to see it, and its remarkable features were so admired that copyists almost immediately set out to capture its appearance.

Artists and patrons and admirers all across Italy knew about *The Last Supper*, and word spread from there to Northern Europe, and then all the way to the Middle East, where the Sultans of Turkey learned of it and referred to it by name in documents written in 1502.

The *Last Supper* became a standard, iconic image almost as soon as it was finished, and its popularity and power have never waned since. In our next lecture, we'll see why this has been the case, as we look at the message and meaning of *The Last Supper* in order to divine from Leonardo's monumental masterpiece the ideas that he wished to convey to us.

The Meaning of *The Last Supper*

Lecture 21

Popular conspiracies to the contrary, some of *The Last Supper*'s most remarkable features are its most traditional, from its composition to its symbolism. Leonardo's work is a masterpiece because of his mastery of the human form, which allows him to portray his figures' psychology through expression and gesture, as well as the wealth of details he packed into this seemingly static image that condense the entire Passion narrative into a single moment.

The Last Supper in Its Original Context

- What has made Leonardo's mural such an icon of Western art? Although a forward-looking painting, The Last Supper can only be understood within the tradition of image-making and narrative painting that gave birth to it.

- Consider the refectory environment in which it was placed: Monastic refectories were large, rectangular rooms with tables arranged in a ring parallel to the walls. Diners all sat outside the ring, facing toward the center of the room, while the tables were served and cleared from inside the ring.

- Monastic diners usually ate in silence. Sometimes, they might listen to one of their brethren reading from the scriptures or to announcements from the head table, but they did not chat or even whisper among themselves.

- Paintings of the Last Supper were considered to refer directly to concepts of leadership and obedience. Members of these communities would connect the image of Christ and his disciples to the actual prior, abbot, or abbess of their community and his or her lieutenants, who were usually positioned directly beneath the painting.

- Images of the Last Supper were, first and foremost, understood as illustrations of the most important scriptural passages from the Gospels. Like most Last Suppers, Leonardo's picture adheres quite strictly to these texts.

The Textual References

- Leonardo places his 13 characters in the setting described in the Gospels, the upper room of a public inn. Daylight dwindles, casting his figures into deep relief, indicating that the time is near sunset. Christ occupies the heart of the composition, with his head placed in the middle of a triple window that probably refers to the Trinity.

- At first glance, this seems to be an early moment in the narrative. Christ points to a wine glass with his right hand and bread with his left—the symbols of Christ's own body and blood. This is the moment when Christ teaches his followers about the **Eucharist**.

- However, the dramatic gestures and expressions of shock on the faces of Christ's disciples are not appropriate responses to this ephemeral theological concept. They are reacting to something else entirely—the second phase of the narrative that Leonardo illustrates.

- On either side of Christ are two sets of six disciples—or rather, four sets of three disciples, grouped as mini-units within the larger context. The physical and emotional actions of each group forms a crescendo from left to right, from a subdued reaction to an explosion of physical energy.

- At the core sits Jesus, isolated from the others by gaps that Leonardo has placed there to emphasize the great gulf that separates the Son of God from mortals. Christ's face reveals little; he is dejected and quiet, but we cannot tell from his lips whether he breathes a word of his inner knowledge to his company.

- According to the Gospels, immediately after the Eucharistic lesson, Christ announces, "One of you will betray me." The disciples respond with mild surprise, then disbelief, then shock, and finally horror—just as the figures do from left to right across the picture plane.

    - The trio of figures at the far left, the Bartholomew group, are quite subdued. All three figures show concern, but their bodies convey little physical animation.

    - The second trio, the Judas group, contains Judas, Peter, and John the Evangelist. Peter holds a knife, both appropriate for a dinner scene and an emblem of an act of violence in his near future. John—shown sleeping in one preparatory drawing—seems sleepy; here he leans toward Peter, in a moment described in John's Gospel, when Peter asks him, "Tell us who it is of whom [Jesus] speaks." Judas, unusually on the same side of the table as Christ, reaches with his left hand for a chunk of bread. In his right he holds a small bag containing the 30 pieces of silver. The interweave of these figures' bodies gives them more energy than the Bartholomew group, but not coincidentally, they form another triangle.

    - The third trio, called the Thomas group, includes a visually riveting collection of disciples in postures of shock and distress, along with another reference to the future: Thomas's finger, which he will later use to inspect the resurrected Christ's wound.

    - The fourth and final trio, the Matthew group, is the most physically dramatic. They no longer look at Jesus because they have already seen his prediction confirmed. Their reaction has as much to do with Judas's reaching for the bread as it does with what Christ has said.

- What we have, then, is a single painting that is more than just a single painting; it forces viewers to use their memories and deductive skills to piece together fragments of the story and reconstruct a vast and sweeping narrative.

- There was a long history of this sort of image in Italian art. One very popular example was the Man of Sorrows–type painting. **Lorenzo Monaco**'s *Man of Sorrows*, from 1404, manages to allude to the chalice of the Last Supper, the 30 pieces of silver, the arrest of Christ, Peter's denial of Christ, the scourge used to beat Jesus, Pilate washing his hands, the cross, Longinus's lance, the tongs that pulled the nails out of Christ's body, the mourning Mary and John, and the resurrection in a single painting.

- Missing from Leonardo's *The Last Supper* as a sequential narrative of the Passion is the Crucifixion itself. This is one major reason to conclude that the commission for the opposite wall was for a painting of the Crucifixion, which would complement and complete this image.

The Legacy of *The Last Supper*

- Images all have lives of their own. They grow and change and do things and have things done to them, and sometimes the life that the image leads after its completion is just as interesting as the message that the image bears. This is one of those cases.

- Leonardo's painting was an immediate sensation. Only a few months after its completion, it was the subject of an engraving by Giovannni di Pietro da Birago, who distributed his reproduction all across the Italian Peninsula.

- The form became quite popular as the 16th century progressed and as champions of Leonardo tried to employ his lessons. Marco da Oggiono, for example, painted a close copy on canvas, and **Andrea del Sarto** painted a Last Supper mural in the Florentine church of San Salvi that is a clear homage.

- Despite its popularity, the mural began to frustrate its admirers quite soon after its completion. Leonardo's experiment in technique had gone horribly awry. The topcoats of oil first started to bubble, and then to blister. The egg underneath was pulled by the weight of the oil glazes, and the picture started to crack from underneath.

- By 1517, chroniclers were praising Leonardo's great invention but lamenting its horrible condition. By 1547, they were calling it ruined, and when Vasari wrote his second edition of *Lives of the Artists* in 1568, he described *The Last Supper* as "a spot on the wall."

- In 1652, a doorway was cut into the wall, just where Christ's feet had been. That was soon bricked up again, but all that pounding caused even more damage. Two projects in the 18th century attempted to repair the damage and stabilize the colors, but both of those did more harm than good.

- When French troops invaded Milan and occupied it in 1796, soldiers threw rocks at the mural and climbed up ladders to scratch out the eyes of the disciples. Twenty years later, attempts were made to detach the painting from the wall and move it to safety, but the process was botched. Central sections of the painting were badly damaged, and chunks of wall and paint were glued back in place.

- The closest the painting came to complete ruination occurred in August of 1943, when an Allied bomb struck the refectory and almost destroyed the building. *The Last Supper* survived because its caretakers had jammed sandbags up against it for just this reason.

- By the 1970s, *The Last Supper* was understandably in horrible condition, and most specialists believed that there was less paint on the wall applied by Leonardo than there was paint applied by the legion of restorers who had tried to fix it.

- In 1978, an extensive conservation project was undertaken, and in 1999, the restoration was complete, revealing a brightness and vividness that had been unseen for generations—but it also unflinchingly allowed bare spots to remain bare.

Important Term

Eucharist: The sacrament of the Lord's Supper, celebrated in the Mass.

Names to Know

Lorenzo Monaco (c. 1372–1424): Monk who left his cloister at Santa Maria degli Angeli in Florence to pursue a career as a lay painter. Among his most important works were panels of *The Coronation of the Virgin* (1414) and *The Man of Sorrows (Vir Dolorum)* (1404)—both in Florence today.

Sarto, Andrea del (1486–1530): Follower of Raphael and Leonardo who worked in the classical idiom, primarily in Florence. His best-known work is *The Madonna of the Harpies* (1517).

Suggested Reading

Barcilon and Marani, *Leonardo: The Last Supper*.

Heydenreich, *Leonardo: The Last Supper*.

Steinberg, *Leonardo's Incessant Last Supper*.

The Meaning of *The Last Supper*

Lecture 21—Transcript

Now that we've looked at the formal traditions that influenced Leonardo's thinking as he composed and produced his painting of *The Last Supper*, it's time for us to turn our attention to what has made the mural such an icon of Western art. In this second lecture on Leonardo's *Last Supper*, we will explore the heart of the painting's message and its meaning. This lecture is designed not to reveal the "Real da Vinci Code:" but rather, to examine this most forward-looking of pictures from within the appropriate context of the tradition of image-making and narrative painting that gave birth to it.

Now the context for the painting is important to review, and we need to consider the refectory more closely in order to understand the initial motivation for this project.

As we know, the picture decorated the dining hall of the Dominican monastery of Santa Maria delle Grazie, located in the heart of Milan, but about a mile away from the Castello Sforzesco and the court of Duke Ludovico. By the 1490s, the monastery was considered by Ludovico to be an important landmark for himself and his family, for it had been his father's wish to see this monastery built, back in the 1460s.

Now, in addition to wanting to celebrate his family's importance in Milan, as well as his father's role in making the city what it had become, Ludovico wished to make Santa Maria delle Grazie the site of the Sforza family burial ground, a key monument in what he hoped would be a string of physical memorials to himself and to his family.

Refectories in cloistered communities were large rectangular rooms with tables usually arranged in a ring corresponding to the contours of each of the room's four walls—thus forming a smaller rectangular box that ran parallel to the larger one that formed its borders. Friars or monks or nuns—depending on the kind of community—customarily ate while seated on benches or stools that were placed in between the table and the wall behind them. Everyone dining in the refectory faced inwards, toward the center of the room.

There were a few good reasons for setting up dining halls this way. This arrangement made serving and clearing both food and cutlery efficient and effective: The brothers responsible for those tasks could move freely between tables without having to negotiate the backs and necks and heads of diners who would otherwise get in their way. Now, monastic diners, habitually and by rule, ate together silently. Depending on the customs of their particular community, they might listen to one of their brethren reading from the scriptures, and there might be an announcement or two made from the head table. But sidebar conversations or gossip or even sotto voce mutterings were strictly forbidden—and they were hard to get away with when everyone was facing inward: they'd be in plain view of everyone on the other side of the room, and that only invited reprimand and punishment from the superiors, seated together at the central table.

Inside the refectory, paintings of *The Last Supper* were considered to refer directly to concepts of leadership and obedience within the hierarchy of that cloister. We're pretty sure that it was common for monks and friars and nuns, when looking at their own refectory's *Last Supper* image, to connect the image of Christ and the disciples to the actual prior or abbot or abbess of their community. For during meal times, these leaders of the cloister were usually flanked by their lieutenants and seated at the head table of the dining hall, which was in turn usually positioned directly beneath the painting of *The Last Supper* for precisely this reason.

But images of *The Last Supper* weren't seen primarily as references to common eating practices, although that certainly was an indirect connection that made them popular in the setting of a refectory. Instead, images of *Last Supper*s were, first and foremost, understood as illustrations of some of the most important scriptural passages from the Gospels of Matthew, Mark, Luke, and John.

Like most *Last Supper*s, Leonardo's picture adheres quite strictly to the texts from which it was gleaned. Leonardo places his 13 characters in precisely the setting described in the gospel accounts—the upper story of a public inn—with a table placed in a room that has been elevated enough to look over the landscape behind it. Daylight dwindles, casting his figures into deep relief, indicating that we are seated at a table right at or near sunset, which in an Italian April is about 7 pm—which is supper time.

Christ occupies the very heart of the composition, with his head placed in the middle of a triple window that most probably refers to the concept of the Trinity, of which Jesus is a main element. He sits in that perfect triangle with his two hands stretched out at either side of his body, and toward each group of his followers. What's he saying as does this?

Well, this is actually one of the early moments from the narrative of *The Last Supper*, and by the looks of things, Christ is pointing to the menu of the day. One of his hands, his right, moves toward a wine glass. The other, his left, presents the bread.

Yes, these are the things they are all about to eat, and it's true that they comprise the main course of this very simple meal. But they are also the symbolic representations of Christ's own body and blood, and Jesus makes it very clear, early in the story of *The Last Supper*, that his followers must pay attention to these elements not only as food to nourish the body, but as ritualistic elements that nourish the soul.

The Gospel of Luke notes that Christ takes a cup in his hands and says to them, "Take this, and divide it among yourselves; for I tell you that from now on I shall not drink of the fruit of the vine until the kingdom of God comes." He then breaks the bread and passes it among them, saying, "This is my body."

Leonardo's Christ calmly, peacefully accepts the fact that he will not be able to stay with them much longer, and he shows Christ gesturing to these two symbols that bring eternal life to those who partake of them. At this, core moment, Christ seems to be teaching his company about the symbolic significance of the Eucharist, and thus, in this first narrative phase of the painting, Leonardo shows us the earliest Communion and the context in which it came about.

But that cannot be the only event that's being captured here. For the dramatic gestures and expressions of shock on the faces of Christ's disciples are not at all appropriate responses if this central figure has just announced a rather abstract theological concept. They're reacting to something else entirely: the second phase of the narrative that Leonardo illustrates.

Now let's look at these men on his flanks. Beside him appear two sets of six disciples—or, rather, four sets of three disciples—that have been grouped together to act as mini-units within the bigger context. Each of them has his own emotional state, each one gestures in a particular way, and each one acts and reacts according to his relationship with the other disciples in his mini-group. They are individuals, yes, but they are part of a larger group (of three), that is part of a larger group (of six), that is part of a larger group still (of 13).

Despite the centrality of the composition, balanced symmetrically with Christ at the core, the physical and emotional actions of the painting form a crescendo from left to right, as the initially subdued positions of the trio at the left end of the table are increased in dramatic feel in the left center, energy y at the far right.

This movement, of course, conforms to the way we read books in the west, and even though Leonardo asks us to begin our reading of his picture with Christ at the center, he is mindful of our natural inclination to read pictures, like books, from left to right.

Yet at the core of it all sits Jesus, like the eye of a storm, isolated from all the others by spatial gaps that Leonardo has placed there to emphasize the great gulf that separates the Son of God from the mortal figures who join him on earth. Christ's expressionless face reveals nothing about his own state of mind at this key moment: He's dejected and he's quiet, it's true, but we can't tell from his lips whether he breathes a word of his inner knowledge to his company. But it's those outstretched arms of his that come to our rescue again, as they once more help us understand what this second phase illustrates.

According to the texts, in literally the very next breath after this Eucharistic lesson, Christ announces the big bombshell of the evening. Now he says, with his eyes cast low in Leonardo's painting, "Verily, verily. One of you will betray me."

Now the disciples respond, first with mild surprise, then with disbelief, then with shock, and finally with horror—that one big crescendo of emotion that moves us from left to right across the picture plane, in the same direction that our eyes take every time we traverse any written text, like the Bible, for example.

The collective reply begins with the trio of figures at the far left, to whom I will refer as "the Bartholomew group" due to the inscriptions found in Leonardo's earlier sketch of the composition. Bartholomew stands up in surprise as he hears Christ's announcement. He seems puzzled by the news, and he leans forward on both of his hands to make sure he's understood correctly. James the Minor turns his head toward the middle, also reacting a little mutely to this strange accusation. Andrew, however, raises both of his hands in an act of displeasure: He is the first of the 12 now to show a really physical response to Christ's news—but even this response is muted. All three show concern on their faces, but their bodies retain a certain verticality that conveys little physical animation. And as a result, their psychological states seem subdued right now because their physical forms tell us so.

Things begin to get a little more active with the next trio, the so-called "Judas group."

At its center we see Peter in his traditional blue robe and white beard. Before him, and to our left, appears a knife in a hand that points awkwardly away from his body. It's an appropriate utensil for a dinner party, so from that standpoint it certainly belongs here. But it's also an emblem of a future act that soon will be attributed to Saint Peter. Within a few hours of *The Last Supper*, Peter will use just such a weapon—maybe even this very one—to slice off the ear of a servant boy who leads Roman Centurions to Christ's hideaway in Gethsemane.

Peter places his left hand on the shoulder of a younger man, who is unquestionably John the Evangelist, shown beardless with his customary long hair, just like he always is in Renaissance depictions of *Last Supper*s.

But we might recall that John is also the sleepy member of this entourage—do you remember the drawing, with John's face down on the table? Well that might explain his reclined position that moves him away from the edge of the table, back towards Peter.

Now this vignette, where Peter beckons to the reclining Evangelist, is actually described in the Gospel of John: Peter asks John to get Jesus to clarify his claim of betrayal—"Tell us who it is of whom he speaks," Peter says. Now this the only time in the entire story of *The Last Supper* when Peter and John actually address one another directly, so we're on very firm ground when we say that this interaction represents that specific passage from the scriptural text.

And with these two disciples, just at the table's edge, we see the culprit. Judas, now on the same side of the table as Christ—perhaps to remind us that this king of all sinners was, at first, a believer—Judas reaches with his left hand for a chunk of bread before him. In his right he holds a small bag or sack in his clutches—the 30 pieces of silver he has just received as a payment for his future betrayal.

Now we have three different bits of this longer narrative referenced in the painting—the moment earlier in the story, before *The Last Supper*, when Judas accepted the silver payment; his ultimate demise, after Christ's arrest, when Judas will commit suicide over his ill-gotten gains; and finally yet another passage that appears in all four of the gospels, who quote Christ as saying, "He who reaches for the bread shall betray me." By now, we realize that what we have here is more than just a single frozen moment time, illustrated by an artist who wants to present only one important scene at the exclusion of so many others. Embedded into this composition by Leonardo is a whole constellation of moments.

The interweave pattern of Judas group offers a more complex artistic solution to the grouping of three figures than what we've just seen in the Bartholomew group. Judas leans toward us, John moves away from us, and Peter cuts horizontally across our visual field—the combination has an energetic effect that moves us away from the more rigid response of the first trio at the far left. But it also, not coincidentally, forms another triangle in the composition that grounds the linear quality of the ensemble grouping—and it subtly connects these three figures together thematically, for these are the only three disciples who actually play supporting roles in the scene, and who are identified by name for their roles in the text: John is the sleeper, Peter is the denier, and Judas is the traitor. Leonardo brings them all together so we can focus our attention on this element of the narrative with one, concentrated gaze, rather than have to go searching across the composition for the three apostles who have individual parts in this play.

The third trio, called the "Thomas group" includes a visually riveting collection of disciples. The interweave solution is not employed here, but rather we now have James the Major throwing his hands back as though both holding off his colleagues from jumping at Jesus in disbelief, while at the same time he physically demonstrates his own shock at what he's heard. Behind him stands the apostle Thomas, who sticks into the air that provocative index finger that he'll later plunge into the side of the resurrected Christ to inspect his wounds.

And behind James the Major's barrier-like arms stands Philip, head tilted, beseeching and pointing toward himself—indeed, maybe even beating his own breast, like Leonardo's Penitent Jerome does in the undercoat painting from 1480 that Leonardo never finished. And this penitential pose indicates to us that yet another line from the dialogue contained in the Gospels has been alluded to, this one uttered by all 12 of the disciples, at different intervals: "Lord, is it me?" they ask.

And finally we move the fourth and final trio, the Matthew group, in which that apostle by that name throws his right arm toward the center and echoes it with a left hand that's equally demonstrative, in what amounts to the most physically dramatic act in the entire composition. Thaddeus gazes at Simon to the far right, who in turn repeats Matthew's horizontal hand gesture as a way of bringing our eyes back to the core. These apostles don't even bother to look at Jesus—they have already heard him, they have already heard what their colleagues have said, and they have already seen the single act which has confirmed Christ's prediction: Their horrified reaction has as much to do with Judas's reaching for the bread as it does with what Christ has said. This is the end of the scene, the final collective expression of outrage that builds in intensity, from left to right, from surprise, to disbelief, to shock, to horror.

What we have, then, is a single painting that is more than just a single painting: It's an image in which a number of scenes have been alluded to, and in a way that forces viewers to use their memories and their deductive skills to piece together important pieces of the story to reconstruct a vast and sweeping narrative—and it's one of the most compelling in the history of mankind.

Think about all the things we've just referenced here. Jesus has invoked the ritualistic concept of the Holy Eucharist. Christ has announced that he will be betrayed. Judas, with his sack of silver coins in his hand, alerts everyone at the table—and everyone in the refectory—that he's the culprit. The disciples recoil at what they've just heard. A knife appears to signal the fight that will ensue when Judas and the Roman Centurions arrest Christ in Gethsemane. And then Thomas arrives, with his finger in the air, to inspect the wound of the resurrected Christ when he appears at the Supper at Emmaus.

Leonardo has intentionally packed into a single painting references to a variety of moments in the Passion sequence. It's all here—not as an actual narrative cycle that explicitly represents these scenes in full, but rather as an abbreviated montage of snippets that jog the memory and help tell a bigger, broader story than the one represented before our eyes.

Indeed, there was a long and proud history of doing precisely this sort of thing in Italian art, and Leonardo was surely aware of it. In the late 14th and early 15th centuries in Florence and in Tuscany, a very popular type of painting called the Man of Sorrows was created to do exactly the thing that Leonardo did in his *Last Supper* of the late 1400s.

One excellent example of the Man of Sorrows picture is this one, painted by Lorenzo Monaco in 1404, which succeeds beautifully in demonstrating the way a single painting can allude to an entire narrative sequence by using mere signs and symbols. Lorenzo shows us the Chalice of *The Last Supper*; the 30 pieces of silver collected by Judas to betray his Messiah; the arrest of Christ, including the kiss of Judas and Peter's knife slicing off the ear of the servant boy; Peter's denial of Christ and the cock that crows at the moment he utters his third lie are shown here; so is the scourge used to beat Jesus; Pilate washing his hands; the cross upon which Christ was nailed; the lance that Longinus used to stab the victim; the tongs that pulled the nails out of Christ's hands and feet; and the mourning Mary and the beardless John the Evangelist, who prepare him for burial, just as Christ simultaneously seems to lift out of his tomb in an act of resurrection and ultimate triumph.

Now this is a tradition that Leonardo knew, for he was about the most knowledgeable art historian of his age. He knew there were subtle, but effective, ways to tell a long story by referring to it briefly, in small sound bites, to an audience that was just as aware of these types of pictures as he was. He knew that they'd understand the multiple episodes that he was referencing, and he felt comfortable laying out for his educated viewers—those friars in the refectory—the entire Passion story, from start to finish, in this one, single mural painting.

But missing from our reading of *The Last Supper* as a sequential narrative of the Passion of Christ is the actual moment of Crucifixion, the key part of the story around which everything else revolves. Without that, it's hard to see this as a complete cycle that covers all the important bases. So why is that missing, you might ask?

This is a major reason why I believe that the likely image on the other wall of the refectory, would have been a scene of the Crucifixion, the other type of image that so often ornamented refectories in monastic institutions during the Middle Ages and the Renaissance. That's where the subject of Crucifixion was supposed to appear in the dining hall of Santa Maria delle Grazie, and that's why it's not here in Leonardo's *Last Supper*.

Now one thing to keep in mind every time you look at a sculpture in a museum or see a painting in a church: Images all have lives of their own. They grow and they change and they do things and they have things done to them, and sometimes the life that the image leads after its completion is just as interesting as the message that the image bears. And this is one of those cases.

Leonardo completed *The Last Supper* in early 1498, and when he did, it caused a furor. Painters and printmakers came to see it. Art lovers and collectors asked for entry into the refectory. Visitors to Milan and citizens of the city came in for viewings. Only a few months after its completion, *The Last Supper* was the subject of an engraving made by an artist named Giovannni di Pietro da Birago, who copied it and distributed this reproduction all across the Italian peninsula.

It's not a completely faithful copy—he has added a couple of extra tiles along the floor, a placard with lines from Matthew that is noted there—but he gets most of the gestures and he understands the main themes that Leonardo aimed to capture. The form became quite popular as the 16th century progressed and as champions of Leonardo's innovative skills tried to employ his lessons.

Marco da Oggiono, for example, painted this large canvas as a close copy of Leonardo's version in Santa Maria delle Grazie, although the background seems to be harsher in this copy.

In 1520, a Florentine painter named Andrea del Sarto began working on a *Last Supper* in the Florentine church of San Salvi, the same one that owned the painting of the Baptism of Christ that Leonardo had helped painted back in 1472. Much of this composition depends on Leonardo's Milanese example, and Andrea del Sarto makes sure that he pays close attention to the physical and emotional responses that his disciples reveal, and he retains that triangular pose of Christ, and he obeys the distance observed by his closest apostles. Moreover, he remembers to set on the upper quadrant of his painting three windows leading out into a background. It's not a direct copy, of course, but it was a fitting homage to Leonardo's *Last Supper*.

And Pieter Paul Rubens, the most influential artist of the 17th century, visited Milan and produced a drawing that his followers came to copy—and here we see a print of one of those copies by the Flemish artist Pieter Claesz, in which the figures have been reversed due to the nature of the printing press (that captures all things backwards). It's a pretty faithful rendition of the scene, save for the Baroque flourishes and the limited spatial recession.

But despite its popularity, Leonardo's *Last Supper* began to frustrate its admirers quite soon after its completion. Leonardo's experiment, it turns out, had gone horribly awry. His application of oil pigments, layered onto on dried egg tempera that had been laid onto its dry surface, soon began to show signs of instability. The topcoats of oil first started to bubble, and then to blister. The egg underneath was being pulled by the weight of all those oil glazes, and the picture started to crack from underneath. Even during Leonardo's own lifetime, flakes of pigment were starting to be swept up by the custodians in the refectory of Santa Maria delle Grazie.

By 1517, chroniclers were praising Leonardo's great invention, but in the next breath they would lament its horrible condition. By 1547, they were calling it "ruined," and when Vasari got around to writing his 2nd [edition of the] *Lives of the Artists* in 1568, he described *The Last Supper* as nothing more than "a spot on the wall."

Other interventions marred its surface over time. In 1652, a doorway was cut into the wall, just at the place where Christ's feet had been located. That was soon bricked up again, but all that pounding against the painting's support shook the wall and the flaky pigments, causing even more damage. Two projects in the 18th century attempted to repair the damage and to stabilize the colors, but both of these did more harm than good. Missing areas were filled in by painters in 1726, and the entire surface was sealed with varnish—which, in turn, soon yellowed, and then began to pull even more paint off the surface.

Another project was initiated in 1770 that called for all of the earlier varnish and repainted sections to be stripped away from the original, but with the result that some of Leonardo's original paints from 1497 were also removed in the process.

When French troops invaded Milan and occupied it in 1796, the refectory of Santa Maria delle Grazie was used by those soldiers of the Revolution as an armory. Perhaps in an act of anti-Catholic defiance, they threw rocks at *The Last Supper* and climbed up ladders to scratch out the eyes of the disciples.

Twenty years later, attempts were made to detach the painting from the wall so that it could be placed in a safer environment. But the process was botched, and central sections of the painting were badly damaged before chunks of the wall and the paint were glued back in place.

The closest it came to complete ruination occurred in August of 1943, when an allied bomb struck the refectory and almost destroyed the building entirely. The *Last Supper* only survived because its caretakers had jammed sandbags up against it, from floor to ceiling, to prevent its destruction from just such an attack.

By the 1970s, *The Last Supper* was understandably in horrible condition, and most specialists believed—with reason—that there was less paint on the wall applied by Leonardo da Vinci than there was paint applied by the legion of restorers who had tried to fix it in the intervening years.

In 1978, an extensive and highly technical conservation project was undertaken by Italian restorers to remove centuries of dirt and grime, layers of varnish, glue, and topcoats of paint that had been placed on in previous generations. Finally, in 1999—21 years later—the restoration was complete, revealing a brightness and a vividness that had not been seen for generations—but it also unflinchingly allowed bare spots to remain bare.

As an intellectual experiment, Leonardo da Vinci's *Last Supper* was an extraordinary success, maybe one of the most extraordinary of all time. But the painting wasn't loved or admired because of the unusual way in which Leonardo composed it or painted it. If anything, the recognition it received during Leonardo's day, and right up until our own, was earned more in spite of its experimental nature. Instead, the painting succeeds because of what it tells us about human nature, about ourselves, and about the world in which we live.

In Leonardo's Christ we see what we aspire to be: courageous in the face of death and resolute in a time of peril. In each of the apostles we can see something of ourselves, both as individuals and as members of a collective, hearing bad news and recoiling from the emotional pain it causes us. And in Judas the Betrayer, we see all that we fear the most within us: the capacity for evil, the ability to succumb to temptation, and the weakness to give in to the darker side of our nature.

The *Last Supper* is more than just a great painting: It's one of the world's most important and enduring cultural monuments. Kenneth Clarke famously called it "the keystone of Western art," and this evaluation has never been challenged. Its message of supreme hope, even in the face of utter disaster, lives on inside us as an exemplum of how to carry on, even in our darkest hour.

Mantua, Isabella d'Este, and Venice

Lecture 22

When Milan fell to the French in 1499, Leonardo's association with Ludovico Sforza ended. For the next eight years, he was constantly on the move, but his first stop was the city of Mantua. Mantua's ruling family, the Gonzaga, was known for its cultural sophistication, and the family's leading light was its duchess, Isabella d'Este, who had long admired Leonardo's work. Leonardo's stay in Mantua was brief, but marks an important period of artistic and personal transition in his life.

The Fall of Ludovico Sforza

- *The Last Supper* became famous very quickly, and it confirmed for those in the know that Leonardo was the greatest living artist of his day. Although he must have had a list of projects awaiting him in the wake of this success, Leonardo was no doubt gearing up to paint the second wall of the refectory next.

- Meanwhile, King Charles VIII of France had died in 1498 without a male heir. To settle the succession, his widow, Anne of Brittany, married his cousin, the Duc d'Orleans. This king took the name Louis XII and embarked on a campaign to retake Milan from Ludovico Sforza.

- Louis's troops met little resistance, and Ludovico fled the city in October of 1499, retreating to the town of Novara. He hired Swiss mercenary troops and made one last attempt to retake the city in the winter of 1500, but Louis's troops were also Swiss, and Ludovico's troops betrayed him rather than fight their own countrymen. Ludovico died in French captivity in 1508.

Departure from Milan

- There were aspects of life as courtier that irritated Leonardo, yet he also likely appreciated the freedom to work as an intellectual free agent under certain conditions, switching loyalties to another leader almost at will. In this sense, it is rather surprising that Leonardo neither fled Milan for greener pastures nor followed Ludovico to Novara when the French arrived.

- Some sources indicate that the French were impressed with Leonardo and interested in keeping him around. It has even been suggested an offer was dangled before Leonardo almost as soon as Louis entered the city. However, the soldiers' destruction of the clay colossus could not have gone well with him.

- In mid-December of 1499, Leonardo sent the significant sum of 600 florins to the hospital of Santa Maria Nuova in Florence for safekeeping—the equivalent of a few years' salary for a courtier. Within a few days, he packed his bags and left Milan.

- Travel was not a simple proposition. Although unmarried, Leonardo was responsible for the well-being of an assistant named Gian Giacomo Caprotti da Oreno, or **Salai** ("the little devil"). He was a notorious mischief-maker but skilled with the pen and brush. He understood his master's interests and eccentricities, and he was utterly, unshakably loyal.

- Luca Pacioli, the Milanese mathematician that Leonardo had befriended at court, was also part of Leonardo's entourage because they were finishing a book together. So, too, were countless drawings for Leonardo's unfinished projects—15 years worth. That said, an enormous chunk of Leonardo's life was also left behind.

Arrival in Mantua

- The group's first stop was the small, remote, and relatively poor sovereign duchy of Mantua, ruled by a member of the Gonzaga family. It lay between Milan to the north and Florence to the south.

- The Gonzaga boasted one of the finest collections of paintings, medallions, and manuscripts in Italy. They also patronized a brilliant young painter named Andrea Mantegna, who captured his patrons in portraits as figures of exquisite taste, high fashion, and cultural superiority.

- In 1500, the duke of Mantua was Francesco Gonzaga. He was married to a woman of tremendous intellect and cultural sensitivity named Isabella d'Este who, as we have seen, was well aware of Leonardo's talents. The daughter of the duke of Ferrara, Isabella was learned, erudite, and one of Europe's most dedicated and skilled art collectors.

- A portrait of Isabella, painted by the Venetian artist Titian in the 1530s, captures her appearance at a much younger age—and an idealized appearance at that—in the style of Leonardo's portrait of Cecilia Gallerani that Isabella so admired.

- Isabella was a logical person for Leonardo to call on when he was forced to flee Milan. She was the sister of Beatrice d'Este, Ludovico's late wife, and already a fan of Leonardo's work. This incident is a prime example of Leonardo's distinctive associations with the women of Ludovico's court.

- Leonardo, by now, also had quite a reputation; he was the High Renaissance equivalent of a rock star. Popular artists had attracted the attention of major patrons in the past, but Leonardo was not only skilled in the arts; he was head-and-shoulders above everyone in the arts and sciences, and a cult of personality began to circulate about him.

Leonardo and Isabella

- Soon after Leonardo arrived—we are not sure when—Isabella asked Leonardo to paint her portrait. Leonardo, contrary to his own rule of quick and effortless preparatory sketching, produced a remarkably refined and finished drawing of the duchess in profile.

- Leonardo has draped her in fashionable clothes, with a low but not untoward neckline. Her hair is carefully arranged to reveal her neck. She holds her head up with an air of dignity. She appears as a leader at court, despite being shown in old-fashioned profile.

- Perhaps Leonardo felt that the profile was Isabella's most attractive angle, or perhaps this was only one of an intended series of preparatory sketches, or perhaps this pose was Isabella's choice and not Leonardo's. Perhaps it was a combination of some or all of these things.

- Leonardo did not take this drawing with him when he left Mantua, however, which implies that it was not preparatory work. We might then surmise that the drawing was so finished because Leonardo never intended to linger in Mantua and knew he would not have time to paint Isabella from life, yet he wanted this important collector to own a display-worthy work.

From Mantua to Venice

- Leonardo left Mantua in March 1500 and set off north for the city of Venice. It has been suggested that his intent was to print the book he and Luca Pacioli had been working on, since Venice was home to Italy's most advanced and active publishing houses. Alternatively, Leonardo may have had official business in Venice, for his arrival was met with great fanfare by the government.

- The Republic of Venice quickly employed Leonardo as a military consultant. Within weeks of his arrival, he produced a white paper warning that the Turks' best approach to the city would be over land, across the River Isonzo, and urging the construction of defenses there. It appears they followed his advice.

- It may have been during his six-week stay in Venice that Leonardo dreamed up a diving apparatus—another one of his quick but brilliant concepts that, as far as we know, was never put to use.

- Leonardo's time in Venice was short before he packed up and headed south once more. He left no traces of his contacts, no hints of commissions, and no preparatory drawings that suggest he was trying to find work there. This venture seems to have been intentionally brief.

Name to Know

Salai (a.k.a. **Gian Giacomo Caprotti da Oreno**; 1480–1524): Salai, or "the little devil," was Leonardo's assistant and colleague for 30 years. In 1519, he inherited from Leonardo *Mona Lisa, Saint Anne Madonna, John the Baptist,* and the now-lost *Leda and the Swan,* all of which passed into the hands of his sisters on his death. They, in turn, sold the pictures to King François I of France.

Suggested Reading

Clark, *Leonardo da Vinci: An Account of His Development as an Artist.*

Kemp, *Leonardo da Vinci: The Marvellous Works of Nature and Man.*

Mantua, Isabella d'Este, and Venice
Lecture 22—Transcript

Leonardo's completion of *The Last Supper* for the refectory of Santa Maria delle Grazie was the cause of much discussion in art circles of the day. In it, Leonardo had captured not only the essence of the subject in ways that were both extremely clear and profoundly sophisticated, but he had managed to illustrate the very concept of the High Renaissance in one coherent picture. It was famous very quickly, and it confirmed for those in the know that—simply put—Leonardo da Vinci was the greatest living artist of his day.

Surely Leonardo had a whole list of projects lined up and waiting for him once *The Last Supper* was completed. Now Leonardo doesn't reveal to us what his most pressing task was at the time, but when we remember that Ludovico Sforza was eager to commence work on the painting of a second wall in the refectory of Santa Maria delle Grazie, I think we can speculate that Leonardo must have been gearing up for that project in 1499. Of course, knowing him, there must've been others in the pipeline, as well. I'd love to tell you what some of these projects were, in 1499. But I can't. History gets in the way of these kinds of questions sometimes.

The king of France, Charles VIII, had died in 1498, without a male heir to inherit his throne, and under normal circumstances this would have resulted in a power struggle. But not long after Charless death, his wife, Anne of Brittany, agreed to marry the one person in France who had the most logical claim to the throne, Charles's cousin, the Duc d'Orleans. When she did this, all the other claims to the throne faded away, and the Duc d'Orleans was recognized as the new king of France—and he took the name of Louis XII.

It didn't take but a few months for Louis XII to embark on his campaign to avenge the dishonor done to his cousin Charles by Ludovico Sforza back in 1495, and the new king quickly convened an army to lay claim to what his predecessor, Charles, had briefly conquered four years earlier.

Louis's troops essentially repeated the expedition that Charles had led in 1494: again, Pope Alexander VI favored the action, in the hopes that the French would defeat Ludovico Sforza and expel him from the Milanese throne. These hopes in fact were realized in quite short order, for Louis XII's French troops met very little resistance as they marched into Milan. Rather than face what appears to have been a daunting military force, Ludovico Sforza fled the city he governed in October of 1499, and he left a garrison of troops behind him the Castello Sforezesco. After a brief siege, and a healthy bribe, the commander of the garrison handed over the entire kit and caboodle to the French. It was the only genuinely defensive position in the city, and that was that.

Ludovico retreated to the town of Novara, to serve a self-imposed exile. But his pride got the better of him, and in the winter of 1500 he hired an army of Swiss mercenary troops and led a counter-attack that briefly expelled the French from Milan. But his victory was only short-lived. Those Swiss mercenary soldiers soon announced to him that they no longer wished to fight against the opposing mercenary forces that Louis XII had just bought to defeat them. It turns out that both armies—the one commanded by Ludovico and the one commanded by Louis—were of Swiss descent, and the two armies didn't much feel like killing each other.

After a brief siege and a yet another hefty bribe, Ludovico Sforza was handed over by his own mutinous mercenaries to the French occupiers in April of 1500, and they now kept the duke in captivity for the remainder of his life. He would die isolated, lonely, and utterly humiliated in a French dungeon in 1508. The portrait of Ludovico by Boltraffio that we see here from the 1490s—shows us here a noble, confident, and even learned humanistic prince—but it doesn't do justice to the wretchedness of his condition after his final capture by the French.

Now there were many things about the life of a courtier that irritated Leonardo da Vinci. As a bastard, he would have been susceptible to the condescension and envy of contemporaries who were not yet quite accustomed to the concept of a meritocracy. With no chance of social advancement and always dependent on the salary promised to him by his patron, Leonardo had not enjoyed the luxury of financial independence or official title to celebrate his vast achievements.

And, of course, he was basically required to do the bidding of his patron when asked to perform for him, so there were moments when Leonardo had been forced to execute projects that were not necessarily of his own choosing. But there was one very good thing about living the life of a hired gun, working for a foreign prince: Leonardo had the freedom to move from court to court as an Intellectual Free Agent when certain conditions allowed him to do so.

It was never lost on Leonardo, never, that his current employment—wherever, whenever, and for whomever that might be—was essentially temporary, and that the agreement he had with his patrons was essentially non-binding. Both parties knew that a prince's star could very easily crash and burn at literally any given moment, and few courtiers were expected to crash and burn with them. Once disaster struck, courtiers were free to flee.

That's why it's something of a surprise to me that Leonardo chose to remain in Milan when the French arrived there in the fall of 1499, for you'd think that an invading force trooping through the main streets of your city would be a pretty good enticement to run for your life. Why he didn't pack his bags immediately and head out to the nearest Italian court is anyone's guess.

Of course, we might also wonder why Leonardo didn't accompany Ludovico to Novara, or why he wasn't on hand to accompany the Swiss mercenaries when they drove the French out of Milan in 1500. One would think that both the courtier and his patron would have recognized an opportunity to build and test at least some of the innovative weapons of destruction that Leonardo had invented during his tenure in the Sforza court. But this never seems to have even entered into Leonardo's mind in the last weeks of 1499.

Some sources indicate that the French, once they had initially occupied Milan, were quite impressed with Leonardo and that they were interested in keeping him around to exploit his tremendous talents—it's also been suggested that some sort of offer or tacit agreement was dangled before Leonardo almost as soon as Louis XII entered the city.

But it was also at just about this time that French soldiers began taking aim at the clay colossus that Leonardo had sculpted and installed in the Milanese cathedral on the occasion of the marriage of Maximilian and Bianca Sforza, and Leonardo may even have witnessed them shooting their arrows into his equestrian sculpture. That could not have gone over very well with him.

In mid-December of 1499, Leonardo sent the significant sum of 600 florins to the hospital of Santa Maria Nuova, in Florence, for safekeeping. This was the equivalent of a couple years' salary for a well-to-do courtier, and it seems that Leonardo was setting up funds that he could use in his old stomping grounds. He had obviously had enough of Milan, and he wanted no part of the French who were now entrenched there. Within a few days he packed his bags, and he left town.

But leaving Milan and going on the road was not a simple proposition, and it would have required quite a bit of preparation. Although unmarried, Leonardo was responsible for the well-being of an assistant named Gian Giacomo Caprotti da Oreno, also known by his nickname of Salai (or "the little devil"). Salai had been in Leonardo's service for about 10 years by 1499, and Leonardo felt responsible for the boy's well-being.

Salai was a notorious mischief-maker, and when he first arrived in Leonardo's studio he turned out to be something of a headache—Leonardo actually wrote down a list of his transgressions in 1491, just to document Salai's shortcomings, and apparently Leonardo read his assistant the riot act. But Salai was skilled with the pen and brush, he understood his master's interests and eccentricities, and he was utterly, unshakably loyal. Leonardo had no children of his own, but in Salai he saw just about the closest thing he had to family: And Salai would have to come along.

Luca Pacioli, the Milanese mathematician that Leonardo had befriended at court, would also form part of the traveling entourage, for he was busy finishing a book that Leonardo was involved in creating. He would stay with Leonardo during most of this journey, as well. So too would all the drawings of unfinished projects that Leonardo had been working on for over 15 years, which must have filled trunks-worth of space. Those drawings, I think we can safely say, were Leonardo's children, as well.

But that said, an enormous chunk of Leonardo's life was also to be left behind, and he must have been at least somewhat rueful as he looked over his shoulder and watched the rooftops of Milan gradually fade into the white nothingness of one of his painted landscapes. He must have been more than just a little concerned about the future, what with his past laying in tatters at the feet of the French.

On one hand, there was really nothing that courtiers dreaded more than being set adrift from their moorings, floating in the countryside with no new court to latch onto. Leonardo had to have felt a little disoriented in December of 1499, what with no one to support him and with no prospects lined up for the immediate future.

But at the same time, for really the first time in his life, Leonardo was free to go where he wished: And while he had no salary coming to him, it wasn't as though he was destitute. He had obviously saved enough money over the years to survive on his own, he had sent a good sum of money to Florence to support him there, and he was clearly able to support Salai through all of this.

Their first stop was the small, remote, and relatively poor sovereign duchy of Mantua, owned and operated by one of the members of the Gonzaga family—one of the few princely operations in the Renaissance to last into the 17th century.

Now Mantua was a quaint little town that sat in between Milan to the north and Florence to the south. It retains much of the same charm today as it did then, and then as now, was marked by the imposing structure of the ducal palace of the Gonzaga family.

The Gonzaga had, for years, thrived as the ruling autocrats there. They had wisely invested their money in objects of art and culture, and boasted one of the finest collections of paintings, medallions, and manuscripts in all of Italy. They had also snapped up a brilliant young painter from the area named Andrea Mantegna, who had joined the Gonzaga court in 1465 and spent the next 40 years of his life celebrating the glory of his patrons.

Mantegna, whose brilliant fresco of the ducal family I show here, knew how to make his subjects look wise, powerful, and very well connected. In this picture, painted sometime around 1470, we see Ludovico Gonzaga receiving news from a messenger that his son has just been named to the position of cardinal. That, in and of itself, sends a message about the family that emphasizes their importance in a political sense.

But the Renaissance style employed by Mantegna was similarly intended to indicate that his patrons were people of exquisite taste, who knew what was fashionable and stylish, and who paid good money for court artists to promote their cultural superiority. The garments of the ladies in waiting, the rather plump duchess, the attendants in their silks and breeches, and even the dwarves who attend this entourage, all carry an air of nobility that only an artist like Andrea Mantegna could've captured.

Mantua was small, and the area governed by the Gonzaga family was not terribly important strategically. But what it lacked in prosperity it more than made up for in cultural sophistication.

Now in 1500, when Leonardo appeared at the front gates of the city, the latest duke of Mantua, named Francesco Gonzaga, was not coincidentally married to a woman of tremendous intellect and cultural sensitivity. Her name was Isabella d'Este; she was quite well aware of Leonardo's talents; and she admired his abilities as a painter.

Now Isabella d'Este is a person of some interest, and she commands our attention in ways not unlike Ludovico Sforza. Born in 1474, Isabella was the daughter of the duke of nearby Ferrara, and she married into the Gonzaga family in 1490 when she was 16 years old. Isabella was learned, erudite, and she became, at an early age, one of Europe's most dedicated and skilled art collectors. She took this hobby of hers very seriously, and she was almost pathologically obsessive about acquiring works from the day's most gifted painters.

I show here one of her most treasured pictures, a portrait of her that was painted by the Venetian artist Titian in the 1530s, at a time when Isabella would've been around 60 years old. Now I know we're getting ahead of ourselves just a little bit, as this portrait was painted by one of the shining stars of 16th-century, who produced this portrait of Isabella d'Este at least three decades after Leonardo made his trip to see her in Mantua. But the painting, and the brief story behind it, help us understand who Isabella was, what was important to her, and why she behaved the way she did whenever she had dealings with Leonardo da Vinci.

Now the picture by Titian is a brilliant and beautiful portrait. The sitter, young and pretty and decidedly blonde, emerges from a darkened background wearing a brocaded garment of silk, a magnificent hat, and what appears to be an enormous feather that stretches diagonally from her right hand to her left shoulder. She appears to us almost as a vision or an apparition, and Titian seems to be taking as a model the template that Leonardo had used when painting his portrait of Cecilia Gallerani back in 1491. We'll get to that issue in a minute.

Isabella has been shown here in all the grace and vivacity of her youth, and she has been placed on display here in an almost completely frontal pose—but not as an object to be ogled, but rather as a wealthy, prestigious member of the ruling class who deserves the deference she demands.

In other words, this picture has very little to do with the actual appearance of Isabella d'Este when Titian was paid to paint her portrait. According to contemporary reports, Isabella d'Este was rather stout, gruff, and just a bit unpleasant. Plus, she was about 60 years old when this portrait was delivered to her, and the sitter we see here is not 60 years old.

Moreover, it turns out that the painting by Titian that we see here was not the original one that he delivered to her: Rather, it was a second attempt by the famous painter. The first one had been delivered to Isabella in a timely manner, but when she saw what Titian had produced, in all its accuracy—warts and all—she returned it to him and demanded that he try again—and this time with an eye peeled more toward flattery than accuracy. This tells you a whole lot about Isabella d'Este.

Despite her vanities, Isabella was a logical person for Leonardo to call upon when he was forced to flee Milan in the last days of 1499. Isabella was the sister of Beatrice d'Este, who had married Ludovico Sforza in 1491 and acted as his duchess of Milan during the 1490s. It was Isabella who had requested and received the *Portrait of Cecilia Gallerani* as a loaner back in 1498, where she mentioned Leonardo by name in her letter to Cecilia, who was the mistress of Ludovico that her sister, Beatrice, had always loathed. And when Isabella received that portrait, she had a faithful copy of it rendered by one of her court artists. Thus, Isabella—in the 1530s—had on hand a replica of Leonardo's portrait of Cecilia Gallerani, and it wouldn't surprise me one bit if Isabella specifically requested that Titian use that image by Leonardo as his thematic guide. The end result suggests that that's exactly what she did.

I have spoken earlier in this course about Leonardo's distinctive associations with the women of Ludovico Sforza's court, and I maintain that it was through them that Leonardo had gained the trust and respect of the entire entourage in the Castello Sforzesco. Now I want to extend that line of argumentation just a little bit farther and say that I believe this network of clientele now came to Leonardo's assistance in the wake of his flight from Milan.

Social networks in Renaissance Italy were indescribably important. People of all stations depended on their social betters to help them advance through their lives—professionally, romantically, and domestically. In times of trouble, it was hoped that one's contacts would be willing to advocate for them—to help them find employment, to intercede with a reluctant father of an eligible bachelorette, or to avenge a wrong done to them by an enemy.

It's no coincidence that Leonardo sought out Isabella. He knew that Isabella knew him; he knew that they were bound by the mutual bond of Beatrice d'Este; and he knew that Isabella liked his work and respected his artistry. That last item alone would make the duchess of Mantua thrilled to admit Leonardo into her court.

For Leonardo, by now, also had something else going for him that transcended the social network of patronage that put him, as a Sforza courtier, in an advantageous position. For by 1500, Leonardo had acquired a reputation that preceded him wherever he went. In fact, I like to think of him at this point in his career as the High Renaissance equivalent of a 21st-century rock star:

Artists had already begun to make the trek to Milan to see his *Last Supper*, and copies were being made of it only a few months after the scaffold had been taken down in 1498. Poems had been written about his pictures and his artistic genius. And his abilities as a painter were known among the day's most important patrons, thanks in no small part to correspondences and gossipy conversations between the noblemen and women who governed the various sovereign city-states of late 15th-century Italy.

Now there had been popular artists who had attracted the attention of major patrons in the past, and we've already encountered a couple of them in this course—Giotto and Donatello and Verrocchio all commanded respect across Italy during the 14th and 15th centuries, and their works were known from Naples in the south to Venice in the north, and in numerous points in between.

But Leonardo, at the dawn of the 16th century, was now in a league of his own. He wasn't just a famous painter who had done good works, and he wasn't just a skilled sculptor to be lodged in one's city to produce an important work. Leonardo was head-and-shoulders above literally everyone in the field of the arts and sciences, and his reputation as a painter, a sculptor, and an engineer preceded him wherever he traveled. Like a rock star, Leonardo was famous for his outstanding works, but he was also famous just for being Leonardo. There was something of a cult of personality that began to circulate about him.

There was no way that Isabella d'Este could've turned him down. Isabella didn't disappoint, either. It may have taken her days, it may have taken her weeks, but it didn't take Isabella long to ask Leonardo to paint her portrait. She clearly wanted to have a genuine Leonardo in her collection of paintings instead of merely the copy of her brother-in-law's favorite mistress; and she clearly wanted that genuine Leonardo to be a portrait of herself. And Leonardo obliged, first offering a verbal promise to paint her likeness in short order, and then actually sitting down to produce this finished drawing of the duchess in profile.

Now we've seen Leonardo's drawings before in this course, and we've heard the words he's written about the medium—mostly polemical admonitions warning his fellow artists about the dangers of devoting too much time and attention to a single drawing. They should be done quickly and effortlessly so there will be no emotional attachments to them to prevent the artist from changing them later on.

But here Leonardo defies his own directives. This drawing is beautifully executed, with Isabella's features expertly reproduced—although with some elaborations included. Isabella, according to sources, wasn't nearly this well-kept, and Leonardo is reputed to have put Isabella on a pretty significant diet in this portrait of her. Still, he has brought into this human form all of the lessons he had learned from his studies in Milan.

The figure has been expertly executed, with the sitter appearing to possess physical charms of distinction. Leonardo has draped her in fashionable clothes, with a neckline that drops an appropriate depth that is attractive without being overt or crass. Her hair has been carefully arranged to reveal her neck, but she does not wear it loosely, down her shoulders, which would have been considered unseemly. She holds her head up in that profile pose with an air of dignity. She appears as a leader at court, a sophisticated and cultured woman who handles her role with nobility.

But that profile pose, I must say, is a bit of a puzzler. It harkens back to that old-fashioned approach to female portraiture that Leonardo had avoided in literally all of his earlier pictures, and it raises questions about its employment here. Perhaps he felt that the most attractive features of Isabella's face and torso were best represented from this angle.

Perhaps this drawing was only one of an intended series of sketches that, when combined, would form a composite three-dimensional portrait that Leonardo could take with him and, in more secure times in the future, produce a painted representation of her: He did, in fact, promise to do just this during his stay in Mantua.

And perhaps this pose was Isabella's choice and not Leonardo's—perhaps she wanted an old-fashioned portrait of her to conform to the traditions she clung to as a member of the aristocracy. Or maybe it was a combination of some or all of these things.

But this story contains a curious note: Leonardo did not take this exquisite drawing of Isabella d'Este with him when he left Mantua, and instead left it there to reside with the sitter. Now it's no wonder that Isabella loved this drawing as much as she did, and it's no wonder that Isabella continued to pester Leonardo in the coming years to paint the portrait of her that he had promised he would. But if Leonardo had intended to use this drawing as a preliminary work to help him build up a painted portrait, he would have taken it with him for future use when he left.

Still, this story tells us something very important about Leonardo, about this drawing, and about the issues of the day. It's clear that Leonardo never intended to remain in Mantua for very long. The drawing was meticulously finished because Leonardo knew he wouldn't have time to paint her picture during his short stay, but we can also speculate that he wanted this important collector of contemporary art to have one of his images in her collection. He was no fool, and he knew that having a work owned by Isabella d'Este would be a feather in his cap. And, of course, the drawing would keep her interested in him and his work even after he left town.

But the painted portrait that Leonardo promised to paint for Isabella would never come to pass. Leonardo never had a chance to build Isabella's drawing into the picture that we know the sitter wanted desperately to possess, and he left Mantua able only to assure the duchess that he would get around to it as soon as he could.

So now, in March of 1500—only a few weeks after he had arrived—Leonardo set off north for the city of Venice. There are a couple of possible reasons for Leonardo's decision to go there in March of 1500. It's been suggested that Leonardo's friend from Pavia, the mathematician Luca Pacioli, wanted to publish a book on proportions that the two of them had been working on for about 10 years. As Venice was home to Italy's most advanced and active publishing houses, this would have been a logical place for them to get their work into print.

But it's also been suggested that Leonardo visited that city on official business, for Leonardo's arrival was met with great fanfare by the Venetian Republican government. They quickly employed Leonardo as a consultant to aid them as they considered ways to defend themselves against the military threats that they saw building up against them—the French were setting up camp in nearby Milan, while the Turks to the east were a constant source of concern.

It's not hard to imagine a Venetian emissary visiting Leonardo in Mantua with an invitation for him to visit Venice should the proper opportunity present itself. And it's not hard to imagine Leonardo accepting such an invitation, either.

The Venetians seem to have put Leonardo to work immediately, and within weeks of his arrival there, he produced a white paper report in which he warned his new clients that the Turks would be smart to stage an attack against them on land, moving through the area of Friuli. But he also remarked that, in order to do so, the Turks would need to cross the River Isonzo in order to approach Venice. Leonardo urged the Venetians to build up river defenses there as a natural impediment to such a campaign, and it appears that the Venetians followed his advice.

As was his custom, though, Leonardo also saw fit to consider a number of unusual and innovative projects that he thought might interest his new hosts in his spare time. It may have been during his six-week stay in Venice that Leonardo dreamed up this unusual invention. It's a diving apparatus that employs long tubes, joined by leather and metal rings to resist the high pressure of the sea under water. The tubes are attached to a floating bell that stays on the surface, and then connects to the facemask of the suit that's strapped onto the shoulders of the diver down below.

As you might have come to expect from Leonardo, this wasn't an invention intended to help local fishermen catch more lobster. As Venice was a sea-faring city, and as Venice depended on its navy for protection, Leonardo probably considered the diving suit as a military weapon that could permit the user to approach enemy vessels undetected, either to reconnoiter the size and strength of a fleet or to perform all sorts of mischief on a hull below the waterline. It's another one of those quick, but brilliant concepts that, as far as we know, was never put to use by clients who just weren't ready to understand what Leonardo was trying to do.

But neither Leonardo nor his hosts had much time to think about the Diving Suit he'd drawn, or even the white paper report on Venice's state of defense in 1500. Leonardo's time there was short-lived, and he was barely able to unpack his bags and take in the sights of one of the most unusual cities in all of Europe, before he had to pack up again and head back south once more.

He left no traces of his contacts, no hints of negotiated commissions, and no preparatory drawings like the one of Isabella d'Este that suggest he was trying to find work in Venice. This venture seems to have been intentionally brief, for Leonardo da Vinci had other places to go and other things to do.

Return to Florence—Sfumato and an Exhibition

Lecture 23

Leonardo's Second Florentine period—although that may be a misnomer—was among the most productive of his career. It also marked an important departure in his painting style, where he abandoned tenebrism and embraced sfumato completely. Leonardo was now so admired that he could almost do no wrong in the eyes of his patrons or the public. Other artists deferred to him, and the public came to see one of his preparatory drawings on display—an unheard-of event in the 16th century.

The Second Florentine Period

- Leonardo da Vinci reinvented himself a number of times during his 50-year career as a painter. Each phase of his professional life brought with it significant changes in the way he produced images for public audiences.

- When we take a wide-angle view of Leonardo's painterly output, we can point to moments when Leonardo took deliberate steps to breathe new life into his works. In Florence, *St. Jerome* and *The Adoration of the Magi* mark a significant leap from his earliest style; In Milan, his tenebristic portraits depart from *Adoration*, then *The Last Supper* presents a more sophisticated handling of form and content than anything that had come before it.

- The success of *The Last Supper* and that approach were abandoned almost immediately when he returned to Florence in 1500 and began working on inventive easel paintings like *Madonna of the Yarnwinder*. Thus the last great transformative phase of his career occurred during a period of great upheaval in his life.

- Between 1500 and 1508, Leonardo was rarely in one place longer than 12 months at a time, traveling from great city to great city all over the Italian Peninsula. We often call this Leonardo's Second Florentine Period, but it could just as easily be called Leonardo's Nomadic Period.

- Some of this movement was due to Leonardo's own choices. But he was also in very high demand by some of Europe's most powerful people, and when those sorts of players called on him to drop whatever he was doing to join them, he had little choice but to acquiesce.

- All this travel should have taken a physical toll on Leonardo, but oddly enough he was incredibly productive throughout all of it. He produced three beautiful Madonnas; a massive fresco; military plans for at least three sovereign states; two sensual figures of strikingly originality; books on painting, flight, and anatomy; the first one-man exhibition in modern history; the foundations of modern medical science; and the most famous painting of all time.

- We know a surprising amount about Leonardo's wanderings. Some information has come down to us in the form of legend and hearsay, but some appears in chronicles, letters, and official statements. It seems his fame was such that people preserved documents that referred to him.

- Leonardo was not oblivious to all this attention, but he did not let it affect his work. He continued to produce good works for his patrons in a reasonably timely fashion and accepted commissions from common people.

Isabella d'Este and *Madonna of the Yarnwinder*

- Leonardo arrived in Florence in May and quickly settled into a new life in his old home. By the summer, he had secured a position as an architectural advisor to a local church and to sketch a villa on the outskirts of Florence so that Francesco could build a duplicate one near Mantua.

© Hemera/Thinkstock.

Florence welcomed its famous son back in 1500, but Leonardo was never truly able to settle there again.

- Leonardo set up a studio in the venerable church of Santissima Annunziata, near the Duomo. Vasari tells us that this workspace was already in use by Filippino Lippi, who happily surrendered it to his more famous colleague.

- Another indicator of his success and notoriety was the continued interest of Isabella d'Este. Impatient for her promised portrait (her husband had, rashly and without her permission, given away the sketch), she wrote to a Florentine friend, a cleric named Fra Pietro, asking him to negotiate with Leonardo for a change in their contract. She would now accept a Madonna in place of her portrait.

- Fra Pietro reported back to her twice within 11 days about Leonardo's doings. In the first letter, Pietro said Leonardo had almost completed a preparatory cartoon of Saint Anne, the Virgin, Christ, and a lamb. This was good news for Isabella, but the bad news was that Leonardo was now distracted by his studies of geometry and mathematics.

- In his second letter, Pietro said he had finally spoken with Leonardo and had communicated Isabella's wishes. Leonardo wanted to "immediately make the portrait" of Isabella, if only he could "detach himself from his obligation to the King of France without dishonor."

- Fra Pietro went on to describe the picture that Leonardo was then painting for his French patron, a Madonna to be given to Louis XII's secretary of state, Florimond Robertet. That painting is now known as *Madonna of the Yarnwinder*.

- Standing only 19.5″ × 14″, this intimate portrayal of the Holy Family is one of the most important paintings not only in Leonardo's career but in the art of the Florentine High Renaissance. Here we have a young Mary in a seated contrapposto and a chubby human Christ, their bodies forming a pyramidal composition. Christ gazes at the yarnwinder, which is an upside-down cross, a reminder of what is to come. In the background are the beautiful landscape features we have come to expect from Leonardo.

- What is innovative is how this painting brings together Leonardo's interests in light, optics, movement, and dramatic narrative all at once and points us in the direction his art will take for the rest of his life. After years of tenebrism, Leonardo now turned to a more subtle approach to light. His figures are seated in a natural landscape, brilliantly illuminated by the shining sun. Hard outlines have been replaced by fuzzy intersections of colors that dissolve, one into the next. Shadows still cover their limbs, but the distinction between illuminated and shaded areas is no longer cut and dried.

- These effects are a development of the sfumato technique Leonardo had periodically experimented with during his youth, which could only be captured through oil paints, not egg tempera.

- This painterly effect corresponded to an optical effect Leonardo had studied for much of his adult life: that human beings can rarely distinguish the outlines of objects positioned at even a modest distance from the eye.

- Sfumato creates a naturalistic effect that gives specific items, and the overall composition, a quality we recognize from our daily experience. Sfumato brought Leonardo closer than anyone before him replicating not the world itself but the viewer's experience of the natural world.

The Second and Third Florentine Madonnas

- As Leonardo worked on *Madonna of the Yarnwinder*, he set up a second easel next to this painting to produce a second version—not a copy but an additional interpretation of the same image.

- Now known as the *Lansdowne Madonna*, it has more distinct outlines, less covert shadows, and a higher vantage point. The vast sea in the background is replaced by a mountain range.

- There are three views on why Leonardo painted this second image. He may have simply made it for quick sale; he may have made it in case *Yarnwinder* was too innovative for Monsieur Robertet's tastes; or it may have been for Isabella d'Este, in place of the promised portrait.

- The first option is probably the best explanation. Monsieur Robertet liked the *Madonna of the Yarnwinder*, and Leonardo kept the second version to do with as he pleased. There is evidence that it was noticed by other painters working in Florence, including Raphael di Sanzio, and its influence can be seen in their works.

- There may have been a second source from which Raphael drew: The cartoon that Fra Pietro mentioned in his letter to Isabella d'Este. The one described by Fra Pietro has disappeared, but we have a sketch related to it, and Leonardo reproduced this composition a number of times during his career.

- In this classical composition, Anne, the mother of Mary, occupies the central position. Mary sits on Anne's lap with her legs extending in one arm of the pyramid. Christ is in Mary's arms in what is called the swimming Christ pose. He looks down at John the Baptist, who forms the right edge of the classical triangle. The interacting figures are modeled by deep shadows and bright white chalk highlights.

- Leonardo's drawing may have been seen by many artists and viewers in Florence in a remarkable setting. According to Vasari, when Leonardo had finished it, he put it on display in Santissima Annunziata for the public. For two days, Vasari says, the drawing was visited and admired by "men and women, young and old, as if they were going to a solemn festival."

- Exhibiting one's works outside their finished setting was unheard of at this time. Moreover, we have no precedents for an artist presenting a drawing as a finished work of art, suitable for public consumption.

- Vasari cannot be trusted completely, but if this tale is true, then Leonardo's public showcase is one of the earliest examples of a modern art exhibition. We can surmise that Raphael saw it and was influenced by it.

- An exhibition also suggests that Leonardo not only recognized the importance of works as art objects in and of themselves but that he wanted the general public to recognize them, too.

Suggested Reading

Bell, "*Sfumato* and Acuity Perspective."

Kemp, ed., *Leonardo da Vinci. The Mystery of the Madonna of the Yarnwinder.*

Nathan, "Some Drawing Practices of Leonardo da Vinci."

Wasserman, "The Dating and Patronage of Leonardo's Burlington House Cartoon."

Return to Florence—Sfumato and an Exhibition

Lecture 23—Transcript

Leonardo da Vinci reinvented himself a number of times during his 50-year career as a painter. Each of the different phases or stages of his professional life brought with it significant changes in the way he produced images for public audiences. He evolved constantly, he was never content to repeat himself, and he worked extremely hard to make sure that everything he did was fresh, original, and utterly new. Moreover, the eclecticism of Leonardo's overall career, as a jack-of-all-trades, was matched by an eclecticism that he embraced as an artist. All of this explains why every single painting that he produced has demanded our attention.

In fact, when we take a wide-angle view of Leonardo's painterly output, I think we can see distinctive junctures where Leonardo shifted gears in an attempt to breathe new life into his works. In Florence, the *St. Jerome* and the *Adoration of the Magi* from 1481 mark a significant leap from his earliest style, while in Milan his deeply tenebristic portraits, with their sharp contrasts between dark and light, point him in a direction that departs from the *Adoration*.

The *Last Supper* presents a more sophisticated handling of form and content than anything that had come before it, but the success of that picture and the approach that he took, were abandoned almost immediately when he returned to Florence in 1500 and began working on inventive easel paintings—like the *Madonna of the Yarnwinder*, that forms a key element of our discussion today. Leonardo wasn't just unafraid of change: He welcomed it, he sought it out, and then he celebrated it once he had embraced it.

But that said, the last great transformative phase of his career as artist was developed during a period of great upheaval in Leonardo's life. Between 1500 and 1508, the artist was rarely in one place longer than 12 months at a time. He frequently traveled vast distances in a matter of weeks, and bounced back and forth between Milan and Florence so often that it's easy to get completely turned around when considering his chronology.

I want very much to call this Leonardo's Second Florentine Period, but it could just as easily be called Leonardo's Second Milanese Period, Leonardo's Nomadic Period, or Leonardo's Where's Waldo Period.

Here's what I mean: From the end of December, 1499 until April of 1500, Leonardo was in Mantua and Venice. But we know he was in Florence by May of that year, and he stayed there for about 18 months.

He spent the summer of 1502 in the Romagna, working for the Dark Lord, Cesare Borgia, until October, maybe even until January of 1503. He then disappears from view entirely for a good six months, during which time we know about neither his movements nor his professional pursuits.

He reappears in Florence, in March, 1503, and in July he was in the Tuscan hills with Machiavelli, trying to destroy Pisa. He returned to Florence before the summer's end, and stayed there for roughly 14 months, until November of 1504. He then spent time in the town of Piombino to serve as a military consultant for the Florentine government, but he returned to Florence in 1505, for another 14 months or so.

In May of 1506, he was forced to go back to Milan, where he stayed at least through the month of February in 1507. He went back and forth between Milan and Florence for the remainder of 1507: In March he was in Florence; in May he was in Milan; in August he was in Florence again—and this time for a full year.

He stayed in Florence until September of 1508, but then he went back to Milan—this time for a quite good chunk of time—basically until about 1513. But after 1508, Leonardo would never again return to Florence for any considerable length of time.

The problem doesn't necessarily lie with Leonardo personally. True, he often had some alternatives laid before him from which to make some choices, and the great distances he traveled were at times traversed voluntarily. But he was also in very high demand by some of Europe's most powerful people, and when those sorts of players called upon him to drop whatever it was that he was doing, he really had little choice but to acquiesce.

Leonardo could go about 50 miles per day when he was traveling, but only if he were riding hard on the back of a horse. In a carriage or a cart, his average daily distance might be about 35 miles, depending on how many hours he was willing to spend each day on a wagon that had no shock absorbers to ease the jostling and bumping that came with travel on the dirt roads of 16th-century Italy. It's too bad he didn't invent those when he was in Milan. In any event, all this travel should have taken its toll on him physically; but, oddly enough, he seems to have been incredibly productive through all of it.

During this phase of his career, Leonardo produced three beautiful Madonnas, a massive mural for the Republic of Florence, some military plans for at least three separate sovereign states, two sensual figures of strikingly originality, separate books on painting and flight and anatomy, the first One-Man Art Show in modern history, the foundations of modern medical science, and the most famous painting of all time.

All this activity makes us rethink his various projects during his first period of activity in Milan, between 1482 and 1499. One wonders whether his talents might have been poorly managed, if not wasted outright, by Ludovico Sforza. We have to ask ourselves if he might have been more productive as a painter (or more successful as an engineer) had he been able to focus on only one or two of the multiple tasks that he took on during his tenure there.

Now Leonardo arrived in Florence in May of 1500 and quite quickly settled into a new life in his old home with great ease. By the summer, he had secured a position as an architectural advisor to a local church that was in desperate need of repair. At the same time, he abided by a promise that he had made to Isabella d'Este's husband, Francesco Gonzaga, to draw a villa on the outskirts of Florence so that the duke could build a duplicate one near his home in Mantua as a vacation retreat.

Both projects required a good bit of drawing, and while we don't have the final products to inspect, we can say with certainty that Leonardo's skill with the pen was just as important for his patrons as was his skill with the brush.

We know that it took Leonardo little time to set up a studio in the venerable church of Santissima Annunziata, about 150 yards from the Florentine

Cathedral. This was a perfect location for Leonardo to work on projects of his own choosing and on those offered to him by important clients, for while it was still in the city center, Santissima Annunziata was just enough outside the heart of Florence to give him a little peace and privacy.

Vasari tells us that Leonardo was actually given a workspace there that was already in use by the artist Filippo Lippi, who was, at the time, working on the painting of a double-sided altarpiece for the church. Filippo, you might recall, was the painter whose Adoration of the Magi had recently been installed on the altar of Santa Donato a Scopeto to fill the void that had been created by Leonardo's inability to complete his original version back in 1481. Filippo Lippi, Vasari tells us, believed it would be an honor to surrender his studio in Santissima Annunziata to the famous Leonardo da Vinci, and out of deference to him, Filippo offered up the space.

That's one of the bits of information we have that supports the idea that Leonardo's status was demonstrably increasing at the turn of the 16th century. It wasn't normal for one artist to surrender a work space in one of the city's most important cultural centers, and Filippo Lippi would not have just done this for anyone. Leonardo must have been very special.

Another indicator of his success and notoriety was the continued interest shown in him by Isabella d'Este, the wife of Francesco Gonzaga and the duchess of Mantua. You remember that Leonardo had drawn her portrait in profile during his visit to Isabella's ducal palace in the winter of 1500. Perhaps he produced this finished drawing to satisfy Isabella's desire to own something by his hand. Or perhaps the drawing acted as some sort of promissory note to indicate his intention to paint her portrait before too long.

But that painted portrait didn't materialize. Isabella waited for Leonardo to make good on his promise through the remainder of the calendar year and on into the next year. But by the end of March 1501, she had had enough.

Annoyed by Leonardo's inability to produce what he had said he would, Isabella wrote a letter to one of her contacts in Florence, a cleric who went by the name of Fra Pietro. In her letter, Isabella explained that she needed a painted replacement for the drawing that Leonardo had done the previous year: for, remarkably, it seems that Francesco Gonzaga, her husband, had rather rashly given it away to someone else as a gift without Isabella's permission.

Realizing that Leonardo really had no interest in painting her likeness, Isabella now rather directly asked Fra Pietro, her Florentine contact, to act on her behalf in an effort to change the nature of her agreement with Leonardo in a way that would make it easier for him to provide her with a picture.

She wanted the friar to meet with Leonardo, to negotiate a deal, and to secure for Isabella's private art collection a painting of the Virgin Mary. Perhaps she felt that Madonna pictures, what with their popularity during the period, might be easier for the artist to dash off in his spare time—and she might even have believed that Leonardo, like other painters of the period, actually had a Madonna picture already completed and preserved in his workshop. Maybe Leonardo could be convinced to surrender that one to her.

Fra Pietro reported back to her within 11 days—twice—about Leonardo's doings. In the first letter, Pietro noted that Leonardo had almost completed a marvelous large cartoon, or a finished drawing, of a representation of Saint Anne, the Virgin Mary, the Christ Child, and a lamb. This must have been considered good news, for Isabella was in the market for just this kind of painting. Better yet, Leonardo had apparently told Fra Pietro that he wasn't currently painting anything for anyone else. There were no patrons lining up at his door—or, at least, there were no projects that interested Leonardo enough to cause him to accept their offer. This must have been music to Isabella's ears.

But then she must have frowned just a bit when the friar went on to report to her that Leonardo seemed so utterly consumed by his studies of geometry and mathematics that he had effectively turned his back on the visual arts altogether. This was a conflicting report—on one hand, Leonardo is deeply engaged in a picture of the Madonna. On the other, it looks like he's not pursuing its completion at all due to mathematical distractions.

But in the second letter that he sent, Fra Pietro clarified the situation, and essentially retracted a portion of his last statement. He reported that he had finally been able to speak with Leonardo directly and had communicated Isabella's wishes to him. Although, Leonardo had replied favorably, he had also added a substantial caveat. Fra Pietro indicated that Leonardo would "immediately make the portrait" of Isabella, if only Leonardo were able to "detach himself from his obligation to the King of France without dishonor."

Well! This little note tells us two important things: first, that—as far as Leonardo was concerned—the promise he had made to paint her portrait was still operative in his mind. Leonardo was not prepared to disappoint the duchess of Mantua, at least not so soon after she had shown him her hospitality when he had arrived at court the year before.

But second, and just as important, it's clear that Leonardo was working on a project for a French patron, who was either the king himself or someone in his service.

But Fra Pietro's letter to Isabella didn't stop there. Perhaps as a way of stoking her interest, Fra Pietro went on to describe the picture that Leonardo was then painting for this French patron. Leonardo, he wrote, was just then beginning a little picture of the Madonna and Child for Louis XII's secretary of state, a man named Florimond Robertet. Now this was exactly the kind of picture that Isabella d'Este had stated she wanted for her private collection should her portrait not be forthcoming. To read Fra Pietro's report about a Madonna picture in the works that was unavailable to her must have frustrated her to no end.

The picture in question was this one, the so-called *Madonna of the Yarnwinder*. It's another one of those domestic Madonna types that Leonardo had produced with some frequency back in the 1470s. It was fairly modest in size, standing only about 20 inches tall by 14 inches wide, and its familiar subject matter makes it easy to overlook, when compiling a list of works by Leonardo to study.

Yet this intimate portrayal of the holy family is one of the most important paintings, not only in the career of the artist, but for the very development of the Florentine High Renaissance in art. Alongside his more famous *Last Supper* and *Mona Lisa*, the *Madonna of the Yarnwinder* marks a specific turning point in the life and career of its maker—and, by extension, it signifies an important moment for Leonardo's followers and admirers, too.

The painting displays a subtly new direction of painting. Leonardo shows us this young Virgin Mary, who leans to her right, yet twists her body to her left. She seems to form a sort of seated contrapposto pose. She begins to raise her right hand. We see those foreshortened fingers, not unlike those that Leonardo painted on the Virgin Mary in the *Madonna of the Rocks* from 1483.

The Christ child is chubby, and his big cheeks cast shadows down his face. His torso is almost completely hidden in darkness. Now Jesus's genitals are barely visible. And that's important for us because it reminds his viewers that Jesus is human, born of a human mother. But he swings up and away to his left, causing a separation with the Virgin Mary and thus causing her right hand to raise, almost in surprise. She must catch him before he squiggles out of her arm. Jesus gazes at that yarnwinder that points up in the air, and he holds it lovingly: Why?

Well, if you take a close look at that yarnwinder, we can see that, in fact, it's a double crucifix—top and bottom—which both tells us what is to come in the story, but also that we are at an opposite moment of that story as we look at the picture.

Now it seems kind of sad to look at the image of the Christ child embracing the object of his death, but it's also actually a happy scene, because it reminds us that in the end Christ beats death, and that he ultimately lives resurrected in heaven. He may have been human, but he's also divine. Finally Leonardo shows us in the background a group of mountains that ultimately form a V toward our figures, an inverse to the pyramidal triangle that's been formed by the Virgin and her child. And there in the distance we see a shoreline and water, with the hint of an island out on the horizon.

It's here where I think we can truly begin to discuss one of Leonardo's great inventions of the early 16th century. With the *Madonna of the Yarnwinder*, Leonardo brings together his interests in light, optics, movement, and dramatic narrative all at once, and he points us in the direction he will go for the rest of his life.

After years of experimenting with tenebristic transitions between bright spotlights and total darkness, Leonardo now turned to a more subtle approach to his scenes and figures. His subjects no longer emerge suddenly and dramatically from the midst a black sea, a stylistic choice that had marked almost literally every single painting he had done since the beginning of his Sforza tenure.

Instead, Leonardo positioned his figures seated in a natural landscape, brilliantly illuminated by the shining sun, and moving confidently in the space he creates for them. Like the *Madonna with a Cat*, both Mary and Christ seem to slide away to their left, with the child strikes a pose that will soon become known as the Swimming Christ figure, due to its extended torso and stretching limbs. (You'll see it again later on in Leonardo's works in the 16th century.) Mary contains her son with her left hand, but with her right, she reveals her level of surprise at the boy's ability to squirm so powerfully out of her grasp. She turns her head to follow him.

That movement has inspired Leonardo; for now, rather than carefully delineating the contours of their bodies, Leonardo has intentionally blurred the edges of their faces, their bodies, and the things that surround them in the painting's background. Hard outlines have been entirely eliminated here, and have now been replaced by fuzzy intersections of colors that dissolve, one into the next. Shadows still cover their limbs, but now the distinction between illuminated and shaded areas is no longer so cut and dry. He doesn't reveal the cause of the shadow that hides the baby's midsection, for example, but he allows our intuition to guess the answer: It must be Mary's head and hand that cast those shadows, which in turn indicates that there's a natural light source above and behind the Virgin's head.

The indirect sunlight creates a softness in Mary's eyes, her nose, lips, and cheeks, while Christ's supple body moves in her hands as naturally as a real child. In Italian, this quality is known as "sfumato," and it's something that Leonardo had periodically experimented with during his youth in Florence and his early career as an artist in Milan.

Painting a picture with this kind of sfumato effect could only be done through the use of oil paints, the pigments that Leonardo employed as a young artist in the 1470s and 1480s. Unlike egg tempera paint, oils allowed him to layer microscopically thin glazes of pigment onto a painting's surface, to work up shadows or allow light to penetrate through them to the yellow undercoat beneath.

In the *Virgin of the Rocks* from the middle years of the 1480s, Leonardo had played with this technique, and his employment of soft light sources had caused his murky figures to float on the darkened surface of the panel. It had also taught him how to produce forms in a distant landscape that broke apart and dissolved into nothingness. And this painterly effect corresponded to one of those important optical effects that Leonardo had studied for much of his adult life: that human beings can rarely distinguish the outlines of objects positioned at even a modest distance from the eye, either because those objects are in motion or because our eyes really aren't that sharp—especially when we get older and lose the power to see clearly.

Sfumato creates a naturalistic effect that gives specific items, and the overall composition, a quality we seem to recognize from our daily experiences on this earth. Sfumato gave Leonardo a technique that brought him closer than anyone else before him to an exact replication not of the natural world necessarily, but of the viewer's experience of the natural world—which is a very different thing altogether.

Now Leonardo seems to have recognized that he was truly onto something with the *Madonna of the Yarnwinder*. As he worked on it for Louis XII's secretary of state, Leonardo appears to have literally set up a second easel next to the one holding that picture in order to produce a second version—not a copy, mind you, but an additional interpretation of the painting for Monsieur Robertet.

This one, now known as the Lansdowne Madonna, is a bit of a sharper image, as the outlines of the figures seem more distinct, the shadows less covert, and the vantage point considerably higher. The vast sea behind the *Madonna of the Yarnwinder* has now been replaced by an Alpine mountain range, and a winding river with a bridge spanning it appears about halfway up the picture plane. Why did Leonardo make this second version? Why did he make so many compositional changes to it? Did he have another owner or viewer in mind?

These are good questions, and there are three alternative views on this matter: Leonardo liked the *Madonna of the Yarnwinder* and clearly knew it would be popular. He made the second version of it so that he'd have one around for a possible sale once the first one was sent off to the French secretary of state. The second suggestions is that Leonardo wasn't sure whether Monsieur Robertet would like the *Madonna of the Yarnwinder*—the sfumato technique he employed there may not have been to the patron's tastes. And thus, Leonardo hedged his bets by making a second Madonna that he could easily send to his French customer should the first one be sent back.

And third, Leonardo may have been mindful of the promise he had made to Isabella d'Este, who in turn had made clear her willingness to alter their agreement and accept a painting of a Madonna rather than her portrait. Knowing that he wasn't likely to paint her portrait any time soon, which would require the two to be in direct contact with one another, Leonardo did this second Madonna intending to send it to Isabella and get her off his back.

Since he didn't get rid of it when he completed it around 1507, it seems like option number one is probably the best explanation. And, in fact, it turns out that secretary of state of Milan liked the *Madonna of the Yarnwinder*, and Leonardo had on hand the second version of the picture to do with as he pleased. And, indeed, the second version seems to have gotten a little notice.

One of the major artists working in Florence during the first decade of the 16th century was the Umbrian painter named Raphael di Sanzio. Like many people of the day, Raphael had traveled widely by the time he was in his early 20s. By 1505 or so he was living in Florence, and the paintings that he produced during his stay there indicate quite clearly that Raphael was profoundly influenced by Leonardo. It's a topic to which we'll return soon enough, but for the time being I want to show you this picture that indicates Leonardo's impact on his younger colleagues.

It's called the *Madonna of the Goldfinch*, and it shows us an image of the Virgin Mary complete with John the Baptist on our left, and Christ on the right located in between Mary's knees. Now we can spend a lot of time talking about the picture, but what I want to point out here is how Raphael has employed that classical composition, that pyramidal structure with the Virgin's head at the apex, her body extending and arms going down the edge of this isosceles triangle. And then her body containing those figures, who strike contrapposto poses that are laminated but also modeled with light and shadow, all the while standing in a Leonardesque landscape.

On the one hand, we can look to the *Madonna of the Yarnwinder* and its sibling, the *Lansdowne Madonna*, as the inspiration for Raphael (and others) who working and imitating him in Florence during the first decade of the 16th century. The comparisons are pretty clear, and the connections are very real.

But there may have been a second source from which Raphael drew. Remember the first letter written to Isabella d'Este by her Florentine contact, Fra Pietro, in April of 1501? The one that describes a cartoon of the Madonna, Anne, Christ, and a Lamb? Well, it turns out that that cartoon was a pretty big deal. The drawing was surprisingly complex, and Fra Pietro included a brief description of it in his letter to Isabella. He writes this:

> The cartoon depicts a Christ child of about one year, who almost climbs out of his mother's arms and seizes a lamb, which he appears to embrace. His mother, almost rising from the lap of Saint Anne, seizes the Child to separate him from the little sacrificial lamb, which signifies the Passion. Saint Anne rises slightly from sitting, and it seems as if she would wish to restrain her daughter so that she should not separate the baby child and the lamb, which perhaps may be intended to represent the Church, who would not have the Passion of Christ impeded.

Now the drawing I'm showing you here was probably not the one described by Fra Pietro, as we're now quite sure that the cartoon he mentioned in his letter has disappeared.

This image, though, is surely related to it. It's more of a quick sketch than a fully formed cartoon, as we can see by the bold strokes around the bodies and the undefined areas in the background, the landscape, and the draperies. But the same figures are there, and they've been arranged in a way that approximates Pietro's description—so we can at least get a sense of what he may have seen in Leonardo's workshop.

In fact, Leonardo reproduced this composition a number of times during his career. One of them is this finished cartoon—which is decidedly not the one Leonardo produced in 1501—but which most of us believe is again a pretty good approximation of it.

The cartoon reminds us of Leonardo's original interests in the classical composition. Anne, the mother of Mary, occupies the central position of the grouping. The Virgin sits on her lap, side-saddle, with her legs extending in one arm of the pyramid, down toward the lower left corner. In her arms appears her blessing Son, who strikes the Swimming Christ pose—seemingly emanating from the very womb of his mother. He looks down at his cousin, the youthful John the Baptist, whose languid slouch helps form the right edge of the classical triangle.

The figures interact with each other: Anne tilts her head toward Mary, who tilts her head toward Christ, who gazes down at John—who returns the favor. All of these figures have been carefully modeled by deep, dark shadows that have been juxtaposed with bright highlights—some of which are colored with white chalk; Other areas that catch the light are actually, just bare spots of the paper that appear to be spotlit only because they haven't been touched by Leonardo's hands at all. The void becomes the light.

Now what's interesting about this cartoon that Fra Pietro described in his letter to Isabella is that Leonardo's drawing appears to have been seen by other artists and viewers in Florence in a remarkable setting. Now it's Vasari who tells us that Leonardo was greeted in Florence by Filippo Lippi, who surrendered his studio in Sant' Annunziata so that Leonardo could use it. Leonardo accepted the offer, and busily went to work on the large cartoon that Fra Pietro saw there.

According to Vasari, when Leonardo had finished it, he actually mounted the drawing in Sant' Annunziata and put it on display for the public. For two days, Vasari says, the drawing was visited and admired by "men and women, young and old, as if they were going to a solemn festival."

Now this is utterly remarkable, for exhibiting one's works outside the specific context of its intended setting was unheard of at the time. Moreover, we have no precedents for an artist being able to show a drawing of all things as a finished work of art, suitable for public consumption.

Now you know by now that I don't exactly trust Vasari completely, and there's always room for skepticism when dealing with his anecdotes. But I actually kind of like this one, and I want to believe Vasari here.

For if this tale is true, then Leonardo's public showcase is one of the earliest examples that we have of a modern art exhibition, where a painter displayed his work outside the context of its setting or its intended viewership, expecting that his audience would be able to appreciate it for its aesthetic merits alone. Certainly, Raphael is one person who saw it and was influenced by it.

An exhibition also suggests that Leonardo not only recognized the importance of graphic works as art objects in and of themselves, but that he wanted the general public to get on board with him and appreciate them, too. It makes him someone who could see the future of art just as clearly as he saw the future of hydraulics, flight, and military science. And I like that.

It would be so nice if we had the drawing described by Fra Pietro that Vasari claimed was the object of this one-man show. But the cartoon is lost, perhaps due to over-handling, perhaps due to a careless owner, or perhaps it was simply one of Leonardo's many papers that were scattered and lost after his death.

I've focused in this lecture mostly on the first two years of what I've called Leonardo's "Second Florentine Period." But this Florentine Period was, in fact, interrupted by travels that took him to places far beyond the borders of his homeland and, on occasion, directly into the arms of patrons whose virtues were highly suspect.

And in the true spirit of the High Renaissance, it was in this crucible of instability and political intrigue that Leonardo da Vinci absolutely thrived.

Leonardo, Cesare Borgia, and Machiavelli

Lecture 24

Finding little paid work in Florence, Leonardo took work as a courtier to Cesare Borgia in 1502. As Cesare's chief architect and engineer, he advised on everything from border defense to the customs of the French court. He used his mathematical and inventing skills to create some of the most accurate city maps heretofore known. Leonardo also met and collaborated with another of the era's most famous figures while in Cesare's employ and for a time thereafter: Niccolò Machiavelli.

The Political Landscape of 1502

- Sometime in 1502, Leonardo made an interesting drawing in red chalk of a single figure displayed in three different poses. The drawing looks to be the kind of multiple-view sketch that painters and sculptors liked to do in anticipation of a larger project.

- The figure is bearded and gruff; the hair on his head and the whiskers on his chin form brackets on either side of his face—and create a fierce appearance, but what is most interesting is the figure's identity: He is Cesare Borgia, known in his day as the wickedest man in Italy. Leonardo not only knew him well but worked for him.

- When Leonardo arrived in Florence in May 1500, he was an old man by Renaissance standards, nearing the end of his career and returning to his roots to spread his wisdom. To some, he was a symbol of the establishment who needed to be outdone, outshone, and then put out to pasture.

- However, Leonardo still needed a paycheck, not to mention stimulating projects and to prove his worth. His return to Florence had not been a triumph: He had garnered zero official commissions from the Florentine government or any other institution in the city by 1502, and so he went looking for work as a professional courtier.

- At this time, Alexander VI was still pope, making the Borgia among Italy's most powerful families. Isabella d'Este wrote many diplomatic letters, trying to secure the borders of Mantua and negotiating with both Alexander's allies in Italy and the French in Milan to preserve its independence. By far, the biggest threat to any Italian state in this period was Cesare Borgia.

Leonardo and the Wickedest Man in Italy

- Cesare Borgia was reviled for his cunning, ruthlessness, and cruelty, but he was also unusually crafty, fiercely loyal to his men, and reputedly one of Europe's most charismatic and charming leaders. As the son of the pope, he had family connections that gave him entry into any court in Christendom. He was also one of the wealthiest men in Italy, thanks to his family's estate, his willingness to commit extortion, and his father's deep pockets.

- To be fair, Cesare Borgia was extremely well educated and by the age of 17 had proven himself so capable that his father could elevate him to the position of cardinal. Cesare used this rank, however, to carry out threats, tortures, and assassinations on his father's behalf and, in 1498, renounced his position and the wealth it brought with it to seek out a dukedom.

- Cesare set out to gobble up cities and towns on the eastern side of the Italian Peninsula just north of Rome, an area called the Romagna. His ultimate goal was to conquer the rest of Italy, too.

- It might seem strange that Leonardo—who valued virtue, honor, and dignity—would approach a man like Cesare Borgia, but Leonardo also had a brilliant military mind, was down on his luck, and had experience working with political potentates, irrespective of their virtues. It was not such an unusual move.

- Cesare hired Leonardo on the spot, and it wasn't long before he began referring to his prize employee as General Leonardo. Others may have been put off by Cesare, but Leonardo was not, at least at first.

- Leonardo joined Cesare in the early summer of 1502, just after Cesare had taken the city of Urbino from the Montefeltro family, who had ruled there for more than two centuries. Cesare then set out to scout and plan attacks on Imola and Piombino, secure the defenses of towns he had conquered but not yet fortified, and prepare to defend his gains against the French. Leonardo could help in all three areas.

- Leonardo's experiences in Milan made him, in Cesare's eyes, an expert on French affairs, so he was asked to advise Cesare on mores, customs, and personalities at the French court, which Cesare would use on his diplomatic mission to Milan in August 1502.

- Just as important was Leonardo's great experience as a military engineer. He was immediately set to the task of fortifying defenses in Cesare's border towns.

- Yet another benefit was Leonardo's understanding of geography, geology, and geometry, which gave him the tools he needed to survey new territories and gain vital environmental intelligence about the towns Cesare wished to annex.

- Leonardo toured Cesare's encampments and towns, which he and his assistants sketched with an eye toward improvement. In short order, his suggestions were put into place, which must have pleased Leonardo, who was more accustomed to having his ideas ignored by Ludovico Sforza.

- Leonardo also drew one of the most precisely crafted aerial views of any given location known to contemporary eyes—a bird's eye view without the bird—of the city of Imola. He used a surveying disc mounted at a central vantage point to measure the radial angles of major features of the city, coordinated with distances carefully measured with a device Leonardo invented, called a **hodometer**.

Leonardo and Machiavelli

- In October 1502, **Niccolò Machiavelli** arrived in Imola as an emissary of Florence. Like everyone else, the Florentines wanted to dissuade Cesare from looking their way. Unlike most others, Machiavelli found much to admire in Cesare, though he later critiqued Cesare's flaws as well.

- Machiavelli met Leonardo as well and saw with his own eyes the things Leonardo could do. The two appear to have formed a relationship grounded in mutual respect and admiration.

- Within a few months, their respective connections with Cesare evaporated. By January 1503, both had left Cesare's court and returned to Florence—Machiavelli as a diplomat and strategist, Leonardo as a military engineer.

- The new republican government of Florence had begun a war of conquest against its long-time rival—the neighboring city of Pisa. Leonardo and Machiavelli convinced the government that they had the technical know-how to redirect the Arno River at key points in its course in a way that would cause it to bypass Pisa altogether, starving the city into submission.

© iStockphoto/Thinkstock.

The Arno River is the life blood of Florence, and it inspired many of Leonardo's most ambitious engineering projects.

- Leonardo began drawing maps of the Arno River, looking for places to alter its course as well as thinking about how the river wanted to move through the terrain. Thanks to his work with hydraulics in Milan, Leonardo knew that water was not as controllable as many believed.

- In Milan, he had devised massive water-moving and canal-digging machines; now, he had the chance to use them. In 1503 and again in 1504, 2,000 Florentine laborers were employed to dig trenches in and around the Arno River, literally carving out a new river bed.

- The plan failed in the end. The new bed only filled with water during the rainy season; when the season was over, all the water drained back into the original route.

- The project was called off, but Leonardo did not despair. He used this failed attempt to divert the Arno as a catalyst for another project that had a better chance of success: designing a canal to bypass the twists and turns of the Arno, giving Florence a navigable route for large cargo ships to reach the Mediterranean Sea.

- If Leonardo's earlier folly had not happened, there was a chance the government might have built the canal. But the city of Florence commissioned him for a quite different project—an enormous fresco that would put his artistic talents to good use instead.

Important Term

hodometer: A device used to measure distances traveled by foot. Leonardo's design for one resembled a wheelbarrow.

Name to Know

Machiavelli, Niccolò (1469–1527): Government official and political theorist. Machiavelli took on a number of diplomatic posts as a representative of the new Florentine republic during the early years of the 1500s. During this time he met and collaborated with Leonardo da Vinci on a number of projects. He was arrested when the Medici returned to take control of Florence in 1513 and wrote his political treatise *The Prince* and a number of plays during a self-imposed exile.

Suggested Reading

Heydenreich, "The Military Architect."

Kemp, *Leonardo da Vinci: The Marvellous Works of Nature and Man.*

Masters, *Fortune is a River.*

Strathern, *The Artist, the Philosopher, and the Warrior.*

Leonardo, Cesare Borgia, and Machiavelli

Lecture 24—Transcript

Sometime in 1502, Leonardo da Vinci made an interesting drawing in red chalk. Currently located in the Biblioteca Reale in Turin, the sheet of paper shows us a single figure displayed in three different poses. The drawing looks to be the kind of multiple-view sketch that painters and sculptors often liked to do in anticipation of a larger project in paint or marble or bronze, as the profile, the three-quarter, and frontal poses, when taken together, can create a three-dimensional impression of the sitter that can then be worked up into a finished image from the confines of an artistic workshop.

The figure is bearded and gruff, and we see that the hair on his head and the whiskers on his chin form brackets on either side of his face—and create a fierce impression when taken together. And this fierceness seems to be an important part of the image, for the figure represented here was known in his day as the wickedest man in Italy—his name was Cesare Borgia, and Leonardo da Vinci not only knew him well, but actually offered him assistance in historically important ways.

Let's think back to what had happened when Leonardo arrived in Florence in May of 1500. He was widely admired as a successful artist of extraordinary expertise in many different fields. But, by Renaissance standards, he was also an old man, probably nearing the end of his career. Yet here he was, returning to his roots to spread his wisdom and his ideas to those who would listen. To some, he was a symbol of the establishment who needed to be outdone, outshone, and then put out to pasture.

To Leonardo, this 48-year-old man still needed a paycheck, still needed stimulating projects, and still felt he had something to prove. I don't think it's a stretch to say that whereas the 1490s may have been the most important decade of Leonardo's life as an intellectual, the following decade—the first of the new century—was probably his most productive and innovative as an artist; and that's saying something for a guy who was considered by most of his peers to have already set the gold standard in painting.

Still, Leonardo's return to Florence wasn't entirely a triumph. On one hand, he produced two lovely Madonnas for the French secretary of state, drew a lovely cartoon that apparently attracted the Florentine art public in droves, and commanded the very special attention of no less a figure than Isabella d'Este. But by the same token, Leonardo garnered approximately zero official commissions from the Florentine government—or any other institution in the city, for that matter—during his first two years back, and as the Italian spring began to turn into summer in 1502, Leonardo set out to change his situation.

As someone still intent on earning a living, Leonardo returned to the approach that had worked well for him in Milan. Leonardo went looking for work among the politically powerful in Italy as a professional courtier. Leonardo had actually been quite astute during his years as a courtier for Ludovico Sforza, and his thorough understanding of the political and cultural needs of Italy's princes now served him well.

Princes, of course, wanted stability and craved cultural prominence among their peers. They wanted respect and prestige and notoriety for their deeds and attributes. They wanted nice things inside nice houses that were filled with pretty mistresses. But mostly, princes wanted to retain power and control over their domains, and in this period they needed even more help than usual. We must remember that after 1494, these men and the women they were married to were under constant threat of attack and imprisonment from any number of malevolent opponents. Literally no one could be trusted, and no one was safe, from the time Ludovico and Alexander VI had first encouraged the French to invade Italian soil.

And while Ludovico had fallen to the French, ultimately due to the strategic importance of his duchy, Pope Alexander survived to cause further mischief. The pope was obsessed with self-interested policies, his nepotistic promotions of unsuitable relatives smacked of corruption, and he openly flaunted both his own personal decadence and his political ambitions to secure Italy as a Borgia state.

The letters that Isabella d'Este wrote (some of which I show here), both to her husband, Francesco Gonzaga, and to Cesare Borgia, the brother of her husband's lover, show that she knew all too well the vices of the papal family. She tried hard through shuttle diplomacy to secure the borders of her adoptive city of Mantua, and negotiated with both Alexander's allies in Italy and the French forces to the north to preserve Mantua's independence.

Now the French, firmly entrenched in Milan, seemed content there in 1502, but their aggressive policies were well known in Italy. Meanwhile, Venice had all but conceded its interests in Constantinople and the former Byzantine Empire, and was instead now quite openly considering expansion into the smaller duchies and territories to the west and the south, along the Italian peninsula that it had ignored for so long ignored.

Florence was now among the weaker entities in the area, when Leonardo arrived there in 1500, and the quite recent restoration of the Republic had left the city too disorganized to contend as a major power. But in 1502, probably the most threatening of the wolves prowling the Italian countryside was neither the Pope nor a prince. Rather, it was a strange mixture of the two.

This man was Cesare Borgia, whose portrait I show here, was reviled by his rivals for his cunning, his ruthlessness, and his cruelty. But Cesare was also unusually crafty, fiercely loyal to his men, and reputedly one of Europe's most charismatic and charming leaders. It was his combination of charisma and cruelty that earned him the title of "the wickedest man in Italy." And it was to Cesare Borgia that Leonardo da Vinci appealed in the spring of 1502.

Now Cesare was truly a character of enormous appetites and vices, and in many ways he embodied all of the things that a Renaissance prince was supposed to represent, although in sometimes backwards and excessive ways.

As the son of Rodrigo Borgia, Cesare had always enjoyed the powerful genealogical connections that he had working for him. As the son of a cardinal who became a pope, Cesare had entry into every court in Christendom. Cesare was also one of the wealthiest men in Italy, thanks to his family's estate, his own willingness to extort treasure from his victims, and his father's habit of funneling money to him whenever he needed it.

But, to be fair, Cesare Borgia was extremely well-educated, so much so that by the age of 17 he had proven himself capable enough to make possible his own elevation to the position of cardinal by his father. Though what Cesare actually did as cardinal was another matter.

In the late 1490s, when his papal father decided to consolidate his power in Rome, Cesare was the one who carried out the threats, enacted the physical tortures, and probably handled the assassinations of his father's enemies in and out of the papal entourage. And Cesare seemed to revel in this lifestyle. He had been handed the keys to Rome and had been given carte blanche to make the city tremble before him, and he absolutely loved it!

He loved it so much that in 1498, to the utter astonishment of even those who feared and despised him, Cesare Borgia actually renounced his position as cardinal—and all the riches it brought with it—in order to pursue what was becoming his true love: physical and political domination, utter control over vast regions, and the happy joys associated with autocratic tyranny.

Thrilled to be rid of him, his father, the pope, happily granted Cesare's petition and set him out on a course to gobble up a series of cities and towns on the eastern side of the Italian peninsula just north of Rome, called the Romagna. Cesare accepted the challenge, along with lots of money from papal coffers, and left Rome to begin his conquest of the Romagna. It wasn't long before everyone else realized that his true goal was to conquer pretty much the rest of Italy, too.

This was the man to whom Leonardo presented himself in the spring of 1502. And because Leonardo had submitted this kind of job application before, we shouldn't be surprised to learn that his application was compelling, too. Leonardo had the qualifications, and he knew how to appeal to the vanities and neuroses of princes in need of a good courtier's services. Now it might seem strange to us now, with 20-20 hindsight, that Leonardo elected to approach Cesare Borgia at all. Leonardo valued virtue and honor and dignity, and Cesare Borgia, I'm afraid, possessed these qualities only in abbreviated form.

But let's look at this from Leonardo's perspective. We've already learned three things about Leonardo at this stage of his life. First, he had a brilliant military mind. He understood tactics, engineering principles, and the needs of princes who had conquest on their minds. Second, he was down on his luck in Florence just then. Leonardo wasn't getting the commissions he wanted, and he wasn't producing work that interested him. And three, his entire career had been devoted to working with political potentates—irrespective of their virtues—ever since his days as an emissary for Lorenzo the Magnificent.

Cesare hired Leonardo on the spot. Others may have been put off by Cesare Borgia, but Leonardo seems not to have been, at least at first. He was used to princely braggadocio, princely arrogance, princely ambition, and he obviously wasn't terribly bothered by Cesare's reputation for being the poster child for all of these characteristics. (And this, by the way, might tell us a little bit about Leonardo's impression of Ludovico Sforza: If Leonardo felt that Cesare didn't sound so bad, maybe it was because he felt that his former employer in Milan hadn't been much better. But I digress.)

In Leonardo, Cesare Borgia saw the most famous courtier of the age, a man gifted in more professional trades and intellectual pursuits than any other single person in Europe, and an experienced advisor who knew how to handle adversity. Leonardo was, quite literally, the smartest guy in the room, no matter where the room was or who else was in it.

Now, in our heart of hearts, we really don't want this marriage to work very well, do we? We want Leonardo, a hero of art and science, to be disgusted by the infamous Cesare Borgia. We want Leonardo to consider employment with Cesare Borgia as something akin to making a pact with the devil, and we want him to take the higher path by turning it down. But it didn't happen. Not at first, at least.

Leonardo, remember, was much more politically savvy than we give him credit for. He knew that Cesare was the current flavor of the month; he knew that he could make some money from a desperate prince willing to part with handsome sums in return for a few ideas; and he knew that as a free agent he could leave Cesare's side just as quickly and easily as he had joined it, if he played his cards right. Because remember, Leonardo served a prince only as long as it suited him.

And Cesare surely knew this too, and Cesare was perfectly content with the arrangement. It's just how things worked at a time when princes couldn't guarantee lifetime job security. And so it was that Leonardo da Vinci went into the service of Cesare Borgia, who had by 1502 collected around him a bevy of robust and highly skilled soldiers and military advisors.

Unlike other princes who merely bought their troops, Cesare fostered the devotion of his mercenaries through the cult of personality. Contemporary chronicles speak of his magnetic personality, his tremendous charisma, and his dashing comportment. Men wanted to be with him, and they wanted to fight for him when he took the field.

Leonardo joined Cesare sometime in the early summer of 1502, just after Cesare had secured his presence in mid-eastern Italy by taking the city of Urbino from the cultured Montefeltro family, who had ruled there for more than two centuries. But Cesare was not content with his position, and he set out to do three things in short order. First, he needed to scout and plan attacks on towns on his frontier, namely Imola and Piombino. Secondly, Cesare needed to secure the defenses of towns he had already conquered, but hadn't yet fortified. And third, he needed to make sure the French weren't going to come crashing down through the Italian peninsula again and take away all of his gains before he could mount an effective defense. Leonardo could help in all three of these areas, and when he arrived in Urbino in July of 1502, he was put to work immediately.

Leonardo's former employment in Milan and his brief flirtation with the French government there back in 1499 made him, in the eyes of Cesare, an expert on French affairs. Leonardo was asked to advise Cesare on mores, customs, and personalities at the French court. What the "wickedest man in Italy" hoped, was to gain insights that might help tip the scales at the negotiating tables, especially when Cesare embarked on a diplomatic mission to Milan in an effort to woo his French rivals in August of 1502.

Just as important as Leonardo's first-hand knowledge of the French in Milan was Leonardo's great experience as a military engineer. Combined with his gifts as an architect, the amount of man hours he had spent thinking about ways to destroy an enemy on the field and behind a drawbridge made him the perfect candidate to fortify defenses on Cesare's border towns. Leonardo took on this task almost immediately upon his alliance with Cesare, and we're told that he set about doing so with great gusto in the summer of 1502.

Still another benefit was Leonardo's understanding of geography, geology, and geometry, fields that gave him the tools he needed to survey new territories and gain vital environmental intelligence about the towns that Cesare wished to annex.

Before Cesare embarked on that diplomatic mission to Milan in August of 1502, he bestowed upon Leonardo the official title of Architect and Engineer ("Architecto e Ingegnero Generale") at the Borgia court in Urbino. And Leonardo was given free and total access to every military installation in Cesare's possession.

In short order, Leonardo left Urbino to tour Cesare's encampments and towns, which he and his assistants not only sketched, but inspected with an eye for improvement. In short order, his suggestions were put into place—a quick response that must've pleased Leonardo, who was more accustomed to having his ideas ignored by Ludovico Sforza.

It was during this time that Leonardo put his artistic talents to use in the name of cartography, of all things. In addition to fortifying defensive positions, Leonardo was expected to employ his talents in an aggressive posture. Cesare had his eye on a whole string of towns and cities along the eastern section of Italy, and he made plans to attack their walled fortresses in 1502.

But Cesare had no interest in charging ahead blindly, particularly against fortified towns that had the potential to withstand a siege and wait out an impatient aggressor, like Cesare Borgia. He needed inside information, and he needed it badly. And that's where Leonardo again came in handy.

Either of his own accord or in response to a directive from Cesare Borgia, Leonardo went ahead to draw one of the most precisely crafted aerial views of any given location known to contemporary eyes. It was not only remarkably precise, it was executed without the benefit of an aircraft from which to view his subject. It was a bird's eye view, without the bird.

The town in question was the modest community of Imola, and it was feared not as much for the garrison inside, as it was for the walls that ringed it, for Imola was a fairly well-protected little town. It was Leonardo's job to learn everything about it, from its geographic setting to its urban plan to the contours of the city walls to the bends in the creeks and streams that surrounded it. Cesare needed a map he could use as he approached his victim, and Leonardo went out and got him one.

The map that Leonardo produced required the use of a surveying disc that he mounted at central vantage points to measure the radial angles of major objects and features of the city. The readings he collected from these vantage points were then coordinated with carefully measured distances around the edges of the city so that a proportional plan could be worked out.

Leonardo had his assistants equipped with a device he invented called a "hodometer"—basically a surveyor's wheel that was pushed by handles—like a wheel-barrow. He then had them infiltrate the town to step off the distances of the roads, the buildings, and piazzas so he could coordinate them with the arcs he made from his central vantage point.

He then created 64 equally spaced lines from the center point of the town, which corresponded to the two old Roman avenues that met at its heart. Eight of the lines he traced in bold outlines, and labeled North, Northeast, East, etc.

Within this circular grid he showed Cesare the churches, the shops, apartment buildings, and villas of the town, along with the layout of their gates, towers, walls, and the moat. He even added the town castle in the lower left corner. This map could not have been anything but spectacularly useful for Cesare Borgia, who clearly knew now what he had in his hands. Here was as precise a record of a town and its defenses as anyone had ever seen before. Here was a blueprint for Cesare to inspect portals, walls, sight lines, batteries, and potential weak spots.

The terrain of the area surrounding the town was also noted, so that Cesare could avoid curves in the river, focus on roads and flatlands for an attack, and use the landscape to his advantage.

Now when we compare this with other maps being produced by artists of the day, Leonardo's solution becomes all the more impressive. The Chain Map of Florence is more of an impression of how the artist knew the city to be, based on experience, than it is an accurate plotting of every inch of its turf. But this was all that could be expected of people who took advantage of only things they knew, and were unable to venture beyond the things they could see.

Leonardo's most authoritative biographer of the last 50 years, the British scholar Martin Kemp, has referred to this map as "amongst the most magnificent surviving products of the Renaissance revolution in cartographic techniques." And when we think about how Leonardo managed to convey the plan of the entire town so accurately without stepping foot inside it, we can understand why the Map of Imola was such a breakthrough in the history of mapmaking.

One of the great political strategists and military chroniclers of the day, Niccolo Machiavelli (whose portrait we see here) commented that Cesare Borgia had the ability to "arrive in one place before it's known he's left another." Maybe it's maps like the one of Imola that made Machiavelli say this. And Machiavelli, in fact, didn't just observe from afar, he was a part of our story, too.

In October of 1502 Machiavelli arrived in this town of Imola as a diplomatic emissary on behalf of the Republic of Florence, which was interested in learning of Borgia's intentions. Like just about everyone else, the Florentines wanted at all costs to dissuade Cesare Borgia from looking their way, as the rapacious desires of the "wickedest man in Italy" almost always resulted in attack.

It was there that Machiavelli got to know Cesare Borgia. Unlike many other observers, Machiavelli found much to admire, although he later critiqued Cesare's flaws as well. And it was here, too, that Machiavelli met Leonardo da Vinci and saw with his own eyes the things that Leonardo could do with his mind, his eye, and his pen. And it was here that Machiavelli came to understand the great potential that Leonardo da Vinci possessed as a military asset. The two appear to have formed a relationship grounded in mutual respect and admiration.

But within a couple months, their respective connections with Cesare Borgia evaporated. By the month of January 1503, both men had left Cesare's court. The cause of Leonardo's defection may have had something to do with his patron's successful campaign against the Tuscan town of Siena, which resulted in Cesare's forces occupying the city briefly. As the Borgia prince had a reputation for punishing his lieutenants whom he suspected of cowardice or betrayal, a squabble within the confines of the court may have caused Leonardo to realize that his days there were numbered.

Or maybe Leonardo anticipated new opportunities back in Florence, since that's where both he and Machiavelli ultimately wound up by the winter of 1503—Machiavelli would carry on as a Florentine diplomat and a strategist, two areas of expertise that would ultimately guide his thinking when, 10 years later, he wrote his famous book of political theory, called *The Prince*.

As for Leonardo, the former architect and engineer of the Borgia Court received a new kind of commission from his home town; for now Leonardo was employed to work for the city of Florence as the new government began a war of conquest of its own. This one was directed against its long time rival—the city of Pisa. Now exactly why the Florentines wanted to fight this war isn't really important to us. Pisa and Florence had been fighting each other since ancient times, and natives from each city basically loathed each other on principle alone.

Now, in 1503, Leonardo the engineer and Machiavelli the strategist teamed up together to devise a scheme to destroy the city of Pisa by natural means, in a plan that was equal parts brilliance and foolishness. The two theoreticians, together with an array of other advisors and assistants deeply interested in the project, convinced the Florentine government that they had the technical know-how to redirect the entire Arno River, at key points in its course, in a way that would cause it to bypass Pisa altogether.

Now, the route of the Arno River does suggest that it can be manipulated. It begins high in the Apennine Mountains, proceeds west through Northern Tuscany, winds its way in and out of Florence, bounces around some just beyond Prato and Pistoia, and then moves fairly smoothly onto Pisa and the Mediterranean Sea. While it would be tough to divert it in the mountains, by the time it opened up toward the plains of the west coast, there was actually an opportunity to change its course.

By redirecting it before it got to Pisan soil, Machiavelli and Leonardo argued, they could dump the fresh water normally consumed by the hated Pisans into the salt water of the Mediterranean, and thus basically starve the Pisans into submission.

It was kind of a diabolical plan from the minds of two geniuses—one of whom had earlier conceived of weapons to cut off the legs of multiple soldiers at the knees and the other who would later write about cruelty and intimidation as desirable political character traits for a perfect prince.

In anticipation of this project, Leonardo began drawing maps of the Arno River—sometimes in sections, and once in awhile in its entirety. He was looking here for places to alter its course, but was also thinking about how the river wanted to move through the terrain. Thanks to his work with hydraulics in Milan, Leonardo knew that water wasn't nearly as controllable as many believed, and his plotting of the circuitous route of the Arno took suggests that Leonardo was thinking about the strategy he would need to employ in order to make his plan work.

It's in the plan to divert the Arno River that Leonardo's experience as a frustrated inventor finally came in handy. In Milan he had worked on ideas for a whole series of hydraulic machines that either used water power to move wheels and cogs or had conceived of ways to move the water itself from one place to another. He had devised massive canal digging machines with just such an idea in mind, and he was always eager to try out some of the ideas that he had worked up on paper. And now he got the chance.

In 1503 and again in 1504, 2000 Florentines laborers were employed to go ahead and do the back-breaking work of digging huge pits and trenches in and around the Arno River, with an eye toward giving mother nature a facelift.

The amazing thing here is that they almost pulled it off. The 2000 ditch-diggers literally carved out a new river bed for the Arno, carting off God-knows how many tons of dirt and mud, as this geological reformation project plugged along. But their plans were foiled in the end. The new basin of the Arno that they'd created with their cranes and ditches, it turned out, only filled up with water during the rainy season—but when that subsided, all the water in their artificial river only drained back into the original source. After months of generally getting nowhere and sapping the Florentine treasury of vital resources, the project was called off: It was all for naught, and the Florentine government went back to more conventional modes of warfare against the Pisans—by which I mean intense propaganda, bald threats, and a whole lot of bluster, but very little actual combat.

But, given Leonardo's precise mind, his understanding of the importance of scientific inquiry, and his dogged determination, the artist did not despair. In fact he used this one failed attempt to divert the Arno as a catalyst for another project which actually had a better chance of success than the first one had.

Combining his knowledge of the Arno River's flow and his now-expert abilities as a cartographer, Leonardo now set about to find a way to address one of the truly big economic problems that had always faced the city of Florence. It turns out that the Arno River, while a natural source of water for hygiene and power, was not a very good avenue of commerce.

The twists and turns of the riverbed to the northwest, in between Florence and Pisa, made the Arno literally unnavigable for vessels of any modest size or capacity, which meant that there was no way for Florentine goods to pass easily to the Mediterranean Sea and then off to markets abroad: The

Florentines always needed to use land routes to export their wares, or depend on middle men to ship their materials elsewhere.

Leonardo, trying to address this problem, proposed to carve a large arc that would serve as a canal that would bypass the crazy twists and turns of the Arno that made it impossible for ships to sail through. He wanted to build a new waterway that would run a straighter course from Florence to western Tuscany, and then reconnect with deeper, more docile parts of the river near the sea.

Leonardo reckoned that such a project would bring 200,000 ducats to Florence annually through tolls and taxes, along with increased sales and direct shipping for all local goods to foreign markets. Curiously, though, he didn't think they'd have to worry that Pisa might work to block the entrance of the Arno to the Mediterranean, but I suppose he figured that Florence would just have to secure that access by conquering Pisa, which did eventually happen in 1509.

So this was a project that had some potential, and had the city been in a little better financial situation, and if Leonardo's earlier folly of redirecting the Arno hadn't happened, there's a chance the government might have gone for it. But in the end, they didn't, and all that training in civil engineering and hydraulics wasn't put to use.

But Leonardo seems not to have been terribly bothered by this decision—for now that he finally had the attention of the government, the city of Florence became interested in him for a quite different project, an enormous fresco that would instead put his artistic talents to good use. And that project would be of enormous symbolic importance. For in addition to celebrating the city's independence from Milan and its power over Pisa, Florence would put on display the talents of Europe's greatest painter and Europe's greatest sculptor, one next to the other, side by side, for all the world to compare.

Michelangelo and Leonardo

Lecture 25

If Leonardo has any rival in the history of Renaissance art, it is Michelangelo, who was the young upstart to Leonardo's old sage when they met in Florence at the turn of the 16th century. Although they never got along, Michelangelo's work shows both profound influence—and profound departure—from that of Leonardo, particularly when we look at the former's sculpture *Pieta* and the drawing for the fresco *Battle of Cascina.*

The New Republic of Florence

- Although Leonardo is generally considered the artistic founder of the High Renaissance in Italy, there is one person whom contemporaries and later generations have thought might be the greater artist: **Michelangelo Buonarotti**. In the first decade of the 1500s, the city of Florence contrived for these two masters to compete with each other in a tremendous project of unusual design.

- The Florence of 1500 was quite different from the one Leonardo had left in 1482. Lorenzo the Magnificent had died in 1492, and his arrogant son, Piero, was roundly despised by those he governed. When the French army threatened Florence in 1494, its citizens rose up against the young Medici prince and forced him into exile.

- Piero was replaced by a cleric named **Fra Girolamo Savonarola**, who set up a republican government with himself at its head. Savonarola was a reactionary who openly condemned the corruption of the Borgia papacy and the Neoplatonic culture supported by Lorenzo the Magnificent.

- It took four years for more moderate voices to rise up against Savonarola, but in 1498 they succeeded, and he was executed on charges of treason. Florence turned to a purer form of Republicanism, but with some serious growing pains.

- With no princely family around to make executive decisions and fund major projects, these burdens fell on the tailors, doctors, and wool merchants of the city, who had no training or experience in politics or economics.

Michelangelo's Early Years

- Leonardo's hopes for an official commission when he returned to Florence in 1500 did not come to pass at first, either because the government did not know what to do with him, felt they could not afford him, or decided to commit their resources to Michelangelo Buonarroti.

- In 1501, the government commissioned the 26-year-old sculptor to create a statue of the biblical King David. They had already secured a block of marble and another sculptor for the project, but that contract had fallen through after the sculptor determined that the block was too flawed to withstand the punishment of hammer and chisel. This was precisely the kind of challenge that Michelangelo relished.

- Michelangelo, like Leonardo, was an adopted son of Florence. Trained in the workshop of Domenico Ghirlandaio, he had made a name for himself during the late 1480s as a precociously talented prodigy.

- If we believe his biographers—Vasari being one of them—Michelangelo was brought under Medici patronage in 1490 as a 15-year-old apprentice. Like many others, he had to leave Florence in 1494 when Fra Savonarola came to power; the city simply wasn't safe for him.

- Michelangelo went first to Bologna, then Rome, at which time he caught the attention of local art collectors. By 1497, Michelangelo's reputation was great enough that he was commissioned to sculpt the *Pieta* for a chapel in Old St. Peter's.

- The *Pieta* shows us how Michelangelo was indebted to the classical movement Leonardo had helped invent. An enormous effigy of the Virgin Mary holding a diminutive adult Christ, who has just been detached from the cross and placed in her arms in preparation for burial, the two figures form a pyramidal composition.

Michelangelo and Leonardo

- His return to Florence as a famous and opinionated artist in 1501 caused something of a stir. Leonardo's presence kept him on his best behavior at first, and the pair stayed at arm's length. We have no record of them cooperating or exchanging ideas.

- They did not have to deal with each other during the summer and autumn of 1502, when Leonardo was working for Cesare Borgia But when Leonardo returned in the winter of 1503, the tension between them intensified.

- A document records a bizarre and petty public argument between them. Leonardo and a group of his colleagues were sitting together in the Piazza della Signoria, talking about **Dante**'s poetry. Leonardo was not a classically educated man, and as he fumbled for something to say, he noticed Michelangelo walking past. Leonardo admitted he could not speak intelligently on the subject but suggested that Michelangelo—who was known as a leading expert on Dante—might be able to educate them.

- For some reason, Michelangelo took offense to this remark and called Leonardo a "failed old fool" who "never finish[ed]anything." The remark must have stung Leonardo because there was some truth to it, and the two appear to have had little or no direct contact with each other afterward.

- At some point during his stay in Florence, Michelangelo took a crack at the Saint Anne, Virgin, and Christ figural grouping that Leonardo had made famous. But ever the sculptor, Michelangelo turned the figures, considering them from an angle that not even Leonardo had imagined.

Michelangelo's *David*

- In 1504, Michelangelo enjoyed his own one-man show, although not as intentional as Leonardo's. Originally, *David* was supposed to be installed 60 feet off the ground on the exterior of the Florentine Cathedral. But when the figure was unveiled, it was clear that such a remarkable work deserved to be seen by the public at close range.

© iStockphoto/Thinkstock.

Michelangelo's *David* was instantly recognized as a masterpiece.

- The statue was moved to the façade of the Palazzo della Signoria, where it was placed on a pedestal and considered a symbol of the Florentine state—an underdog willing to take on all challengers courageously, violently, and successfully.

- The figure is nude, in keeping with the biblical description of David's confrontation with Goliath. He stands in a perfect contrapposto, turning his head to the left to size up the giant. This emphasizes the latent power of the rock about to be hurled from his sling.

- The proportions of the figure, its striking musculature, and its intense gaze have no equal in the annals of Western art. Leonardo knew and admired *David.* He drew it, probably soon after its installation.

The Salone dei Cinquecento Murals

- Leonardo and Michelangelo might have avoided each other completely if not for one project that not only brought them together but put them into competition. In October 1503, Florence's governor, **Piero Soderini**, commissioned Leonardo to paint a mural in the Palazzo della Signoria called the Salone dei Cinquecento, or the Big Room of the 500.

- Leonardo's work is no longer visible. Some scholars claim it fell apart not long after Leonardo took the scaffolding down; others think it lasted until the mid-16th century. But thanks to Leonardo's preparatory drawings and copies made by others, we know more or less what it looked like.

- The space was absolutely enormous. The fresco that now occupies the space, produced by Vasari in 1565, measures 50′ × 50′. By comparison, Leonardo's largest previous painting, *The Last Supper*, measures 15′ × 28′.

- The picture by necessity would have to be a mural painted on plaster, but Leonardo hated the traditional fresco technique. The subject matter—a battle scene, namely the Battle of Anghiari, in which the Florentines had defeated Milan in 1440—was also unfamiliar for him. Finally, he was required to work rapidly; his contract demanded that paint had to be applied to the wall within 15 months of the signing.

- Leonardo settled on depicting the moment when the Florentine army captured the Milanese flag. He worked out a wide range of compositions very quickly, focusing primarily on the selection of his moment, the relationships between specific figures, and broad gestures and expressions of individual characters, combining the physical freneticism of combat with the drama of the historical narrative while focusing on individual soldiers and their personal struggles.

- Leonardo decided to employ a technique called **encaustic**. Popular in antiquity, it had fallen out of favor by the 16th century due to the extremely sensitive nature of the process. The pigments are mixed with piping hot wax, which serves as the binding agent. While the wax is hot, one can paint somewhat leisurely, but once the pigments are on the surface, they are pretty well fixed there.

- In September 1504, Michelangelo was commissioned to paint a picture on the other half of the same wall, to the left of Leonardo's *Battle of Anghiari*. His drawing was dedicated to a similar regional conflict, the Battle of Cascina, fought against Pisa in 1364.

- Having the advantage of seeing Leonardo's initial work, Michelangelo focused on themes of motion, terror, confusion, and rage, all conveyed through an expressive and descriptive gestural body language. But unlike Leonardo, Michelangelo's figures twist and turn in unusual poses, reach out to each other awkwardly, and respond to this call to arms in excessive ways. It is Michelangelo telling us that Nature must be respected and can be improved on by the skilled and imaginative artist.

- Michelangelo's **cartoon** for the painting was 20′ high by 60′ long, but before he could start on the fresco, he was called to Rome by Pope Julius II. The drawing was left behind in Florence, and it became an artistic sensation, passed around from artist to artist for years. Individual figures were cut out of the drawing for art students to study and copy. By 1600, the entire cartoon had disintegrated due to mishandling and overuse; all that is left are copies and copies of copies.

- In January 1505—more or less on schedule—Leonardo began applying his encaustic pigments to his half of the wall. We do not know how much of the painting he finished; only a portion was copied by his contemporaries, which suggests that ether it was never completed or that it disintegrated quickly, like *The Last Supper*.

- Nonetheless, the picture was impressive and instantly celebrated. A number of artists brought brushes, easels, and pigments into the room to copy it; a number of others obtained and copied the cartoon.

- As for the picture itself, nothing remains. The encaustic method could not withstand the atmospheric conditions of hot and humid Florence, and by the mid-16th century, Leonardo's wall was covered over by a new one, on which Vasari was hired to paint a fresco in 1563.

Important Terms

cartoon: From the Italian *cartone* ("cardboard"), a full-size preparatory drawing from which a design is transferred to a surface for painting.

encaustic: A painterly process whereby pigments are mixed with melted wax and applied to a dry surface.

Names to Know

Alighieri, Dante (1265–1322): Florentine thinker, poet, politician, and social critic. Dante wrote theologically driven love poetry and treatises on modern government but found himself on the wrong side of a civil war in Florence and was exiled from his homeland in 1301. During his itinerant years as persona non grata, Dante penned the most important work of literature of the early modern period, *The Divine Comedy*, which was the very first work of literature written in Italian.

Buonarroti, Michelangelo (1475–1564): One of the most prolific artists of all time, who revolutionized the world of the visual arts through his drawings, paintings, sculptures, and architectural works—primarily in Florence and Rome. Among Michelangelo's most famous and influential projects were the frescoes for the Sistine Chapel, the sculptures for the Tomb of Julius II, and his designs for the New Sacristy in the Church of San Lorenzo, Florence.

Savonarola, Fra Girolamo (1452–1498): Fiery preacher who opposed the humanistic interests of Lorenzo de' Medici and led the reactionary movement against the family in the 1490s. He organized bonfires of the vanities, in which common people burned the material possessions they were ashamed to own. He led the Florentine government from 1494 until 1498, when moderates overthrew him and burned him at the stake in the middle of the Piazza della Signoria.

Soderini, Piero (1450–1522): Gifted politician and a favorite of Lorenzo de' Medici, after Lorenzo's death in 1492 and the execution of Fra Savonarola in 1498, Soderini helped organize and then presided over the new republican government of Florence until its fall at the hands of the Medici during the coup d'etat of 1512. Soderini worked with both Leonardo and Michelangelo during the project to paint murals in the Salone dei 500 of the Palazzo della Signoria from 1503 to 1505.

Suggested Reading

Farago, "Leonardo's *Battle of Anghiari*."

Gould, "Leonardo's Great Battle-Piece."

Kemp, *Leonardo da Vinci: The Marvellous Works of Nature and Man.*

Travers Newton and Spencer, "On the Location of Leonardo's *Battle of Anghiari*."

Wallace, "Michelangelo In and Out of Florence Between 1400 and 1508."

Michelangelo and Leonardo

Lecture 25—Transcript

Although Leonardo da Vinci is generally considered the artistic founder of the High Renaissance movement in Italy, there is one person who rivaled his artistic brilliance. That person was Michelangelo Buonarotti, and in this lecture we will see how the city of Florence, borrowing from the playbook of earlier Renaissance governments, contrived for these two supreme masters to compete directly with each other in a tremendous project of unusual design.

The city of Florence that Leonardo entered in 1500 was quite different from the one he had left in 1482. Lorenzo the Magnificent had died in 1492, and his arrogant son, Piero, had done little to carry on his legacy. He was roundly despised by those he governed, and when the French army of Charles VIII threatened Florence, its citizens rose up against the young Medici prince and forced him into exile in 1494.

Piero was replaced by a fiery preacher named Girolamo Savonarola, who set up a republican government in Florence with him at its head. Savonarola was a reactionary cleric who openly condemned the corruption of the Borgia papacy and the Neo-platonic culture that had been supported by Lorenzo the Magnificent. He was famous for staging what were referred to as Bonfires of the Vanities, where citizens were urged to take from their homes all the possessions they had amassed which celebrated the hedonistic ways of the Medici family and toss them into a fire.

It took four years for more moderate voices to rise up against him, but in 1498 they succeeded, and Fra Savonarola was executed on charges of treason, and his body was burned on a bonfire not unlike the ones he had formed during his reign.

Now Florence returned to a purer form of Republicanism than it had seen in over 60 years, but it did so with some pretty serious growing pains. With no princely family around to make executive decisions—and put up the money needed to fund those major decisions—the burden of handling finances, maintaining law and order, and maintaining some form of national defense system was placed squarely in the hands of tailors and doctors and wool merchants who really had no kind of training for this sort of thing.

By the time Leonardo arrived in Florence in 1500, this new government had been in existence for fewer than 20 months, and while there were no French troops clamoring at the gates for booty, the situation there was tenuous, which may have been attractive to Leonardo. He had, after all, spent the last 20 years working for dukes in trouble, and I suspect he felt that he'd be able to find work for this new government fairly quickly.

But, as we've seen, Leonardo's hopes for an official commission did not come to pass, and Leonardo brooded, mostly unemployed, until the opportunity to work for Cesare Borgia came along, and Leonardo's courtier instincts took over. But what of this other fellow, Michelangelo? Well, oddly enough he did manage to secure an official commission from the city of Florence at precisely this time.

In 1501, the Republican government approached the 26-year-old sculptor to ask him to accept a commission to take a piece of marble and carve a statue of a biblical figure the city had long considered its symbolic ancestor: the Old Testament king, David.

Now Michelangelo was in Rome when he was approached with this opportunity, and the more he learned about it, the more interested in it he became. The Florentines had already secured a block of marble that they wanted him to use, but it was widely thought that the block of marble they had purchased was too seriously flawed to withstand the punishment it would receive from a hammer and a chisel. This was precisely the kind of challenge that Michelangelo relished.

Now Michelangelo, like Leonardo before him, was an adopted son of Florence. The son of a professional bureaucrat, Michelangelo had been born in 1475 out in the hills of Tuscany, and had been reared in a nearby suburb called Settignano. He had been trained in the workshop of our old friend, Domenico Ghirlandaio, during the late 1480s and had made a name for himself even then as a precociously talented prodigy.

If we believe his biographers—Vasari being one of them—Michelangelo was identified as a worthy candidate for the Florentine court maintained by Lorenzo the Magnificent, and in 1490 the 15-year-old apprentice was brought to the Medici villa.

For two years, Michelangelo honed his skills as a marble carver during the day, and at night listened to dinner conversations and debates that were staged between the likes of Marsilio Ficino, Poliziano, Pico della Mirandola, and Lorenzo himself—who was no slouch when it came to Platonic philosophy. But like these courtiers, Michelangelo left the Medici villa when Lorenzo the Magnificent died in 1492, and then quit Florence altogether in 1494 when Fra Savonarola had come to power. The city simply wasn't very safe for him.

Michelangelo landed in Bologna for a little less than two years before going on to Rome in 1496, at which time he caught the attention of local art collectors there who gave him his first commissions in that city. By 1497 Michelangelo's reputation was great enough to cause a member of Alexander VI's court to commission him to sculpt the now-famous *Pieta* for a chapel in the Church of Saint Peter's. The *Pieta* was Michelangelo's introduction to the artistic community in Rome. The sculpture is among the most tender-fully beautiful creations ever made. The white marble statue features an enormous effigy of the Virgin Mary. Stretched out across her lap appears a diminutive adult Christ, who has just been detached from the cross and placed in her arms in preparation for burial. The two figures combined form the pyramidal composition that we have now come to identify as inherently classical and as an indicator of a High Renaissance mentality.

Mary's head, of course, forms the apex of the pyramid, and her right arm extends diagonally to support Christ's body under her arm, thus forming one of the arms of this isosceles triangle. Her left arm, meanwhile, reaches for Christ's legs, which bend at the knee just beyond Mary's thigh, and drop at an angle—thus extending that arm of the triangle. The core grouping of Leonardo's *Adoration of the Magi* can be seen in this composition, and it signals to us Michelangelo's adherence to the principles espoused by Leonardo da Vinci.

The sculpture was justifiably praised for its subtly when Michelangelo installed it in St. Peter's in 1498, and he enjoyed the recognition he received from audiences and patrons in Rome, who congratulated him for his work. But Michelangelo quite obviously missed his homeland, and with Fra Savonarola out of the way, and a newer, safer Republican government installed in his place, Michelangelo decided to return to Florence.

Now Michelangelo was no shrinking violet, and his arrival in Florence in 1501 caused something of a stir. This short, wiry, but powerful sculptor had been educated in the Medici court by the smartest men in Europe, and he had very precise opinions about art, about life, and about his own status as a master of both. His presence in the city was the cause of some excitement, and the figure of David that he was charged to sculpt became a notable topic of discussion.

But the presence of Leonardo in Florence put Michelangelo on his best behavior, at least at first. The two of them seem to have kept each other at arm's length in 1501. Although we know they were aware of each other's work, we have no record of them cooperating or exchanging ideas. They shared a city, but they did not share a friendship.

Naturally, they did not have to deal with each other during the summer and autumn months of 1502, when Leonardo was working for the reviled Cesare Borgia. But when Leonardo returned in the winter of 1503, the tension between these artistic giants intensified.

Now Leonardo's ego by this time had mellowed enough to the point where he didn't seem to care much that there was a talented sculptor in his midst. Leonardo didn't feel he had anything to prove to anybody, as his *Last Supper* in Milan had basically secured his position as Europe's greatest painter. And he seemed content to let Michelangelo—or anybody else, for that matter—take credit as the greatest sculptor of the age. The failed project of the Colossus of Milan had made Leonardo painfully aware that he could never stake a claim to that title.

But Michelangelo, the younger upstart, wasn't quite as comfortable in his own skin, and he seems not to have handled Leonardo's return to Florence in 1503 as graciously as he could have. There's actually a document that survives that records a bizarre, and quite terse, little argument between the two of them that, on the surface of things, seems fairly petty; but upon further review, we can perhaps see a little bit of Michelangelo's personality coming out in a not-terribly flattering light.

The story goes like this: Leonardo and a group of his colleagues were sitting together in the Piazza della Signoria, in the very heart of the Florentine city, talking about the writings of Dante, the greatest poet in Italian history. But Leonardo, as we've seen, was not a classically educated man, and as he fumbled for something wise to say about Dante's extremely complicated writings, he noticed Michelangelo walking past him. Leonardo apparently turned to his colleagues and announced that he didn't know enough about Dante to speak intelligently on the subject. But Michelangelo—who had literally memorized the *Divine Comedy* and was known as a leading expert on Dante—he might be able to educate them.

We're not sure why Michelangelo took offense to this remark, but he obviously did: Michelangelo retorted with venom, saying something along the lines of "well of course you don't anything you failed old fool, who had to run from Milan without doing anything, for fumbling the Sforza horse, for never finishing anything." Well!

We're not sure how Leonardo replied, or whether he replied at all. But the remark must've stung because, indeed, there was some truth to it. And the two appear to have had little or no direct contact with each other after that interaction. But it doesn't mean they weren't aware of each other's art.

We're told by Vasari that Leonardo staged his one-man show in 1501 by presenting to the general public an image of the Saint Anne Madonna that was probably based somewhat on Leonardo's cartoon of the same subject that we see here.

At some point during his stay in Florence, Michelangelo took a crack at it. Here's a drawing of the figural group that Michelangelo produced, which includes all the characters that Leonardo had probably included in his drawing that he exhibited in 1501. But ever the sculptor, Michelangelo can't prevent himself from thinking about Leonardo's work in three dimensions. He chooses not to copy the picture and its vantage point perfectly, but rather chooses to turn the figures so that he can consider them from an angle that not even Leonardo had imagined when he drew them in the first place.

In 1504, Michelangelo had enjoyed a certain type of one-man show of his own—although not as intentionally planned as Leonardo's had been three years earlier. When the sculptor had finished his enormous statue, the Florentine government revisited the agreement they had made with him with an eye toward changing the venue of the figure of David. Originally, the *David* was supposed to be installed some 60 feet off the ground on the exterior of the Florentine Cathedral. But when the figure was unveiled by Michelangelo in 1504, it became quite clear that such a remarkable work had no business being that far off the ground and away from a curious viewing public. It was moved to the front of the façade of the Palazzo della Signoria, where it was placed on a pedestal and considered a symbol of the Florentine state—an underdog willing to take on all challengers courageously, violently, and successfully.

And that's exactly what Michelangelo's *David* does. The figure stands before us, brazenly nude in keeping with the description of his confrontation with Goliath. He stands with all his weight balanced on one foot, which causes his hips to rise and his shoulders to sag in an absolutely perfect contrapposto pose. Michelangelo has David turn his head to the left and size up the giant he's about to encounter, thus emphasizing the latent power of a rock about to be hurled, but not yet tossed from the sling. The proportions of the figure, its striking musculature, and the intense gaze of this Old Testament warrior have no equal in the annals of Western art. Just as *The Last Supper* represents a perfect painterly representation of the cultural movement of the High Renaissance, so too does the *David* celebrate the period and its sensibilities in sculpture.

And Leonardo obviously knew it and admired it. Here's a drawing that he made of it, probably soon after its installation in front of the government palace in 1504. We see the same contrapposto pose and shift of weight, the same hairstyle, and the identical proportional relationships between the torso and the legs—it's clear that Leonardo was drawing Michelangelo's *David*, either out of admiration, curiosity, or study.

They knew each other and each other's works, and they clearly respected each other's abilities. They were professionals co-existing in the same space. But they might have been perfectly happy to have had nothing to do with one another at all, in any context. And they probably could've gotten away with it, had it not been for one project that caused both of them to have to deal with the other. It also allowed them to compete with one another, though, and that seems to have suited both Leonardo and Michelangelo just fine.

In October of 1503, Leonardo received a commission from the new republic of Florence, which had at its head a governor named Piero Soderini. Although elected to his position for life, Soderini seems to have been genuinely committed to preserving Florentine autonomy, and he did and said all the right things about republican rule. Now back in the 1490s, when the Medici had left Florence, a number of rooms in the Palazzo della Signoria were expanded to seat the growing number of Republican representatives who now ruled the city. The biggest meeting hall in the building, the so-called Sala dei Duecento, or Room of the 200, was expanded in 1495 and was renamed the Salone dei Cinquecento, or the Big Room of the 500.

But given the climate in the city in the 1490s, with Savonarola increasingly condemning the vices of the Florentines, no one got around to actually decorating the Big Room of the 500 when it was finished. And it wasn't until the fall of 1503 that Piero Soderini decided that he wanted to do something about that.

Leonardo had, by now, been working for the government for a few months to divert the River Arno away from Pisa. He was, therefore, on Soderini's radar as he began to think about this project. When the Florentine governor finally decided to move forward with his plans, Leonardo—as the most famous painter in Europe—was Soderini's painter of choice.

Leonardo was charged with the task of painting a fresco on one of the long walls of the trapezoidal Salone dei Cinquecento: There's some debate about which wall it was, but most of us now agree that it was probably the east wall, just opposite the main entrance, and thus facing Florentine Republican representatives as they walked into the room for debates and votes.

Now before we move into a discussion of this project, we need to address a singular problem that clouds much of what's to follow. The picture that Leonardo was supposed to paint (and the portion of it that he completed) is no longer visible: Some scholars claim that it fell apart not long after Leonardo took the scaffolding down, for reasons we'll discuss in a moment. Others think it lasted until the middle of the 16th century. But we're all in agreement that no one has seen this painting for over 400 years.

However, due to copies that were done of while it was still visible, and due to the drawings that Leonardo did in preparation for its execution, we actually have some pretty interesting things to say about it. Now as the details of this project to paint a wall in the Big Room of the 500 began to come out, Leonardo could quickly see that he had some challenges ahead of him.

The wall space that was given to him, first of all, was absolutely enormous. The fresco that now occupies the space was produced by Vasari in 1565, and it's a good 50 feet by 50 feet, an enormous stretch of wall. Leonardo's painting wasn't much smaller than that, and that means that the painting for the Salone dei Cinquecento would've dwarfed every other picture that Leonardo had ever produced, conceived, or considered—and by a lot. The *Last Supper* had only been 15 feet by 28 feet.

Now because the wall space given to Leonardo was inside a room, the picture by necessity would have to be a mural painted on plaster. This immediately must have given Leonardo pause, for we've already seen that Leonardo's only other adventure in fresco painting turned into a prolonged experiment that was already beginning to show signs of failure up in Milan by 1503. Leonardo would either have to get over his dislike of egg tempera paint or find a new way to fix his pigments to the wall.

And the subject matter posed a bit of a problem, too. Leonardo was charged to commemorate a single, minor battle fought by the Florentines in the hills of Tuscany back in 1440 against, ironically, the city of Milan, when it was still governed by the Visconti family. By our standards it would be considered a fairly modest contest, as it didn't result in an expansion of the Florentine state or the elevation of a military hero celebrated for tactical brilliance or uncommon bravery in the field.

But in 1503, the Battle of Anghiari was considered a noble defense of all that was good about the city, and the fact that it had been conducted and won against another city-state that was ruled by a tyrant only underscored the idea that Republics were virtuous and powerful, and therefore not to be messed with.

Leonardo went straight to work on the massive space he had to fill, for the contract very specifically stated that paint had to be applied to the wall within 15 months of the signing of the contract. In order to abide by this time frame, Leonardo would need to finish all his drawings and studies by the middle of 1505 and begin painting his scene shortly thereafter. Of course, Leonardo had a couple of other pressing problems to work out, but those were problems that faced all painters when considering a blank tableau that had to be filled with figures.

How was he going to capture the Battle of Anghiari? Would it be a generic battle scene with lots of action, chaos, and melodrama? Would it focus on a single hero or a single moment? How many figures would he need to paint? What would their state of mind be? Would they be desperate at the unknown moment when the outcome is still undecided, or tensing in anticipation of death, or triumphant in victory?

Unlike other artists, though, Leonardo also found himself thinking about how he wanted to lay down his pigments on the surface of that massive wall. Leonardo was quite well aware that his biggest challenge would be fighting the temptation to experiment with a technique he didn't much like while simultaneously working under a deadline.

So, in addition to thinking about which moment to depict, the number of figures he needed to paint, and the emotional content of those figures, Leonardo was also rethinking the entire painterly method he had used in Milan when painting *The Last Supper* on the walls of Santa Maria delle Grazie.

The sketches we have, like this one, show us an evolution of themes and moments with which Leonardo experimented in 1503 and 1504. Using his standard approach, Leonardo worked out a wide range of compositions very quickly, focusing primarily on the selection of his moment, the relationships between specific figures, and on broad gestures and expressions of individual characters within the bigger composition. And here we see in this sketch, exactly what Leonardo was trying to accomplish as we see figures in different poses of violence, some of them swinging what appear to be axes or swords, others who seem to respond or recoil from them, and up above this great cacophony of motion as horses and riders merged together in this great swirl of violence.

An evolutionary approach emerges from these drawings, as Leonardo experimented with a variety of different moments and combinations of form. In this one we have a whirlwind of activity: horses charging toward one another in what almost seems to be something of a joust; riders try to spear soldiers underneath them. This truly is a vicious battle that Leonardo's describing.

He ultimately settled on the moment in the Battle of Anghiari when the Florentine army broke through the attacking formation of the Milanese and captured their flag—thus symbolizing their victory over the invaders. In so doing, Leonardo smartly recognized that he could combine the physical freneticism of combat with the drama of the historical narrative he was telling, while focusing on individual soldiers and their personal struggles. In this way he could represent a group psychology that reflected the realization within both camps that one of them was winning and the other losing.

For months Leonardo developed both the broader composition and the details within it, now relying quite heavily on his earlier studies of individual human facial features that he had drawn in all those caricatures of everyday people that he had compiled over the years. But now he didn't emphasize the comical or the beautiful, but rather the extremes of emotional states that only those who themselves have experienced the heat of battle can fully understand.

In these two drawings we see remarkable expressions of anger, of fear, even of chaos, and those expressions match the physical positions of the faces that Leonardo has drawn. There's even a sense of contortion in some of them as those muscles converge around the forehead, around the chin, around the mouth. There's a holistic combination here of emotion, of psychological fury, of visceral panic, and terror, and even death.

As for the wall, well that was another exercise in experimentation. Leonardo decided to employ a technique rarely used then or now, called encaustic. It had been quite popular in antiquity but had fallen out of favor by the 16th century due to the extremely sensitive nature of the process.

Encaustic painting is basically an application that involves pigments that are mixed with piping hot, melted wax, which serves as the binding agent. The wax paint is applied to a surface before it dries, which allows one to paint somewhat leisurely: As long as the paints are hot, you can go at your own pace. But, of course, once they're on the surface, they're pretty well fixed there. So you've got to know exactly what you want to paint, and you can't really change anything once you've put your paints down.

Leonardo seems to have worked out all of these problems in fairly short order, but still it seems that both Piero Soderini and Leonardo knew that tackling this one gigantic surface on half of the east wall of the Salone dei Cinquecento would pretty much exhaust the artist's patience.

In September of 1504, Michelangelo was now commissioned to paint a picture on the other half of the wall that Leonardo had not yet conceived. Michelangelo began working intensely on the compositional format of the picture that he wanted to place on the side of the wall just to the left of Leonardo's *Battle of Anghiari* in 1504.

His drawing was dedicated to a similar regional conflict that had gone Florence's way—this one called the Battle of Cascina, which was fought against Pisa in 1364. Like Leonardo, Michelangelo wanted to make a statement, and having the advantage of seeing Leonardo's initial work, Michelangelo built on what he saw there in the Big Room of the 500.

Like Leonardo, Michelangelo focused on themes of motion, terror, confusion, and rage, all conveyed through an expressive and descriptive gestural body language. But unlike Leonardo, who worked to ground every movement and emotion in the experiences he had had in the natural world, Michelangelo began to experiment with figures and poses that accentuated the natural. His tightly muscled figures twist and turn in unusual poses. They reach out to each other awkwardly, and they respond to this call to arms in excessive ways. It's Michelangelo telling us that Nature must be respected, but that Nature can be improved upon by the skilled and imaginative artist.

The drawing that Michelangelo composed was unbelievably large—and I mean that: It was 20 feet high by 60 feet long. It was an enormous cartoon that suggests it was produced as a finished, final expression of his intensions for the wall in the Palazzo Vecchio.

But Michelangelo, like Leonardo, was never able to complete the fresco for his portion of the wall. As soon as he completed the drawing of the Battle of Cascina, Michelangelo was called to Rome by Pope Julius II, who had some very specific plans in mind for the Florentine sculptor.

So Michelangelo left his home in 1505 and made his way south, to Rome. But the drawing of the Battle of Cascina was left behind in Florence, and it became an artistic sensation. It was so famous for its originality and innovative approach to figural studies that it was passed around from artist to artist for years after it had been completed. Individual figures were cut out of the drawing for art students to study and copy. By 1600 the entire cartoon had disintegrated due to mishandling and overuse: All that's left of Michelangelo's drawing are copies, and copies of copies, like the one you see here.

But Leonardo didn't seem to pay much attention to this furor over Michelangelo's cartoon, and in January of 1505—pretty much on schedule—Leonardo began applying his encaustic pigments to the half of the wall designated for his image of the Battle of Anghiari.

We're not entirely sure how much of the picture Leonardo finished during the year he worked on it in the Palazzo Vecchio. Most believe that the entire space designated for Leonardo's painting was used and filled by the artist; but the fact that only a single portion was copied by contemporaries and early 16th-century painters, like this one, similarly suggests that only specific selections were actually finished—or were done in ways that didn't disintegrate soon after Leonardo took the scaffold down from the wall in the Salone dei Cinquecento.

But we know that the picture was immediately impressive and instantly celebrated. A number of artists brought brushes, easels, and pigments into the Big Room of the 500 and copied Leonardo's painting, and a number of other artists managed to get their hands on the cartoon that Leonardo had produced for various segments of the fresco, and they copied that. And here's one of them.

We can see here that a couple of horses bear riders that are in acts of extreme violence. We see swords being held aloft by soldiers who grimace and try to swing them at their counterparts. We see others who shy away; one rider to the far left almost seems to be trying to flee from the scene. Down below, two foot-soldiers—infantrymen—struggling against one another, a dagger about to go into the throat of a victim. This is one of those moments when Leonardo is experimenting both with nature and human nature, where we see the emotion of figures—even emotion of horses—coming through in violent acts, violent gestures, violent facial expressions. This must have been an extraordinary painting in the big room of the 500, and it must have struck at the hearts of viewers intensely.

And those cartoons and copies, we know, survived into the 17th century, when Pieter Paul Rubens took it upon himself to interpret Leonardo's battle scene through the lens of one of these intermediaries, giving us probably one of the most faithful conceptual renderings of the Battle that has been passed down to us. But of the picture itself, nothing remains.

As had happened with *The Last Supper* in Milan, Leonardo's insistence on bypassing traditional methods of fresco painting resulted in disaster. The picture's surface simply could not withstand the atmospheric conditions of the hot and humid Florentine climate, and by the middle of the 16th century, Leonardo's wall was covered over by a new one. A new painter—no less a figure than Giorgio Vasari—was hired in 1563 to paint a brand new fresco of a completely different military engagement to celebrate the glory of his patron, the Duke Cosimo I de'Medici, and what was left of Leonardo's Battle of Anghiari was lost behind the plaster and the paint that Vasari layered on top of it.

The *Battle of Anghiari*, like *The Last Supper*, was a remarkably inventive work of art that allowed Leonardo to experiment with figural poses, gestures, emotional representation, motion, and, above all things, a brand new technique for large-scale mural painting. Although it did not stand the test of time, Leonardo's work in the Big Room of the 500 lived on in the hearts and minds of future generations as a brilliant example of his courageous approach to art.

In our next lecture, we'll see how Leonardo used his inventiveness to develop yet another new way to approach the genre of portraiture, and wound up creating the most famous painting in the world.

Mona Lisa—La Gioconda

Lecture 26

Few paintings in the world are as famous as Leonardo's *Mona Lisa* (in Italian, *La Gioconda*), but despite its notoriety, many mysteries swirl around its origins and meaning. The majority of scholars now identify the sitter as Elisabetta Giaconda, the wife of a Florentine silk merchant, but why did Leonardo paint her, when and how he did, and why is the image so captivating? The answers lie, in part, in Leonardo's studies of optics, anatomy, and engineering.

The Most Famous Painting in the World

- When we encounter an old friend, do we dwell on past experiences or move forward toward seeing one another with fresh eyes, to experiencing anew what made that particular acquaintance so intriguing in the first place? This is the great challenge facing us whenever we look at the *Mona Lisa* or, as it is known in Italian, *La Gioconda*.

- Your visual memory of the painting is probably quite vivid, but what do you know about the conditions of its production? Have you ever wondered about the sitter's identity, who the patron was, or what the inspiration for the artist might have been?

- All of this leads to perhaps the most important questions: Why is the *Mona Lisa* so famous, so important, and so notable? Why should we care about this painting, its appearance, and its history?

- Quite a modestly sized painting at only 21″ × 30″, it is painted on a poplar wood panel, which Leonardo favored during his Florentine years. The woman sits in a three-quarter pose, and her body forms a classical pyramid composition. She wears a dark, velvety gown with ruffled sleeves that catch the light and reveal its fine fabric. A translucent veil is cast nonchalantly over her left shoulder, thanks to an expert application of thin oil glazes.

- She sits on a porch with balustrade. Hidden columns indicate this is a well-appointed villa. The elevated balcony overlooks a wilderness of rivers and alps; we see bridges but no people.

- The painterliness of the picture is readily apparent—its colors merge softly, so imperceptibly that we do not even notice the tiny brush strokes.

Who Is the *Mona Lisa*?

- Documents about the painting's commission, production, and ownership do not exist until the last days of Leonardo's life, when he was revising his will and putting his affairs in order, and even those snippets do not tell us much. Yet more details about the life of the sitter seem to come out with each passing year.

- Six years after Leonardo's death, in 1525, Leonardo's assistant Salai wrote about the things he had inherited from his master, including a portrait he calls *La Ioconda*, or the happy, jocular one. Salai's language makes it sound like the picture had always been called this.

- The painting continues to be called *La Ioconda* from the time it passes from his possession to his sisters, and from them to King François I of France who gives it a French translation, *La Gioconde*, the title it bears in the Louvre today.

- The earliest reference we have to the painting comes from Antonio de' Beatis, who visited Leonardo's studio in France in 1517. He described a picture of "a certain Florentine lady" that had been placed there for the pleasure of visitors and was being painted at the pleasure of Duke Giuliano de' Medici, Leonardo's patron between 1513 and 1516.

- Based mostly on these two sources, specialists have pieced together a speculative history of the painting.

- In 1503, Leonardo took on a commission to paint **Elisabetta Gherardini Gioconda**, the pregnant wife of Francesco di Bartolomeo di Zanobi del Giocondo. Giocondo was a wealthy Florentine silk merchant with good political connections; Elisabetta was of old aristocratic stock. Her family called her Lisa; others called her by the feminine form of her husband's family name—La Gioconda.

- Francesco Giocondo's personal, entrepreneurial, and political skills caught the attention of others. By 1515, he was on the payroll of the Medici family at precisely the time they were making their move to destroy the republican government and restore Medici rule.

- Lisa was not nearly as interested in politics as her husband and lived a life that avoided comment by her peers. We have no record of her movements, interests, concerns, illnesses, hobbies, fears, or pleasures until 1538 or 1539, when Franesco died, perhaps of plague.

- With her husband's passing, Lisa moved into a nunnery called Sant'Orsola, where one of her daughters resided. She lived at least another four years, until 1542, and may even have lived until 1551—the records are not conclusive.

- Features of the painting also hint at the sitter's identity. She is a woman of means; we know this because the setting is a summer estate, and those were owned by members of the aristocracy in 16th-century Italy. The villa overlooks a vast, untarnished landscape, telling us that the sitter is the guardian of that terrain.

- This analysis raises three problems however: Why would Leonardo accept a commission from a local merchant when he had obligations to both the Florentine government and Isabella d'Este? What about Antonio de' Beatis's claim that the patron was Giuliano de' Medici, not Francesco Giocondo? Also, if the de' Beatis letter and the style of the painting date it to the 1510s, could the commission really date to 1503?

- Some have suggested that *Mona Lisa* was Leonardo's attempt to fulfill his promise to Isabella d'Este. The woman portrayed looks nothing like her, however, even accounting for flattery and lost preparatory drawings.

- *Mona Lisa* is one of the most unusual and innovative portraits of the entire Italian Renaissance, which should not surprise us from Leonardo. He deviates from his 15th-century work by softening all the outlines and contours. The blurred edges create a subtle tremor.

- Leonardo's interest in how our eye perceives objects has led him to this intense sfumato. He had long believed that air around was not what everyone thought it was; rather, he knew that particles in the air directly influenced the appearance of sunlight, which in turn affected what the sunlight illuminated.

- This conceptual approach to the relationship between air, light, and objects caused Leonardo to paint in ways that challenged traditional Florentine methods. Leonardo's 16th-century art is all about motion and energy, and not always of the gestural kind. It can be subtle, infinitesimal, a fleeting glimpse or expression.

- This motion and energy can be contained in the minute muscles of the face. The famous smile of the *Mona Lisa* is a case study to show how the muscles in the face move and or what the human eye perceives when they do.

Sfumato versus Tenebrism

- Why did Leonardo decide to deviate from the tenebristic style of portraiture that he had employed in Milan? The first and most obvious reason is his study of the natural world. Painting his sitter against a black background was a good way to satisfy a poet, but painting his sitter within a thriving yet sublime landscape was the way to satisfy the naturalist.

- Perhaps Leonardo was following his Florentine predecessors from the mid-15th century, like Fra Filippo Lippi or Piero della Francesca. These artists placed their sitters in elevated settings that allow them to describe a natural backdrop from above, looking out and over a vast distance. If *Mona Lisa* is a Florentine woman, as Antonio de'Beatis says, then it would make sense for Leonardo to paint her in the local idiom.

- Leonardo was deeply engaged in some pretty detailed and intricate environmental engineering in the early 16th century. The waterways in the background of the *Mona Lisa* speak to Leonardo's desire to address the movement of rivers by placing man's mark on them in the form of a bridge.

- Leonardo also simply loved the natural world and wanted to capture it in all its glories. In painting, that meant finding excuses to depict the natural world whenever possible because painters were not asked to produce pure landscape pictures for another 100 years or so.

Name to Know

Gioconda, Elisabetta Gherardini (1479–1542/51): Traditionally recognized as the sitter of Leonardo's *Mona Lisa* (known as *La Gioconda* in Italian), she was the wife of a political figure named Francesco and was buried in the Florentine nunnery of Sant'Orsola.

Suggested Reading

Greenstein, "Leonardo, *Mona Lisa*, and *La Gioconda*."

Mariotti, *Mona Lisa.*

Pallanti, *Mona Lisa Revealed.*

Mona Lisa—La Gioconda

Lecture 26—Transcript

I want you to picture in your mind's eye the famous painting of the *Mona Lisa*. You know her by now, I'm sure. She seems familiar to you, doesn't she? She's just like an old friend.

What do we do when we encounter an old friend or an acquaintance we haven't seen in awhile? After our greeting, do we dwell on past experiences, recounting the good old days in an attempt to bring those memories back to the surface? Do we try to piece together the fuzzy bits that we can't remember quite so clearly but that, together, can be reconstructed accurately? Or do we move beyond the pleasantries of catching up to move forward toward new experiences, toward seeing one another with fresh eyes, to experiencing anew what made that particular friendship so intriguing, and why we liked that old friend so much in the first place?

This is the great challenge facing us today, whenever we look at the *Mona Lisa* or, as it's known in Italian, *La Gioconda*. Today I'm going to ask you treat the *Mona Lisa* the way you treat an old friend you've just seen again for the first time in about a decade. Are you ready?

Here she is. You remember that captivating smile, don't you? But what else did you remember about her? What did you remember about the appearance and position of her body? Which way she's facing? Or the position of her hands? Did you think of her as sitting or standing? Was she on ground level or was she elevated? What had you remembered about the background? What forms emerge in the distant landscape? Did you remember any buildings? What had you remembered about the mountains and rivers and forests and fields?

Well, so far, all that is just getting reacquainted with your visual memories. You can also move on and ask yourself other questions: Who was she when you last saw her? Was she wealthy or poor? Was she married or single? Did you see her as cloistered or worldly?

You might have asked yourself about the sitter's identity, or who the patron was, or what the inspiration for the artist might have been? And then, because you are re-encountering possibly the most famous person on earth, you may have asked yourself: Why? Why is the *Mona Lisa* so famous, so important, so notable? Why should we care, maybe even care so much, about this one painting and its appearance and its history?

Now, already that's quite a lot. And yet all of those questions merely reactivate old memories. And if your relation to a great work of art is really anything like a friendship, then you also need to move forward into today, to experience new things and to let the painting grow on you in new ways that you haven't experienced before. That's what makes friendships last so long, isn't it? If you can move on and grow, then the friendship continues to thrive.

My challenge today is to get us where we need to be to resume and develop this friendship that you probably already started—or that you've always wanted to have—with the *Mona Lisa.*

First, let's take a quick trip around the painting that Leonardo produced, just to bring together and reassemble all those fuzzy bits of information that we remember and yet also tend to forget. Now physically, the painting is really quite modestly sized. It's only about 30 inches high and 21 inches wide. And it's painted on poplar wood, which was favored by Leonardo during his Florentine years. And of course it features those oil pigments that Leonardo had been experimenting with since the 1470s.

The sitter is obviously a woman, and she sits in a three-quarter pose, with her body angled just enough that it forms that classical composition, that pyramid that we've now come to recognize as a core in the center of the picture. Her hands are clasped together, but she twists herself in space, almost uncomfortably. She wears a velvety, dark gown, and the ruffled sleeves along her right arm catch the light and reveal its fine fabric. A translucent veil has been cast nonchalantly over her left shoulder—it's an expert application of a see-through garment by a painter who really knows what he's doing.

She's located on a porch with a balustrade in front of her. And just on the edge of that picture to the far left we see the base of a hidden column. It indicates that she is probably seated in a well-appointed villa, and that villa is elevated. It looks over a vast wilderness. Rivers twist and turn below. There's a bridge that we can see on the right side of that picture over her shoulder. There are no people in that wilderness, but we do see opening up behind her a vast mountain range.

The painterliness of the picture is readily apparent—its colors merge softly together so imperceptibly that we don't even notice the tiny strokes he uses to apply those veils of paint, those tiny glazes of oil pigment that he can manipulate with his brush, or his knife, or even his fingers.

This much we know—we can see it. But questions about her identity, the purpose of the picture's production, its place in the painter's artistic chronology, and the meaning of the items he painted there all demand a review that digs much deeper than a surface description of the picture.

We'll start this review tentatively, by saying that some of the historical information we are about to discuss cannot be confirmed at all, for documented facts about the *Mona Lisa*'s commission, production, and ownership simply do not exist until the last days of Leonardo's life, when he was revising his will and putting his affairs in order—and even those snippets of information don't really tell us very much. On the other hand, more details about the life of the sitter seem to come out with each passing year. While we have no choice but to speculate about some of the features of the painting, we're on firmer ground when we start taking about the person the painting represents. But let's begin our examination of the *Mona Lisa* by reviewing the very few references we have to it from the period.

Six years after Leonardo's death, in the year 1525, Leonardo's assistant, Salai, wrote about the things that had come into his possession from his master. In this commentary, he includes a reference to a *Portrait of a Woman* that he called, *La Ioconda*, or the happy, jocular one. The famous smile that graces her face makes this title seem rather obvious and appropriate, and Salai's language makes it sound like the picture had always been called this. In fact, the painting will continue to be called *La Ioconda* from the time it passes from Salai's possession to that of his sisters, and from them to no less a figure than King Francois I of France, who bought it from Salai's sister and referred to the picture as *La Gioconde*. It's the title that is still attached to the picture by the French today, who display the image in the Louvre—they call it *La Gioconde* while Italians call it *La Gioconda*. At the most superficial level, then, the painting merely shows us a study of a woman smiling or enjoying herself—*la iocanda*—instead of someone known by that surname.

But this passage by Salai is not the earliest reference we have to the *Mona Lisa*. That distinction goes to a man named Antonio de'Beatis, who in 1517 visited the studio of Leonardo da Vinci in France. When Beatis entered the room, he saw a picture of a woman that had been placed there for the pleasure of visitors by Leonardo himself.

In this passage, which is only a few sentences long, Antonio de'Beatis reveals that the picture portrays "A certain Florentine Lady." He then writes that the picture was being painted at the pleasure of the Duke Giuliano de' Medici, Leonardo's patron in Rome between 1513 and 1516. (We'll meet him a little later on in this course.) Although Beatis declines to offer the sitter's identity (he calls her neither *Mona Lisa* nor La Gioconda), it seems likely that he's getting his information from Leonardo directly—though perhaps, as we'll see, the image itself offers clues to suggest that she's a Florentine.

Based foremost on these two written comments, one by Beatis just two years before Leonardo's death, and the other eight years later by Salai, specialists have pieced together a quite speculative history of this painting—one that should be taken with a grain of salt.

It goes like this. The year was 1503. Leonardo had just returned from his service with Cesare Borgia and had engaged in some pretty remarkable plans with Niccolo Machiavelli to divert the course of the Arno River so that rival Pisa could be starved into submission. He had begun work on an encaustic mural painting for the Republic of Florence and had been placed on a very short leash with definite deadlines that he was working hard to meet.

He had made enemies with a jealous and insecure Michelangelo, whose *David* neared completion in a workshop in the cathedral. The duchess of Mantua was breathing down his neck for him to paint a picture for her. In other words, Leonardo was busy and preoccupied, and he really didn't have much time for nonsense. And yet, at precisely this time, Leonardo took on a brand new project from an entirely unexpected source.

Right around 1503, Leonardo was approached by a man named Francesco di Bartolomeo di Zanobi del Giocondo, who wanted a portrait done of his wife. Giocondo's wife, named Elisabetta, was expecting a child, and this seemed like an appropriate way of celebrating that event.

Now Francesco Giocondo was a wealthy merchant who had made his fortune in the silk trade. He had done a good job of transforming himself from a New Man into a Powerful Man. He had done this in two ways, both of them as familiar to us now as they were back then: First, Giocondo had gotten involved in politics, and had cashed in both his chits and his good name for offices that gave him leverage in the new Republic.

Second, Giocondo married old money—he convinced the noble Gherardini family to part with their daughter, Elisabetta, in order to make an alliance between their aristocratic family (representing old money) and him, this rising entrepreneur (presenting new money). The two were married in 1495, and when Elisabetta, or Lisa, as she was known, entered her new household, she became known by the feminine form of her husband's family name. Thus, she was known in Florence as Lisa Gioconda.

So far, all of this conforms to what we've heard about the picture from the memoirs of both Antonio de'Beatis, who said it represents a Florentine woman and Salai, who said the picture was called "La Ioconda." But there's more to the story.

Francesco Giocondo's personal, entrepreneurial, and political skills caught the attention of others. By 1515 or so, his name begins to appear in documents that list or refer to Florentine allies to the Medici family in Florence. And Francesco isn't just mentioned as a friend of the Medici in passing: He's literally on the payroll of the Medici family at precisely the time they were making their move to destroy the Republican government and return it to Medicean rule. By the middle of the 1520s, Francesco had been named to a key political post, which now allowed him to support Medici policies after they had managed to regain control of the city.

Now Lisa wasn't nearly as interested in politics as her husband was. She came from one of Florence's oldest families, which meant that her father had lots of property at his disposal, but did not have a steady income aside from the rents he collected. In those days, aristocrats did not work.

Lisa had been born in a house on the south side of Florence, but her family moved several times during her childhood, and she was reared in at least two different Florentine homes, both near the church of Santa Croce, which was located in the quarter of the city where Verrocchio and Leonardo had shared a workshop in the 1470s.

But Lisa also spent time on her family's farm in the agriculturally rich Chianti district, south of Florence, which was one of the perks of aristocratic birth in the 1400s. But there was also a downside to this, as her cash-strapped family struggled to pay bills, even with all the land they owned in and out of the city.

Lisa's marriage to Francesco appears to have been unexceptional for the period. The two of them lived in an apartment in Florence for the first eight years of their marriage—until about the time of this picture. They had five children, including a son named, Andrea, who was born in 1503—at just at the time many believe Leonardo's portrait was begun. They also had two daughters who wound up living in local convents, which does become a part of our story in just a minute.

While Francesco made a name for himself as a Medici ally, Lisa lived a life that avoided comment by her peers—we have no record of her movements, her interests, her concerns, illnesses, hobbies, fears, or pleasures. She shared her life with Francesco fairly anonymously until 1538 or 1539, when her husband died, perhaps of plague.

With her husband's passing, Lisa either couldn't or wouldn't remain in their Florentine home. She was moved into a nunnery called Sant'Orsola, where one of her daughters resided. She lived at least another four years, until 1542, and may even have lived until 1551—the records are not conclusive—but by that later date, at the very latest, Lisa Gioconda was dead.

In any event, the surname of Lisa and her husband explains why French and Italian lovers of the portrait refer to it as *La Gioconde* or *La Gioconda.* Francesco's association with the Medici have led others to believe that Antonio de' Beatis may have been onto something when he wrote that there was a Medici connection intertwined in the story of the painting.

There are features in the picture that help us understand a little something about the sitter's identity, and they help us confirm that the person Leonardo has painted is, indeed, Mons Lisa Gioconda.

Leonardo tells us, in a subtle way, that the sitter of this portrait is a woman of means. Her black dress does not convey this, nor does her hairstyle, nor any fashionable accessories. But the sitter has been perched on a porch in an elevated setting, that once displayed a classical column along one side of the picture much better than it does now. She's been placed in a country villa, in other words, that's located out in the countryside. It's a summer estate, and those were owned primarily by members of the aristocracy in 16th-century Italy.

And if she's sitting on a porch in a villa—and she is—and if that villa overlooks a vast, untarnished landscape—and it does—then we can say with some security that Leonardo is telling us that his sitter is the guardian of that terrain. It's the garden that extends beyond the manor house, the orchards and vineyards and pastures that provide for the mansion, the natural playground with fresh breezes and cool evenings that call the aristocracy out to the countryside in the first place.

If we read this picture in this way, then we have to come to the conclusion that this may, in fact, represent *Mona Lisa* Gioconda, who was the daughter of an aristocratic family with property in the Tuscan Hills—but who had limited cash supplies and couldn't splurge on fancy dresses and elegant jewelry.

Now you've got to admire all this super sleuthing, and I'm actually pretty content with what we have here, save for three important problems. First, I'm not sure why Leonardo would accept a commission from a local merchant when he had both the Florentine government and Isabella d'Este incessantly nagging him to finish other projects, and while he was traveling out to the banks of the Arno to figure out how to change its course. Producing a picture of an aristocrat at this moment in his career seems much more likely. Maybe this portrait represents someone altogether distinct from Lisa Giocondo and her new money husband.

Second problem: In the same statement by Antonio de' Beatis in which he calls the picture a Florentine lady, he also says that Leonardo told him the patron was Giuliano de' Medici, and not Francesco or Lisa Giocondo. Now Leonardo worked for Giuliano de' Medici between 1513 and 1516, which is a good 10 years after the dating of this picture. How do we make the leap from Francesco to Giuliano?

And third, de' Beatis suggests that Leonardo was currently in the process of painting the picture when he visited him in 1517, and the stylistic approach taken by Leonardo supports a dating of the picture to the late 15-teens, during the last years of his life, rather than during the very first years of the 1500s.

In other words, there are really good reasons to think that, first of all, this picture wasn't commissioned in 1503 or anytime thereabouts, and secondly, that this picture doesn't even depict Elisabetta Gioconda at all—and that Salai's reference to *La Ioconda* should be taken literally, due to her smile, rather than as a reference to the sitter's last name. And the business about the whole Medici connection throws a real wrench into the whole problem.

Now one part of the puzzle is this drawing that we've seen before of Isabella d'Este. We know that Leonardo not only did this portrait from life and that the sitter was eager to have Leonardo produce something for her, but that the artist had actually indicated to Isabella that he intended to work up a painted version of this portrait for her pleasure at a future date.

I so want the *Mona Lisa* to be Leonardo's attempt to satisfy Isabella, and I so want this painting to show Leonardo's faithful attempt to abide by the promise he made to the duchess of Mantua in February of 1500—and I'm not bothered by the fact that her head here is a profile while her body twists back toward us in a three-quarter position. We've seen enough of Leonardo's working method to know that he was never satisfied, that he was always changing, and that he was perfectly happy to rotate a sitter's pose if he felt it would make a better picture; and the disposability of drawings in the period might help explain why other sketches of Isabella have not survived.

But the facial features of the sitter just don't match, and the rather homely nature of Isabella's physique simply do not correspond with the beauty that Leonardo has shown us in the *Mona Lisa*. The sitter here seems stately and kind, and neither of those two words were ever used to describe the duchess of Mantua. This is no painting of Isabella d'Este, no matter how badly I'd like it to be.

Whoever it was that was represented here was immortalized in one of the most unusual and innovative portraits of the entire Italian Renaissance. But that really shouldn't come as a surprise to us by now. For we've seen that Leonardo had always been at his most innovative when it came to producing portraits.

Ginevra de' Benci's groundbreaking depiction brought her out of the turgid profile pose that had confined female sitters for generations before her. Cecilia Gallerani was shown emerging dramatically from a black background. Both of them were painted as great beauties, and both of them were shown bearing symbolic images that revealed their identities, which in turn emphasized their importance as individuals.

Of course, Leonardo didn't invent these things from whole cloth. He'd been descended from a lineage of innovative portraitists from Antonello da Messina (whose portrait of a man I show here) to the Flemish artists Petrus Christus, Robert Campin, and Jan van Eyck—each of whom used a microscopic attention to detail as a way to convey psychological presence and reveal an emotional sensibility in their sitters.

But Leonardo deviates from both Antonello's model and from his own portraits of the 15th century. Stark outlines and contours, formed first by the distinct outlines that Leonardo applied to the portrait of Ginevra and then, later, to the brilliantly illuminated face of Cecilia Gallerani, have been softened here.

Blurred edges make the woman before us seem to move before our eyes, ever so slightly, in a much more subtle tremor than we see in the jerking hand of the *Virgin and the Swimming Christ Child* in Leonardo's experimental *Virgin of the Yarnwinder*, from 1501. Antonello's close examination of the details of the natural world influenced Leonardo in the way that an optical reality had been captured by the Sicilian painter. But Leonardo's decision to blur those details, rather than zero in on them, signals to us that Leonardo is interested in a different kind of naturalism—his is no longer an exact replication of objects as they exist in the world, but rather an exact replication of how our eye perceives those objects—which is usually a little bit fuzzy and out of focus, especially as we get older. Nature guides both of these traditions, but it's a different kind of nature that Leonardo strives to capture.

In fact, Leonardo's approach to this sfumato technique was based on his close observational powers and his scientific mind. He had long believed that the air around us was not what we thought it was, and he was convinced that its quality directly affected the way our eye perceived the world around us.

He wrote in one of his notebooks, "The blueness we see in the atmosphere is not intrinsic color, but is caused by warm vapor evaporated in minute and imperceptible atoms, on which the solar rays fall, rendering them luminous against the infinite darkness of the fiery sphere which is beyond." He knew that particles in the air directly influenced the appearance of sunlight, and that the qualities of that sunlight in turn influenced the appearance of things that it illuminated.

When translated to painting, this conceptual approach to the relationship between air, light, and objects caused Leonardo to proceed with pictures in ways that challenged traditional Florentine methods of painting. When the brilliant Sandro Botticelli painted the *Birth of Venus* sometime around 1480, he busily made his preparatory sketches, transferred the figures to the surface of his picture, and then dutifully filled in the spaces he had created with his underdrawing with specific colors to represent specific areas and items. The contours of the areas, delineated by the drawing, really mattered, for they showed Botticelli where to put those colors on his painting.

And this type of application caused Leonardo to admonish painters like Botticelli, who he felt were too precious, too rigid, and too disciplined. Leonardo saw outlines as a prison, and he worked to loosen the contours of his images even when they were in the form of drawings.

Leonardo's art from the 16th-century is all about motion and energy—and not always of the gestural kind, either. It can be subtle, infinitesimal, a fleeting glimpse or a look or an expression. The energy can be the imperceptible breath taken by a sitter, causing her head and her shoulders and her chest to move. It can be a breeze gently moving leaves and branches on trees. It can be a light mist in the distance that hovers and shifts before a mountain range.

But most importantly, this motion and energy can be contained in the minute muscles of the sitter's face: in the eyes and lips and cheeks that twitch so slightly that we don't even notice it when they do. And Leonardo tries to show that movement through the blurry sfumato technique that causes him to omit contours and outlines, and replace them only with subtle shadings that turn a neutral mouth into a happy one at the very edges, no matter how slightly.

That's why the *Mona Lisa* smiles: She's being used as a case study to show how the muscles in the face move, and how—or what—the human eye perceives when they do.

Now a really good question that we ought to ask ourselves is: Why did Leonardo decide to deviate from the tenebristic style of portraiture that he had employed in Milan to such great effect? It was clearly pretty popular in the Sforza court then, and both poets and potential patrons were moved to write passionately about the figures that emerged from Leonardo's murky dark backgrounds. It's a good question, and there are a lot of different answers to it.

The first and most obvious one is that Leonardo was by now completely dedicated to the study of the natural world—as an artist, as an engineer, and as a scientist. Painting his sitter against a black background was a good way to satisfy a poet, but painting his sitter within a thriving, yet sublime, landscape was the best way to satisfy the environmentalist. By the dawn of the 16th century, Leonardo saw himself as being more of the latter than the former, and placing his subjects in the middle of a fantastic natural setting allowed him to suggest relationships between the sitter and the world around her—which, in turn, could be interpreted as a more philosophically oriented statement on the relationship between mankind and how it fits in the natural world.

Perhaps Leonardo got this idea by looking at portraits painted by his predecessors in the middle of the 15th century, like Fra Filippo Lippi's Madonna from about 1460 that displays the mother of his child—the nun, Lucrezia Buti. Or maybe he was thinking about the double portrait that Piero della Francesca had painted in 1473 of the former duke of Urbino, Federigo de Montefeltro, and his Milanese wife, Battista Sforza, that Leonardo would've known from his very recent trip to Ubino while working for Cesare Borgia.

In both pictures, sitters are placed in elevated settings that allow the portraitist to describe a natural backdrop from above, looking out and over a vast distance. He can describe the wilderness that he imagines framing his sitters, and in the process he can compare the physical and spiritual features of his subjects to the wonders and glories and virtues of the pristine landscape in the background.

This had become a Tuscan tradition that was followed by portraitists, and we know that, while in Tuscany, Leonardo adhered to it. That's why the painting of Ginevra de' Benci features so prominently a naturalistic landscape behind her. If you ever drive or walk through the hills of Tuscany, even just a couple of kilometers outside the urban center of Florence, you know that the rolling hills and sparkling vineyards and deep green forests warrant the loving attention of environmentalists, naturalists, and artists alike. They tended to emphasize nature and space rather than obliterate it in favor of a microscopic analysis of the human sitter that was preferred in Milan and points north.

And if this is a Florentine Woman, as Antonio de'Beatis says she is, then it would make sense for Leonardo to paint her in the local idiom. If it's Lisa Gioconda of the Gherardini family that owned a summer home in the Tuscan hills south of Florence, than there was even greater reason for the artist to paint her in this setting.

But we can also remember that Leonardo, personally, had been deeply engaged in some pretty detailed and intricate environmental work of his own, the likes of which hadn't been seen in Italy since the days of the building of Roman aqueducts 1500 years earlier. He had been thinking about re-routing the Arno, and he had envisioned the plans and machines to dig new riverways through the hills of his boyhood stomping grounds.

The waterways in the background of the *Mona Lisa* speak very clearly to Leonardo's desire to address the movement of rivers, as they twist and turn, like the Arno at its wildest spots. But he also places man's mark on them in the form of a bridge, a structure that he had designed before in Milan but had never had an opportunity to build. And these lead us to those dramatic mountains we see in the background, that jut out from the ground like the Alpine peaks not far from Milan—and their size in relationship to the sitter probably approximated Leonardo's most common encounter with them while he had lived there: He knew those mountains well, but he knew them only from a distance. Leonardo put all these things in the big, broad context of an entire universe, made up of mysteries and curiosities that even his own mind couldn't completely understand.

Leonardo loved the natural world, and he wanted to capture it in all its glories. And in painting, that meant finding excuses to depict the natural world whenever possible. For in the first decades of the 16th century, painters were not asked to produce pure landscape pictures. The freedom to focus exclusively on landscapes that Leonardo had discovered in drawing very early, in his youthful sketch of the hills outside Florence, wouldn't come to painting for another 100 years or so. In his day, the only chance that Leonardo had to express his full enthusiasm for the natural world he loved so much, was to insert landscapes into his portraits and narratives whenever the opportunity arose.

The *Mona Lisa* captures the very essence—the core truth—of Leonardo da Vinci's entire career as an artist, a thinker, and a scientist. It's a painting that brings together all of his pursuits and all of his interests, all of his dreams and visions, and all of his beliefs about art and nature and the things that make us human. It captures the spirit of the High Renaissance brilliantly, maybe even perfectly, in the way that so many of the great ideas and discoveries of the age are referenced here, in this modestly sized *Portrait of a Woman* of no real historical distinction. The *Mona Lisa* is both the culmination of everything that came before it in the Renaissance—and in Leonardo's artistic career—and a premonition of everything that would follow it.

It is the best-known painting in the world—and a very good friend of ours for some very good reasons.

Raphael and Leonardo

Lecture 27

While Leonardo and Michelangelo were carrying on their silent Florentine feud, a young man from Urbino came to town to make a name for himself. This painter, only 20 years old, quickly adopted Leonardo's style and principles and was so successful that he came to be known first as an artistic hack and then as one of the greatest and most influential painters in Western history. He was Raphael, and thanks in part to Leonardo's teachings, he would shortly be summoned to Rome to be part of that city's great artistic revival.

Raphael Chooses Sides

- For perhaps two years, Florence hosted three of Western history's greatest artists at the same time: Michelangelo, **Raphael**, and Leonardo. At 20 years of age, Raphael was a young upstart but, unlike Michelangelo before him, was eager to learn and more eager to please.

- The project that most directly facilitated this remarkable artistic convergence was the Salone dei Cinquecento between 1503 and 1505. Artists in Florence were presented with a choice: The meticulous naturalism and science of Leonardo versus the emotional and angst-ridden sculptural style of Michelangelo.

- The choice was not difficult for Raphael. He chose Leonardo, and his reasons seem obvious. Leonardo's adherence to the laws of nature, his tendencies to clarify subject matter, and his ability to tell a coherent story spoke to Raphael's inner artist. On a more personal level, Leonardo was the greatest artistic courtier of his generation, maybe of all time. Raphael, too, was destined for life as a courtier.

- Born in 1483, Raphael grew up in Urbino, where his father served as court painter to Duke Federigo de Montefeltro. Raphael spent a good amount of time inside the ducal palace and was taught at an early age about the rules and games of courtly life.

- In the mid-1490s, his father arranged for him to apprentice with Piero Perugino. Raphael learned the rules of painting as devised by Leonardo and his contemporaries, with an emphasis on the importance of good draftsmanship.

- There is an extremely good chance that Raphael traveled a good deal to see the works of other artists, including Leonardo, and Leonardo may have met Raphael when he was serving Cesare Borgia after Cesare had taken Urbino.

Raphael was a devoted follower of Leonardo's style.

- While no documents support a relationship between Raphael and Leonardo, we have visual evidence of Raphael's leanings. The clearest indicators are Raphael's portraits produced in Florence, especially those commissioned to commemorate the marriage of Maddalena and Agnolo Doni in 1507.

- Maddalena and Agnolo are shown at half length, with their torsos twisting in a seated contrapposto and three-quarter gaze. Behind each of them appears a brilliant, naturalistic landscape. Although the sfumato is not apparent here, the composition otherwise strikes one as decidedly Leonardesque.

- Raphael's *Lady with the Unicorn* shows a similar approach: the twist of the body, the frontal gaze, and the deep landscape in the background. Just as the *Mona Lisa* originally contained a column running along the edge of its frame, so did this painting.

Leonardo's *Leda*

- Two other works by Leonardo made a strong impression on Raphael: Sometime between 1505 and 1508, Leonardo began preparing sketches for *Leda and the Swan*—a moment from Greek mythology and an overtly erotic picture, particularly for that day.

- Leda is shown in full frontal nudity, with thrusting hips and a contrapposto pose. She looks out at us knowingly, maybe even invitingly. The swan swings his neck and beak up toward her. The forms are sinuous and supple. To emphasize the point, children emerge from eggs: Castor and Pollux, Helen and Clytemnestra. The painting was completed at some point before he left Florence for Milan in 1508.

- We have become increasingly numb to the depiction of the nude female form, but in the early 16th century, such depictions were likely thought of as highly charged erotica, particularly when shown in the context of a pagan story about seduction. Leonardo was not the first to show female nudity, but earlier Renaissance depictions tended to use this image as a metaphor for concepts like purity or as part of a creation story.

- In December 1499, only four months before Leonardo and Luca Pacioli went to Venice, an openly pornographic poem was produced anonymously in Venice, probably by a Dominican friar named Francesco Colonna. Called *The Fight for Love in the Dream of Poliphili*, it recounts a wild vision by a girl of that name and was accompanied by a number of erotic and fetishistic prints.

- The book was a best seller. Even if Leonardo did not read it, he surely knew of the illustrations. Leonardo was more subtle and legitimized his erotic painting by grounding it in a story from pagan mythology. Yet the raw sensuality reminds us that Leonardo was human and perhaps more aware of the emotional side of nature than some critics have wanted to see in him.

- The original painting traveled with Leonardo for the last years of his life, went north to France with him, and ultimately landed in the hands of King François I of France, whereupon sometime in the 17th century, it disappeared.

- *Leda* was famous in its own day—so much so that Raphael copied the drawing, unknown painters did the same with Leonardo's finished product, and it was considered the most valuable of all of Leonardo's pictures when he died in 1519. Leonardo's contemporaries saw it as an opening salvo in what could become the rapidly emerging genre of erotic painting.

Leonardo's Madonnas and Raphael's Copies

- The most influential Leonardo painting of this period for younger artists like Raphael was completed around 1508. Like *Leda*, it seems to have had no patron, no predetermined setting, and no particular function. This *Saint Anne Madonna* was based on the sketch we saw earlier, the one Vasari tells us he put on display for the public.

- Like in a preparatory sketch, we see the familiar classical composition forming a family tree, with each generation emanating from the legs, or womb, of the predecessor. Mary tries to hold Christ back, but he squiggles out of her reach toward John the Baptist and his destiny.

- This cartoon builds on an idea that Leonardo had wanted to pursue for 30 years: the concept of motherly love, the infuriating independence of children, danger, self-sacrifice, and tenderness.

- The popularity of Madonna paintings had never been higher in the city of Florence. Madonna of the Goldfinch by Raphael, now in the Uffizi Gallery, shows his understanding of classical composition: Mary creates that solid core in the center. She reaches down to caress Christ, who strikes an elegant contrapposto pose while stroking a Goldfinch held by the John the Baptist, which symbolizes the soul. The landscape transitions from green to blue to white, as a picture by Leonardo might, although not with the same use of sfumato.

- People bought small Madonnas for their homes at a pretty crisp rate at this time, and Raphael's popularity grew by accommodating their needs—adding all the requisite figures: Mary, Christ, and John the Baptist.

- Once in a while, he would try something unusual, as he did with *Madonna of the Meadow*. Mary is shown on a stool, and Christ is squeezed between her arms. Symbolically, this composition may allude to a birthing stool and childbirth. It may have been meant to comfort a woman who was pregnant for the first time, for childbirth was, by far, the number one cause of death among adult women.

- Between 1505 and 1508, Raphael churned out handfuls of Madonnas, most of them of modest, unintimidating sizes, like the *Louvre Madonna* and *Madonna of the Pinks*, all along Leonardo's model. But with the sole exception of that one-man show in 1501, the only way Raphael could have seen Leonardo's drawings was to have visited his workshop.

- The fact that Raphael blatantly borrowed from Leonardo and Leonardo let him indicates a couple of things: Leonardo was not particularly interested in churning out Madonnas or in a formal partnership with a younger painter. However, while the borrower showed proper deference and respect to the one whose ideas he was borrowing, the creator did not insist on recognition.

The End of an Era

- Then, just as abruptly as this remarkable confluence of artistic synergy emerged, it was broken, or at least reconfigured. In 1503, Julius II came to the papal throne and embarked on a bold plan to revitalize Rome.

- He began calling the greatest artists and architects of the day to the city. First, in 1504, he called Bramante to the papal court. Next, in

1505, came the call for Michelangelo. Then, in 1508, Julius called for Raphael.

- Leonardo never received a similar call, for by then he was committed to a different master on the opposite end of Italy, back in Milan—the king of France.

- When Raphael came to the papal court, Michelangelo interpreted this as a threat to his prominence, for here was a Leonardo protégée in his midst.

Name to Know

Raphael (a.k.a. **Raffaello Sanzio** or **Raffaello Santi**; 1483–1520): Enormously talented painter and deft courtier who earned a reputation for artistic elegance and diplomatic skill during his years in Florence and Rome. A member of Julius II's entourage of artists from 1508 to 1513, Raphael painted frescoes in the Vatican (*The School of Athens*, 1512), portraits of his papal patrons (*Julius II*, 1512; *Leo X*, 1516), and altarpieces for Roman churches (*The Transfiguration of Chrst*, 1518), before his sudden death at the age of 37.

Suggested Reading

Allison, "Antique Sources of Leonardo's *Leda.*"

Brown, "Raphael, Leonardo, and Perugino: Fame and Fortune."

Hochstetler Meyer, "Leonardo's Hypothetical Painting of *Leda and the Swan.*"

Raphael and Leonardo
Lecture 27—Transcript

For a very brief time, maybe for two years or so, the city of Florence hosted three of Western history's greatest artists, all at the same time. In 1504 and 1505, Michelangelo, Raphael, and Leonardo da Vinci resided in the tightly compact city by the Arno River. The first, Michelangelo, was in his late 20s and preoccupied with the intricacies of carving his David. He remained aloof and distant. The second, Raphael, was a young upstart, barely more than 20 years old. He was eager to learn and more eager to please. And the third, now in his fifties, had more experience—and more kinds of experience—than the other two combined. If these three artists could at all be said to represent a kind of artistic godhead in the High Renaissance, Leonardo would clearly have been God the Father.

The three of these artists looked and stared at each other's ideas, since there was so much to see and so much consider. This was the time when Michelangelo's *David* was nearing completion, and when Leonardo was in the middle of his work on the *Mona Lisa*. It was also the time when Raphael painted his picture of *Agnolo Doni*, which signaled his entry into Florentine high society as a portraitist of the nobility. Only Michelangelo's departure in 1505 for Rome and the papal court of Julius II snapped the extraordinary intersections of these three giants of art history.

The one project that most directly facilitated this remarkable artistic convergence was the competition staged by the Florentine government inside the Salone dei Cinquecento from 1503 to 1505. There, Leonardo's classical approach to figures and scenes was put to the test by Michelangelo's ultra-naturalistic alternatives. Although Michelangelo was unable to finish his painting, and Leonardo seems only to have produced a portion of his, the drawings that described their visions of how pictures ought to look inspired artists for generations to come.

But it also presented a challenge to them, at least it did in 1505 when Michelangelo left for Rome and his papal appointment. Artists in Florence immediately realized that there was a fairly distinctive choice being presented to them. One was offered by the meticulous naturalist and scientist from Vinci. The other was offered by the more emotional and angst-ridden sculptor from Settignano.

Anyone with any experience in the field of drawing or painting could see, just by looking at the designs for the wall in the Big Room of the 500, that these two alternatives were radically different. Leonardo's centralized compositional approach emphasized an immediately familiar emotional sensibility that was grounded in natural experience. Michelangelo offered a twisting, turning, contorted composition that featured characters who surpassed the mundaneness of that natural experience. Artists began to feel as though they had to make a choice between the two, and it was an extremely difficult one for many of them to make.

But not for Raphael. This young painter quickly made his choice, and in the years of his activity in Florence—and really right up until just before his death in 1520—Raphael elected to follow the inspiration of the Greatest Painter in the World.

The reasons for this choice seem obvious at first. On one hand, Leonardo's adherence to the laws of nature, his tendencies to clarify subject matter, and his ability to tell a coherent story spoke to Raphael's inner artist. A young and impressionable painter, Raphael saw in Leonardo a grand master who had enjoyed great success for very good reasons.

But on an even more personal level, Leonardo must have been the very exemplum of what Raphael aspired to be. Leonardo was the greatest artistic courtier of his generation, and maybe of all time, and he had shown everyone just how a painter could survive in a modern day court setting. Leonardo was the role model for Raphael, due both to his elegantly classical painterly style and to his ability to thrive in the Medici, Sforza, and even Borgia courts. Leonardo had a vast wealth of experience for precisely the kind of court painter that Raphael longed and expected to become. And Raphael already knew about the kind of culture better than almost any artist his own age.

Raphael was born in 1483 and grew up in the town of Urbino, where his father served as a fairly undistinguished court painter for the local duke, Federigo de Montefeltro. Because of his father's position, Raphael spent a good amount of time inside the ducal palace, where he had an opportunity to observe his father's colleagues, as they formed what later would become considered to be the model of a 15th-century Italian court. As a result, Raphael was taught at an early age about the rules of the games that were played in a courtly setting, and the early part of his career was spent preparing himself so that he might one day receive a call to serve in a similar setting as the courtier/painter of a noble prince.

And in fact, as a child, Raphael had shown tremendous skill with the pen and brush, and in the mid-1490s his father arranged for him to apprentice with the painter Piero Perugino, whose drawing of the Virgin Mary we have already noted for its delicate use of line and subtle hints of modeling. With Perugino as his master, Raphael learned the rules of painting as devised by Leonardo and his contemporaries at the turn of the 16th century—with an emphasis on the importance of good draftsmanship.

There's an extremely good chance that Raphael, as a student of Perugino, traveled quite a good bit to see the works of other artists, living and dead, whose works were on display in nearby cities. Florence would have been a natural destination, and there's good reason to believe that Raphael made the journey to see Leonardo's cartoon of the Saint Anne Madonna when he put on his one-man show in Santissima Annunziata in 1501.

But, in an interesting twist of fate, it seems that Leonardo actually may have come to see Raphael. In 1502, when in the service of Cesare Borgia, Leonardo was stationed in the town of Urbino, and there is a strong likelihood that Raphael maybe made an effort to see him. In any event, when Raphael moved to Florence in 1504, it was Leonardo to whom the young painter looked for inspiration. No documents support this claim of mine: We don't have a diary or letters from Raphael's hand indicating his preference for Leonardo's approach to painting. But we do have some pretty strong visual evidence to demonstrate the choices that he made.

The clearest indicator of Raphael's deep appreciation for Leonardo's art comes in the form of the portraits that the young painter from Urbino produced while in Florence. Raphael was commissioned to commemorate the recent marriage of Maddalena and Agnolo Doni, whose images I show here.

Both sitters have been posed in ways that remind us of the sitters that Leonardo painted in both of his Florentine periods. Maddalena and Agnolo are shown at half-length, with their torsos twisting in a seated contrapposto position. They gaze out at the viewer in the now-familiar three-quarter pose, and Maddalena's hands press down, one on top of the other. Behind each of them appears a brilliant, naturalistic landscape.

The figural positioning of Maddalena Doni alone indicates that Raphael knew and valued the work that Leonardo was currently doing on his portrait of the *Mona Lisa*. Raphael has intentionally borrowed Gioconda's pose from Leonardo, and he jettisons the profile position, just as Leonardo had in his portraits of women. Moreover, Raphael places Maddalena in a countryside setting that seems awfully familiar. Although the sfumato technique preferred by Leonardo is not apparent here, the composition otherwise strikes one as decidedly Leonardesque.

Soon after he had produced the *Maddalena* portrait, Raphael painted this portrait of a woman, now known as the *Lady with the Unicorn*. Similar approaches have been taken here, as the twist of the body, the frontal gaze through the three-quarter shift, and the deep landscape in the background all suggest that Raphael had learned well Leonardo's lessons about female portraiture. And when we remember that the *Mona Lisa* originally contained a column running along the edge of its frame, the same architectural feature in the *Lady with the Unicorn* now indicates a very close reading of Leonardo's painting by Raphael.

Raphael looked at the older, more experienced artist and he copied him, and this made him very attractive to clients eager to have a painting that looked something like a Leonardo, but was only a little bit cheaper. It also seems that two other works by Leonardo made an equally strong impression on the painter from Urbino during this same period. Sometime between 1505 and 1508, Leonardo began working slowly on a brand new image, and one that he seems to have produced with no specific patron or owner in mind.

Working up a series of sketches, each one showing the main figure in different positions and attitudes, Leonardo began composing a scene that featured the forms of *Leda and the Swan*—a moment from Greek mythology when the maiden, Leda is wooed and won by the god Zeus, who appears before her in the form of an elegant white swan.

What Leonardo has produced, in fact, is an overtly erotic picture, particularly for that day. Leda has been shown fully nude, thrusting her hips out one way, contrapposto pose informing that shape of the body. She looks out at us, knowingly, maybe even inviting us to play along with her now in this engagement that she has with a swan that has appeared before her to her left. The swan swings its neck and its beak up toward her, almost pecking at the side of her head, maybe whispering into her ear. There's a decidedly sensual content here, a sinuosity of forms that appear to the curves of the body, the suppleness of the skin.

And, just to make sure that we don't miss the point of this picture, actual byproducts of this sexual union are here announced. Children emerge from eggs in the lower left: Castor and Pollux, Helen and Clytemnestra, they all appear. If we have any doubts at all about what this picture is about, those nude children wipe it all away. This is a picture about gods and nymphs and the naughty things they do.

Knowing how Leonardo worked, we would expect that this composition change, and it did. This version is a little bit less sexually charged: Leda turns her head away from the swan, and seems to be rejecting him just a bit with the inclination of her head. But that sentiment is overridden, both by the fact that her nudity is so brazenly displayed to us and because, even though she turns her head away, her arms grab Zeus by his neck and pull him toward her.

Raphael obviously saw Leonardo's highly charged drawing, and he slavishly copied it. Here's his version of the same theme. Not much is different here, save for the fact that Raphael has used a stylus, which creates a much sharper outline than the chalk employed by Leonardo in his original.

Now Leonardo, as we've seen, used paper like it was free, and it was absolutely normal for him to craft compositions and then abandon them forever. But not this time. Now Leonardo actually put some of his drawings to use and took the time to dip his brushes into pigments and apply them on to a surface. At some point during his second Florentine Period, before he left for Milan permanently in 1508, Leonardo completed his painting of *Leda and the Swan*. It's one of the most tenderly beautiful pictures Leonardo could have even painted or even could have imagined painting. The uses of colors here are dramatic—where we see blues mixed with greens, browns, whites, and reds. There's a genuine sinuosity and sensuality to these figures, all of them posed in delightful positions that sometimes suggest to us again that sense of sexuality but also of playfulness as we see in the lower left corner with those two children.

There's a genuine tactility to the figures and their interaction, as Leda seems to thrust her hip out to accommodate that bent neck of Zeus disguised as a swan, but also of course, wraps her arms around it, clutching it, stroking the neck, making it seem as though these two are not merely lovers but actually have a relationship that goes beyond the sexual.

Now the nude children in the lower left corner become accentuated, not only through their increased size and the playfulness that we've just remarked on but also because Leda's gaze, previously interpreted as being a demure rejection of the Swan, now we can see that instead she's nodding down to them, noting to us that these children has are the products of her union with Zeus.

We in the digital age of mass media have become increasingly numb to the depiction of the nude female form in works of high art and in low art, as well. We look at Leda and shrug our shoulders, at least at the idea that this might be considered a titillating image. But in the early 16th century, such depictions were much more likely to be thought of as highly charged erotica, particularly when shown in the context of a pagan story.

Mix into the batter the fact that, indeed, this is a story about seduction, intercourse, and the offspring produced by it, and Leda's nudity can only be seen in the light of 16th-century erotica. And this was new, in a sense, quite new.

Now, Leonardo was certainly not the first to show the female figure nude and positioned frontally for all to see: Examples from antiquity littered sculpture collections up and down the coasts of Italy, and painters like Masolino and, more recently, Botticelli had been painting them for a good 80 years by now.

But normally the appearance of the nude woman was also formulated in the context of some highfalutin ideals: Sometimes they told a story about innocence, sometimes they represent naked truth, and sometimes they appeared as representations of Creation myths—like *The Temptation of Eve* by Masolino in 1425 and the *Birth of Venus* by Botticelli.

Nudity was both an unavoidable physical condition and a metaphor for emotional vulnerability or unadorned purity, and it was an acceptable subject when used in one of those contexts. But rarely was it about the pleasure of the sex act, which was referred to either euphemistically or symbolically—or it was shown through very chaste (and clothed) embraces with lots of cheek petting. It was only in the first decade of the 16th century that artists and poets alike began to experiment with the topic of erotica in their formal works.

The turn of the century actually marks a convenient starting point for this. In December of 1499, only four months before Leonardo and his friend, Luca Pacioli, fled from Milan and arrived in Venice, seeking a publisher for their book on mathematics, an openly pornographic poem was produced anonymously in Venice, probably by a Dominican friar named Francesco Colonna.

This poem, called "The Fight for Love in the Dream of Poliphili," recounts a wild vision enjoyed and endured by a girl of that name.

The book included a number of prints to illustrate the titillating content of Polyphili's erotic dream, and many of them featured brazenly sexual and violent forms—nude men and nude women, to be sure, but also enormous phalluses, pictures of masturbating figures, dismembered human corpses, and multiple images of rape. The book, as you can imagine, was a best seller.

It is this tradition into which Leonardo's *Leda and Swan* fits, I think. Even if Leonardo didn't read the poem—and I'd be shocked if he didn't, frankly, seeing as how he was in Venice at the height of its popularity—he surely knew of the illustrations in it, and the paintings that were derived from it.

But Leonardo was more subtle than the Franciscan friar who wrote the *Dream of Polyphili*.

First of all, Leonardo legitimized his erotic painting by grounding it in a story from pagan mythology. His story had a long and proud literary history, and his picture was merely an illustration of something had been set down in writing long ago.

There's also none of the fetishistic stuff that we read and see in the *Dream of Polyphili*, which gives Leonardo's picture a more acculturated quality. It's not a dirty picture, in other words, even though it might not take much to turn it into one.

Leonardo easily could've hidden Leda's nudity—indeed, he could have shown her fully clothed—and he didn't need to curl Zeus around her bare skin quite so brazenly. But Leonardo not only left in these tantalizing bits of the story—he foregrounded them; which immediately forces us to ask why he made that decision.

This is a pretty raw and unexpected kind of image when you think about it, and I actually kind of like that about it: It reminds us that Leonardo was human, three dimensional, and perhaps a little more aware of the emotional side of nature than some critics have wanted to see in him.

But we need to recognize that, once again, Leonardo experimented here with a new subject matter for painting, and one that had been essentially taboo from the days of Rome's fall right up to 1500. Openly sexualized pictures existed, to be sure, but famous, world-class artists just didn't do those sorts of paintings until Leonardo in the latter part of the first decade of the 16th century.

Of course, I also need to come clean with you and say that the painting we're looking at here is not Leonardo's original—rather, it is a close copy of that original, which traveled with Leonardo for the last years of his life, went north to France with him, and ultimately landed in the hands of Francois I, the king of France—whereupon sometime in the 17th century, the original picture simply disappeared. I wouldn't be surprised if it's right now sitting in the private vault of some European nobleman, who's been charged with the task of keeping it hidden in the family collection at all costs.

But the *Leda* was so famous in its own day that Raphael copied the drawing, unknown painters did the same with Leonardo's finished product, and it was considered the most valuable of all of Leonardo's pictures when he died in 1519. I think Leonardo's contemporaries had an idea that the *Mona Lisa* offered new solutions to problems in the world of portraiture: but it's clear that they saw in *Leda and the Swan* a vital opening salvo in what could become the rapidly emerging genre of erotic painting. And, for all we know, Leonardo may have intended it to be so, and produced it as a discussion piece for his close circle of artistic friends and colleagues to dissect. That would have been entirely in character for Leonardo.

An example of Leonardo's influence in this genre may be seen in the work of one of Venice's true revolutionary painters, a man known as Giorgione, or Big George. Roughly a decade after the publication of the *Erotic Dream of Polyphili*, and roughly five years after Leonardo's *Leda*, Giorgione painted this influential picture. In the 19th century it was dubbed *The Dresden Venus*, or *The Sleeping Venus*.

Here we find Giorgione painting us this nude figure reclining in a lush landscape on top of a red pillow. She exposes herself to us but also, tantalizing, places her left hand over her genitalia. Is it to cover it or to touch it?

I won't try to claim that Leonardo invented the genre of erotic art with his painting of *Leda and the Swan*—to do so would be to ignore a raft of precedents dating back to the very earliest art objects produced by Paleolithic cave dwellers, 25,000 years ago. But I will say that Leonardo helped legitimize it as a subject in the culture of Renaissance Italy. He takes it out of the realm of the taboo and gave other artists, like Giorgione, and their patrons permission to experiment with their own ideas and projects in a similar vein. And for that, Leonardo deserves some credit. But that's not the most important thing that younger artists like Raphael were paying attention to during their period as Leonardo protégées.

Sometime around 1508, Leonardo came to the conclusion of yet another project that seems to have had no patron, no predetermined setting, and no particular function. This was his *St. Anne Madonna.* It was a familiar theme, and one that Leonardo had already displayed in another format to his fans in Florence. But this particular composition seems to have lived within Leonardo, and he needed it to come out.

In this cartoon, we see that familiar classical composition, which forms a triangle or pyramid of action. Here we have our genealogical family tree, with generations not only represented together, but also even emanating from the legs or the womb of their predecessor. Anne and Mary form the core of this group, with Anne sitting in the background and Mary on her lap, while Christ emerges out from Mary's belly toward the figure of John the Baptist.

Leonardo was not the first person to do this kind of picture. Masaccio had also formed a genealogical family tree back around 1423—it was one of his first paintings in Florence, in fact. And in this painting the very same notion had been translated into paint. Once again, we have something of a pyramidal form, now these figures, though, are stacked one behind the other: the Virgin Mary and Christ both emanate from their respective mothers, which in turn suggests the notion of bloodline, lineage, and family.

But Leonardo's version is different, and not only because it's not as static or rigid as Masaccio's work from 85 years earlier. In his cartoon, Leonardo included the small figure of John the Baptist, who stands and receives the blessing of his cousin, who doesn't just swim out of his mother's arms, but now actually dives out of them.

She's smiling. She's clutching him. She reaches out. Mary tries to hold Christ back, but he squiggles out of her reach. Christ stretches his hands out for John the Baptist, his cousin, who will be the first person in adulthood to recognize Jesus as the Son of God. Jesus leaps out toward him causing Mary to support him before he tumbles to the ground.

This cartoon builds upon an idea that Leonardo had wanted to pursue for 30 years: the concept of motherly love, the infuriating independence of children, danger, self-sacrifice, and tenderness. The cartoon got an audience, somehow, and other artists in Florence studied Leonardo's composition and his message very closely.

There was good reason for them to do this, of course, because the popularity of Madonna paintings had never been higher in the city of Florence than it was in the early 16th century.

We know that lots of people—very often fairly young women or their husbands who were just starting their wedded lives together—became interested in owning these types of pictures and setting them up in their homes. We've heard how ideas about the power of images were fixed in the minds of many owners of Madonna pictures—they believed they could influence the quality of their future children by gazing into the eyes of painted holy figures during the act of conception. They believed that the figures painted in their private devotional panels could hear their prayers and then answer them. And they believed they would gain the respect of their neighbors if they demonstrated their piety by purchasing and displaying these domestic pictures in their homes.

The *Madonna of the Goldfinch* by Raphael (which I show here) is a great example. This lovely painting in the Uffizi Galleries of Florence shows us Raphael as both a capable and a confident young artist. He understands the importance of Leonardo's classical pyramid, and he goes to great lengths to make sure the twisted and bending figure of Mary strikes a pose that creates a solid core in the center. She reaches down to caress Christ, who strikes an elegant contrapposto pose while stroking a goldfinch, held by the little John the Baptist, the goldfinch symbolizes the human soul—it's something we humans can hold onto for a little while, but at death we must release it, and the soul, like a goldfinch, flies up and away to heaven.

It's a beautiful painting, set in a landscape that transitions from green to blue to white, just as a picture by Leonardo might, although not with the exact same use of the sfumato technique that the older artist would have employed. It's no wonder that Raphael's popularity as an artist grew so rapidly during his stay in Florence. And grow it did. People bought small Madonnas for their homes at a pretty crisp rate and installed them in their bedrooms, where the figures and the subject matter might be best put to use.

And Raphael accommodated their needs by adding all the requisite figures: Mary, Christ, and John the Baptist peopled most of his Madonna images, and they were usually shown outdoors, in a Leonardesque landscape.

Once in awhile he'd try something unusual, as he did with this painting. In addition to showing us our standard figures in this classically pyramidal composition, Raphael also alludes quite specifically to the concerns held by many women who were either about to deliver a child or who had new responsibilities as young mothers.

In Raphael's painting of the *Madonna of the Meadow*, the artist places Mary on a stool. She's not on the ground and there's no seat back. Now right away, that would be seen as a signifier for women of child-bearing ages; for women in this period—and really, right up into the 19th century—did not give birth to babies lying down in a bed: rather, they sat in birthing stools that had half of the seat cut away so that the baby could be pushed down and out of the mother.

Now the position of Mary in Raphael's picture, by itself, does not confirm that that's what Raphael had on his mind. But the way he paints the Christ child does. For now we see Jesus, literally naked as the day he was born, squeezed between two unusually elongated arms of his mother, that serve as a birth canal through which the breech baby passes. There's a line of thought among some specialists today that Raphael is here trying address fearful women about to face their first childbirth—and, thus, about to face their first brush with death: For childbirth was, by far, the number one cause of death among adult women in nearly every corner of the planet. They had good reason to want an image to pray to.

Now Raphael realized a business opportunity when he saw one, and he began churning out Madonnas at a very high rate. As he did, he seems to have been chatting with Leonardo about ways in which to produce these things. If we look at the *Madonna of the Goldfinch* by Raphael and Leonardo's *St. Anne Madonna*, we can see that both of them are focusing on that central pyramidal form but are also now playing with a second pyramid, whereby the Christ-child and John the Baptist form another zone for us to focus our attentions. It seems that these two artists were playing off of each other, and maybe Leonardo was looking at Raphael just a little bit.

Now it's important to remember that in the three cases where we've seen Raphael imitating Leonardo, the template has been in the form of drawings or large cartoons. And with the sole exception of Leonardo's brilliantly staged one-man show in 1501, the only way a young artist like Raphael could've seen the old master's drawings was to have actually visited him in his workshop.

In the workshop, a young artist like Raphael could've looked at Leonardo's drawings together with him, talked about art and life, and perhaps even exchanged some sentiments about the characteristics of Italy's greatest princes and villains—for both them had infinite experience with these sorts of people. The fact that Raphael was so blatantly borrowing from Leonardo—and the fact that Leonardo let him—indicates to us a couple of things: first of all that Raphael admired Leonardo and believed he had formulated the best Madonna type out there. Leonardo wasn't particularly interested in churning out Madonnas for regular Florentine couples like Raphael was so Leonardo didn't mind it so much that Raphael wanted to use his ideas.

And second, the two, while not forming a partnership of any sort, were aware of what the other was doing, and the borrower showed proper deference and respect to the one whose ideas he was borrowing, and the creator of those ideas did not insist on recognition, for he had quite enough of that, thank you very much.

So the two of them had a very nice little relationship going. And then, just as abruptly as this remarkable confluence of artistic synergy had emerged in Florence in the early years of that first decade of the 16th century, the matrix was broken apart, or at least reconfigured.

For in 1503, a new pope named Julius II had finally replaced Alexander VI on the throne in Rome. And this new pope had some very grand ideas about how his reign was going to proceed—and how artists and architects were going to help him reach his goals. First, in 1504, came the addition of Bramante to the papal court. Next, in 1505, came the call for Michelangelo. And then, in 1508, Julius called for Raphael.

But Leonardo never received a similar call, for by then he was already committed to a different master on the opposite end of Italy, back in Milan. This time, though, Leonardo's patron was not the great Sforza family that had dominated regional affairs in the 15th century, but rather the French forces that had usurped Ludovico's power in 1499, had exiled him, and had tossed him in a prison cell to rot.

But for that brief instant in Florence, Michelangelo, Leonardo, and Raphael coexisted and performed a delicate dance between them that was not always cordial, but was not always antagonistic, either. And from 1506 to 1508, the artistic connection between Leonardo and Raphael strengthened, and with it perhaps was forged a personal allegiance that bound the younger artist to the elder.

Which meant that when Raphael got his call to attend the court of Pope Julius II in Rome in 1508, the sculptor who had preceded him there, Michelangelo, interpreted the move as a new threat to his prominence: for here was that Leonardo protégée in his midst, challenging Michelangelo to produce and defend himself once again.

What we've been discussing for most of this lecture is the brief period when Florence was the epicenter for the High Renaissance. In the next lecture, we'll return north, to the city of Milan, and then turn south to Rome, where we'll discuss what happened when Florence began to be eclipsed by those two cities at the climax of the High Renaissance.

Leonardo in Milan and Pope Julius II in Rome
Lecture 28

The French were eager to welcome Leonardo back to Milan in 1506, and they found a way to make his temporary move permanent by 1508. During this time, Leonardo completed a second version of *Madonna of the Rocks*, as well as some other intriguing religious images. Meanwhile in Rome, Pope Julius II was trying to change the way the world viewed the church and the papacy through a grand artistic program that Leonardo did not participate in—directly.

Return to Milan

- In 1506, the city of Milan was still in French hands under a highly competent and successful governor named **Charles d'Amboise**. He recognized the opportunity to get his hands on the one artist who could rival the stable of painters and sculptors being collected by Pope Julius II, thanks to a legal proceeding.

- On April 27, 1506, an independent arbitrator concluded his evaluation of a longstanding dispute between Leonardo and the Confraternity of the Immaculate Conception over the *Madonna of the Rocks*, painted back in 1483. The arbitrator sided with the patrons and decreed the painting had never been finished.

- Leonardo was now obligated to complete the terms of his contract with the confraternity. In May 1506, Leonardo arrived in Milan while Charles d'Amboise and the Florentine government argued over the length of time he was to remain because the *Battle of Anghiari* was not finished yet.

- In August 1506, Charles d'Amboise was forced to write a letter to Florence, asking them to extend their loan of Leonardo. King Louis XII got into the act as well in January 1507, stating that he expected Leonardo to produce a number of small paintings for him, depending on Louis's whims and desires. By July, Louis was writing letters about "our dear and good friend Leonardo da Vinci, our painter and engineer," suggesting that Leonardo was now a French courtier.

The Second *Madonna of the Rocks*

- Even in that era of enhanced individuality and artistic originality, no artist could work alone. Leonardo reached out to an artist involved in the first *Madonna of the Rocks* to complete the second: **Ambrogio de Predis**, who had painted the side panels of the original tryptich more than 20 years earlier.

- With Ambrogio doing most of the work, they finished the painting that is now referred to as the *London Madonna of the Rocks*, due to its current location in the National Gallery. In this new version, there is an emphasis on illumination. The light is more evenly laid. The landscape emerges clearly. The figures are identifiable by iconographic attributes.

- The figures seem bigger and more monumental—perhaps because the panel is a bit smaller than the original. It seems more like a picture of the Holy Family in a landscape than a landscape containing the Holy Family.

- After two years, the painting was not complete, and it never would be, although Ambrogio managed to get it installed at the end of that year, thus closing the book on this litigious commission.

The Confrontational *John the Baptist*

- Leonardo did not spend all of this period exclusively in Milan. He spent time in Florence in the winter of 1507 at the hospital of Santa Maria Nuova performing scientific work. He also traveled to and from Florence in the spring and summer of 1507 to deal with a legal matter pertaining to his father's estate, but in early 1508, Leonardo left Florence for good.

- Around 1509, Leonardo became occupied with an unusual picture that has been a bit of a problem for a lot of art historians over the years. It is a chest-high picture of a male youth, arm extended and pointing to the sky, emerging out of darkness. Sfumato returns as well; there are practically no lines anywhere.

- The figure, identified as John the Baptist, is entirely frontal and addresses us directly. His position recalls his first meeting with Christ as an adult, during Christ's baptism: John sees the dove of the Holy Spirit over Christ's head and says, "Behold the Lamb of God." Remarkably, John's position in this painting addresses the viewer as Jesus.

- Leonardo experimented with this concept before, maybe as early as 1506, in a study of the angel of the Annuciation, which is today in Windsor Castle. Gabriel lifts an arm to the skies, telling us that he brings a message from God. The study puts the viewer in the position of Mary.

- This John the Baptist also reverts to tenebrism for the first time in more than 10 years—the tenebrism that had dominated Leonardo's first Milanese period. Perhaps when Leonardo is in Milan, he adopts the Northern European style of dramatic portraiture, but when he is in Florence, he adopts the natural landscape backgrounds in the southern, Florentine style.

- Leonardo strives to achieve a personal connection between the viewer and the image, with a religious link binding the two together. But this personal connection almost seems to invite the bypassing of intermediaries—like priests and church officials—to achieve personal redemption from heavenly figures. It invites us to wonder whether the move northward is affecting not only his approach to painting, but also his approach to the church.

Meanwhile in Rome

- Pope Julius II was quickly becoming the most important patron of the European High Renaissance. He was busily transforming the city of Rome into a magnificent showpiece.

- Rome's complete refurbishment was carried out by a string of popes—Sixtus IV, Innocent VIII, Alexander VI, Pius III, Julius II, and Leonardo X—and Leonardo never worked directly with any of them, but their interests and actions affected him both directly and indirectly.

- Julius was the most ambitious of these pontiffs. His given name was Giuliano della Rovere, and he was one of the most extraordinary men to ever hold the office. During his nine-year reign, he did more than any other single figure of the period to return the Italian Peninsula to the glory days of the Roman Empire.

- Born in 1453, Giuliano was educated in the ways of the church by his uncle, Francesco della Rovere, who became Pope Sixtus IV. As pope, one of his first acts was to appoint the 18-year-old Giuliano to a bishopric in France, and Giuliano soon joined the papal court of his uncle as a cardinal.

- When he came to the papal throne, Julius embarked on a series of audacious goals. First among these was to return Italy to the Italians and to revive the glory of the Roman Empire, with himself, the pope, as the new emperor. To do this, a number of things had to be accomplished:

  - Destroy Cesare Borgia and conquer his lands in the name of the pope.

  - Expel the French from Milan and the Spanish from Naples and install in their places leaders sympathetic to Julius.

  - Push Venice back to its former borders and destroy her ability to wage war in Italy.

- Vivify the city of Rome as a fitting cultural and political center.
- Celebrate Julius the key figure of it all in any and every way possible.

- Julius needed three things in abundance to accomplish these goals: Soldiers, artisans, and money. So Julius engaged in one of the grandest schemes of simony and the sale of indulgences in the history of the papacy. He then called on Europe's greatest artistic talents to rebuild and redecorate his city.

- Finally, he cobbled together alliances that won a string of victories for him. His need for outside assistance caused him to play fast and free with a number of different devils: the king of France, the Holy Roman Emperor, Ferdinand of Spain, Henry VIII of England, Florence, Milan, and Venice, each of whom agreed to fight each other in various forms and combinations.

- This system gave Julius a series of temporary gains, but in the long run all he did was keep the door open for foreign troops to stay in Italy.

Leonardo's Accidental Revenge

- One thing Julius did succeed at was rebuilding Rome. The first member of his all-star team was Donato Bramante, the architect. He was called to work on the single most important architectural project of the entire High Renaissance, the new St. Peter's Basilica.

- The most important church in western Christendom, it was built in the 4th century and was now 1,200 years old. So the old one was torn down, section by section, with its ancient and medieval artistic masterpieces smashed to bits or removed and installed in other buildings.

- Bramante looked back to designs he had forged in collaboration with Leonardo to create a centrally planned church inspired by Leonardo's Neoplatonic understanding of architectural symbolism.

- In April 1506, the first stone was laid for this dynamic new structure—smaller in scale than Julius had initially envisioned, but much more innovative and modern than the traditional cruciform plan that everyone expected.

- This became a problem for the second all-star to join his team, Michelangelo, who was absolutely apoplectic when he learned of Bramante's design. Michelangelo had a design for Julius's tomb—a full three stories high, with 40 larger-than-life-size figures adorning them.

- When it became clear that Bramante's centrally planned church would not have enough room to fit this free-standing mausoleum, Julius had no choice but to put Michelangelo on hold and instead turn his attention to a different project: the painting of the ceiling of a free-standing chapel in the Vatican that Julius's uncle, Sixtus IV, had built in 1478.

Michelangelo's *Creation of Adam* was a diversion for Michelangelo.

- From 1508 to 1512, Michelangelo bitterly set his energies on painting one of the most famous frescoes in the world. He produced extraordinary figures for this unbelievably complicated fresco cycle, including the one painting that rivals the *Mona Lisa* as the most easily recognizable image in Western history, the *Creation of Adam*.

Raphael in Rome

- The third great artist to join this team was Raphael, who was put to work painting a series of frescoes in a set of rooms called the **Stanze**, built by Alexander VI as papal offices.

- One of this series is *The School of Athens*, which documents the rise of intellectual humanism across Italy in the early 16th century and the actual works produced in the Vatican at the time this picture was produced in 1512.

- The painting is a fantasy of an ideal Renaissance court. The building, with its steps, large piers, and unfinished dome, is clearly the interior of St. Peter's. Aristotle and Plato descend the steps at the center of the composition. Many believe that the model for Plato's face was Leonardo. They are flanked by at least 19 different ancient scholars—including Euclid, Socrates, Pythagoras, Epicurus, and Boethius.

- Down below, literally an afterthought to Raphael, who only included it late in the project, is Michelangelo: alone, aloof, and brooding. Absent from this interpretation of a modern-day court cast in the guise of a Greek symposium is Julius himself, who would have been present in person.

Important Term

Stanze: From the Italian word for "rooms," the rooms built in the Vatican Palace during the pontificate of Alexander VI and decorated by Raphael and his followers between 1509 and 1524.

Names to Know

d'Amboise, Charles (1473–1511): Military leader and skilled diplomat who served in the French royal court and was appointed governor of Milan after the occupation of Northern Italy by the forces of Louis XII in 1499. As head of state, Charles acted as patron and protector of Leonardo da Vinci from 1506 to 1511.

Predis, Ambrogio de' (c. 1455–c. 1508): Milanese painter and colleague of Leonardo's in the 1480s who continued to work with and for Leonardo into the 16th century. The two artists collaborated on both versions of *The Madonna of the Rocks* (Paris and London).

Suggested Reading

Hollingsworth, *Patronage in Renaissance Italy*, pt. 4.

Kemp, *Leonardo da Vinci: The Marvellous Works of Nature and Man*, chap. 5.

Verdon, "Pagans in the Church."

Zwijnenberg, "*St. John the Baptist* and the Essence of Painting."

Leonardo in Milan and Pope Julius II in Rome
Lecture 28—Transcript

In 1506, the city of Milan was still in French hands, although the king, Louis XII, was no longer there. Instead, in his place, was a highly competent and successful government official named Charles d'Amboise, whose portrait I show here was by a follower of Leonardo da Vinci.

Charles seems to have recognized that he had an opportunity to get his hands on the one artist who could rival the stable of painters and sculptors being collected by the dangerous Julius II in Rome. A legal proceeding helped Charles realize this. On April 27, 1506, an independent arbitrator concluded his evaluation of a longstanding legal dispute between Leonardo and the confraternity of the Immaculate Conception over the picture of the *Madonna of the Rocks* that the artist had painted way back in 1483. The arbitrator sided with the patrons, and decreed that the painting had never been finished by Leonardo and was therefore unsuitable for the confraternity's oratory.

Now it would have been fairly easy for Leonardo to rectify this problem when the decision was remanded in 1506, just as it would've easy for Leonardo to settle the case out of court long before then, just by adding the required brushstrokes wherever the confraternity's captains felt they needed to appear. But this was not to be, and it's more likely that, in fact, the real complaint from the patrons was that they didn't like the picture, and they wanted a brand new one. This raises the question: Why didn't they like it? It's one of the most stunningly beautiful works of the entire 15th century, and one of the most important in the history of art. What's not to love?

Well, let's count the ways, remembering to put ourselves into the shoes of the religious confraternity of that day, which means being a little bit stuffy and particular about the way we want our meeting hall to look.

First of all we need to remember that interiors of this period were only illuminated by candles. And when we think about it like that we recognize that Leonardo's painting was too dark. We can't tell what's going on. The subject is darker still. We're not sure who's who in the picture and who the picture is supposed to represent. We also notice that there's a little additional nudity here, which might not have met with the approval of the confraternity. And that one kneeling angel off to the right isn't necessarily obvious. We can't tell who it is. In other words, the community seems not to have understood what Leonardo was trying to say in his painting.

Now the arbitrator made it clear to Leonardo that he was now obligated to complete the terms of his contract with the confraternity—a subtle reminder to us that, despite Leonardo's elevated status as a superstar, he was not so far elevated as to be above the law.

By May of 1506, Leonardo had arrived in Milan, apparently after some negotiations between Charles d'Amboise, who wanted him back, and the Florentine Republic, which didn't want to lose him again. Leonardo began working rather quickly on a replacement piece for the *Madonna of the Rocks* of 1483, while those two political powerhouses argued over the length of time he was to remain in Milan.

The Florentines were serious about getting Leonardo back—probably because the Battle of Anghiari wasn't finished yet in the Big Room of the 500. They seem to have made an official request to the French to send Leonardo back to them, for in August of 1506, Charles d'Amboise was forced to write a letter to Piero Soderini's Republican government, asking them to extend their loan of Leonardo and admitting that it had been a unrealistic of him to have requested his services for only three months.

Louis XII got into the act as well, stating in January of 1507 that he fully expected Leonardo da Vinci to produce a number of small paintings for him, depending on Louis's whims and desires.

And in July of 1507, Louis was now writing letters about "our dear and good friend Leonardo da Vinci, our painter and engineer," which suggests that the artist wasn't just repainting the *Madonna of the Rocks*, but was now fully engaged in other projects for the French in Milan. Indeed, he must have been quite active, for the salary he received for the next 12 months, until July of 1508, was one of the highest of his entire career.

Now even in that era of enhanced individuality and artistic originality, no artist worked alone. Despite Salai's probable assistance, Leonardo sought additional help with the revised *Madonna of the Rocks*, and Leonardo reached out to the artist who had participated in the first project over 20 years earlier, the painter Ambrogio de Predis. Ambrogio had been the one who painted the angels on the sides of the original picture for the confraternity, including this one, and he was very well acquainted with the terms of the commission and the artistic vision of the painter.

The two of them worked out the final designs, and together—with Ambrogio doing most of the work—they finished the painting that is now referred to as the *London Madonna of the Rocks*, due to its current location in the National Gallery.

In this new version, Leonardo worked up some earlier drawings that he had played with back in the middle portion of the 1490s, around the time of his painting of *The Last Supper* in Santa Maria delle Grazie. In this new version, Leonardo and Ambrogio rectified some of the complaints directed at them by the confraternity brothers.

This picture shows a greater emphasis placed on linearity and luminosity. We can see bodies beneath draperies, we can see skin and cloth, ringlets of hair, the whole works.

Light is more evenly laid across the entire surface. And we don't see as much of an emphasis on sfumato. The landscape emerges clearly in the background. And figures are obviously identified by iconographic attributes: John the Baptist holds a cruciform and also wears now a camel hair cloth, while Jesus actually has a halo over his head. And the angel has lowered its hand and the pointed finger, so it's not nearly as obvious a figure, which adds a little naturalism to it.

Just as importantly, though, the figures seem bigger, more monumental—perhaps because the panel is a bit smaller than the original. But this now seems more like a picture of the Holy Family in a landscape than it does a landscape containing the Holy Family. And for a religious organization that wanted to focus its attention on the figures they were venerating, this was probably the most important change that Leonardo made.

Leonardo and Ambrogio worked long and hard on the picture, but even after two years, in 1508, the painting wasn't completely finished—and it never would be, even though Ambrogio managed to get it installed at the end of that year, thus closing the book on this litigious commission: To this day, the angel's left hand, Christ's back and his right hand, and John the Baptist's right foot could stand a little painterly attention.

Despite the demands of this project and the insistence of the French king, Leonardo did not spend all of this period exclusively in Milan. He took some time in the winter months of 1507 to return to Florence, perhaps trying to escape the Alpine winters of Milan for just a few months. He spent much of his time in the hospital of Santa Maria Nuova, the place where he had sent his 600 florins back in 1499, just before his trip to Mantua, Venice, and finally Florence. During this brief period, using the facilities of the hospital, Leonardo did some of the most extraordinary scientific work of his entire career—and I promise that we'll devote all of our next lecture to it.

Leonardo moved back to Milan once the weather began to warm up, but he wound up traveling to and from Florence in the spring and summer of 1507, mostly to deal with a legal matter pertaining to the estate of his father, who had died three years earlier. But in early 1508, Leonardo left Florence for good, and traveled back to what had become his second home in Milan. But this move wouldn't merely be temporary. Now Leonardo settled down in that city as a permanent resident and a salaried member of the French royal court.

Right around 1509, Leonardo became occupied with an unusual picture that has been a bit of a problem for a lot of years for art historians. The painting shows us a chest-high picture of a male youth, arm extended and pointing to the sky, emerging out of the darkness that surrounds him in a circle. The figure smiles at us. He has long hair that cascades down his shoulder. Leonardo spends lots of attention on that skin, on his chest. That quality of sfumato now returns and in a big way—there are practically no lines anywhere, no contours delineating the features of the figure. We look at him now, and we identify him as John the Baptist.

Now this is a rather confrontational picture. The figure is entirely frontal, and it addresses us directly, but it shows us only John the Baptist's face and his hands. He raises them up to the Heavens, recalling his first meeting with Christ as an adult, when Jesus descends from the desert while John baptizes his followers in the River Jordan. John immediately sees the dove of the Holy Spirit flying over Christ's head, and he points to it and says, "*Ecce Agnus Domini*" ("Behold the Lamb of God").

Now this is impressive. John's not looking off into the distance, nor is he pointing to some remote spot to his sides. Rather, John addresses you as though you are Jesus, and John the Baptist now says to you, "Behold, the Lamb of God!"

Now that's quite a shock, I think: to put you, his viewer, in the position of Christ and to have you addressed personally and directly by John the Baptist! It's remarkable! Except that we think Leonardo had been experimenting with this concept before, maybe as early as 1506.

Based on some drawings by students or followers under his direction, we have this study of the *Angel of the Annunciation,* which is today in Windsor Castle.

In the midst of other sketches of horses, standing figures, wheels, and machines, we see a quickly sketched figure of the archangel Gabriel. Gabriel lifts his arm to the skies. He tells us that there's a message from God. Who are we? We are the Virgin Mary. The concept of John the Baptist addressing us was something Leonardo had in the works, at least in his mind's eye, for a couple of years before he painted the picture. But originally that image and that relationship was going to be represented in an annunciation of the Virgin.

But Leonardo reverts back to some earlier ideas and themes. For the first time in over 10 years, Leonardo painted one of his figures emerging from a completely blackened background.

And this, of course, harkens back to his own portraits from the first Milanese period—like the *Belle Ferronniere* here—which invoked his highly focused use of spotlights and shadows to create a dramatic appearance of the sitter.

Now I do want to pause for just a second and make a comment that, I'll bet, has already struck you before. Have you noticed that when Leonardo is in Milan, he adopts the Northern European style of dramatic portraiture—what with all that tenebristic drama of lights and shadows? But when he's in Florence, the natural landscape returns in his portraits and narrative scenes? Leonardo seems to be something of a chameleon, able to change his stylistic approach according to what's fashionable in whichever city he's now living. Interesting, isn't it?

Even if he is borrowing from current trends in Northern European painting, we still have here a suggestion of daring from our artist. Leonardo strives to achieve a personal connection between the viewer and the image, with a religious link binding the two together. But this personal connection almost seems to invite the bypassing of intermediaries—like priests and church officials—to achieve personal redemption from heavenly figures.

In a way, Leonardo invites us to wonder whether the move northward to Milan is affecting not only his approach to painting but also his approach to organized religion.

And it's to this enormous and highly politicized institutional problem that we now turn, for the new pope in Rome was quickly becoming the most important patron of the European High Renaissance. He was busily transforming the city of Rome into a magnificent showpiece of a capital for himself and for his church.

Now Rome was actually refurbished by a string of popes who saw in themselves the true inheritors of the greatness of the ancient imperial city. Leonardo never worked directly with any of them—neither Sixtus IV, Innocent VIII, Alexander VI, Pius III, Julius II, nor Leo X—but their interests and actions affected him both directly and indirectly from start to finish.

Among the most ambitious of these political pontiffs was Julius II, whose given name was Giuliano della Rovere, and who ascended to the throne in 1503. Now Giuliano della Rovere is one of the most extraordinary men to hold the office of pope in the entire history of the institution, and during his nine-year reign Giuliano did more than any other single figure of the period to realize the biggest political dream of the Renaissance—to return the entire Italian peninsula to the glory days of the Roman Empire.

Born in 1453, the year after Leonardo, Giuliano had been thoroughly educated in the ways of the church from an early age, thanks to his Uncle, Francesco della Rovere, who was a highly esteemed member of the Franciscan Order. In 1471, Francesco was elected pope, and he took the name of Sixtus IV—and one of his first acts was to appoint his 18-year-old nephew to a bishopric in France. It wasn't long before Giuliano had risen up through the ranks, and he soon joined the papal court of his uncle as a cardinal.

This painting by Melozzo da Forli shows Sixtus in all of his finery, seated enthroned beneath a spectacular architectural setting that reminds us of the fringe benefits that went along with ecclesiastical office. One of the courtiers surrounding Sixtus is Giuliano delle Rovere, the Pope's nephew, who was destined to hold this office in the next century.

And when this came to pass in 1503, Giuliano—or, rather, Julius II—was faced with a personal choice that he had to make. In this period, newly elected popes tended to take one of two routes: They could either go about the business of effecting substantial reform within their realm—which, was not done very often—or they could sit back and enjoy themselves now that they'd attained the highest office in Christendom, which was much more the norm.

When Giuliano della Rovere took the name of Julius II, he elected to take the first route. Recognizing an opportunity to alter the way things were being done in the Church spiritually and particularly politically, Julius endeavored to remake the entire region with a series of audacious goals.

Julius wanted nothing less than to return Italy to the Italians, to rescind his earlier promises and stamp out the threat of Cesare Borgia once and for all, and to revive the glory of the ancient Roman Empire with himself, the pope, as the new emperor.

But in order to get it done, a number of things had to be accomplished. First of all, Julius would have to destroy Cesare Borgia, the wickedest man in Italy, and then conquer Cesare's lands in the name of the pope. Julius would have to expel the French from Milan and the Spanish from Naples, and install in their places leaders who were sympathetic to Julius. He'd need to push Venice back to its former borders and destroy her ability to wage war in Italy. Julius wanted to vivify the city of Rome as a fitting cultural and political center. He wanted to build and rebuild and decorate every single thing that might be associated with the papacy as the new potentates of Italy. Julius wanted to be the key figure of it all. To celebrate his virtues and his victories, he wanted to have images made in his honor, and he wanted his vision to be celebrated in any and every way possible.

Now it doesn't take a genius to see that Julius needed three things in abundance to accomplish these goals. First he needed soldiers. Popes have great influence and popes have big ideas and popes have great leverage; but popes do not have standing armies. Julius needed troops to do all the fighting that his plans required.

Second, Julius needed artists and architects. If you're going to build things and then make them so beautiful that all the world wants to come see them, and if you want to make yourself the chief character in the meta-narrative contained in them, you need to acquire all the very best talent you can find.

And third, Julius needed money. Points one and two wouldn't come cheap, and even the deep coffers of the papal treasury couldn't account for all the fighting and building and painting that Julius envisioned for his papacy.

So, moving backwards, here's what Julius did to take care of those three things. First, he engaged in one of the grandest schemes of simony and the sale of indulgences witnessed during the history of the papacy. Bishoprics and archbishoprics, cardinals, papal legates, secretaries, scribes—offices of all sorts—were sold to those willing to pay an exorbitant fee for them.

Second, he called upon the very best talent he could find who could help him spruce up Rome. The city had fallen into decay during the Middle Ages, and particularly during the 14th century, when the papal court had been moved to Avignon. New churches were needed, new chapels had to be built, sculptures had to be carved, paintings needed to be produced—you name it—it had to be done.

And third, Julius needed to fight battles and win them. But this was a difficult thing to do, and it forced him to perform some delicate dances. On one hand, he brilliantly cobbled together an array of alliances that won a string of victories for him, including a truly important one in the city of Bologna in 1508 that brought that key city under his control. On the other hand, his need for outside assistance caused him to play fast and free with a number of different devils, one after the other, that included the king of France and the Holy Roman Emperor and Ferdinand of Spain and King Henry VIII of England and the cities of Florence and Milan and Venice, each of whom agreed to fight each other, in various forms and combinations.

One year, a group of them would get together and focus on humiliating one of Julius's enemies, and the next year a different combination would gang up on one of the others. Through most of this period, the French were the ones Julius was most eager to expel. This system gave Julius a series of temporary gains, but in the long run, all he did was keep the door open for foreign troops to stay in Italy as this year's allies. Julius never even remotely approached his dream of expelling the foreigners once and for all, or of uniting the peninsula from Sicily to the Alps under papal leadership.

But one thing that Julius II did succeed at was rebuilding the city of Rome. The first member of the Julian all-star team to get signed up was Donato Bramante, the architect from Urbino and the old associate of Leonardo da Vinci from their days in Milan. Like Leonardo, Bramante had been forced to leave Milan in 1499; but instead of stopping in Florence, like Leonardo had, Bramante had continued on to Rome, where his experiences and abilities made him a desirable commodity in the papal city, even before Julius came to power. Two projects he conducted simultaneously between 1500 and 1504 caught the attention of Julius and the papal court. One of them was the Tempietto (that we've already seen in this course). This work was produced for the Franciscan church of San Pietro on the west side of the Tiber River. In the Tempietto we see that Bramante is playing with this circular and centrally planned design, elevated up on steps and employing ancient motifs and designs.

The second project was the façade of Santa Maria alle Pace, in which we find Bramante producing this exterior for a squared Romanesque courtyard, complete with Roman arches, detached ancient pilasters, and a register above. This turned out to be a fairly peaceful Renaissance haven in the middle of the hustle and bustle of a big urban environment, and it impressed the Romans when it was completed.

Both of these projects earned Bramante considerable notice, and almost immediately after Julius's election to the papal throne, Bramante was invited to work for the pope on the single most important architectural project of the entire High Renaissance.

As Julius considered the grand master plan he had for himself and his papal descendants, the dilapidated condition of St. Peter's Basilica was moved to the very top of his list of priorities. And for good reason: The structure was literally crumbling. It had been built in the 4th century and was now 1200 years old. Bits and pieces of it were falling off during religious services, and people were afraid they'd be hit and killed by them. That's bad for the pilgrimage business. Second, St. Peter's was, in fact, quite old fashioned, designed and constructed according to outdated medieval notions of architectural space that had more in common with early Christian concepts than anything developed by the time of the Renaissance. And third, St. Peter's in 1504 was absolutely crammed full of stuff. There was no space left for new chapels or sculptures or paintings. There were no naming opportunities for sale in this old church, and Julius wanted those.

So, the old St. Peter's was torn down, section by section, with ancient and medieval artistic masterpieces smashed to bits or removed and installed in other buildings in Rome that needed or wanted some vestige of the ancient past to legitimize claims of authenticity or longevity.

It was Donato Bramante who was charged with the task of creating something new in its place, and Bramante looked back to designs he had forged in collaboration with Leonardo in Milan during the salad days of the early 1490s.

Bramante created a centrally planned church that featured a Greek cross, whereby there were wings of equal sizes that revolve around this central harmoniously designed cross. It's a very modern church, inspired by Leonardo's Neoplatonic understanding of architectural symbolism and architectural perfection. Leonardo didn't design the church of New St. Peter's, but his fingerprints are all over the final product.

In April of 1506, the first stone was laid for this dynamic new structure. It was smaller in scale than Julius had initially envisioned, but it was much more innovative and modern than the traditional cruciform plan that everybody expected the New St. Peter's to employ.

But this became a problem for the second all-star to join the team. Michelangelo Buonarroti was absolutely apoplectic when he learned of Bramante's new plans for St. Peter's.

Now Michelangelo had joined the court of Julius II a little bit later than Bramante, receiving his invitation only in 1505. Like Bramante, Michelangelo had been called to Rome to execute one specific project, and like Bramante, Michelangelo was asked to make this project an expression of its patron's greatness. While Bramante was to build a new St. Peter's, Michelangelo was to design and sculpt the greatest burial tomb in the history of the world—a full three stories high with 40 larger than life-size figures adorning them, all chiseled out of marble in honor of the new emperor of the new Rome. Here's one of Michelangelo's earliest designs for the tomb of Julius II. And I think you can see it in the great vision Michelangelo had for his patron.

But when it became clear that Bramante's centrally planned church would not have enough room in it to fit this freestanding mausoleum, Julius had no choice but to put Michelangelo on hold. He told the sculptor to stop his planning and instead to turn his attention to a different project.

Julius, through a combination of cajoling, threats, and pleading, convinced a reluctant Michelangelo to devote his entire attention to the painting of the ceiling of a freestanding chapel in the Vatican that Julius's Uncle Sixtus had built in 1478 to celebrate his victory over the Florentines and Lorenzo the Magnificent.

From 1508 to 1512, Michelangelo bitterly set his energies on painting one of the most famous frescoes in the world. The subject revolved primarily around nine scenes from the book of Genesis, from the Creation story to *The Deluge* and Noah's Ark. Michelangelo produced extraordinary figures for this unbelievably complicated fresco cycle, including the one painting that rivals the *Mona Lisa* as the most easily recognizable image in Western history.

In the Creation of Adam, Michelangelo focused on the singular moment of potency and spiritual energy that infuses all of us with spiritual life. The powerful body of Adam, chiseled from a block of marble in Michelangelo's imagination, reclines in a meadow, unable to move due to a lack of energy. God the Father sweeps in from the right. He extends his hand, and with his finger prepares to zap Adam with the force that will animate the First Man and make him and us different from all the other beasts. It is justifiably celebrated as one of history's most beautiful, influential, and important works of art, and it was unveiled to a worshipful public on November 1, 1512.

But Michelangelo was not the only artist busily working in Julius's Rome. The third great figure to join this Renaissance dream team was Raphael, who had received his invitation in 1508 and was quickly put to work painting a series of frescoes in a set of rooms called the Stanze, that had been built by Alexander VI during his pontificate but never properly decorated. Julius was now using these rooms as work spaces—one was a library, another was a receiving room, another was a personal study—and Raphael was employed to produce pictures in all of them.

Intermittently, from 1509 to 1520, Raphael painted a whole series of murals in these adjacent spaces, including the famous *School of Athens*, which documents the cultural interests of Julius II during his pontificate, the rise of intellectual humanism across Italy in the early 16th century, and the actual works produced in the Vatican at the time this picture was produced in 1512, which was the same year that Michelangelo's ceiling was being unveiled.

The painting is a fantasy of an ideal Renaissance court. The building, with its steps, large piers, and unfinished dome, is clearly the interior of St. Peter's Cathedral that Donato Bramante was building at the time that Raphael was painting this fresco.

Aristotle and Plato descend from this group of figures down those stairs. Aristotle points to the ground, and Plato points to the air. This latter figure holds the Timaeus, his book of space, time, and change, which was considered one of the very few utterly essential texts on science and mathematics of the age.

Many believe that the model for Plato, the most divinely inspired of all the Greek philosophers, was Leonardo da Vinci. It's interesting that Raphael associates Leonardo with those subjects, and with that thinker, isn't it?

Now this core group of Aristotle and Plato is flanked by at least 19 different ancient scholars—including Euclid, Socrates, Pythagoras, Epicurus, and Boethius. It's a balanced composition. It's a perfectly selected moment. It's a true classical composition that Leonardo would've applauded.

And down below, literally an afterthought to Raphael, who only included it late in the project, is Michelangelo: alone, aloof, brooding, contemplating who knows what on the steps of New St. Peter's.

Absent from this interpretation of a modern-day court, cast in the guise of a Greek symposium, was the actual princely patron who would normally be responsible for managing the troop of geniuses. But seeing as how this particular room was used as Julius as a personal library and office, I think it's pretty clear that the prince in charge of all this brainpower was the pope sitting behind the desk in the middle of the room looking at the painting.

It was from this room, and the others surrounding it in the Vatican Palace, that Julius II oversaw the rebuilding of St. Peter's, directed the paintings and sculptures of Raphael and Michelangelo, and led the military campaigns to defeat the enemies of the Church, both foreign and domestic, on the field of battle.

Ironically, one of those foreign foes was King Louis XII and his French army, that was still occupying the city of Milan and hovering ominously over the rest of Italy. For much of the time of Julius's papacy, Leonardo worked for that rival camp, in the service of a French patron whose presence in Italy had inspired the artistic projects that the other three great giants of the High Renaissance produced in Rome.

By the second decade of the 16th century, the epicenter of the High Renaissance was no longer the city of Florence—that distinction now lay with the papal court in Rome, and it reached its apex in 1512, the year when Raphael completed the *School of Athens* and Michelangelo completed his incomparable ceiling for the Sistine Chapel.

But Milan was also a key player in this period, and Leonardo da Vinci was its standard bearer. But the works that Leonardo produced there looked very different from the overtly propagandistic images that were decorating the halls of the Vatican Palace. Next time, we'll concentrate our attention on one of the most important projects of the entire early modern period—Leonardo's groundbreaking studies in the field of human anatomy.

The Anatomical Drawings—His Greatest Works?

Lecture 29

Leonardo's notebooks contain multiple descriptions, drawings, and definitions of the human body, and his understanding of blood circulation was centuries ahead of its time. He obtained the knowledge to make these drawings through dissection—a rare and dangerous practice in Europe in the 16th century. Through this pioneering work, Leonardo can be considered, in many ways, one of the fathers of modern medicine.

The Rarity of Autopsy in the 16th Century

- At the end of 1507, Leonardo returned to Florence for a few months to address some legal matters. While there, he devoted a great deal of his attention to a subject that had never been developed in quite the way he thought it should. He took some valiant risks as he did it and confronted many intellectual taboos.

- Leonardo tells us about his interest in anatomical studies in one of his notes dated to January 1508. He was spending much of his time reading books in the Florentine hospital of Santa Maria Nuova, where he also met an elderly man who caught his interest:

  An old man, a few hours from his death, told me that he had lived a hundred years, and that he felt nothing wrong with his body other than weakness. And thus while sitting upon a bed in the hospital of Santa Maria Nuova in Florence, without any movement or other sign of any mishap, he passed out of this life. And I made an [autopsy] of him in order to see the cause of so sweet a death.

- This was not the first time Leonardo had ever cut into a human being. He regarded this autopsy as a scientific investigation, yet his notes indicate empathy and personal loss at the old man's death, all of which make Leonardo seem a very modern kind of physician.

- Dissections were rare in European Christian societies of the day, although not unheard of. A few manuscript illuminations show physicians performing dissections and assistants and clerics in attendance. One such image was painted in 1483 to document a medical lecture delivered by a professor in Pavia, the town not far from Milan where Ludovico Sforza made his country home. It is possible Leonardo attended such proceedings there.

- In the image, note that none of the attendees take notes or otherwise record their observations, implying that anatomical drawings before the work of Leonardo were rare.

- Medieval medicine was symptom and tradition based. Advances in medical knowledge were tightly restricted by the refusal of some religious leaders to allow for the dissection of human beings—particularly Christians. Medieval Christianity held that, at the impending Second Coming, dead souls would be restored to their bodies; thus their bodies must remain intact.

- Surgical work also presented problems in a society with no real refrigeration or concept of germ theory. Corpses fouled so quickly that members of the medical community refused to deal with them. Their lack of experience meant that, even if they did try to perform autopsies, they did not know what to do or what to look for.

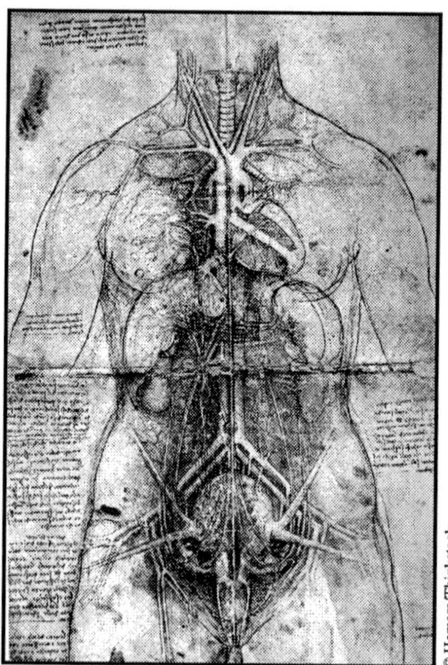

© Hemera/Thinkstock.

Leonardo's anatomical drawings were unprecedented in their level of detail and could only have been achieved with the use of dissection.

- Moreover, the scientific method had not been invented; therefore, which meant that any research on human subjects was truly a fly-by-night operation. if medieval researchers did venture into the body, none of them were prepared to record their findings with any kind of order or accuracy.

Leonardo's Art Meets Leonardo's Science

- A medical treatise from about 1345 by Milanese physician and scholar Guy of Pavia demonstrates why Leonardo's unique talents made him such an effective medical researcher. Guy describes the dissection of the thorax, but the accompanying illustrations seem merely decorative; they would be no use in replicating the procedure or studying anatomy.

- In short, scientists were not artists, and artists were not scientists—until Leonardo—and no one who understood as Leonardo did how a well-executed image can convey information so much more efficiently and effectively than words.

- Second, it is impossible for anyone to learn about everything one needs to know about the human body through studying cadavers, especially under 16th-century conditions. There is too much information, and too few dissections. An artist can capture this information to be studied at leisure.

- We think Leonardo conducted some 30 dissections himself. In his notes toward a possible anatomy treatise, he claimed that mastery of the human anatomy would require someone to perform 18 dissections, with six major topics examined three times and from three different views: once from the front, once from the side, and once from the back.

- This work was dangerous: Not only was Leonardo unknowingly exposing himself to bacteria; many still believed this kind of scientific research was in violation of church law and therefore punishable in the harshest terms imaginable.

- Leonardo was examining—and maybe even dissecting—corpses at least as early as about 1488 in Milan. His earliest drawings are in the Windsor Castle collections and show us primarily what Leonardo did not know.

- The issues that consumed Leonardo's attention in 1488 were the cardiovascular system and the human head. Leonardo produced a drawing of those organs contained within an outline of the human figure, but the drawing has nothing to do with direct observation.

Leonardo's Head Studies

- Leonardo's 1488 studies look at the human skull from two vantage points: The frontal view is a double drawing and focuses on teeth. The right side shows us a perfectly aligned dental arrangement and the left shows us a decayed skull with the mouth bashed in. Four teeth are drawn independently on the left. As with his mechanical drawings, he is showing the smaller parts of the bigger machine.

- The side view shows the relation of the spinal cord to the head. In the drawing above it, Leonardo gauges the circumference of the skull, which allows him to think about the size of the brain and how it sits inside the head. He notes the sunken cheekbones, the recessed eye sockets, and the way the jawline cuts under the mouth at nearly 90 degrees.

- Some scholars have reconsidered *St. Jerome*, wondering whether that painting should be dated later than 1480—that is, coming after the anatomical studies of skulls Leonardo conducted in 1488. However, human bones were displayed in hospitals, churches, and even architectural structures. Whether the studies or the painting came first, the two can be seen as closely related variations on a common exploration.

- We can also look at his portraits from the first Milanese period in the same way. If we consider the head of *La belle ferroniere* from the 1490s in the context of Leonardo's anatomical studies, we notice immediately its sophisticated handling of facial bone structure compared with *Ginevra de' Benci* from the 1470s.

- Leonardo wanted to know how the eye worked, and he theorized about its functions in part so he could paint pictures that would appeal more thoroughly to the human soul. He started to cut into human heads with the intention of learning what the eye was connected to and how images were transferred into the mind.

- Leonardo also came to recognize that the process by which our brains understand things in our field of vision was exactly the opposite of conventional wisdom of the day: Light, he realized, enters the brain through the eye. In the 15th century, medical expertise held that the human eye projected light onto an object.

Leonardo's Studies in Reproduction

- Leonardo's drawing fearlessly explored the act of procreation. In 1493, he drew a cross-section of a couple in the act of conception, with the internal reproductive organs sketched in. In style, they resemble his caricatures, and the pair grin at each other, conveying emotional pleasure.

- At just about the time he was working on a painting for the possibly pregnant Lisa Giocondo, he drew a human fetus; the human female anatomy; and the human male anatomy with veins and muscles added in a three-dimensional model of what happens during intercourse. The proportions of each object have been pristinely calculated so that we see how they appear in relation to others.

- Leonardo adds a little note: "Woman desires that the size of the male member to be as large as possible, while man wishes the opposite of the genital organ of the woman." Leonardo wasn't just drawing anatomy; he was also dealing with the joy of sex.

Treatise on Anatomy

- All of Leonardo's anatomical drawings are masterpieces of draftsmanship. Most of them appear to have been for his own personal edification, not for publication or general consumption.

- Some may have been intended for a treatise on anatomy that he never published. He pioneered the practice of looking at an organ or structure from four different directions and a cross-section.

- Another clue is a drawing of a woman's body that has been pierced to be reproduced through the **pouncing** technique. This implies that at least some of his drawings were distributed for educational purposes.

- The kind of work Leonardo had to do to make these drawings, even in the sanitized laboratories of modern scientific institutions, is not for everyone. He likely had to do the work of cutting, cleaning, and drawing all by himself. He wrote about the challenges facing the medical scientist who might consider conducting these kinds of experiments:

  Even if you love this activity, you may be hindered by your weak stomach; … by fear of being at night in the company of these bodies, torn to pieces and skinned and frightening to look at. And if this doesn't hinder you, you may lack the drawing skill suitable for such representation. Or if you manage the drawing, you may lack the perspective. And if that isn't so, you may fail the arrangement of the geometrical representation or the reckoning of the strength and power of the muscles. Or you may fall short of patience, and thus you will not be diligent. Whether or not I have succumbed to these things you can judge.

- We see in these drawings Leonardo at his most humble, his most reverent, his most introspective, and his most eloquent, but also at his most detail-minded and observant.

- Leonardo invented the cornerstone of modern medical science as we know it, but the only way he could have done this was through his rare combination of talents—as an artist, an engineer, and a scientist.

Important Term

pouncing: A process whereby chalk dust is placed inside a cheesecloth sack and lightly patted against a drawing that has been pinpricked along its contours and laid on top of the surface to be painted. The dust pushes through the pinpricks, forming an exact copy of the original drawing on the new surface. 29

Suggested Reading

Cianchi, *Leonardo: Anatomy*.

Keele and Roberts, *Leonardo da Vinci: Anatomical Drawings from the Royal Library, Windsor Castle*.

The Anatomical Drawings—His Greatest Works?

Lecture 29—Transcript

At the end of 1507, Leonardo da Vinci returned to Florence for a fairly brief stay that would last only a few months, until the end of the winter of 1508. A legal proceeding over his uncle's estate had called him back there, in much the same way that wrangling over his father's estate had earlier forced him home. But as best we can tell, during these several weeks in the city that he knew so well, Leonardo devoted a great deal of his attention to a single subject that had never been developed in quite the way he thought it should. He took some valiant risks as he did it, and he had to screw up tremendous courage in the process. But when he was finished, Leonardo da Vinci had taken the very first serious steps toward what you and I would call "modern medical science."

And when I say he had to screw up tremendous courage, I refer both to his willingness to confront outdated intellectual taboos and the specter of censorship that would similarly face Galileo a century later when had invents the idea that the Earth goes around the Sun. But the issues in anatomy that Leonardo confronted required courage in a second, more timeless way as well, insofar as anatomy, the way Leonardo understood it, goes directly to our existence as human beings—how we are born, how we reproduce, and how we die.

But the developments we'll discuss in this lecture had already been in his mind for a very long time. Already in 1489, he had written in his notes an intention to publish a treatise on anatomy, and his work continued to grow with increasing sophistication, particularly after his brief stay in Florence in the winter of the 1508.

Leonardo tells us about his interest in anatomical studies in one of his notes dated to the month of January of 1508. There he indicates how he was spending much of his time reading books in the Florentine hospital of Santa Maria Nuova, the place where he had sent 600 florins for safekeeping back in 1499 when he was preparing for his flight out of Milan. He apparently had a workspace there, and his hours were spent studying and thinking about the nature of the hospital's mission, which had provoked him to do some related work on human subjects. One man, in particular, had captured his attention, and in his notes, Leonardo wrote about him.

> An old man, a few hours from his death, told me that he had lived a hundred years, and that he felt nothing wrong with his body other than some weakness. And thus while sitting upon a bed in the hospital of Santa Maria Nuova in Florence, without any movement or other sign of any mishap, he passed out of this life. And I made an [autopsy] of him in order to see the cause of so sweet a death.... This [autopsy] I described very diligently and with great ease owing to the absence of fat and humors which, usually, greatly hinder the recognition of the parts.

Now this annotation, written down only a few hours after Leonardo had performed his examination of the old man, tells us a remarkable amount about Leonardo's interest in the human body and the depth of his engagement in anatomical study.

Leonardo clearly talked to patients freely. He gained their trust. He performed autopsies, and he performed dissections.

He knew about the appearance of older bodies and the appearance of younger bodies. He knew about fatty tissues that can obscure muscles, veins, and bones. This was certainly not the first time Leonardo had ever cut into a human being. But also we know that Leonardo drew, and he drew and wrote down what he found. He regarded this autopsy, and others like it, as a scientific investigation.

Now let's be very clear about what Leonardo was doing right from the beginning, for we need to appreciate the challenges and the risks that he faced at nearly every turn as he performed the anatomical explorations during the damp Florentine nights in the winter of 1508.

Dissections weren't exactly the norm in European Christian societies of the day, but this was changing. Vasari tell us that Antonio Pollaiuolo, one of the Florentines of the previous generation who had influenced Leonardo, was the first to perform a dissection for the sake of his art. Physicians did dissections, too, of course, as suggested by this illumination from a French manuscript from about 1475. But note that this miniature was clearly not produced for the purpose of scientific study—rather, it seems to record that an autopsy was conducted, and that assistants and clerics attended the physician of record when it occurred. It shows us a medical school lecture, and it suggests that students looked into the body as it was being cut apart, with the professor present to describe what people saw.

This miniature was painted in 1483 to document a medical lecture delivered by a professor in Pavia, the town not far from Milan where Ludovico Sforza made his country home, and where Leonardo traveled as his courtier. I think that's a pretty interesting little bit of information there, as it's clear that dissections were going on in northern Italy—precisely where Leonardo was spending time as a member of the Sforza court. I can't help but wonder if Leonardo attended some of these proceedings in Pavia from his earliest days in Milan, and whether these types of demonstrations helped spark his interest in conducting experiments on his own.

In the image, though, we can see that none of the students attending this lecture have thought to take any notes or record any of their observations. We see no papers and no stylus in the hands of anyone in the audience. Contemporary approaches to scientific inquiry—and not just medical research—relied upon memory and writing, but not visual materials. In other words, anatomical drawings before the work of Leonardo da Vinci were rare and basically useless even when they did exist.

Now, Medieval medical doctrine had been based on the study of symptoms, previous experience with patients, plus some ancient observations that had been passed down through the generations. Possible advances in medical knowledge were tightly restricted by the refusal of some religious leaders to allow for the dissection of human beings—particularly Christians.

Basically, dissections were not all that common. And here's why. According to widely held doctrine, Christians believed that the connection between body and soul was absolute and binding, both during life and death. All mortals were condemned to ashes and dust, but Medieval Christianity held that at the moment of the Second Coming of Christ and the Last Judgment, the dead would be resurrected, and their bodies would be reunited with their souls, and then they would endure an eternal fate dependent on their level of faith and piety while on earth.

This concept of eternal life after death included a certain understanding of physicality: If one was going to live on in eternity, it stood to reason that one would need a body in which to function. And this meant that the body, after death, had to be kept intact at all costs: If bodies were mutilated or if body parts were buried in separate areas, their reunion with their original souls would be impossible to complete. The judged would spend the rest of eternity living a second life with a distorted or incomplete body.

This, of course, did not exclude surgical work on the living, or dissections of non-Christian cadavers: Nonbelievers presumably weren't going to heaven anyway.

But surgical work itself also presented some problems. In non-sterile environments, human flesh decayed quickly, fouling the physical qualities of internal organs and emitting a stench that was so foul that even members of the medical community refused to conduct them.

Moreover, the lack of experience in cutting into human flesh meant that researchers, even if they decided to do this, really didn't know what they were looking for. In the Middle Ages, knowledge was mostly to be found in the writings of previous scholars than through detailed observation.

And finally, and this is a key point, even if medieval researchers did venture into the body, none of them were prepared to record their findings with any kind of accuracy whatsoever. None had been trained to draw with any kind of fluency, few could write their observations with the sort of detail that might serve future readers, and all of them struggled to find an audience for what they might have been able to figure out from their procedures.

Here's one medical treatise written right around 1345 by a Milanese physician and scholar named Guy of Pavia, in which his dissections and surgical procedures are described. The miniature tells us that this dissection of the thorax was done, but the illuminator doesn't give us any information of use should we decide that we want to perform this activity. It seems to be his job not to record how the procedure was performed, much less whatever it might tell us about the human body, but rather to show that it had happened and that it could be done. But the drawing is so poorly executed that we can't replicate his procedure, and therefore we can't learn from this drawing what he saw, and what was known when he drew it.

In short, scientists weren't artists, and the artists that were employed to illustrate the texts didn't have Leonardo's fidelity to nature, and hadn't observed the procedures the scientists had performed. Artists were basically guessing what the science was trying to tell them.

This caused multiple problems. First, there simply was no body of research conducted by medical scientists that incorporated firsthand observations of the workings of the human body. There were writings about the structure of the skeletal system, the origins and functions of nerve tissue, and the responsibilities of muscles and vital organs, but the written word rarely describes a complicated object as well as an image, as we saw when comparing Leonardo's own convoluted written notes about a machine to one of his drawings. Physicians had no human maps to use when dealing with a medical problem, and as a result, medicine remained among the most primitive of all the sciences.

Second, it was impossible for anyone to learn about the entire human body solely through the study of actual cadavers. There was just too much information contained there to digest all at once.

Leonardo had needed multiple subjects in order to attain the clarity contained in only one of his drawings. In fact, we think he conducted some two dozen dissections all himself, and in notes toward a possible anatomy treatise, he claimed that mastery of the human anatomy would require someone to perform at least18 dissections, with major topics examined three times and from three different views: once from the front, once from the side, and once from the back. But that meant that physicians would need access to lots of cadavers, and that wasn't at all an easy proposition. Leonardo knew that precise drawings were needed as substitutes for those cadavers that most physicians in Renaissance Europe simply couldn't find. If properly represented, anatomical drawings could provide a comprehensive, encyclopedic understanding of all the organs and tissues in the human body and minimize the need for actual dissections.

And there were two other problems as well. First, the work was physically dangerous: Every time he cut into human tissue, Leonardo was exposing himself to bacteria that he didn't know existed. Second, the work was socially dangerous: Many still believed this kind of scientific research was in violation of Church Law, and therefore punishable in the harshest terms imaginable.

For all those reasons, but also just for the degree of difficulty alone, the work on anatomy stands as Leonardo's proudest achievement—both as a scientist and as an artist.

Now Leonardo had become interested in the internal workings of the human body long before 1508, and it's pretty clear that he was examining—and maybe even dissecting—corpses at least as early as about 1488 in Milan. These early drawings, like many of the anatomical sketches that he drew, are from the Royal Collection at Windsor Castle in England. They serve us well in a couple of ways. First and foremost, they show us what Leonardo didn't know, and what he needed to grasp in order to start broader investigations of the world's most ingenious and misunderstood mechanism.

The two basic issues that consumed Leonardo's attention in 1488 were the cardiovascular system and the human head. He knew, of course, that both were essential for human survival. The former pumped a life-energy through every region on the body. The second, was where the human soul—the so-called *sensus communis*—resided.

Of the former, some things had already been written. Avicenna, and before him Galen, had written treatises on human organs and, depending on them, Leonardo produced this drawing of those organs, contained within an outline of the human figure that he drew almost as a framing device for a painting. It's quite clear, though, that the drawing really has nothing to do with direct observation of those organs for it would be largely impossible to draw them in a completely flayed human corpse in the short amount of time required to capture those elements before immediate decay set in. Leonardo seems to be drawing by the numbers, as it were: trying to make visible the words that his predecessors had described in prose.

It was only with his examination of the human head, the skull, and particularly the eyes, that Leonardo really began to take some of those career-threatening risks we outlined a minute ago. Leonardo's early work on the human head seems to have been designed as an exercise in personal edification. In these drawings, both from about 1488, Leonardo looked closely at a human skull from two vantage points. The frontal view is actually a double drawing and focuses on human teeth. Here, he's cut his skull in half, vertically. On the right side he shows us a perfectly aligned dental arrangement, and on the left he shows us a decayed skull with the mouth basically bashed in. Four teeth are drawn independently on the left, where he seems to be teaching himself how these smaller parts of the bigger machine look all by themselves, and then how these smaller parts fit into that bigger machine as a whole when they're placed in their proper positions.

The side view shows Leonardo thinking about the relation of the spinal cord to the head, and he's careful to make sure that he connects the two in a way that demonstrates this relationship. The vertebrae are articulated in his sketch, and move up the spine almost like steps in a ladder, moving toward the casing that holds the brain.

In the drawing above it, Leonardo gauges the circumference of the skull, which allows him to think about the size of the brain and how it sits inside the head. He notes the sunken cheekbones, the recessed eye sockets, and the way the jaw line cuts under the mouth in nearly a 90-degree angle.

Leonardo's new interest in the human skull, in both its functions and its appearance, has led some scholars to return to his paintings to see if any influences of his anatomical work can be seen in them. For example, some scholars have reconsidered the *St. Jerome* to wonder if that painting should be dated later than 1480, that is, as coming after the anatomical dissections of skulls that Leonardo conducted in 1488.

In this approach, Jerome's drawn face and hardened cranial features are seen to follow the contours of the skull that Leonardo studied and drew in his studio in Milan. I think that's an interesting observation, and I like it quite a bit—but I also need to say that Leonardo would've had ample opportunity to look at skulls in Florence, as the bones of the dead were not uncommonly displayed in hospitals, in churches, and even in architectural structures. I still like the earlier 1480 date for the painting, and whether he did the anatomical dissections first, or the painting first, it has become clear that the two can be seen as closely related variations on a common theme.

We can also look at portraits he painted during his first Milanese period in the same way. If we consider the head of *La Belle Ferroniere* from the 1490s in the context of Leonardo's anatomical studies, we notice immediately its sophisticated handling of facial bone structure. And if we compare that with *Ginevra de' Benci* from the 1470s, in the period that predates his close anatomical studies, we can see how Leonardo's understanding of the skull in the later picture has become far more detailed and powerful. His increased ability to capture the nuances of the head only enhances the tenebristic effects of light and dark that make his portraits from that period so dramatic, and together they give the faces of his subjects both a naturalistic and an individualistic quality of unusual depth.

As a painter, Leonardo believed in the adage that the eye was the window to the soul; that is to say, that our experiences as human beings are determined by what we see and how we perceive what we see. Leonardo believed to his core that the eye was the most important of our five senses and was the thing that helped distinguish the human being from the rest of the animal kingdom.

But as an artist, Leonardo also wanted very much to know how the eye worked, and he theorized about its functions as a mechanism, in part, so that he could paint pictures that would appeal more thoroughly to the human soul. Learning about vision, he thought, could make his art that much more powerful. And so he started to cut into human heads with the intention of learning what the eye was connected to, so he could figure out how visions of images were transferred into the mind.

His early examinations of eyes made him realize that the appearance of light was a key to perception, a concept accepted by the scholarly community at the time. But Leonardo also came to realize that the process by which our brains understand things in our field of vision was exactly the opposite of conventional wisdom of the day. Light, he realized, enters into the brain through the eye, which has an opening in it through which that light passes. In the 15th century, medical expertise held that it was the human eye that projected light onto an object, which is what made objects visible to us.

But once he was clear about how light revealed items in our field of vision, things got much more complicated. What happens to the eye when light enters into it and articulates objects before it? How does that information get processed and delivered to the brain? What's the conduit?

Leonardo began dissecting eyes and heads, noticing that nerves and synapses extend back from the retina into the center of the human head, and then are attached to the spinal cord at the base of the neck. This led him to examine the nerve endings in the spine, and in so doing he saw how nerves clustered around disks to form, if you will, a center to and from which signals are transmitted—which explained to him how objects illuminated by light within one's field of vision could travel from the outer skin of the eyeball into the brain for perception and interpretation.

As scientific documents, these drawings amount to a wonderful introduction to the human body, and I am convinced that Leonardo was as delighted to draw them as we are to see the results. Leonardo drew everything. He was afraid of absolutely nothing. So another area that his drawings explored quite fearlessly was the act of procreation itself.

Already in 1493, he had drawn this cross section of male and female specimens in the act of conception, with the internal reproductive organs of both sketched in. These figures and their organs have been drawn with sharp, clearly defined outlines that designate the body parts, almost in the tradition of caricature drawings that Leonardo was by now expert at producing. But, as usual, Leonardo was just as interested in human emotions and the workings of the mind as he was in the body. The figures in this scientific drawing grin at each other in a way that conveys pleasure, as well as the anatomy of the act itself.

Two decades later, these anatomical drawings from 1507 and 1508 are, because of both their extraordinary detail and the highly unusual nature of the study, some of the finest works he ever produced. At just about the time he's working on a painting for the possibly pregnant Lisa Giocondo, he draws a human fetus, curled up according to its correct position, with its arms tucked in and its legs pulled up, with a visible umbilical cord. He examines and illustrates human female anatomy, in as detailed and accurate a drawing as had ever been done before in all of human history. Human male anatomy is similarly defined, now with veins and muscles added in a three-dimensional model of what happens during intercourse.

Cross-hatching has been expertly done to capture the volume of the head of the fetus in utero. Shadows and light patches demonstrate the mass of each part of each organ so that we know exactly what it looks like and exactly what it does. Proportions of each object have been pristinely calculated so that we see how they appear in relation to others.

But Leonardo isn't always rigidly technical in these drawings. If we look back at that drawing of colitis, we see Leonardo also adding a little note or aphorism along the margin: "woman desires that the size of the male member to be as large as possible, while man wishes the opposite of the genital organ of the woman." This is not an anatomical observation, but rather a sensory and psychological one. Leonardo wasn't just drawing the anatomy of reproductive organs and considering the origins of life—he was also dealing with the joy of sex.

But we, in the 21st century, can take for granted what Leonardo accomplished during his most intensive phase of anatomical research between 1507 and 1510. So I want to go back to emphasize the quality of these scientific drawings. All of them are masterpieces of draftsmanship, of course. As we look at a few of them today, we can marvel at their technical precision and the sensitivity with which he handled his figures.

Most of them appear to have been for his own personal edification, as they appear in pages of his notes that contain his familiar backwards scrawl. They were for his own use and his own study, but not for publication or general consumption. But some of them may have been intended for a treatise on anatomy that he never published. He pioneered the practice of looking at an organ or a structure from four different directions, and he used cross-sections of drawings, and other things too, that serve as clues that he wanted these drawings to be reproduced.

I show here one of Leonardo's drawings of a woman's body that focuses on the arteries and blood vessels that travel through it. We have blown up a facsimile of the drawing, and dry mounted it, so you can see it a little better. This drawing contains a series of dots that conform to the contours of the figure. They start underneath the arm, inside that heavy line there. They move inside the drawing and then back out again, now running parallel from outside of the figure that's drawn.

The drawing was then laid down on another piece of paper and secured fast to that piece of paper. Then, a cheesecloth or sack filled with chalk or charcoal dust was gently bounced along all the dots and all the lines in the drawing, so that the dust would poke through the holes and onto the sheet underneath. The technique is called "pouncing," and it allows one to transfer a drawing perfectly from one sheet of paper to another as a direct copy, and thus you're able to disseminate a visual idea quickly—albeit one piece of paper at a time.

And that's what appears to be going on with this particular drawing. For if we turn it over, we can see another piece of paper was attached to it, and that the pouncing technique was employed here by Leonardo, or perhaps by one of his assistants, which in turn transferred that exact drawing on to this one with the same contours of the figure worked in. You can even see some of these dots running in a series along the contours of the body on the outline here. And over here we can see some more of these dots, these pinpricks around the organ that Leonardo has drawn. By doing so allowed a copy of the original drawing, here, to reappear on the other piece of paper, here, which was then worked up in a much more detailed drawing, complete with organs that are shaded to show where the relationship is to other organs, those arteries, and even a spinal cord that appears up at the neck.

Obviously, Leonardo was not hoarding this information, and he wasn't trying to hide it from other people. Some of his anatomical drawings were copied through this pouncing technique and then given out to others who wanted or needed to know about them and how the human body worked.

Now sometimes we forget that each one of Leonardo's drawings was done under duress: The clock was ticking for each of them, and he had to focus his energies entirely on only one section of the body at a time. I'd like to think that Salai or one of Leonardo's other assistants was helping him at the operating table—cutting skin and bone and mopping up blood and holding back flaps of flesh so Leonardo could get a better view of what he was drawing. But we all know that this kind of thing, even in the sanitized laboratories of modern scientific institutions, isn't for everyone—or even for a very few.

Leonardo's assistants were likely in the back of the room, holding their noses from the stench, retching into buckets at the sight of some of the more lurid things Leonardo was uncovering. Or they were cowering at the thought of what might happen to them and their master if news of this shocking work leaked out into the wrong places.

I'd have to think that Leonardo was doing most of the cutting, the gauzing, and the cleaning himself. He was doing the washing and the looking and the thinking too. And he was actually doing the drawing too, sometimes at the table, sometimes a few minutes later, committing to memory what he had seen before him before it was lost, and all of it following what was probably a fitful night's sleep.

Leonardo himself recognized all of these problems, and he wrote about the challenges facing the medical scientist who might consider conducting these kinds of experiments. In one passage, Leonardo notes that the challenges facing the medical researcher revolve around both the environmental conditions he must endure and the artistic skill he must possess in order to do his work.

He writes in one of his notes:

> Even if you love this activity (of dissecting bodies), you may be hindered by your weak stomach; and if you aren't hindered by that, you may be hindered by fear of being at night in the company of these bodies, torn to pieces and skinned and frightening to look at. And if this doesn't hinder you, you may lack the drawing skill suitable for such representation. Or if you manage the drawing, you may lack the perspective. And if that isn't so, you may fail the arrangement of the geometrical representation or the reckoning of the strength and power of the muscles. Or you may fall short of patience, and thus you will not be diligent. Whether or not I have succumbed to these things you may judge for yourself.

Leonardo acknowledges the steep obstacles that faced him every time he conducted an anatomical experiment. But he also says, with pride, that he has never buckled under that pressure.

But in the end, for me, it's the artistry of these anatomical, scientific drawings that should stop us in our tracks. Look at the care with which Leonardo has drawn his subjects. The skin of the elderly man sags just so, but the crown of his head has been tenderly drawn, as have his cheekbones, eyes, nose, and lips. We see he's had some dental problems, as did most people past the age of about 40 in this period, long before oral hygiene became all the rage.

But Leonardo shows his human subject nobly, if not as nobility, per se. There's an elegance and a respectability to him that makes him a sympathetic character in a narrative Leonardo has set up for us, the willing participant, at peace with what is happening to his body by the scientist who hovers over him. I cannot help but feel that we see in these drawings, Leonardo at his most humble, his most reverent, his most introspective, and his most eloquent. And, of course, Leonardo is also at his most detailed and observant. His are the first absolutely accurate analyses of the biceps and triceps muscles ever shown, as the engineer in him recognizes a natural pulley system taking place in the human arm.

His are the first detailed studies ever made of a heart, although here Leonardo is looking at the heart of an ox rather than a human being. His are the first correct drawings of the pulmonary system, including arteries, veins, and capillaries that branch out just under the surface of the skin. He draws the liver, the kidney, and the bladder, the brain, the spinal cord, the joints of the toes and the fingers, the inner workings of the eyeball and eardrum. He seems to have been the first to draw the appendix. His drawings show us how these organs connect to others, how they expand and contract, and even what their function is.

Leonardo invents the cornerstone of modern medical science as we know it and single-handedly pulls the study of human anatomy out of the realm of medieval theory and propels it into that of empirical observation. But the only way he could have done this was through his rare combination of talents—as a painter, who understood line and modeling; as a sculptor who understood mass and volume and proportions; as an engineer who understood how machines worked and what they absolutely required in order to function properly; and as a scientist who knew that the only way to learn about something was to take it apart and examine it, piece by piece. Remove any one of those qualities, and the invention of modern medical science could not have occurred when it did.

I consider these drawings to be Leonardo's greatest accomplishments as a human being—that is to say, as a scientist, an engineer, and an artist, all rolled into one. They are daring, they are noble, they are driven by intense curiosity, and they communicate an immense amount of information. They are motivated by a passion for learning about the unknown; and they are, aesthetically speaking, breathtakingly beautiful.

Anatomy is inherently visual. But in Leonardo's view, the body was also a microcosmos, that is, a lesser world or universe unto itself. Leonardo's eagerness to acquire scientific knowledge, and then to convey what he learned, using all his skill as an artist, provided the first real window into the universe that each of us has within us.

In Praise of Painting—Leonardo's Manifesto

Lecture 30

After one last (unsuccessful) crack at sculpture at the start of the 16th century, Leonardo turned his back on the art form for good. This seems appropriate, given his thoughts on the matter as recorded in his notes that came to be called the *Treatise on Painting*, as well as his *paragone* (or public defense) of painting as the highest art form. Both of these sets of arguments profoundly influenced the painters of the following generations.

Leonardo the Author

- Leonardo planned many publications during his lifetime—treatises on anatomy, bird flight, mechanics, and hydrodynamics—and he published a treatise on geometry with Luca Pacioli. Leonardo almost seemed to be groping toward the creation of a personal encyclopedia.

- The only treatise Leonardo brought close to completion himself was a sort of manifesto, the *Treatise on Painting*. Leonardo never organized this material into a treatise, and his range of topics goes far beyond what we would normally think of as painting. But it unquestionably lays down specific ideas about what matters in painting and what painters ought and need to know to do things the right way.

The Trivulzio Tomb

- Leonardo made a second foray into sculpture around 1509 or 1510 for a **condottiere** named **Giovanni Trivulzio**. Trivulzio had begun his career under Ludovico Sforza during the 1480s, then in 1488 went to work for better wages in the Spanish court of Alfonso of Naples.

- A true mercenary, he joined the French in 1494. When Charles VIII and his troops entered Naples, Trivulzio lured Alfonso into his camp, and then deposed his former employer. Next, Trivulzio turned against Ludovico Sforza. By 1504, he was a wealthy man and designated 4,000 ducats for the design and production of a massive equestrian monument to be installed in a burial chapel that was to be built for him in a church in Milan called San Nazaro.

- In 1510, Leonardo submitted his invoice to Trivulzio, including the cost for marble, metal, clay, **armatures**, assistants, laborers, and his own salary, the total coming in at just over 3,000 ducats.

- From what we can tell from Leonardo's preliminary sketches, the ensemble would have been something of a pastiche of earlier projects he had either seen or done for himself. The base, made of marble, would be freestanding, containing a niche holding Trivulzio's effigy, as was the custom.

- Lashed to each of the niche's columns were full-length male nudes, struggling against their chains to break free—perhaps a reference to Trivulzio's conquests. The figures of the bound prisoners compare quite closely to some of those produced by Michelangelo for Pope Julius II's tomb.

- The focal point was the equestrian monument on top. Leonardo looked to best his old master, Verrocchio, in his monument of Bartolommeo Colleoni. The horse here rears up on its hind legs, improving on Verrocchio's three-legged horse. The rider seems ready to take off into the air. Below him cowers another of the vanquished, stomped under the beastly power of the stallion ridden by the merciless warrior.

- At some point, someone intimately familiar with the plan—maybe even Leonardo himself—produced a small bronze statuette of the rearing horse and rider. This is precisely the kind of preparatory **maquette** an artist might produce for a patron.

- But at this point, the project came to a halt. Charles d'Amboise, Milan's French governor, did not trust Trivulzio, with good reason, and would not allow Trivulzio to immortalize himself as a hero of Milan.

- In fact, when Charles d'Amboise died in 1511, Trivulzio briefly took command of the city. The project did not resume, however; Trivulzio's attention and money were focused elsewhere. Leonardo would never have an opportunity to return to this work.

The *Treatise on Painting*

- For about 10 years, Leonardo wrote down his thoughts about painting on sheets of paper, which were then filed away and kept private throughout his life. They numbered in the hundreds by the time he was finished with them.

- Leonardo's so-called *Treatise on Painting* was never published during his lifetime and was never seen by the general public for well over 100 years after his death. The various sheets were compiled after his death by his disciple, **Francesco Melzi**, and organized into discrete sections. Melzi then transcribed all the notes into a new manuscript of about a thousand passages.

- According to an estimate by the scholar Martin Kemp, only about one-fourth of the transcribed passages have themselves survived in Leonardo's hand; the rest we have only because of Melzi's manuscript, which is held today at the Vatican library and called the Codex Urbinas.

- Melzi passed the manuscript along to those select few painters he trusted with the information. That manuscript was again copied by hand and passed around within the artistic community but was still a well-guarded document. Finally, in 1651, an abbreviated version was published simultaneously in French and Italian as the *Treatise on Painting*.

- Leonardo says in his Introduction,

  I know well that, not being a man of letters, it will appear to some presumptuous people that they can reasonably belabor me with the allegation that I am a man without learning. But they do not grasp that my concerns are better handled through experience rather than bookishness. Though I might not know, like them, how to cite from the authors, I will cite something far more worthy, quoting experience, mistress of their masters. I say that anyone who argues on the basis of ancient authorities does not exploit his insight, but rather his memory.

- In other words, Leonardo believes the only way learn is by doing something yourself and, through trial and error, getting it right. This flies in the face of early Renaissance humanism, which relied heavily on the authority of ancient texts. Leonardo favored a more modern, scientific approach to art and the natural world.

- Leonardo spends lots of time talking about the science of optics and light, in particular how people receive images through the eye. He knew he alone possessed information about sight that painters had to know.

- He also wrote about perspective and distance, which were not new subjects in the 16th century. But Leonardo supplemented Alberti's well-known equations with his own geometrical studies and knowledge of atmospheric and aerial perspective.

- Leonardo's study of nature also helped him articulate his distinctive interest in the interplay of light and shadows, known in Italian as **chiaroscuro**. Unlike earlier theorists, who had argued that figures and objects are naturally illuminated but then obscured by shadows, Leonardo believed that all things exist in a sea of darkness and are revealed only when light strikes them.

- When his notes were passed around beginning perhaps around 1530, Leonardo's ideas fell into the hands of artists like **Carlo Urbino**, who produced a number of drawings based on what they were reading. These sketches help tell us that Leonardo's ideas were getting around and that artists were testing his ideas.

The *Paragone* of Painting

- Leonardo wanted to convey a view of painting as a form of knowledge about all other subjects. He imparted to painters his observations on the human body—including sections on proportions, emotions, gestures, movement, and distribution of weight. His abilities as a musician meant that he could write about harmonies from intellectual experience.

- Leonardo da Vinci, the Renaissance man, was telling his readers that they, too, had to be Renaissance men. In fact, Leonardo was saying not only that art would benefit from greater knowledge, but also that art would itself contribute to the increase of knowledge. We know from Leonardo's own work on anatomy and other subjects that the visual arts were central to his own achievements in science.

- He argued that, "He who despises painting loves neither philosophy nor nature." This kind of sharp discourse comparing, even ranking, one art against another was known in Italian as a *paragone*. This sort of argument mattered a great deal in the Renaissance environment of intense artistic and academic competition.

- Debates were held on these matters with some frequency during the 15th and 16th centuries, usually in the presence of important judges. Leonardo took part in at least one of these debates, on February 9, 1498.

- And at that time, painting had no assigned place in relation to the seven classical liberal arts—grammar, rhetoric, logic, arithmetic, geometry, music, and astronomy. Leonardo wanted to change that.

- The first *paragone* in Leonardo's *Treatise on Painting* involves a comparison between painting and poetry. Leonardo goes to great lengths to demonstrate the shortcomings of verse; poetry, he argues, tries to show with words what only the eyes can properly understand.

- Leonardo then talks about the eye and how it works; he talks about how our senses interpret the world around us. Then he makes an effort to elevate painting to a status equal to that of poetry and philosophy: "Painting represents the works of nature … with greater truth and certitude than do words and letters."

- Painters have leverage here: "Painting immediately presents to you the demonstrations which its maker has intended and gives as much pleasure to the greatest of senses as anything created by nature." By contrast, poetry takes a long time to grasp.

- He has good things to say about music, which is perhaps not surprising, given his own gifts in this field. But in the end he argues that music, which appeals to the ear and is performed by the mouth, is the lesser sister to the more noble art that serves the eye.

- He rather surprisingly decides to take aim against the sister arts of sculpture and architecture. Most of his argument lies in his belief that their practitioners are too bound by their ties to manual labor to escape the label of craftsmen. It is hard not to read these remarks as a reflection of his own disappointments—or a dig at Michelangelo.

- But his most damning critique of sculpture is that it is not a very intellectual medium: Spatial definition arises from the nature of the medium and not from the artifice of the maker.

- Leonardo never published his collection of thoughts on painting. Had he ever published a book, we can feel free to imagine he might have revised his language, as much as he revised and perfected his visual ideas.

Important Terms

armature: A wooden model of a sculpture that an artist covers in clay.

chiaroscuro: Italian word meaning "light-dark"; refers to the dramatic or theatrical contrast of light and dark in painting.

condottiere: A mercenary general.

maquette: A small-scale preparatory sculpture for a larger monument, usually created to garner a patron's approval before moving ahead with a project.

paragone: An Italian word meaning "debate" or "discourse"; a popular form of intellectual inquiry in the Renaissance, in which the author or speaker demonstrated the virtues of one particular theme or concept by comparing it favorably to another.

Names to Know

Melzi, Francesco (c. 1491–1570): A painter of noble birth, Melzi joined the studio of Leonardo as a teenager and became a trusted member of the inner circle for the rest of Leonardo's life. Melzi inherited Leonardo's notes and writings and maintained them carefully until his own death.

Trivulzio, Giovanni (c. 1440–1518): Aristocrat, mercenary soldier, military commander, and political leader. Eager to establish a legacy for himself, he briefly engaged Leonardo da Vinci to produce designs for an equestrian monument in his honor. The project was dropped when Trivulzio took control of Milan in 1511 and focused his energies on matters of state.

Suggested Reading

Clark, *The Drawings of Leonardo da Vinci in the Collection of her Majesty the Queen at Windsor Castle.*

Kemp, ed., Leonardo on Painting.

Radke, *Leonardo da Vinci and the Art of Sculpture.*

In Praise of Painting—Leonardo's Manifesto
Lecture 30—Transcript

Leonardo's astonishing work in anatomy, which we discussed last time, was apparently intended to contribute toward an eventual treatise or book called On Anatomy. But that was very far from being the only publication Leonardo had in mind. As we've mentioned, at one time or another, Leonardo made notes toward a work, On the Flight of Birds, another On the Elements of Machines, another On Water, and so on. He also collaborated with Luca Pacioli toward a treatise on geometry that was published. In an age before encyclopedias, Leonardo almost seemed as though he was groping toward the creation of a personal encyclopedia to contain everything that he'd learned.

It's time now for us to consider what Leonardo had to say about everything that we've seen so far. So in this lecture, I'll be quoting from his own writings a little bit more than usual. In particular, we'll consider the one book or treatise that Leonardo brought closest to completion. It's what I like to think of as his manifesto—a work first published long after his death under the title, the *Treatise on Painting*. That title is somewhat misleading, since Leonardo never organized his material into a treatise, and his range of topics goes far beyond what we would normally think of as painting, or even the graphic arts more generally. But it unquestionably lays down some very specific ideas about what matters in painting, and what painters ought and need to know in order to do things his way—the right way.

But ironically, we'll start this lecture by looking at Leonardo's second foray into sculpture, which occurred just after his dissections in Florence, during what can be called his second Milanese period. Of course, sculpture was an artistic medium that had caused him trouble in the past, but getting back on the horse, so to speak, made some sense when he returned to Milan.

In 1504, a will was drawn up in Milan by a mercenary soldier named Giovanni Trivulzio. Now Trivulzio had had a long association with the city of Milan, although not all of it was good. He had begun his career as a military man under the command of Ludovico Sforza during the 1480s. Whether he had known Leonardo then is anyone's guess, for Trivulzio left that court in something of a snit in 1488 to go work for better wages in the Spanish court of Alfonso of Naples, the Spanish king who was about to be deposed by the French. Trivulzio helped that along, in the true spirit of a mercenary solider, when he happily switched sides and joined the French in 1494. When Charles VIII and his troops entered Naples, Trivulzio joined him, and together they deposed his former employer.

Next, Trivulzio turned against Ludovico Sforza, whom he worked hard to destroy for the next 10 years on behalf of the French. He was rewarded for that treachery in 1500, when Sforza was finally defeated and imprisoned, once and for all.

By 1504, this fairly dangerous knight decided that his legacy warranted commemoration, and he designated a full 4000 ducats for the design and production of a massive equestrian monument to be installed in a burial chapel that was to be built for him in a church in Milan called San Nazaro.

Leonardo appears to have been given the opportunity to try his hand at this project fairly soon after his arrival in Milan in 1506—the French occupation had limited a lot of artistic activity in the city, and there were few sculptors available or capable of producing this work.

It makes a lot of sense that Leonardo was approached to design this colossal equestrian monument. He was known in Milan for his 24-foot clay model of the Sforza horse, and it hadn't been his fault that the bronze casting had never taken place.

But even though Leonardo may have been quite pleased to have a chance at artistic redemption through an equestrian monument for Giovanni Trivulzio, he was also clear with Trivulzio that the statue would have to be put on hold. But the knight was willing to wait, and when Leonardo was able to begin thinking seriously about it in 1509 and 1510, Trivulzio was happy to have him as his lead artist.

Leonardo seems to have actually gotten quite far along in this project, for in 1510 he submitted a list of materials he'd need for the sculpture, including the cost for marble, metal, clay, assistants and laborers, along with armatures (or wooden stick models to mold clay over). He also noted the salary he commanded for crafting each of the eight figures that he envisioned around its base, plus the horse and rider. Even then, Leonardo low-balled his estimate, coming in at just over 3000 ducats (3046, to be precise), and this must've pleased Trivulzio to no end, for he had budgeted 4000 for the project.

It's been suggested that, in addition to this checklist of materials and costs, Leonardo probably also submitted some finished drawings to show the patron exactly what he had in mind.

From what we can tell from Leonardo's preliminary sketches, probably from about 1509 or 1510, the ensemble would have been something of a pastiche of earlier projects he had either seen or done for himself. This drawing, housed in the Royal Collection at Windsor Castle, provides the clearest vision of how Leonardo wished to commemorate the life of his patron.

The base, made of marble, would be a freestanding architectural form, available from 360 degrees, and containing within it the tomb effigy of the patron, lying in state on his marble funeral bier, as was the custom.

This kind of dormition figure, that is, a figure in a final resting position, was prevalent all across Europe, and there would've been no shortage of other examples for him to copy. The tomb of the Duke Giangaleazzo Visconti, initiated by the sculptor Gian Cristofor Romano, in the middle of the 1490s would've been a nice model for both Leonardo and Trivulzio: Its design also featured a niche in the form of a rounded, arched loggia, with an effigy of the deceased place on top of the tomb inside. As it was in nearby Pavia, the progress that Romano was making on the effigy could be monitored and borrowed by Leonardo in nearby Milan without too much trouble.

Along the columns, in pairs, were these unusual figures—full-length male nudes, lashed to columns, struggling against their chains to break free—but to no avail. Their symbolic function remains a mystery, and it's been suggested that they were a reference to Trivulzio's conquests as a military man, and represented the vanquished he had helped control during his life as a soldier of fortune—which the patron no doubt would've liked very much.

While their meaning is a bit of a question mark, their artistic origins are pretty easy to trace. At just this time in Rome, Michelangelohad been called away from his sculptural monument to Julius II—but the drawings he had made for the 40 larger-than-lifesize figures he wanted to carve for it were known to those in the field.

The figure of the bound prisoner that Leonardo drew for the Trivulzio monument, I think, compares quite closely to some of those produced by Michelangelo for the project for Julius's tomb. Their similarities are surprising, and therefore are probably not coincidental. It suggests that, somehow, Leonardo knew of these.

But the main part of this ensemble wasn't the tomb effigy, the loggia that contained it, or the vanquished prisoners that stood guard around it. The key piece of the whole thing was the equestrian monument that Leonardo wanted to conquer for himself and place squarely in the middle of the whole thing.

And now Leonardo was once again looking to best his old master, Verrocchio, who had managed to design the most magnificent equestrian of them all in his monument of Bartolommeo Colleoni.

Leonardo knew Verrocchio's template well, having stayed in Venice for at least six weeks in 1500. In his drawing for the Trivulzio Monument Leonardo now played around much more intensely with that energetic-looking stallion. Rearing up on its hind legs—now improving upon Verrocchio's three-legged version in Venice—that horse carries a rider who seems ready to take off into the air. Below him cowers yet another one of the vanquished, stomped under the beastly power of that stallion ridden by the merciless warrior.

And in his own repertoire, Leonardo had plenty of ammunition upon which to draw. Here are familiar drawings, one of a horse and the other of horses and riders in the heat of battle. Both show Leonardo's sensitivity to the anatomical details of the beast, but also to the effects on the body caused by extreme contortions seen on the battlefield. He knew how to draw warhorses, and one can understand why Trivulzio was willing to wait on Leonardo to finish his other projects between 1506 and 1509 in order to get him to work on this monument for him.

It's pretty clear that Leonardo's designs for a horse rearing up on two legs received the nod of approval from his patron. At some point in the early 16th century, someone intimately familiar with Leonardo's ideas—maybe even Leonardo himself—produced this small bronze statuette, featuring just such a horse rearing up on its hind legs, with a rider positioned properly to balance the figure on its base. This is precisely the kind of preparatory maquette that an artist might produce for a patron, and Trivulzio would've marveled over how Leonardo intended to balance such an inherently imbalanced composition—weighing a good ton in bronze—on a marble base. This may have been an attempt to show Trivulzio how to do it.

But at this point in the project, all things actual were forced to come to a halt. Trivulzio's presence in Milan had caused Charles of Amboise, the French Governor there, to watch the condottiere's movements closely and with grave reservations. Trivulzio wasn't to be trusted, and his record showed that Trivulzio was just as likely to stage a coup d'état as he was to honor an oath of allegiance to someone else. There was no way Trivulzio could get away with initiating a project to immortalize himself as a hero of Milan while Charles of Amboise was still in charge.

Now, when Charles died in 1511, Giovanni Trivulzio did, in fact, briefly take command of the city, and one would think that this would result in Leonardo resuming this project and seeing it through to its completion. But Trivulzio's attention and his money were now focused elsewhere, and the new head of state informed Leonardo that he could spare neither for his monument. And just like that, the project died. Once again Leonardo would not be able to complete a major work of sculpture.

Leonardo would never have an opportunity to return to this work, and his desire to make up for his greatest artistic shortcoming—the failure to cast the *Colossus of Milan*—would never be satisfied.

In hindsight, maybe this was a good thing; for Leonardo was neither a sculptor by trade nor inclination. And we know this, in part, because of the amount of time he spent writing down his thoughts on the importance of painters and the shortcomings of sculptors in a world that, he thought, should place a very high value on painters.

For about 10 years, Leonardo wrote down his thoughts about painting on different sheets of paper, which were then filed away and kept private throughout his life. They numbered in the hundreds by the time he was finished with them. Despite his great interest in the subject, Leonardo's so-called *Treatise on Painting* was never published during his lifetime, and was never seen by the general public for well over 100 years after his death. His musings, observations, and sometimes petulant rants were all collected from the loose sheets of paper on which they'd been scribbled, brought together after his death by Leonardo's disciple, Francesco Melzi, and organized into discrete sections. Melzi, about whom we'll learn more in our next lecture, then transcribed all the notes he had organized into a new manuscript of about a thousand passages. Good thing, too: According to an estimate by the scholar Martin Kemp, only about one-fourth of the transcribed passages have themselves survived; the rest we have only because of this manuscript Melzi created, which is held today at the Vatican library and called the Codex Urbinas. Melzi then passed the manuscript along to those select few painters that he trusted with the information.

That manuscript was again copied by hand and passed around within the artistic community, but it was still a well-guarded document. Finally, in 1651, an abbreviated version of this text was published simultaneously in French and Italian as the *Treatise on Painting*, and Leonardo's ideas finally began to reach a wider public.

Now, as we listen to what Leonardo says in that work, it's important to remember that he was not formally educated; he knew no Greek, he had very bad Latin, and he spent very little time fussing with the out-dated and theoretical guesses of scientists who, for one reason or another, felt unable to engage in actual experimentation.

Here's a part of what Leonardo says in his Introduction:

> I know well that, not being a man of letters, it will appear to some presumptuous people that they can reasonably belabor me with the allegation that I am a man without learning. But they do not grasp that my concerns are better handled through experience rather than bookishness. Though I might not know, like them, how to cite

> from the authors, I will cite something far more worthy, quoting experience, mistress of their masters. I say that anyone who argues on the basis of ancient authorities does not exploit his insight, but rather his memory.

Now this, in a nutshell, is as close to a personal intellectual manifesto as Leonardo ever gives. He's clearly uninterested in bombastic sycophants who aim to impress by reciting all the great things other people have said. He wants to get at the heart of things, and he believes the only way to do that is by doing it yourself, through trial and error, until you get it right.

Still, it's striking that Leonardo criticizes those around him who depend on ancient sources for their information and as the basis for their beliefs. In the early 15th century, this would have been considered not only a noble practice, but a sign of great learning and a mastery of humanistic inquiry. In short, it would have signaled that the speaker was, if you will, a Renaissance thinker. But now, in the early 16th century, this kind of slavish dependence on other writers—no matter how old or how respected—was ripped apart by Leonardo, who favored a more modern, scientific approach to the natural world. It's one of the things that distinguished the Age of the High Renaissance from the earlier phase that immediately preceded it, as the newer generation increasingly looked to go beyond old book learning to advance the cause of knowledge in new and original ways.

Not surprisingly, Leonardo wanted to impart new knowledge about painting. He spent lots of time talking to painters about the science of optics and light: Because of his experiments on the human body, which had begun in the late 1480s with his dissection and examination of the skull and the eye, Leonardo felt comfortable talking about how people receive images through these all-important mechanisms.

But he also knew that he alone possessed information about sight that painters had to know, which is what inspired Leonardo to write it all down in the first place. He wanted to tell them something new that they could then apply to painting that normally wasn't considered important to the field. He also wrote about perspective and distance, which were not new subjects in the 16th century.

But Leonardo supplemented Alberti's well-known words of wisdom with his own geometrical studies to argue that laws of mathematics could be used both to calculate diagonal, orthogonal lines in architectural structures and to produce an aerial perspective by diminishing the size of objects in an accurate way as they receded into the distance.

Leonardo's study of nature also helped him articulate his distinctive interest in the interplay of light and shadows, known in Italian as *chiaroscuro*. Unlike earlier theorists, who had argued that figures and objects are naturally illuminated, but then obscured by shadows, Leonardo believed that all things exist in a total sea of darkness, and are revealed only when light strikes them. The earth needs the sun to illuminate it, he saw, and painters need to approach their figures as existing in a state of darkness, who can then be revealed only when a specific light source strikes them and allows us to see them as we can see here in his painting of John the Baptist.

When his notes were passed around by Melzi beginning perhaps around 1530, Leonardo's ideas fell into the hands of artists like Carlo Urbino, who produced a number of drawings in their own manuscripts based on what they were reading in Leonardo's. These sketches help tell us that Leonardo's ideas were getting around, and that artists were not only paying attention, but were trying to figure out what he was trying to say through the written word by actually drawing his descriptions.

In addition to imparting new knowledge about how to be a better painter, Leonardo also wanted to convey a view of painting as itself a form of knowledge about all other subjects. For example, Leonardo imparted to painters his observations on the human body—including sections on proportions, emotions, gestures, movement, and distribution of weight. Leonardo's work as a mathematician let him include within the subject of painting a knowledge of ratios, and his abilities as a musician meant that he could write about harmonies from intellectual experience. Proportions, he knew, had to be calculated according to these ratios and harmonies, which would in turn allow the painter to create natural, believable figures—everything was all bound up together in this world, which meant that good painters had to know a lot about, well, everything.

Leonardo da Vinci, the Renaissance man, was telling his readers that they, too, had to be Renaissance Men. In fact, Leonardo was saying not only that art would benefit from greater knowledge, but also that art would itself contribute to the increase of this knowledge. This might sound like vague platitude, but we now know from Leonardo's own work on anatomy (and other subjects) that the visual arts had been utterly central to his own achievements in science.

It's in light of what Leonardo had learned about the importance of the visual arts in the pursuit of science that we can perhaps better understand him when he says, "He who despises painting neither loves philosophy nor nature." It sounds pretty severe, but his argument makes a little bit of sense: Because the actual and symbolic qualities of things are apprehended by the naked eye, painters, become interpreters of the natural world—like poets. Because painters show us precise renderings of organisms and objects as they appear to us, they must also be seen as scientists. And because painters show us, through narrative and conceptual themes, how those organisms behave within the grand scheme of the universe and, arguably, God's plan, painters must also be seen as philosophers.

In short, painters needed to be mentioned in the same breath as poets and scientists; and in order to prove it, he started to compare his own field to those that enjoyed a higher status than his did in the 16th century.

Now this kind of discourse wasn't at all rare for the time: It was known in Italian as a *paragone*, and it had become quite popular in the 16th century as writers of different stripes had tried their hand at it.

Arguing about the place of one art against another, or even one academic discipline versus its counterparts, seems a little silly to us today. We don't spend our time worrying about whether music more capably captures the yearning of our hearts than poetry does, or if photography is a worthier medium for human expression than interpretative dance. There's value in everything and room for everyone in this big world of ours.

But in Renaissance Italy, where practitioners had been raised in an environment of intense competition, and where courtiers vied for the favors of patrons who rewarded them for their prominence, this sort of argument mattered a great deal. Whether the subject was art versus science, philosophy versus poetry, or sculpture versus painting, the great minds of the High Renaissance took comparative considerations very, very seriously.

In fact, we know that debates were held on the matter with some frequency during the 15th and 16th centuries, and usually in the presence of important judges, whose job it was to determine who had brought to light the most important matters that ought to be understood by the general public. We also know, from the notes of Luca Pacioli, that Leonardo took part in at least one of these debates, on February 9, 1498, just as his *Last Supper* was being completed in the Milanese cloister of Santa Maria delle Grazie. This was something that leading thinkers did, and Leonardo entered into the fray happily and with great success. I imagine he was quite good at it.

At that time, painting had no assigned place in relation to the seven classic liberal arts—which were grammar, rhetoric, logic, arithmetic, geometry, music, and astronomy. Leonardo wanted to change that. The first *paragone* in Leonardo's *Treatise on Painting* involves a comparison between painting and poetry. As one might expect, Leonardo goes to great lengths to demonstrate the shortcomings of verse when compared to painting. Poetry, he argues, tries to do with words what only the eyes can properly understand: Verbal descriptions of objects and scenes and gestures and emotional responses will always fall short of the mark because those are things that humans need to see in order to understand fully.

Leonardo then talks about the eye and how it works; he talks about how our senses interpret the world around us, with a recognition that science is wholly dependent on our ability to see and interpret the things we see clearly and objectively and truthfully; and then he makes an effort to elevate painting to a status level with that of poetry and philosophy. "Painting," he writes, "represents the works of nature … with greater truth and certitude than do words and letters."

Painters have some leverage here; Leonardo writes that "Painting immediately presents to you the demonstrations which its maker has intended and gives as much pleasure to the greatest of senses as anything created by nature." By contrast, poetry takes a long time to grasp, as words gobble up precious time. Paintings allow viewers to understand something instantaneously, without all the noise of fumbling prose or gross inaccuracies.

Leonardo has good things to say about music, though, which is perhaps not surprising, seeing as how he was reputed to have been quite gifted in this field. But in the end Leonardo argues that music, which appeals to the ear and is performed by the mouth, is the lesser sister to the more noble art that serves the eye, namely painting. And he says, "He who loses his eyes leaves his soul in a dark prison, in which every hope is lost of seeing again the sun, the light of the world." And this is important, too, since the argument suggests that painting belongs ahead of music, which was one of the seven liberal arts studied at University.

Now that Leonardo has informed us of painting's place among, and superiority to, the noble fields of music and poetry, he rather surprisingly decides to take aim against the sister arts of sculpture and architecture: oddly, to our way of thinking, he's not willing to let them share equally in the glory that he has brought to painting.

Most of his argument lies in his belief that sculptors, as a group, are too bound by their ties to manual labor to escape the label of craftsmen. Because of the sweat that goes into the production of a marble statue, Leonardo argues that sculpture is the lesser of the two arts, and he works hard to set a mental image for us that is powerful and memorable:

> The sculptor undertakes his work with greater bodily exertion than the painter, and the painter undertakes his work with greater mental exertion. When making his work, the sculptor uses the strength of his arm in hammering, to remove the superfluous marble or other stone which surround the figure embedded in it. This is an extremely mechanical operation, generally accompanied by great sweat, which mingles with dust and becomes converted into mud. His face becomes plastered and powdered all over with marble dust, which makes him look like a baker, and he becomes covered in minute chips of marble, which makes him look as if he is covered

> in snow. His house is in a mess, and it's covered in chips and dust from the stone.

The Leonardo contrasts this by describing those in his, more noble profession:

> The painter's position is quite contrary to this, because the painter sits before his work at the greatest of ease, well dressed and applying delicate colors with his light brush, and he may dress himself in whatever clothes he pleases. His residence is clean and adorned with delightful pictures, and he often enjoys the accompaniment of music or the company of authors of various fine works that can be heard with great pleasure without the crashing of hammers and other confused noises.

Did you see what he just did there? Sculpture is dirty, manual, and akin to construction work. Painting is in the hands of men who wear garments similar to those worn by educated men, whom Leonardo presumes will account for his readership. Moreover, the painter, he says, can enjoy those lesser arts of music and poetry to help him produce that more noble activity of replicating nature for the eye. He's managed to condemn three of painting's rivals in one clean sweep.

It's hard not to read these remarks, at least a little bitr, in light of Leonardo's disappointments with the Sforza and Trivulzio monuments. Moreover, Leonardo's broadsides against sculpture reveal a genuine sense of disdain for the medium and for its practitioners, perhaps especially for the figure of Michelangelo, for whom he felt little affection.

But the worst for sculpture is yet to come, for its most damning drawback, quite simply, is that it's just not a very intellectual medium. He writes:

> There is no comparison between the innate talent, skill, and learning within painting and within sculpture, inasmuch as spatial definition in sculpture arises from the nature of the medium and not from the artifice of the maker." In other words, as long as the sculptor knows the measurements of the human body and how it fits together, he

> will be able to create something that looks like a representation of nature. But painters have to go beyond just the figure to capture the entire world, including mountains, fields, and streams, clouds and rain and forests, sorrow and joy and anger, beauty and ugliness and all the things of nature and of human nature.

For Leonardo:

> The painter should weigh and consider everything he sees, and choose the best parts thereof. He should accomplish this in the manner of a mirror, which changes itself into as many colors as are contained in the objects placed before it. And if he does this, he will be like a second Nature.

Painters have the power to tell us everything we need to know about our world, and in that sense they are the greatest scientists of them all.

As with all the other treatises Leonardo envisioned, the *Treatise on Painting* is not a work he ever prepared for publication. Had Leonardo ever published a book, we can feel free to imagine he might have revised his language, as much as he revised and perfected his visual ideas.

In any case, Melzi's compilation was eventually published in 1651, and was soon translated into all major European languages, thereby making Leonardo's musings available to a wider public for the first time. Leonardo's claim that the visual arts are, and ought to be, regarded as fully-fledged contributors to knowledge began to be given wider consideration. Artists read him closely, taking to heart, in a hundred different ways, his advice that it's "a poor pupil who does not surpass the master."

Leonardo and the Medici in Rome

Lecture 31

Leonardo came under Medici patronage once again when Giovanni de' Medici became Pope Leonardo X and his brother, Giuliano de' Medici, became the ruler of Florence. Nominally attached to the Florentine court but living in Rome, Leonardo spent his time in the Vatican doing mostly as he pleased, more ornament than advisor, and finally began to paint a subject that had long occupied his imagination: the *Saint Anne Madonna.*

The Final Departure from Milan

- Charles d'Amboise died in 1511, and Giovanni Trivulzio stepped into the breach. Sensing weakness, Pope Julius II attacked the city and, by July 1512, had installed a new ruler, Massimiliano Sforza.

- As a former courtier of both d'Amboise and Trivulzio, Leonardo disliked this turn of events and left Milan with an entourage that included Salai, his new apprentice Francesco Melzi, and two others.

- Leonardo was more relaxed about this journey than previous ones, perhaps because his reputation now preceded him and finding a new home would not be difficult. The group first journeyed northeast to the small town of Vapprio d'Adda, to a villa owned by Melzi's parents.

- Melzi's decision to apprentice to Leonardo speaks to the newfound status of the visual arts , and visual artists, during the early modern period. It would have been almost unthinkable only 20 years earlier for an aristocrat like Melzi to pursue a career in painting.

- During their stay, Leonardo produced a couple of drawings of the estate with an eye toward improvements and additions, but otherwise, it appears that the group was just biding its time before moving on to Florence.

The Return of the Medici

- **Giuliano di Lorenzo de' Medici,** the son of Lorenzo the Magnificent, was a highly regarded poet, humanist, and dilettante known for his unusual interest in the lives of women and an interest in defining a feminine ideal.

- Giuliano was not only a son of the wealthy Medici family; on the death of Pope Julius II in 1513, his brother, Giovanni de Medici, became Pope **Leonardo X**. Thus he was supremely well connected.

- The Medici had retaken Florence in 1512 and installed Giuliano as its ruler, thanks in part to help from internal Medici allies, including Francesco Giocando. Florence would remain in Medici hands for another 200 years, until 1737, when the family line finally died out. This batch of Medici were unlike the 15th-century gang, however. Giuliano was more interested in power, wealth, and prestige than diplomacy, benevolence, and charity.

- At some point in 1513, Leonardo became Giuliano's courtier, but he did not move back to Florence. Rather, Leonardo was to live in Rome, where Giuliano actually spent most of his time. Rooms in the Vatican's Belvedere Palace were prepared for his use, which Leonardo was working in by July 1514.

Leonardo in Rome

- Giuliano de'Medici was head of the papal militia, so Leonardo once again became a military engineer. He designed improvements for the port of Civitavecchia and drew up plans to drain the mosquito-infested marshes that lay south of Rome. Leonardo might have assisted the elderly Bramante with his work on St. Peter's, but there is no evidence to support or refute this idea.

- Raphael was in Rome as well and probably endorsed the addition of Leonardo to the papal court. Raphael, the silver-tongued courtier, became a favorite among his new Medici patrons. Leonardo was now the visitor and Raphael was the established power broker in the city.

- The one person in Rome who could not have been happy about Leonardo's arrival was Michelangelo. He had detached himself from Pope Leonardo X's court to concentrate on Julius II's tomb, and around 1515 he completed two figures for it: *The Dying Slave* and *Moses.*

    - *The Dying Slave* aligns with Michelangelo's earlier declarations that artists were obliged to experiment with the natural order, from the accentuated contrapposto pose, the elongated torso, and the overly delicate hands.

    - In *Moses*, Michelangelo added a physical power to convey the psychological intensity of the narrative moment: Moses grasps the two tablets of the Ten Commandments and rises up to address his followers, whom he has discovered worshiping a golden calf.

© Hemera/Thinkstock.

Michelangelo's *Moses* tomb monument for Julius II.

- We have no evidence that Giuliano gave Leonardo any artistic projects to work on whatsoever. Scholars have tended to see Leonardo as an advisor to the artists and philosophers in the papal court, but we have no evidence to suggest he played this role, either.

- We know from his sketchbooks that he designed costumes and temporary architectural structures for Medici parties and theatrical productions. We also know that he continued his medical dissections, under the nose of ecclesiastical authorities, focused more intensely than ever on the human fetus, the female reproductive system, and the spinal cord.

- Sometime in 1514, a research assistant was assigned to Leonardo by someone in the papal court. This assistant began telling his superiors that Leonardo's anatomical studies were diabolical—literally the work of the devil. Leonardo brought his anatomical studies to a halt shortly thereafter.

Return of the *Saint Anne Madonna*

- Leonardo directed his energies toward at least one painting while in Rome, and maybe as many as three simultaneously. One was the painted version of the *Saint Anne Madonna.* Leonardo may not have had an owner or an audience in mind; rather, it may have been an experiment for the *Treatise on Painting*—allowing him to work out his ideas in practice while describing them in words.

- The cartoon from 1508 focuses on the combination of Saint Anne, Mary, Christ, and John the Baptist. Some of the painting's features are absolutely identical to the cartoon. However, in the painting Mary bends at the waist and crosses over the torso of her mother. She reaches down with both arms to clutch her child and pull him back into her arms. John has been replaced by a lamb, whom Jesus grips by the ears. He throws one leg over its back, as if riding a horse.

- Although the facial expressions of the women are still peaceful, and while Christ's return glance seems to be a cheerful one, the presence of the lamb indicates an ominous theme. The lamb was understood to be a sacrificial animal, a symbol of Christ's sacrifice as the Lamb of God. Leonardo tells us that Christ knew and embraced his fate from the moment of his birth.

- The painting is a sophisticated theological statement that makes clear what early Madonna paintings from the 1300s and 1400s had only alluded to: that images of Mary and the Christ child were intended to be a little sad.

- Leonardo took his time with this painting, and it was in his possession right up until his death in 1519. Significant areas have not been finished. This adds to the suggestion that it was a personal exercise.

More on the *Mona Lisa* Mystery

- Recall that Antonio de Beatis wrote in 1517 that Leonardo was working on paintings of "a Florentine woman … and one of the Madonna and Child, who take positions in the lap of Saint Anne." The latter is the *Saint Anne Madonna* we have just examined, and the former is the *Mona Lisa.*

- The relationship between Giuliano de' Medici and the Giocando family may have been a close one. Francesco Giocando helped restore the Medici to Florence, and he was on the Medici payroll for many years thereafter.

- Were the families close enough, as de Beatis suggested in his letter, might Giuliano de' Medici commissioned a portrait of Lisa Giacondo himself? Perhaps the clue lies in Giuliano's personality. Giuliano was a poet, and the subject of many of his poems was the virtue of women. Leonardo had a track record of capturing the essence of women in portraits.

- This web of connections tie in nicely with some of the stylistic choices Leonardo made in the *Mona Lisa*, which point toward a period of execution in the 1510s rather than the decade before, such as the advanced state of the sfumato.

Leonardo Leaves Rome

- In Rome, Leonardo enjoyed a new level of artistic freedom. He had no major obligations or responsibilities, nor any pressing deadlines, nor any distasteful genuflections to pompous patrons.

- On the other hand, sometime later, Leonardo wrote, "The Medici made me, and the Medici destroyed me." Lorenzo the Magnificent, of course, gave him his earliest opportunities. But the second half of that statement is cryptic indeed, as Giuliano (and by proxy Pope Leonardo) would be his last Medici employer.

- It could have been because his pursuit of anatomical studies was forced to a halt, or perhaps it was because in 1516, when Giuliano de'Medici died unexpectedly no one in the papal court made an attempt to retain his services.

Names to Know

Leonardo X (a.k.a. **Giovanni de' Medici**; 1475–1521): The second son of Lorenzo the Magnificent; he succeeded Julius II to the papal throne in 1513. Whereas Julius II initiated a systematic program of "revenue enhancements" to help pay for the rebuilding of Rome during his pontificate, Leo expanded on these approaches to cover the expenses of his personal art collection and parties.

Medici, Giuliano di Lorenzo de' (1479–1516): The third son of Lorenzo di Piero de' Medici (a.k.a. Lorenzo the Magnificent), Giuliano was one of the leaders of the coup d'etat that reinstated his family as the governors of Florence in 1512. One of the characters in Baldassare Castiglione's *Book of the Courtier* and the person to whom Machiavelli's *The Prince* was originally dedicated, Giuliano was both a poet and a diplomat. He spent much of his time in Rome at the side of his brother, Pope Leonardo X, and was the patron of Leonardo da Vinci from 1513 to 1516.

Suggested Reading

Budny, "The Sequence of Leonardo's Sketches for *The Virgin and Child with Saint Anne and Saint John the Baptist.*"

Partridge, *Renaissance Rome.*

Leonardo and the Medici in Rome

Lecture 31—Transcript

In the second decade of the 1500s, the High Renaissance converged on Rome. Now, by 1511, Leonardo was a well-traveled veteran of about five different Italian courts, and he was about as jaded as could be after leaving each of them just as things were falling apart there. And as he looked out at the political landscape from his perch in French-controlled Milan, the view couldn't have been very good.

Charles of Amboise had managed to control the city effectively for the first decade of the 16th century, but had become growingly wary of Giovanni Trivulzio, whose presence marked for Charles a genuine threat to his authority. Sure enough, when Charles died in 1511, it was Trivulzio who stepped into the breach to take control of the city on behalf of its French occupiers.

That didn't last long. Sensing weakness there, Pope Julius II combined forces with a Swiss army to attack the garrison in Milan. Both had good reasons for the attack—the Swiss, we're told, were feeling rather badly about how Ludovico Sforza had been turned over to the Frenchd way back in 1500 and were itching for a chance to make up for it, while Julius, being Julius, was interested in expelling the French from Italian soil altogether.

Just as importantly, Julius wanted to add Milan to the string of Italian cities he hoped to conquer in order to unify Italy and revive the Roman Empire—with Julius as its leader.

This army attacked Milan in December of 1511, and Leonardo was there to watch it. The Swiss succeeded in taking much of the city, and by July of 1512 they had installed as the ruler of Milan the son of Ludovico Sforza, named Massimiliano in honor of the Holy Roman Emperor. French forces managed to hold out in the Castello Sforzesco for over a year, but they were finally forced to abandon it on September 19, 1513.

As a courtier in the employment of first, Charles of Amboise and, second, Giovanni Trivulzio, Leonardo feared that he was in a bad position. So he packed his bags once more, and fled from Milan on September 24 with an entourage in tow that included Salai, a recently added apprentice named Francesco Melzi, and two others.

Unlike his flight of 1499, this time Leonardo seems to have been somewhat more relaxed about his journey: Maybe it was because he knew his reputation now preceded him wherever he went. Maybe he believed that finding work would not be difficult in this bellicose time. Or maybe it was because Francesco Melzi, one of the young men in his entourage, just so happened to be of high birth, was well-educated, and was the son of wealthy parents. The group journeyed northeast to the small town of Vapprio d'Adda, where for most of the autumn of 1513, Leonardo and his stable of assistants lived in the villa owned by the parents of Melzi, his new apprentice.

Now Melzi had only recently come into the orbit of Leonardo, having been added to the studio either in 1506 or else sometime between 1509 and 1510. We're not entirely sure. Melzi's decision to join Leonardo speaks to one of the other big developments during the High Renaissance—the elevation in status of the visual arts and visual artists, during this early modern period. It would've been almost unthinkable, only 20 years earlier, for an aristocrat like Melzi to pursue a career in painting, which had previously been considered by many to be a manual labor unworthy of educated people.

We don't know much about that visit with Francesco Melzi's parents, save for the fact that Leonardo produced a couple of drawings of the estate with an eye toward improvements and additions. He may have done them as a gift of thanks for their hospitality, and he just as likely may have been commissioned by Francesco's parents to do them, or perhaps he merely did them out of boredom—all three are equally possible, in my view. But the project wasn't terribly complicated in any event, and it appears as though Leonardo and his assistants were basically biding their time before moving on to bigger things.

The travelers now continued on to Florence, ostensibly to visit Leonardo's half-brothers, who were ill. During this stay, Leonardo came into contact with one of the most important and powerful men in Italy—the son of

Lorenzo the Magnificent, named Giuliano de' Medici, whose portrait I show here.

Giuliano was a highly regarded poet, humanist, and dilettante, who became quite well known for what was in his day a rather unusual interest in the lives of women and in the qualities that he believed comprised a feminine ideal. He was a poet of some renown, and he liked to write about the virtues of women that distinguished them from men. Baldassare Castiglione, the author of the extremely important text called the *Book of the Courtier*, described Giuliano as the very embodiment of the ideal Man of Elegance, graced with education, wit, manners, and a heightened sense of grace.

Giuliano de' Medici also happened to be very well connected. He was born in 1479, four years after his brother, Giovanni, and seven years after his eldest brother, Piero—the one who had been forced to flee Florence in 1494 and had been replaced by Fra Savonarola. Piero had died in a military campaign in 1503, forever known in the annals of history as "Piero the Unfortunate." But his brother, Giovanni, more than made up for Piero's sad life.

Born in 1475, Giovanni had been named a cardinal in 1491, at the tender age of 16, to satisfy the wishes of his father, Lorenzo the Magnificent. Giovanni had watched two popes profit enormously from their position, and he learned from Alexander VI and Julius II that with their office and title came rights and privileges unheard of anywhere else in the world. Like most of his fellow cardinals, this appealed to Giovanni de' Medici .

And, to his great pleasure, in the winter of 1513, Giovanni was elected to the papal throne after Julius II's unexpected death from a fever. Giovanni took a new name at the time of his election: Pope Leo X.

Now sometimes it's tempting to feel a little badly for the brothers of highly successful people—sibling rivalry can be a killer—but in Giuliano's case, no tears shall be shed, for Giuliano de' Medici was, by the fall of 1513, the brand new ruler of Florence.

On orders from Julius II, Giuliano and his brother, Giovanni, had directed a military campaign against Florence in 1511 to punish Piero Soderini and his

Republican government for its opposition to Julius II's policy of imperial unification. The Medici attempt to oust the members of the anti-papal Republic had failed then, but the desired effect was realized a few months later, in September of 1512, when a successful coup d'état was staged by members of the Medici family and their supporters—one of whom was named Francesco Giocando.

That's when Giuliano de' Medici took control of Florence. For the first time in 18 years, the Medici family were again in control of Florence. It would stay that way for another 200 years, until 1737, when the family line finally died out.

So when Leonardo and his entourage left Melzi's family estate and entered the city of Florence in the fall of 1513, his former home was not at all like the one in which he had worked the previous decade—nor was it much like the one in which he had worked during the 1470s, either.

This batch of Medici weren't like the 15th-century gang. Although Giuliano was a man of letters, like his brother he was more interested in the acquisition of power, wealth, and prestige than he was in diplomacy, benevolence, and charity. These Medici had more in common with Rodrigo Borgia and his children than they did with Cosimo the Elder and their father, Lorenzo the Magnificent.

Leonardo doesn't comment about his brief stay in Florence during the autumn of 1513, and we're not completely sure why he left the city as abruptly as he did. But we do know that at some point, Leonardo came into direct contact with Giuliano de' Medici—and his encounter with the ruler of Florence changed the course of Leonardo's life.

How and why and where, exactly, Leonardo met Giuliano is still unknown to us. It's been noted that the Medici brothers had visited Milan in 1496 and in 1497 on a diplomatic mission, and that there they had met Leonardo for the first time.

It has also been suggested that Giuliano and Leonardo met in Venice in 1500, when both were in that city during the tumultuous months surrounding Louis

XII's French invasion of Northern Italy. But their most important meeting surely occurred in the fall of 1513, when Giuliano learned that Leonardo was out of work and looking for a patron.

And as his brother, Giovanni, was now the pope, well, all things were possible. Giuliano invited Leonardo to join him as a courtier in his own court, but this court would not be in Florence, the city that Giuliano ruled, but rather would be in the city of Rome, where Giuliano actually lived and spent most of his time. He obviously sold Leonardo on the idea that he would be able to enjoy the fruits of the Medici's remarkable successes of late, and that working in close concert with the court of Leonardo X would have its benefits.

Things moved fairly quickly once an agreement between patron and painter had been confirmed. On Dec. 1, 1513, rooms in the Vatican's Belvedere Palace were being prepared for his use, and Leonardo seems to have occupied them soon after that. In July of 1514, Leonardo writes that he's been working in a studio provided for him by Giuliano de' Medici, although he doesn't indicate the project that he's working on.

But it seems that his earliest responsibilities revolved around a familiar theme, for in addition to overseeing affairs in the city of Florence, his patron, Giuliano de'Medici, was also the head of the papal militia. Leonardo's experience in military matters, as an engineer who had helped fortify Cesare Borgia's strongholds back in 1502, now came in handy. In September of 1514 he visited the cities of Parma and Civitavecchia. Civitavecchia was of particular importance, and Leonardo designed improvements for the port town, which were greatly needed. A few months later, in December of 1514, he combined his interests in civil engineering and hydraulics by drawing up plans to drain the mosquito-infested marshes that lay south of Rome.

Many have argued that Leonardo occupied a good portion of his time helping out with the project to rebuild the church that was now being called New St. Peter's. Donato Bramante, his old colleague, was still hard at work there. Bramante's central plan for the church was still being followed pretty closely, and the core of St. Peter's was already considered a modern day marvel, thanks to his references to classical Roman architecture—like the fluted pilasters and antique capitals and horizontal entablatures above, and, of course, the Neoplatonic central plan that he employed. But Bramante was eight years older than Leonardo, and his health was failing so badly that he would die within a year.

Raphael probably endorsed the addition of Leonardo to the papal court in Rome, although by now he had made a name for himself as the best painter in the city and was considered by some to be superior to Leonardo in his innovative approaches to figures and scenes. Paintings like the *School of Athens*, completed one year before Leonardo arrived in Rome, had made Raphael the toast of the town.

We remember that in this painting that Raphael had envisioned a perfect ancient court, filled with history's greatest intellectuals. But Raphael was also commenting here on the great collection of thinkers currently working in Rome during the High Renaissance of the early 16th century. As befitting one who was so deeply enmeshed in court culture, Raphael was the perfect person to comment on this. He did so ingeniously by including portraits of his fellow Vatican courtiers in the guise of those ancient thinkers. We've already seen Leonardo as Plato and Michelangelo as Heraclitus, the poet. But Raphael also painted Bramante as the stooping figure of Euclid, Perugino as the painter, Protogenes, and himself as Apelles, the Greek court artist in the service of Alexander the Great.

Raphael, the silver-tongued courtier who painted life at the Renaissance court, became a favorite among his new Medici patrons. Indeed, the tables had now turned in favor of Raphael, who was now 30 years old when the 60-year-old Leonardo arrived in Rome. The old Florentine was now the visitor, and Raphael was the established power broker in the city.

The one superstar in Rome who could not have been terribly inspired by Leonardo's arrival was Michelangelo. Now Michelangelo had managed to detach himself from Pope Leo's court in order to concentrate on the tomb of Julius that he'd been forced to abandon in 1508. But with the completion of the frescoes on the ceiling of the Sistine Chapel in 1512, the sculptor could now concentrate on a few of those figures for the tomb. Right around 1515

Michelangelo completed two of them that were intended to ornament the monumental, freestanding mausoleum to the now-deceased pope.

The *Dying Slave* is a luscious example of Michelangelo's interest in a sensualized interpretation of the human figure. His earlier declarations that artists had the obligation to experiment with the natural order that God had created—first announced in his drawing of the Battle of Cascina—comes out clearly in this work: the accentuated contrapposto pose, the elongated torso, and the overly delicate handling of hands and figures reminds us of his drive to move beyond the static naturalism of his 15th-century predecessors—like old men, like Leonardo da Vinci, who slavishly copied only the things that they could see.

The figure of Moses was also carved for the tomb of Julius. Here, Michelangelo added a physical power to his Moses that conveyed the psychological intensity of the figure at the specific moment he had selected: Moses grasps the two tablets upon which have been written the Ten Commandments, and now rises up to address his followers, who have grown weak during their journey and now worship a golden calf—in direct defiance of God's law. According to scripture, Moses will smash these tablets in the next instant, and we can see the rage building up inside him as he prepares to vent his anger. It's a major achievement in the art of early 16th-century Italy, and it was admired by all who saw it in Michelangelo's studio.

Despite his fame, Michelangelo was the sort of person who tended to feel that one city wasn't big enough to hold both him and an equally famous competitor. There seems to have been very little contact between the two during Leonardo's Roman period, from 1513 to 1516.

Now one of the interesting issues that face us at this juncture is that we have no evidence that Giuliano gave Leonardo any artistic projects to work on, whatsoever. Scholars have tended to see Leonardo as something of an "advisor" to the artists and philosophers in the papal court at Rome, but we also have no evidence to suggest he actually conversed with his fellow court artists or, if he did, that they listened to what he had to say.

We do know from his sketchbooks that Leonardo designed costumes and temporary architectural structures for Medici parties and theatrical productions, most of which hinged on themes remarking on the family's status as the leading clan in Italy. This drawing in Venice shows Leonardo imagining a dance performance, presumably to be held at court, with women dressed in billowing garments and spinning around each other in poses that Botticelli had made famous in his painting of the *Primavera* in the early 1480s. The dancers balance on their toes, join hands over their heads, and turn in a clockwise, circling motion. One figure, echoing Botticelli's figure of Zephyr in the *Primavera*, comes racing in to join them, and the central dancer opens her position to allow that to happen. It's a wonderful study of motion and energy, and it builds upon the earlier work of a Florentine colleague from the 1470s. But where this drawing led Leonardo, we cannot say.

We also know that the dissections that Leonardo had conducted in Milan and Florence were continued when he arrived in Rome, despite the fact that Leonardo was now doing them quite literally under the nose of ecclesiastical authorities. That didn't deter him, at first, as Leonardo now focused more intensely than ever on the human fetus, the female reproductive system, and the spinal cord. His drawings became more direct and explicit, probably revealing the nature of his own scientific experiments to learn more about the origins of human life. But in order to do so, of course, Leonardo had to conduct the necessary dissections—and this was a touchy subject.

It's reported to us that, sometime in 1514, a research assistant was assigned to Leonardo by someone in the papal court—maybe Giuliano, maybe even the pope himself—and that this assistant began telling his superiors that Leonardo's studies were literally diabolical—the work of the devil.

We don't know if word of these accusations got back to Leonardo, whether he was warned by friends to watch his back, or whether he was asked by his patrons to cease and desist for the good of Leonardo's reputation. But we do know that Leonardo brought his anatomical studies to a halt shortly thereafter.

Although his medical research came to a close, his painterly work continued right along, unimpeded. Leonardo appears to have directed his energies toward at least one painting, and maybe as many as three simultaneously. At some point in the 15-teens, Leonardo once again took up the theme of the *Madonna and Child with St. Anne*.

This time, however, Leonardo chose to approach the problem not in the form of a drawing, but rather as a completed painting worthy of public display. Like his other works from this late period, we are not at all sure whether Leonardo had an owner or an audience in mind for this picture, for there are no documents connecting the painting with a specific patron or setting.

It may simply be that Leonardo, working for Giuliano de' Medici, considered the picture the property of his patron; or, Leonardo may have painted the image for himself as a grand experiment that he worked on while writing his *Treatise on Painting*. It would have been just like Leonardo to work out his ideas on a surface while writing his thoughts down on paper, and I rather like the idea that this picture was produced at literally the same time that he was describing optics, light, oil pigments, perspective, and the representation of nature in a three-dimensional way on a two-dimensional surface.

We remember that Leonardo had already addressed this basic conceptual theme. His cartoon of the subject, from about 1508 or so, focuses on the combination of Anne, Mary, Christ, and John the Baptist, with the two cousins interacting in the drawing's lower right corner. The pyramidal composition, beautifully mapped out in this finished drawing, features the gentle smiles of the two older women as the toddlers squiggle and squirm and fawn over each other.

The painting obviously has much in common with the cartoon, and reveals Leonardo's desire to continue working on this theme that had consumed him since at least 1501, when he had worked up this idea in the now-lost drawing that he exhibited in that one-man show to the general public from his studio in Santissima Annunziata.

Some of the painting's features are absolutely identical to those of the cartoon. The pyramid retains its place of primacy in the composition's center, grounding it and liberating Leonardo to place objects around it with ease. Three of the characters reappear here, with Anne, Mary, and the Christ child featured as the core players of the symbolic narrative. And the familiar atmospheric haze that we recognize as the sfumato effect informs the contours of both the figures in the foreground and the mystical, dissolving Alpine Mountains in the background.

But clear changes have been made here, as well. Now Mary bends at the waist and crosses over the torso of her mother. She reaches down with both arms to clutch her child, and now—instead of stabilizing the swimming Christ, as she does in the cartoon—now she tries to pull the baby back up into her arms and on her lap. And that's because the fourth character in the painting has been changed from John the Baptist now to a little lamb, the ears of which Jesus grabs hold of like a child grasping the handlebars of a tricycle.

Although the facial expressions of the women are still peaceful, and while Christ's return glance seems to be a cheerful one, the presence of the lamb indicates an ominous theme.

The lamb, in Leonardo's day, was an extremely important symbol, and could be read in two different ways. The first had to do with the moment from his adult life when Jesus descended into the River Jordan from the mountains of Palestine, which caused John the Baptist to look at him, see the dove of the holy spirit over his head, and exclaim, "Behold, the Lamb of God!" As the earlier cartoon from 1508 has the youthful John the Baptist positioned in this spot, there's a good chance that Leonardo references that particular moment, with the lamb standing in for the person who connects Jesus to this animal.

But the second symbol of the lamb was even more pronounced. The lamb was traditionally understood to be a sacrificial animal, slaughtered by followers of pre-Christian faiths as a gift to their gods. Now one of the main features of the early Christian church was to do away with blood sacrifices, and they interpreted Christ's crucifixion as the only sacrifice that was needed to appease God the Father. And, as such, Christ was seen as The One Sacrificial Lamb, killed on behalf of others in a ritualistic offering to the Almighty. Of the two interpretations of the symbolic importance of the lamb, this second one was the more common. And that suggests that Mary, here, reaches down to pull her son away from his impending death, as any altruistic mother would do. She mourns his passing at the crucifix, we know, so her impulses to save her little boy—that we see in Leonardo's picture—are consistent with the character sketch we have of her from the Gospel texts.

But what's equally important is the response of little Jesus, who not only embraces the lamb but slings his leg over its back as if to mount it and ride it off into the sunset. Leonardo tells us that Christ knew about his fate from the moment of his birth—and maybe even before that, at the time of his conception, at the moment of the Annunciation. Leonardo wants us to know that Christ accepted his destiny from the beginning, and even welcomed it, knowing what its implications were for the rest of humanity. He knew he had to die, for his death would save us all.

The painting is a sophisticated theological statement that makes clear what early Madonna paintings from the 1300s and 1400s had only alluded to: that images of Mary and the Christ child were intended to be a little bit sad, for they were supposed to be a reminder of Jesus's human nature—which, by necessity, must end in his death. Leonardo's picture represents the most explicit illustration of that sentiment, and in an extremely poignant way.

It's not hard to see that Leonardo took his time with this painting, and it was in his possession right up until his death in 1519: Significant areas have not been finished, and the blue draperies around Mary's lap seem to be in only a preliminary state. And this turn suggests that perhaps Leonardo produced it as a personal exercise—maybe as a way to put into practice the advice he was writing in his *Treatise on Painting*, or maybe just to paint a compositional concept that had been gnawing at him since his early days as a painter of Madonnas.

We've already heard about the report made by Antonio de Beatis in 1517 after he visited Leonardo's studio in France and spoke with the painter directly about the works there. Beatis noted that Leonardo was working on "a Florentine woman, made from nature at the insistence of Giuliano de'Medici; another, a picture of a young John the Baptist; and one of the

Madonna and Child, who take positions in the lap of Saint Anne; all of them are done perfectly."

One of these pictures is the *St. Anne Madonna* that we've just examined. The second is clearly the half-length, mischievous teenaged John the Baptist that Leonardo probably started earlier in his career, right around 1510, but which Leonardo never finished and never parted with. And the third is the *Mona Lisa*, to which we now return for one added layer of interpretation.

Recent archival discoveries by Josephine Rogers Mariotti indicate that the relationship between Giuliano de' Medici, Leonardo da Vinci, and the family of Mona Lisa Giocando was much closer than previously believed.

We now know that Lisa's husband, Francesco, was one of those Florentines working behind the scenes in 1512 to bring down the Republic, and that he was a staunch ally of the Medici during the coup d'état that brought Giuliano to power there. Francesco received payments from the Medici for years thereafter, and Francesco Giocando was clearly a Medici favorite in Florence.

It has been suggested that Giuliano de' Medici commissioned the portrait of Mona Lisa because, as Baldassare Castiglione notes in *The Book of the Courtier*, Giuliano was a poet—and the subject of many of his poems, in fact, was the virtue of women. Now Giuliano had in his court Leonardo da Vinci, an artist who had a track record of capturing the essence of women, as he did in the portraits of Cecilia Gallerani and Ginevra de' Benci. And thus, just as Ginevra de' Benci's portrait addressed the concept of the muse and her poet, in her case the Bembo, Mona Lisa's painting was commissioned by Giuliano de' Medici also as a muse to promote the notion that he was a poet on par with Bembo—and Dante and Petrarch, too—all of whom had their muses.

Now a few lectures ago, we noted that some of the stylistic choices made by Leonardo in the *Mona Lisa* point toward a period of execution in the 15-teens rather than the decade before.

This later dating may well be confirmed by Antonio de Beatis' statement that Giuliano commissioned the work, for the relationship between the Medici family and the Giocondo family at a crucial moment in the history of Florence during the 15-teens might help explain the advanced state of the sfumato approach in this picture. And, of course, the fact that Leonardo had it in his studio and on display for Beatis in 1517 suggests that this was the period of its production, rather than, or in addition to, the period from 1503 to 1506.

Another problem for us to end on has to do with Leonardo's own perceptions of his patrons and the life he was leading in Rome. On one hand, he enjoyed artistic freedoms that even he had never quite enjoyed. There were no major obligations or responsibilities for him to attend to, no pressing deadlines to meet, and no distasteful genuflections he had to make to pompous patrons—aside from having to stop the dissections he was conducting in his studio in 1514, Leonardo was pretty much free to do as he pleased.

But on the other hand, Leonardo himself, later in his life, made the rather cryptic remark that "The Medici made me and the Medici destroyed me." The first half of that statement seems pretty clear: Lorenzo the Magnificent had supported Leonardo in his bid to acquire a courtly patron in the figure of Ludovico Sforza back in 1482 and perhaps had saved Leonardo from prison long before that. But the second half of Leonardo's comment is more difficult to understand, for we have no record of any significant conflict or dispute between Leonardo and either Giuliano or Pope Leonardo X. We just don't know what happened to make him feel betrayed by the Medici family.

It could have been because this was the time when his pursuit of anatomical studies was ground to a halt, and I can certainly understand why that would've bothered him. But I suspect it may have had more to do with the fact that, in 1516, no one in the papal court of Leonardo X made any attempt to retain his services when his patron, Giuliano de'Medici, died unexpectedly. Maybe Leonardo blamed them for the chain of events that ultimately took him away from his homeland forever.

And we'll soon see how and why Leonardo left Rome, and all of Italy, taking the High Renaissance to the unknown valley of the Loire River in the northern European court of King Francois I of France.

High Renaissance Art from Rome to Venice

Lecture 32

During the 1510s, a new generation of painters, sculptors, and architects adopted and disseminated this classical style that we now refer to as High Renaissance, which was largely Leonardo's creation. These included other Florentine artists like Raphael, but they also included the breakout artists of the Venetian Renaissance, like Giovanni Bellini, Giorgione, and Titian, who were the first painters to bring naturalism to an artistic tradition heavily influenced by the Byzantine world.

Leonardo's Artistic Principles

- Leonardo's artistic legacy in Italy was felt from Rome to Venice. Even in cities he only visited briefly, he changed the way art was seen and valued forever. The ideas and concepts that Leonardo embraced became popular among an entire generation of skilled and innovative artists.

- A few things mattered deeply to Leonardo when it came to painting: that compositions were focused and balanced; that figures were properly proportioned; that their motions and gestures were believable; that natural forms and objects were emphasized; that perspective was correct; and that grace and elegance dominated the whole image.

- Leonardo had many imitators. These painters generally tried too hard to copy both the style and the substance of his work and captured neither very well.

- Sometimes entire compositions were lifted by Leonardo's admirers, but usually these quotations added some features that made them, at the very least, interesting to viewers.

- What is particularly interesting is that Leonardo was able to influence so many artists in so many different Italian artistic centers. One place that was unusually keen to borrow Leonardo's ideas was Venice, where he had visited briefly in 1500.

Venetian Art in the Early 16th Century

- Venice had a long and complicated history as both the westernmost city of the Byzantine Empire and the easternmost outpost of the Italian culture.

- Venice had a longstanding tradition of mercantile ingenuity, territorial ambitions, and lots and lots of money, but until the very end of the 15th century, its art had been tightly bound up with medieval Byzantine traditions.

- A couple of decades after the fall of Constantinople in 1453, Venetian painters and audiences finally became comfortable naturalistic representations in art. The painter who did the most to bring this about was **Giovanni Bellini**.

- Bellini was admirably prolific during his career, which was from the early 1460s until his death in 1516. His *Madonna of the Meadow*, from about 1500, provides a nice example of his mature work. It uses a pyramidal composition, sfumato, and an elegance of forms and gestures. Bellini had the ability to paint lovingly, carefully, and slowly by using oil glazes, as Leonardo had.

- Venetians could not take the same approach to their art as their Florentine colleagues. Frescos did not hold together well in the salty air of the lagoon, and pictures on wood panels tended to warp within mere years of completion. So by 1500, Venetian painters had become adept at employing oil paints on canvas.

- This also meant that Venetian artists were often less interested in drawing figures on their canvases because pencils tend to jump around on uneven surfaces. Venetian painters made their preparatory drawings in sketchbooks but then translated them a little more freely onto canvas. Hence in Venetian painting of the High Renaissance, we tend to see a looser handling of paint and an emphasis on color and brushstroke over detail.

Giorgione and Titian—Rebel Sons

- Among the very best Venetian painters during Leonardo's lifetime was a young and highly enigmatic artist known today as **Giorgione**. His meteoric rise to prominence was matched only by his sharp and inexplicable departure from the art world sometime around 1510 when the so-called *Dresden Venus* was completed.

- Giorgione was active from the late 1490s, and it is no small matter that one of Leonardo's stops in 1500 was in Venice. In Giorgione's paintings, we can see quotations from Leonardo's precedents. *The Old Woman*, complete with disheveled hair, plain dress, and beleaguered face, is utterly inconceivable without Leonardo's caricatures.

- Giorgione's painting of a woman in the guise of Laura, the muse of the 14th-century poet **Francesco Petrarch**, captures the figure in the same three-quarter pose as Leonardo's *Ginevra de' Benci*, gives her a similar facial expression, and employs a deep tenebrism to soften the contours of his figure. Giorgione combines the best elements of Leonardo's Florentine and Milanese styles.

- The softness of Giorgione's was also employed by an even more accomplished painter named **Titian**, who was Giorgione's contemporary and perhaps his partner at the end of Giorgione's life. They borrowed heavily from each other (and from Leonardo)—so much so that art historians often have a hard time deciding which one of them painted which pictures.

- *The Concert in the Open Air* has been attributed to both Giorgione and Titian, separately and as a joint production. We see Leonardo's influence in the central core of the composition and the attention to the details of the natural world. There is also an undeniably erotic component to the picture that recalls Leonardo's *Leda*.

- Titian's debts to Leonardo sometimes appear in more subtle ways. One of his earliest paintings, made for a Venetian official in 1514, is an allegory called *Sacred and Profane Love*. Titian emphasizes the nude female form, using the same twisting pose from *Leda* and the *Concert*. The landscape has the atmospheric haze of Leonardo's earliest works from Florence. The figures incline their bodies toward each other in a way reminiscent of Leonardo's *Annunciation*, and between them is positioned a marble object—not a lectern this time, but a fountain.

- Titian seemed uncomfortable relying on formula, and his entire career, which lasted until 1576, can be interpreted as a massive trajectory of innovation and change. Among his most important inventions was the **figure-eight composition**, which he developed at about the same time that Raphael was working on something similar in Rome.

- Titian's altarpiece for the Franciscan church of Santa Maria Gloriosa dei Frari in Venice is a large lunette-shaped picture that depicts the Assumption. Mary rises toward Heaven, surrounded by apostles, who marvel at her ascent. As she moves, Mary begins to twist, forming a midair contrapposto. Her arms are slightly elevated, and their alignment leads us through and around the composition.

- Whether by coincidence or because he had been influenced by Titian, Raphael used the same compositional idea in his *Transfiguration of Christ*, which was largely painted in 1516 but completed after Raphael's death in 1520 by an assistant named **Giulio Romano**.

- In this moment from the Bible, Jesus levitates and begins to speak to apparitions of the Old Testament patriarchs Moses and Elijah, much to the surprise of Peter, John, and James, who cower beneath him. Christ's outstretched arms lead the eye around the image.

- Both of these artists embraced Leonardo's decree for balance and clarity, but they also experimented with ways to reduce the rigidity of Leonardo's classical pyramid. They injected movement, energy, and physicality in ways that not even Leonardo had foreseen.

- They also were not replicating something viewers already knew from personal experiences but attempting to excite the soul and elevate the mind by showing viewers things they had never dreamed possible.

Raphael and Andrea del Sarto—Obedient Students

- Raphael's approach to painting solidified Leonardo's theories of art in the most successful way. He became an accomplished and highly sought-after portrait painter who knew how to capture the essence of his fellow courtiers with neither flattery nor fiction.

- Raphael's religious pictures were equally peaceful. His *Sistine Madonna* is both dependent on Leonardo's rules for painting and a departure from his preferred approach. The composition is balanced, with Mary and Christ at the core, but Raphael omitted both the evocative atmospheric qualities and all references to a landscape because the scene takes place in Heaven.

- One artist generally considered a tremendous advocate of the High Renaissance style was **Andrea del Sarto**, who worked in Florence during the 1510s and 1520s. He was a follower of Raphael and, by extension, Leonardo.

- *The Madonna of the Harpies*, an altarpiece painted for a Florentine convent in 1517, contains a balanced composition through an elevated core. The figures poses, movements, and gestures, while highly elegant, are not strained or unnatural. The painter uses light expertly, models his figures in a naturalistic way, and he creates a believable space. His *Last Supper* for the Church of San Salvi is similar but not identical to Leonardo's version.

© Photos.com/Thinkstock.

Andrea del Sarto's *Madonna of the Harpies* shows Leonardo's influence.

- The demands that Leonardo placed on artists came in a variety of formats, but none of those came from his actual writings, which were kept closely guarded in his studio until well after his death. Mostly, these ideas were conveyed by Leonardo through the paintings themselves.

- Later, when successive generations of painters began to move in a different direction than was being charted by Raphael and Titian, it was Leonardo that they used as their foil.

Important Term

figure-eight composition: Created simultaneously by Raphael and Titian, a compositional pattern that causes the eye to move in a circular interweave across a picture's design.

Names to Know

Bellini, Giovanni (c. 1430–1516): Painter and son of another important artist, Jacopo Bellini, Giovanni pioneered the oil technique in Venice through his depictions of Madonnas and landscapes. He was the master of Titian and influenced Giorgione with his subtle forms and balanced compositions.

Giorgione (a.k.a. **Giorgio da Castelfranco**; c. 1476/8–1510): The extraordinary career of this talented Venetian artist was mysteriously cut short in 1510, yet his allegorical pictures remain among the period's most innovative and influential paintings, and his employment of oil paint was rivaled only by that of his master, Giovanni Bellini, and his colleague Titian.

Petrarch, Francesco (1304–1374): Bibliophile, poet, and philosopher, and one of the founders of early modern humanism. A keen student of ancient Roman history, Petrarch helped revive the study of antique Latin during the 14th century.

Romano, Giulio (1499–1546): Painter and printmaker of great creativity and ingenuity who trained with Raphael and spent his youth assisting his master on the frescoes painted inside the Vatican Stanze. Romano left Rome after Raphael's death and spent 10 years designing and decorating the Palazzo del Te in Mantua.

Sarto, Andrea del (1486–1530): Follower of Raphael and Leonardo who worked in the classical idiom, primarily in Florence. His best-known work is *The Madonna of the Harpies* (1517).

Titian (a.k.a. **Tiziano Vecellio**; c. 1488/90–1576): Along with Giorgione, Titian is widely regarded as the greatest of all Venetian painters. After completing his studies with Giovanni Bellini around 1510, he went on to produce a series of highly influential oil paintings on canvas, including the *Assumption of the Virgin* for the church of the Frari, the *Venus of Urbino* in the Uffizi Gallery, and a series of portraits of Holy Roman Emperor Charles V.

Suggested Reading

Farago, "'Three ducats in Venice.' Connecting Giorgione and Leonardo."

Goffen, *Renaissance Rivals*.

Rosand, *Painting in Cinquecento Venice.*

High Renaissance Art from Rome to Venice

Lecture 32—Transcript

Before we follow Leonardo to France, I think it's highly useful—essential, even—to take a broader look at the artistic legacy that Leonardo would leave behind him Italy. His influence was felt all across the countryside, from Rome to Venice, and the lessons he taught his fellow painters changed the way art was made, changed the way art was seen, and changed the way art was valued forever.

Leonardo da Vinci was in effect the elder statesman of Italian art when he prepared for his departure from Rome in the spring and summer of 1516. He had spent three years in Rome thinking about anatomy, flight, and hydraulics, but also about the intellectual merits of his original vocation—the art of painting. He had reputedly consulted with the artists and courtiers working for the pope in the Vatican, counseling and advising them as they moved forward with their projects.

And Rome in the 15-teens was at the very center of European culture. With Raphael and Michelangelo and Bramante there, Leonardo had the ability to mold and shape the solutions that artists settled on when considering their artistic problems, and it is my intention with this lecture to demonstrate how this impact was felt among his colleagues, in and out of Rome, as the most celebrated painter in the Western world.

Naturally, Leonardo had his followers. In fact, the ideas and concepts that Leonardo embraced were becoming popular among an entire generation of skilled and innovative artists from Sicily to the Alps. His formula for replicating the natural world in brush strokes and pigments caught hold all across the Italian boot in the decades that framed the turn of the century.

Let's review those principles here. First Leonardo made it quite clear, in both his paintings and in his writings about paintings, that a few things mattered to him deeply. He wanted to make sure that compositions were focused. He valued the pyramid above all things, but second to that, he looked for general balance. The proportions of figures had to be correct. The motions of had to be identifiable and believable. Gestures had to be taken from observed examples, and nature simply had to be the guide for whatever decisions the artist would make. Natural forms and objects had to be emphasized. And perspective had to be correct. And grace and elegance had to dominate.

The artistic style employed by painters in the High Renaissance generally revolved around these rules of painting, and if they didn't, then they fell outside Leonardo's paradigm of what constituted worthy art. Leonardo had many imitators. These tended to be painters who tried almost too hard to copy both the style and the substance of his work, and who wound up capturing neither very well. As Galileo said, there were those who knew Leonardo's rules but could not paint a stool.

This *Nursing Madonna* by an anonymous painter shows us the monumental Virgin and bulky Christ child that Leonardo had preferred during his early days in Florence, and the mountainous background interrupted by the large central tree recall both his landscapes of the 1470s and the massive core of that first *Madonna of the Rocks* from the mid-1480s. But the figures are stilted and awkward, as the strange, twisting body of Christ bears no semblance of naturalism whatsoever, and the faces of both figures have little to do with the structural qualities of the human head that Leonardo knew so well. Moreover, there's an emotional detachment between these figures that matches their figural rigidity, and that tells us that this painter just doesn't quite understand what Leonardo is all about.

Similarly, the painter of the woman who emerges from the darkness depends heavily on Leonardo's Milanese portraits. The figure's shoulder and forehead leap from that murky background lit by spotlights that shine off her skin, and her lowered, almost demure eyelids focus her gaze down to the lower right. We're not sure who she is—maybe she's Mary Magdalene in her pre-repentant state as a prostitute—but she has been modeled on Cecilia Gallerani's tenebristic portrait, along with the deeply introspective figure of Christ in Leonardo's *Last Supper*. Why exactly she appears before us is not entirely clear in the painting, and neither her state of nudity nor the dramatic apparition of her body make much sense as a result. It's a sensitive portrayal of nude figure, that but, it is also a largely derivative painting that shows us an anonymous artist who knows what he's supposed to be doing, but isn't exactly sure how or why he's doing it.

In fact, the ideas and concepts that Leonardo embraced were becoming popular among an entire generation of skilled and innovative artists from Sicily to the Alps, and the formula for replicating the natural world through brush strokes and pigments caught hold all across the Italian boot in the decades that framed the turn of the century.

We've already seen the influence that Leonardo had on his colleagues in Florence, like Lorenzo di Credi, and also in Milan during the late 15th and early 16th centuries. Sometimes entire compositions were lifted by Leonardo's admirers, as we can see here in Lorenzo di Credi's theft of the Annunciation composition in this smaller panel from right around 1480 or so. But usually these quotations added some features that made them, at the very least, interesting to viewers who were seeking a little originality from their artists—in this case a genuflecting Virgin, a lectern that divides the Madonna and angel somewhat equally, and a more pronounced set of benches to the far left that serve as orthogonals back into the distance.

What's particularly interesting is that Leonardo was able to influence so many artists in so many different Italian artistic centers, for he inspired the imaginations of painters not only Milan and Florence and Rome, where he spent most of his time, but in other places, too. And, in fact, one of the artistic centers in Italy that was unusually keen to borrow Leonardo's ideas was that of Venice.

Now we've encountered Venice in passing in this course already. It was the place where Leonardo had briefly visited in 1500, and it had a long and complicated history as both the westernmost city of the Byzantine Empire and the easternmost outpost of the Italian peninsula. The city in the lagoon had a longstanding tradition of mercantile ingenuity, territorial ambitions, and lots and lots of money. But until the middle of the 15th century, its artistic traditions had been tightly bound up with the distinctly old-fashioned approaches taken by Byzantine artists of the Middle Ages.

It was only a couple decades after the fall of Constantinople in 1453 that Venetian painters and audiences became comfortable with the idea that naturalistic representations were just as meaningful as those passed down by tradition. And the one painter who did the most to bring the city and its cultural leaders into the early modern age was the artist Giovanni Bellini.

Born in 1430, Bellini realized the potency of treating that the picture as windows onto space, where the eye could happily deceive the brain if invited to do so. Bellini captured as well as anyone of his age the delicacy of the human figure, the textures of clothing, and the luminosity of light and shadow, Bellini ushered into the Venetian visual vocabulary the same basic principles that Leonardo da Vinci had promoted in Florence and Milan and Rome.

Bellini was admirably prolific during his career, which spanned six decades from the early 1460 until his death in 1516. The *Madonna of the Meadow*, from about 1500, provides a nice example of his mature work from the very middle of the High Renaissance. Mary and Christ sit in the middle of a northern Italian landscape: The flat middle ground is reminiscent of the territory surrounding Venice on terra firma, while mountain tops can be seen off in the deep distance. There's a certain softness of forms and facial features that indicates Bellini's use of Leonardo's sfumato technique, and the natural elegance of gestures indicates an attention to the behavior of human beings in the real world.

And Bellini has the ability to paint areas—both large and small—lovingly, carefully, and slowly, employing the approach used by Leonardo of layering glazes of pigment one at a time over areas of his picture to build up colors, shadows, and but also microscopic details.

Looking at this Madonna by Bellini, we can see the Venetian working toward the same ends that Leonardo strived to attain. Both wanted to produce figures and settings that brought viewers into a believable space in an effort to entice them to have a familiar experience with the image in an effort to spark an effective devotional moment in the hearts and minds and imaginations of worshipers.

Bellini's picture places the Virgin behind a marbleized ledge and emerging from a deep, dark background akin to Leonardo's portraits of courtiers and mistresses from the 1480s and 1490s. She has very little emotional stake in the fact that her child sprawls out on that ledge, and this might be due to that highly formalized Byzantine tradition of gold-ground icons that so informed Venetian painting right through the 15th century. Still, the monumentality of the Madonna, her technically expert facial features, and the employment of that tenebristic relationship between lights and shadows reveals Bellini's adherence to Leonardo's laws of classicism. Of course, we need to remember that this particular interest could also be connected the art of Antonello da Messina and the Northern European painters who so expertly produced these types of paintings—but the closer proximity of Leonardo—in Milan at the time this picture was probably produced—suggests to me that he was probably the greater influence.

Now we have noticed some of the ways that the style of Leonardo changed from place to place. His early works in Florence were largely based on the laws of draftsmanship that Verrocchio taught him in the workshop. These laws were followed faithfully by the other artists who learned and painted alongside Leonardo during the 1460s and 1470s, like Domenico Ghirlandaio, whose *Sassetti Altarpiece* I show you here, and Sandro Botticelli, whose famous *Birth of Venus* appears here—both of them probably painted in the middle of the 1480s. These Florentines emphasized sharp contours to their figures, distinctive outlines that set them apart from other figures and areas in the composition, and a bright palette that allowed them to use colors that made the surface seem to jump out at viewers.

The difference, though, was that Ghirlandaio and Botticelli and their Florentine contemporaries never really advanced beyond this stage. Even in works produced during their maturity they neither ever grew or nor changed according to what they were seeing coming out of other artistic centers beyond the borders of the Florentine state. This work by Botticelli from the late 1490s, called the *Calumny of Apelles*, still has him replicating both his own style of the 1470s and even the same figures from the 1480s, including the nude female form he had used in his *Birth of Venus*. It's a harsh picture, filled with animosity and even paranoia that were born of his own allegiance to Fra Savonarola and his reactionary movement of the mid-1490s.

This is how they painted for pretty much the duration of their careers, and while they're good and talented artists, neither one of them can compare to Leonardo's sense of ingenuity, daring, and innovation.

Venetians, however, couldn't take the same approach to their art that their Florentine colleagues could down in Tuscany. In a climate so damp and humid, and with air so salty from the Mediterranean Sea in which they lived, Venetians had very little success with fresco paintings, which didn't hold together very well in that climate, and they had an equally tough time producing pictures on wood panels, which tended to warp within only years of completion. It's really hard and really rare to find a wood panel in Venice from before 1450; and even though a few have managed to survive, most were ruined by a climate that has very little patience for wood.

So, by 1500, Venetian painters had become adept at employing oil paints on canvas surfaces—oil, because it was malleable and not as susceptible to damage in harsh climates, and canvas because it was innately flexible: Their paintings wouldn't bend, and the pigments they used wouldn't crack and flake off of it.

But this also meant that Venetian artists were often less interested in drawing figures on their canvas surfaces for, as you know, canvas tends to be bumpy, and pencils will jump around on uneven surfaces. Venetian painters came to be trained to make their drawings in sketchbooks, and then to translate those drawings a little more freely on the canvas when they took to painting them with pigments.

Hence, in Venetian painting of the High Renaissance, we tend to see a looser handling of paint than we do in pictures by artists working in Florence or Milan or Rome. They weren't as tied to the demands of linearity as their peers in central Italy, and thus they emphasized color and brushstroke over detail.

Among the very best of the painters that Venice had to offer during Leonardo's lifetime was a young and, in fact, highly enigmatic artist known today as Giorgione. Born only in 1477 or so, Giorgione's meteoric rise to prominence in Venice was matched only by his sharp and inexplicable departure from it, sometime around 1510, when this picture of the so-called *Dresden Venus* was completed.

Giorgione was active only from the late 1490s, so his most mature works coincide precisely with Leonardo's nomadic period after his flight from Milan. And it's no small matter that one of Leonardo's stops in 1500 was in Venice, where the painter unquestionably came into contact with the art and artists of that city, including Giorgione, and where Leonardo both influenced this new generation of painters that he met and was influenced by the Venetian interest in brushstroke and color and luminosity.

In Giorgione's paintings, we can see some rather direct quotations from Leonardo's precedents. The painting of the elderly woman, complete with disheveled hair, plain dress, and beleaguered face, are utterly inconceivable without the caricatures by Leonardo and his explorations of different human types in his sketches and in his paintings. The unfinished pictures of *St. Jerome* and the *Adoration of the Magi* from about 1480 come immediately to mind as large-scale works in this genre.

Even more obvious is Giorgione's decision to paint a picture of this woman in the guise of Laura, the muse of the 14th-century poet Francesco Petrarch. Giorgione captures this striking figure in the same three-quarter pose as Leonardo's *Ginevra*, gives her a similar facial expression, and even arranges the branches and leaves in the form of a halo around his sitter's head in a way that recalls Leonardo's similar solution. But he also employs that deep tenebristic quality to the picture by having Laura emerge from that pitch-black setting. And this, in turn, helps the artist soften the contours of his figure to give her a suppleness that makes her a sympathetic character for viewers. Giorgione combines the best elements of Leonardo's Florentine and Milanese styles to create his image of Laura.

The softness of Giorgione's figures, in turn, was employed by an even more accomplished painter named Titian, who was Giorgione's contemporary and, perhaps, his partner at the end of Giorgione's life. Now the impulses of Titian, who was born in 1488, were initially quite similar to those of Giorgione. The two of them borrowed heavily from each other (and from Leonardo)—so much so that art historians often have a hard time deciding which one of them painted which pictures. The *Concert in the Open Air* has been attributed to both Giorgione and Titian, separately and as a joint production, due to confusion over painterly styles and artistic impulses. For our purposes, though, the subject and the poses are what matter.

The *Concert* contains some basic High Renaissance ideals, but also shows a willingness to expand upon them somewhat. There's certainly a central core to this composition, what with the four figures occupying the middle of the field, and they've been arranged in a balanced way that helps our eye move around that core pretty easily.

Light illuminates all four characters, with special attention placed on the nude female forms, who most of us now believe represent the muses of the two musicians who play their lutes together in this summer picnic.

The painter, or the painters, understand how to capture the natural world, and they obey the rules of the High Renaissance by depicting grass, trees, clouds, and the deep distance according to the guidelines set forth by Leonardo and also by Giovanni Bellini.

But there's also, undeniably, an erotic component to this picture, which we see appearing in paintings with increasing frequency as the 16th century progresses. Those nude bodies, even if they are visions in the minds of two youthful musicians, appear before our eyes literally and full-bodied, and it's tough for us to ignore those curvaceous figures.

I don't think it's too difficult to find a precedent in the work of Leonardo da Vinci. His designs for the figure of Leda, which were later transferred to a painting that was lost in the 17th century, not only form the precedent for the appearance of the nude figures in this picture, but quite literally influence the actual pose of the standing muse to the left.

Even during his own lifetime, Leonardo's Leda was provoking artists to begin spending time drawing the nude from life; and the nude models they were drawing to practice and improve upon their abilities to capture the human form in a naturalistic way were both male and female models. And this was a dramatic departure from the old days, when such a practice would've been considered not only highly inappropriate, but borderline litigious. Leonardo's lost painting of *Leda and the Swan*, and the drawings that led up to it, were profoundly influential for the creation of this burgeoning genre of erotic painting that, by the end of the 16th century, would form a key element of the visual arts in Europe.

Titian, just as much as Giorgione, looked to Leonardo for inspiration, but his debts sometimes came out in more subtle ways. One of Titian's earliest paintings was for a Venetian official, painted in 1514. It's called the *Sacred and Profane Love*, and the allegorical picture reminds us of a Leonardo composition.

Again, Titian emphasizes the nude female form, and does so with the same twisting pose that we've seen in the *Leda* and in the *Concert*. But he now focuses on only two figures in his beautifully appointed landscape, which has the same atmospheric haze seen in Leonardo's earliest works from Florence. The women incline their bodies toward each other in a way reminiscent of the Annunciation, and between them is positioned a marble object—not a lectern this time, but rather a fountain that represents love.

It's probably an allegory of virtue; the Nude figure, unadorned and needing absolutely no artificial accessories to beautify her, is Sacred Love. The clothed one, conversely, represents Profane, or merely erotic love. Those things which are holy and true can be understood and appreciated with no additional ornamentation whatsoever, while those things that are base and earthy can only be enjoyed after they've been burnished and dandified. It's a surprising twist on the subject, as I think most people today would assume that it's the other way round.

High Renaissance paintings are all different, of course, and the people who painted them had their own interests to pursue and their own clients to please. But when you look at a picture produced between about 1480 and another from about 1520, chances are pretty good that you're going to see a lot of the things that we've just noted about these horizontal paintings by Leonardo and Titian.

But that's not to say that the High Renaissance was a period of repetition or rigid adherence to rules. Titian himself seemed uncomfortable relying on formula, and his entire career, which lasted until 1576, can be interpreted as a massive trajectory of innovation and change. Among his most important inventions was the so-called figure-eight composition, which Titian developed at just about the same time that his older contemporary, Raphael, was also working on something similar in Rome.

Between about 1516 and 1518, Titian produced this very large altarpiece for the Franciscan church of Santa Maria Gloriosa dei Frari in Venice; it's truly one of the singular masterpieces of High Renaissance painting anywhere on the planet, and fortunately it may still be seen today in its original setting in the sanctuary of the Frari.

The large lunette-shaped picture rises up from the choir of the Franciscan church, and it's framed by windows that add a natural light source to the supernatural one that Titian paints. The Virgin Mary has been depicted on her flight up into heaven—it's her Assumption—and she's surrounded by apostles who marvel at her ascent. As she moves, Mary begins to twist in her own space, creating a contrapposto pose in midair that suggests she's actually standing on that cloudbank beneath her, even though you and I both know that clouds can't support a human being. But that's not just any old cloud, as a flash of light announces that she's being born aloft by a supernatural force that can defy all logical explanation from mere mortals—like us.

Mary's arms are elevated to form visual lines that lead us through and around the composition, and as we follow the path of Titian's composition, including those gesturing apostles at its base, we realize that we are no longer looking at a classically oriented, High Renaissance composition. Instead, we have before us a figure-eight design, filled with movement and energy, that cause our eye to move up and around and back and forth across this picture—but still doing so within the framework of a stable setting. It is a groundbreaking and exciting elaboration on Leonardo's classical theme, and it announces that a break with the old master is about to occur.

Whether by coincidence or because he had been influenced by Titian, Raphael was also working out exactly the same ideas in his painting of the *Transfiguration of Christ*, which was largely painted in 1516, but was only completed after Raphael's death in 1520, by an assistant named Giulio Romano.

In his picture, painted for a Medici cardinal in Rome, Raphael focused on the scene of the Transfiguration of Christ, a moment when Jesus suddenly levitates off the ground and begins to speak to apparitions of Old Testament patriarch Moses and Elijah—much to the surprise of Peter, John, and James who cower beneath Christ, on that little hill there.

Just as we see in Titian's picture, Raphael has employed a not-so-subtle figure-eight design that leads us from Christ's outstretched arms, back down through his body, and on below, where a new set of arms reach out to help carry our eye down and around and back up again on the other side. Like *The Assumption of the Virgin* in Titian's Venetian work, Raphael's *Transfiguration* announces a departure from the rules that Leonardo had so forcefully presented. While both of these artists have embraced Leonardo's decree for balance and clarity, they've also experimented with ways to reduce the rigidity of Leonardo's classical pyramid and his overly attentive focus on balance.

These painters inject movement and energy and physicality into their forms in ways that not even Leonardo had foreseen, and their impulse was not to ground figures in a setting that merely replicated something viewers already knew from previous experience, but rather to excite the soul and elevate the mind by showing viewers things they'd never dreamed possible.

We've already spoken a little bit about Raphael in this course, as his early career in Florence was unquestionably influenced by Leonardo's ideas and works, and his transfer to Rome in 1508 helped secure that city as the artistic successor to Constantinople in Christian culture.

Because we're now talking about the High Renaissance in Italy during the first two decades of the 16th century, it's time to return briefly to him, for it's Raphael's approach to painting that solidified Leonardo's theories of art in the most successful way.

Like Leonardo, who earned the trust primarily of women orbiting around Ludovico Sforza, Raphael became an accomplished and highly sought after portrait painter. His portrait of Pope Leo X with two cardinals, show us the ease with which Raphael captured his human subjects, the delicacy of his handling of line and pigment, and the way the courtier knew how to capture the essence of his fellow courtiers with neither flattery nor fiction.

Raphael's religious pictures were equally peaceful, as we can see in the so-called *Sistine Madonna*, painted in 1513 to honor the memory of his first papal patron, Julius II. The picture is both dependent on Leonardo's rules for painting and a departure from his preferred approach.

The composition is certainly balanced, with Mary and Christ standing not only in the picture's center, but in an elevated position that causes both the figures around them and our own eyes to lift them up and hold them at the core. The flanking saints and the two angels below circle around the main characters, and I think Leonardo would have appreciated the theatrical curtains that are pulled back in the upper corners to reveal this vision to the viewer.

But Raphael has omitted both the evocative atmospheric qualities that Leonardo loved so much, and all references to a landscape that could've helped us see the natural world, which Leonardo felt was the sole painter's guide. Granted it's a scene that takes place in Heaven, which is, by definition, a supernatural world, but I think Leonardo would've been a little ambivalent about this picture when he saw it.

One artist generally considered to be a tremendous advocate of the High Renaissance style was Andrea del Sarto, who worked in Florence during the 15-teens and 1520s. He was a follower of Raphael and, by extension, a disciple of Leonardo.

The *Madonna of the Harpies*, an altarpiece painted for a Florentine convent in 1517, contains some of those now familiar forms that we expect to see in a High Renaissance painting. There's a balance to the composition that's created by an elevated core, flanking saints of similar postures, and a series of poses and movements and gestures that, while highly elegant, are not strained or unnatural. Andrea del Sarto uses light expertly, he models his figures in a naturalistic way, and he creates a believable space in which his forms reside. This picture gets the seal of approval from the High Renaissance panel of judges.

Andrea del Sarto was not only a disciple of Raphael, though, but also an ardent admirer of Leonardo da Vinci. We can see quite clearly his deep interest in Leonardo's precedents in a number of his pictures, and perhaps best of all in his *Last Supper* for the church of San Salvi, the home of Verrocchio's *Baptism of Christ* that includes Leonardo's angel.

That long table, covered with the white cloth, provides the barrier behind which sit all the actors on the stage, arranged in a fashion that's similar to, but not identical with, Leonardo's version in Santa Maria delle Grazie. Andrea acknowledges the mastery of Leonardo's painting by trying to replicate the various individual responses of the apostles to the news of Christ's betrayal, and we see the action transpiring inside a room that has some of the same features of the one painted in Milan.

Leonardo formulated the basic principles of the classical style that informed the High Renaissance as a cultural period, and he was powerfully influential during his own lifetime. The demands that Leonardo placed on artists came in a variety of formats, but none of those included his actual writings, which were kept closely guarded in his studio until well after his death. Mostly, these ideas were conveyed by Leonardo through the paintings he made—especially his public pictures of the *Annunciation*, *The Last Supper*, and the *Battle of Anghiari*—but he also showcased his ideas through the drawings that he exhibited publicly and displayed privately. Mostly by example, Leonardo laid down some very basic rules, and he consistently abided by them in his own work.

And later, when successive generations of painters began to move in a different direction that was being charted by Raphael and Titian during his own lifetime, it was Leonardo that they used as their foil, believing that he had already perfected his style and had left little room for them to develop. And that, while backhanded, may be the greatest compliment any artist can receive from his peers.

In the next lecture, we'll follow Leonardo to France.

Last Years—Leonardo in France

Lecture 33

Late in his life and amidst the turmoil of European politics in the early 16th century, Leonardo received an invitation to take his talents to the French court of François I. There he spent the last years of his life working on some of his most famous paintings—including not quite finishing the *Mona Lisa*—and advising on architectural projects. But his real purpose at François's court was to lend polish to a kingdom that was, culturally, far behind its peers.

Rome in Decline, France in Ascendance

- Leonardo's time in Italy permanently ended in 1516. For 64 years, he had thrived in an environment that was fluid and unstable: The Pandora's box opened by Alexander VI in 1494 had not been closed by Julius II.

- Pope Leonardo X inherited a realm still under threat by France, the Holy Roman Empire, Spain, England, and even Venice, all of whom used agents, spies, assassins, and armed forces to wrest control from each other in an ever-shifting web of alliances and leagues.

- The northern powers were now wise to the papacy's needs and strategies. They began working to undermine Rome's authority, and a number of people began to listen. Leonardo X was soon deeply in debt to creditors he could never hope to repay. He intensified Julius's practices of simony and the sale of indulgences.

- Desperate to maintain their power, the Medici looked almost everywhere for support, and in 1515, the pope's new strange bedfellow was France, under its new young king **François I**, who had not yet made a name for himself as the daring, cultured, and highly regarded Renaissance king he would later become.

- To secure the alliance Giuliano de' Medici married François's aunt, Philiberta of Savoy, in February 1515. To return the gift, Giuliano had his talented courtier Leonardo make a mechanical lion for François, which apparently pleased François I enormously.

Leonardo Moves to France

- In March, 1516, Giuliano de'Medici died suddenly and unexpectedly at the age of 37 with no legitimate heirs to inherit his estate. Philiberta was not in a position to retain Leonardo's services at court.

- Sometime in August of 1516, Leonardo was transferred to the French court at the castle of Amboise, to begin the last phase of his career as the most famous courtier in the entourage of King François I of France.

- François not only had to confront a host of European rivals on the battlefield and negotiating tables, but also in the imagination of the common people. Henry VIII of England was demonstrating an interest in expanding his interests beyond his shores. In Spain, King Charles I was shortly to become Emperor Charles V of the Holy Roman Empire. François wanted the prominence of his court to match his political exploits.

- Nearly all of François's predecessors had focused on maintaining power. The kings of France did not spend money on art, and they only commissioned buildings for defensive or political purposes. This disregard for cultural commissions is obvious when we examine works produced at this time, like those of Jean Clouet, whose paintings of François I from about 1525 reveal a certain ability to capture a face and display some charm, but have none of the naturalistic sensitivity that we see in the works of Italy's best artists.

- Failure to invest in objects of luxury, style, class, and culture had caused a vacuum of quality within the borders of France. So François quickly came to the conclusion that the best thing to do when you do not have stallions in your own barn was to take the stallions in the poorly guarded barn of a neighbor.

- François attacked Milan in September of 1515 and looked into the possibility of moving Leonardo's *Last Supper*. Once it became clear that it could not be done, François made an overture to the picture's painter instead. Getting a giant of Italian art into his court would give this new monarch instant credibility.

The Deluge

- At this time, Leonardo was working on some studies that allowed him to consider some new and important issues. *The Deluge* is a drawing of a massive, active, ferocious storm as it passes over a country setting.

- The loosely handled, gestural swipes of his pen only create an impression of what is happening below from his elevated vantage point. The storm envelopes his vista so completely that the blackened clouds and the driving, swirling rain obscure the very landscape.

- Leonardo annotated this drawing in his *Treatise on Painting* in great and elegant detail. It is one of the few times when a written passage by Leonardo compares favorably to a corresponding drawing.

- The sketch of *The Deluge* was not the first time Leonardo drew while outdoors, but a lot had changed since that 1473 landscape. The drawing from 1473 is essentially a teaching tool. *The Deluge* is a completed work in itself. It is not only a study of how the world looks but also how the world works.

- Leonardo did not date this drawing, but in this case, the looseness of the composition and the freedom of its handling indicate that it is a late work. It is a useful rule of thumb, when trying to set up a chronology of works by a single artist, that the tighter the composition and the handling of details, the earlier the image was made. The older an artist gets, the less concerned he is about playing by the rules.

A Quiet Retirement

- François does not seem to have had anything in mind for Leonardo, at least at the outset, save for enhancing the reputation of the French court. Leonardo and his retinue arrived at Amboise, southwest of Paris, in the early spring of 1516.

- Leonardo's trusted inner circle included Salai, who had been with him for 25 years, and Melzi who had been with him for seven. Salai was quite skilled as a painter, and Melzi, the educated nobleman, could carry on an intellectual conversation.

- Leonardo was now free to work on his unfinished paintings, including the *Mona Lisa*, *John the Baptist*, and the *Saint Anne Madonna*. None of them was ever quite completed.

- As soon as he arrived at Amboise, Leonardo threw himself into some architectural projects that interested François. François's palace, the Chateau d'Amboise, was in need of repair. The extent of his participation in the project is unknown, but scholars see his touch in a royal fountain that was built there in 1518.

- In 1517, Leonardo drew plans for a chateau near Blois called Romorantin and has been credited with advising builders on the unique chateau at Chenonceau, which traverses a river on a series of arches and takes advantage of water as a source of power.

- Two other chateaux where the inspiration, if not the actual structure, of two double helix staircases built between 1515 and 1530 have also been credited to Leonardo's imagination. The first is an exterior staircase at the Chateau de Blois; the second is about 12 miles away at the Chateau de Chambord, which was begun a year after Leonardo died. Here, some have also suggested that Leonardo's presence is visible in the use of open-air loggia and other features typical of northern Italy.

© iStockphoto/Thinkstock.

Leonardo may have been an advisor to the architects and builders of Chenonceau Chateau, which incorporates the river into its design.

- We have no set of drawings to indicate his participation in these projects specifically, but they are reminiscent of one of his drawings of the Castello Sforzesco, which includes a revolving stairway.

- As he had done for the Medici, Leonardo was also charged with designing theatrical stages and costumes. In 1518, when François's niece, Maddalena de la Tour d'Auvergne, was married to Lorenzo de' Medici, the nephew of his former patron Giuliano, he designed the bride's ring, as well as a stage set for the entertainment.

Death and Burial

- In 1517, Leonardo was plagued by partial paralysis on his right side—fortunately not his dominant hand—after what seems to have been a stroke.

- In April 1519, Leonardo acknowledged the contents of his last will and testament, a clear indication in that era that the testator believed he was mortally ill. On May 2, just two weeks after his birthday, the 67-year-old Leonardo passed away.

- Salai was left a vineyard that Leonardo had acquired during his Florentine years, along with the unfinished paintings—*Mona Lisa*, *Leda and the Swan*, *John the Baptist*, and the *Saint Anne Madonna*. Melzi was left with literally thousands of pages of notes, all of them loose sheets of paper in unbound and uncatalogued stacks. Each bequest was suited to the assistant's talents and needs.

- Not present at Leonardo's deathbed was François I, who was off riding with a hunting party dozens of miles away. A monarch was neither expected nor wanted at such a delicate time.

- Leonardo's body was placed in a casket and interred in the cloister of a church next to the Chateau d'Amboise called Saint-Florentin, where his tomb was largely forgotten for centuries. During the Napoleonic era, an architect declared that there was nothing salvageable in the church and he ordered the stones to be removed to repair the adjacent chateau. Leonardo's tomb was lost.

- Sixty years later, the site was explored by archaeologists, who found a tomb bearing an inscription containing letters of Leonardo's name. Inside were skeletal remains, including an unusually large skull, which were removed and transported to the nearby chapel of Saint-Hubert. There Leonardo da Vinci may—or may not—rest today.

Name to Know

François I (1494–1547): French king of the Valois dynasty and distant relative of Louis XII, who preceded him on the throne. François ascended to power in 1515 and gradually enjoyed a political and military career that made him one of the most important and successful figures in early modern history. He was well educated and politically savvy. One of François's early acts as head of state was to invite Leonardo da Vinci to serve as his courtier. Leonardo accepted the invitation in 1516, thus giving François's court instant credibility.

Suggested Reading

Heydenreich, "Leonardo da Vinci, Architect of Francis I."

Kemp, *Leonardo da Vinci: The Marvellous Works of Nature and Man*, chap. 5.

Pedretti, *Leonardo da Vinci: The Royal Palace at Romorantin.*

Last Years—Leonardo in France

Lecture 33—Transcript

Leonardo's time in Italy officially and permanently ended in 1516. He had spent all of his 64 years there, and he had thrived in an environment that was largely fluid and highly unstable for most of those 64 years. By the time of his departure he was the most famous thinker in Italy, and maybe the greatest artist in the entire Western world, and his exit from Italian soil meant that the field was basically clear for Raphael and Michelangelo to claim as their own.

But if Leonardo rued the day that he left his homeland forever, he never seems to have shown it—unless, of course, his journey to France was the cause of the bitterness that comes across in that little phrase of his, "The Medici made me and the Medici destroyed me."

It could be that this statement is more a reflection of what transpired more generally within the Medici court than of Leonardo's personal issues with the family.

We must remember that the Pandora's box opened up by Alexander VI in 1494 had not been closed by Julius II in quite the way he had hoped by the time of his death in February of 1513. Pope Leo X inherited a realm still under threat by France, the Holy Roman Empire, Spain, England, and even Venice, all of whom used agents, spies, assassins, and armed forces to wrest control from each other in a never-ending string of alliances and leagues.

And because of Julius II's aggressive policies and leadership role in arranging so many of these leagues, the northern powers were now wise to the papacy's needs and strategies. They began working to undermine Rome's authority, first by publicly condemning the rather bald political motives of the papacy's actions and then by suggesting that that the entire office was corrupt: and a number of people began to listen.

It wasn't hard to see the point. Whereas Julius II had raised money to build Rome and deal with invaders, Leonardo X had reverted back to Alexander's more profligate ways. Pope Leo spent on parties, exotic food and wine, elegant clothing, and a growing personal art collection (that Raphael alludes to in this portrait—both in the grandeur of the picture that he's painting but also in the priceless Medieval manuscript that Leonardo inspects with his golden magnifying glass). And all this came at a massive expense.

The hundreds of thousands of ducats that Leo X received in salary each year melted away more quickly than they could be raked in, and Leo X was soon deeply in debt to creditors he could never hope to repay. The pope now intensified Julius's practices of simony and the sale of indulgences to record proportions: In one year alone, he stocked the College of Cardinals with a shockingly high number of noblemen, each of whom paid more than the last one had for his title. The Medici bought allies for the papal court and filled their personal coffers in one deft move. The papacy was once again was open for business, and now its enemies north of the Alps began to use this to their advantage.

Desperate to maintain their power, the Medici looked almost everywhere for support, and they always seemed but in odd places. In 1515, the pope's new strange bedfellow was France—yes, the same country that Julius II had been so desperate to expel from Italian soil only a few years earlier. Now this alliance may have been initiated by the French, for in January of 1515 King Louis XII died and was succeeded by young Francois I, who had not yet made a name for himself as the daring, cultured, and highly regarded Renaissance king he would later become.

By way of securing an alliance with the Medici family—the rulers of Florence and Rome, and with a College of Cardinals willing to do their bidding—the French arranged a marriage between the aunt of King Francois to Giuliano de' Medici, Leonardo's patron in Rome. The political connections that this implied were too tempting to resist, and in February of 1515, Philiberta of Savoy was wed to Giuliano de' Medici.

Keen on maintaining good relations with his in-laws, Giuliano tried his best to flatter the French royal family. When Francois I made a triumphal entry into the city of Lyons, Giuliano arranged to send to the occasion a mechanical lion, designed by his court artist, Leonardo da Vinci, as a token of his respect. When Francois entered the city on July 12, 1515, there was the lion, which took a couple of threatening steps on its own toward the king, stopped, and automatically opened two doors in its chest to reveal clusters of fleur de lis, symbols of both France and of Florence, and reminders of the alliance that had linked these two states since the 13th century. This primitive robot, of which we know only through verbal descriptions, pleased Francois I enormously, and it seems to have made quite an impression on the young king.

And then, Leonardo's world was turned on its head, and with absolutely no warning whatsoever. In March of 1516, Giuliano de'Medici died suddenly and unexpectedly at the age of 37, and with no legitimate heirs to inherit his estate. This was a big problem for Leonardo, for it turns out that Philiberta, the aunt of Francois I, and now the widow of , Giuliano de' Medici, was not in a position to retain Leonardo's services at court.

Instead within a few months of Giuliano's death, Leonardo was on the move again, this time to a brand new patron—and he may have had Philiberta to thank for it. An arrangement was made, and sometime in August of 1516, Leonardo—now 64 years old—was transferred from the Roman court of Giuliano de'Medici to the French court at the castle of Amboise, to begin the last phase of his career as the most famous courtier in the entourage of King Francois I of France.

Now Francois was an extremely important and powerful European ruler; but he wasn't the only one, to be sure. As Francois took control over his nation, it was becoming clear that he would have to confront a host of European rivals on the battlefield and at the negotiating tables. But also Francois would have to capture the imaginations of common people who wanted good reasons to respect their leaders.

In London, the youthful and vibrant king, Henry VIII, was expanding his interests beyond the shores of England. In Spain, Ferdinand of Aragon was succeeded by his grandson, Charles, who also happened to be the grandson and heir of Maximillian, the aging Holy Emperor. And when Maximilian died, King Charles of Spain also inherited Maximilian's possessions, making him Holy Roman Emperor, over a realm that stretched from Spain to the Netherlands to Bohemia—the largest empire Europe had known since the days of ancient Rome.

Leonardo's invitation to come north to France was extended to him in 1516, at exactly the time that Charles was preparing to inherit a wealthy and expanding Spanish state. Francois knew that the survival of his realm in France depended on a strong army and a network of diplomats and spies to keep his rivals at bay, but he also believed that the prominence of his court would have to match his political exploits.

Born the son of the Count of Angouleme and the Countess of Savoy, Francois came into this world in September of 1494, as the troops led by his great uncle Charles VIII were making their way into Milan and on toward Naples. Given his rather distant relationship to Charles, and to Louis XII who succeeded him, Francois really shouldn't have been a contender for the throne when Louis died. But neither Charles nor Louis had been able to produce a male heir during their martial careers, and Francois found himself to be the only legitimate claimant to the French throne when Louis XII died late in 1514.

And this must have been quite a daunting thing for Francois, for at this time France was battling with the papacy, Spain, and England, all at the same time. In addition to conducting an exceptionally complicated foreign policy, Francois was responsible for modernizing his new court and bringing it up to date with those in all the other political centers with which he was constantly doing battle.

During his minority, Francois seems to have come into contact with a number of humanistic instructors and role models, and while his education cannot be considered truly innovative in this sense, it is equally true that Francois was one of the more cultured monarchs to govern France in the history of Valois line.

When Francois I ascended to the throne on New Year's Day of 1515, nearly all of his predecessors had focused on three things. They wanted to maintain power internally by striking bargains with various barons and bishops in France. They needed to fend off foreign threats to French soil by raising vast armies to defend their borders. And third, they needed to build massive stone structures to placate the stakeholders in France who either wanted to promote themselves or protect the things they had procured during their tenures.

The French crown, in other words, was woefully bereft of things like paintings, tapestries, and sculptures—and one historian has claimed that in 1515, when Francois took control of the state, not a single royal residence in all of France was decorated with a single work of sculpture, ancient or modern, of any sort whatsoever. None.

The kings of France historically didn't spend money on art, and the only time they commissioned buildings was for defensive or political purposes. The idea of official French patronage hadn't been invented yet. That didn't happen until Francois I came along in 1515. And this disregard for cultural commissions becomes highlighted when we examine works produced at this time, like these pictures by the French painter Jean Clouet, whose paintings of Francois I from about 1525 to 1530 reveal a certain ability to capture a face and display some charm, but have none of the naturalistic sensitivities that we see in the works of Italy's best artists.

Failure to invest in objects of luxury, style, class, and culture had caused something of a vacuum of quality within the borders of France. There just weren't very many artists running around there who had studied or trained with the finest masters that Europe had to offer, for there wasn't much money to be had in that line of work. Young men inclined to go in that direction either left their homeland for greener pastures in Flanders or in Italy, or they ditched their artistic dreams altogether for other trades where they might actually make a living.

The dilemma for Francois was that he knew the value of art patronage for matters of diplomacy and power brokerage. But he also knew that he didn't have the horses in his own stable to win a race he knew would gain the respect of his allies and enemies alike. And so Francois rather quickly came to the conclusion that the best thing to do when you don't have stallions in your own barn, was to take the stallions in the poorly guarded barn of neighbor for your own personal use.

Now one of Francois's earliest military campaigns as king of France involved a brief, but successful attack on the city of Milan. In September of 1515, French soldiers reentered the city, expelling the Swiss army that had briefly occupied it with Massimiliano Sforza as their figurehead. Once there, Francois actually looked into the possibility of moving Leonardo's *Last Supper* from its fixed place on the refectory wall of Santa Maria delle Grazie; but once it became clear that it could not be done, Francois made his overture to the picture's painter, instead, and he invited Leonardo to France.

Now this was an important move on Francois's part. Getting a giant of Italian art and science to cross the Alps and come to a country with little art and no sculpture there would give this new monarch instant credibility as a prince of learning. His court would immediately be considered among the very best in all of Europe. But he was also asking the world's greatest painter to come to a vast cultural desert where there was an embarrassing dearth of riches.

Just when Francois was making his intentions known to Leonardo, the artist was working on some important studies that had allowed him to consider some new and important issues.

During his last months in the court of Giuliano de'Medici, Leonardo produced this drawing of a massive storm that we now call *The Deluge*, and that has excited so many geologists who have studied it over the years.

Leonardo produces an active, ferocious storm as it passes over a country setting. The drawing is only barely recognizable as a landscape, as the core elements of the work suggest either a rock formation or a cityscape. Instead, Leonardo has focused on the dramatic event that threatens the structures, the objects, and potentially the people below.

The loosely handled, gestural swipes of his pen create only an impression of what's happening below him, from an elevated vantage point. Crashing down on this landscape is a rainstorm that envelopes his vista so completely that the blackened clouds and the driving, swirling rain obscure the very landscape that he has hinted at. Geologists love this drawing, in part because it helps illustrate the observations about storms that he wrote in his *Treatise on Painting*. Leonardo had said:

> The air is seen tinged with nebulous darkness at the approach of a tempest or storm at sea. This is a mixture of rain and wind, with serpentine twistings in the tortuous course of threatening lightning

> bolts. The trees bend to the earth, with the leaves turned inside on the bent branches, which seem as though they would fly away, as if frightened by the blasts of the horrible and terrifying wind, amid which is diffused the course of the turbulent dust and sand from the seashore. The obscure horizon of the sky makes a background of smoky clouds, which, struck by the sun's rays and penetrating through an opening in the clouds opposite, descend to the earth, lighting it up with their beams. … Claps of thunder, created by the globular clouds, throw off infuriated bolts of lightning, and their light illuminates the shadowed countryside in various places.

It's a wonderfully colorful description of a powerful event, and I'd argue it's one of the few times when a written passage by Leonardo the unpublished author compares favorably to a corresponding drawing by Leonardo the artist.

Now the sketch of *The Deluge* was certainly not the first of these landscapes that Leonardo drew while outdoors. We remember that he'd begun such drawings at least as early as 1473, when he drew this Tuscan landscape at the age of 21. It was already in his repertoire, and Leonardo returned to this subject matter easily and seemingly without any hesitation.

But a lot had changed in the meantime. The drawing from 1473 is essentially a teaching tool that Leonardo uses to practice his hand at drawing landscapes that can, presumably, then be reused for paintings. By contrast, this drawing of *The Deluge* contains a narrative all for itself.

Now we see a genuine weather event, complete with those heavy clouds and sheets of rain driving heavily down across the hills. This isn't your basic, normal bucolic landscape, in which the artist is interested in showing us how the world looks, but rather it's another one of Leonardo's intensive scientific studies of the natural world and how the world works. And there's a big difference between the two.

There's another interesting little tidbit here, too. Leonardo didn't write down the dates of his drawings, with the notable exception of the *Landscape of 1473*, and sometimes it's hard to tell when he did what. But in this case, the looseness of the composition and the freedom of its handling indicate that it's a late work. It's a useful rule of thumb, when trying to set up a chronology of works by a single artist, that the tighter the composition and the handling of the details, the earlier the image was made. The older an artist get, the less concerned he is about playing by the rules or adhering to traditional formats. As this drawing of *The Deluge* is about as loose as it gets in the 16th century, I think it belongs at the very late end of Leonardo's career.

While in Rome, Leonardo had also continued his examination of flight: In one of his experiments, he had crafted wax models of small birds and animals that were filled with compressed air and then he shot through the air. He watched them as they flew, considering problems of flight and aerodynamics, a variation of the problems that had consumed him for decades in Florence and Milan.

But Leonardo probably was not completely comfortable in this environment. Unlike Ludovico Sforza, who had appreciated Leonardo's inquisitiveness from a pragmatic perspective, hoping one of his inventions might actually work and tip the scales in his favor someday, Giuliano seems to have paid practically no attention to Leonardo whatsoever—the experiments and scientific dabblings of the elderly tinkerer didn't really appeal much to Giuliano de' Medici.

News of Francois's interest in Leonardo must have struck him as something of a godsend in 1516.

Like Giuliano de'Medici, Francois had no major paintings that he wanted Leonardo to produce. He didn't want a colossal bronze equestrian monument erected in his honor. He didn't need inventive war machines or solutions to dire agricultural predicaments caused by the terrain or by foreign armies poised on his flanks.

In fact, Francois doesn't seem have initially had anything in mind for Leonardo, save for this very famous artist to come live with him at court north of the Alps and make France a new center of European intellectualism.

Oh, and get paid a whole lot of money to do so, for Francois was prepared to toss in the highest salary Leonardo had ever seen in his life. It seems to have been a nice retirement package that would allow Leonardo to spend the last years of his life in great comfort.

And Leonardo, now 64, thought this was a pretty good deal. He accepted, and off he went to the French Loire Valley in the summer of 1516, finally passing beyond the Alpine mountains that he had seen from afar so often in Milan, and which had made appearances in so many of his paintings over the years.

Now Leonardo arrived at Francois's court in Amboise, south and west of Paris, in the summer of 1516 with his now familiar retinue of associates close at hand. By now they had formed an inner circle of friends and colleagues whom Leonardo both trusted and respected greatly for their abilities and, more importantly, for their loyalty. Salai, for one, had been with him for 25 years and Francesco Melzi another seven—and while Salai was quite skilled as a painter, Melzi, the educated nobleman, could carry on an intellectual conversation with Leonardo on the master's own level. They would stay with Leonardo until the very end, and be rewarded for their faithful service to their master in ways that only they could possibly appreciate.

It sounds like this was the Renaissance equivalent of a golden parachute, what with Leonardo getting so much money to come to a lovely royal villa to live out his final days in peace and comfort. But Leonardo went to Amboise with absolutely no intention of fading gracefully into retirement. Nor was he treated by his French patron as someone who should by now be put out to pasture, despite his advanced age for this period.

It's pretty clear that Leonardo was free to continue working on those paintings he still hadn't finished during his years of service for the Medici in Rome and his French patrons in Milan. The *Mona Lisa* was with Leonardo in his studio when he was visited by Antonio de Beatis in 1517, and so were both the small picture of *John the Baptist* and the larger *St. Anne Madonna.* The painting of *Leda and the Swan*, which disappeared in the 17th century, was also in his possession, although Leonardo didn't set it up for Beatis's inspection, for unknown reasons.

The three pictures that were set up were obviously either put on display to commemorate the visit or, more likely, were actually installed on easels in a working environment so that Leonardo could tend to them as the spirit moved him. Still, it must be said that none of them was ever brought to an absolutely final state of completion during his stay in France. Even the *Mona Lisa* has areas that need some attention, including a final set of touchups on the hands, the eyebrows, and the hills in the background just over her left shoulder, just beyond the arched bridge.

Instead, as soon as he arrived at Amboise, Leonardo seems to have thrown himself into at least two architectural projects that interested the French king, Francois I.

First, was probably the palace used by the court of Francois himself, the Chateau d' Amboise, which was in need of repair and rebuilding. We don't know for sure whether Leonardo was involved in discussions about how these apartments were designed, or the extent of his participation in the project if he was. Among the candidates for Leonardo's signature touch would have been a royal fountain that was built there in 1518. This was precisely the kind of thing that Leonardo would've been good at, given his history of experimental hydraulics, and precisely the kind of thing that Francois would've identified as something worth Leonardo's time and energy.

Second, we're also told that in 1517 Leonardo drew plans for an altogether different chateau, near Blois, called Romorantin. He's been credited with advising builders on the unique chateau at Chenonceau, which traverses a river on a series of arches and takes advantage of water as a source of power. The arches we see today were added later, but I really like this idea, as his participation in this beautiful and unique French chateau would have allowed him to put his interests in hydraulics and civil engineering to very good use.

And there are two other chateaux, where the inspiration, if not the actual structure, of two double helix staircases built between 1515 and 1530 have also been credited to Leonardo's imagination. The first is an exterior staircase at the Chateau of Blois that has two staircases wrapping around each other, in two separately twisting pathways.

The second is about 12 miles away at the chateau of Chambord, which was begun a year after Leonardo died. In this case, the double helix staircase is now embedded in the architectural setting. But it, too, employs that pair of steps leading up around each other in an upward spiral to the floors above. Here, some have also suggested that Leonardo's presence in France is perhaps also visible in the use of an open-air loggia and other features typical of northern Italy, but absent from French architecture before this time.

Now, we have no set of drawings or plans or even references in the books to indicate his participation in these projects. But the uniqueness of this form is one of the reasons why Leonardo gets credited, at the very least, for advising the designers of the double helix staircase. In his drawing of the Castello Sforzesco from his first Milanese Period with Ludovico, Leonardo had included in the upper right corner this kind of revolving stairway, contained within an upright rectangular box. His drawing envisions this as more of a linear design that employs right angles at each turn, but the basic concept is the same. Seeing as how double helix stairwells just weren't being done in France before this time, and how Leonardo had already envisioned this architectural form in his notes, he has been a logical choice as the moving force behind its construction at both Blois and Chambord.

As he had done for the Medici, Leonardo was also charged with designing theatrical stages and costumes. One such opportunity came to Leonardo in 1518 when the niece of Francois I, named Maddalena de la Tour d'Auvergne, was married to Lorenzo de' Medici, the nephew of his former patron Giuliano. Not only did Leonardo design the wedding ring for the bride, but the Florentine artist was also charged with the task of designing the stage set for a play called "The Feast of Paradise" by the Italian poet Bellincioni—the very same poet who, in 1491 or 1492, had praised Leonardo by name in his verses about the beauty of his portrait of Cecilia Gallerani.

I think this kind of work on staged performances gave Leonardo great pleasure: It was the one thing he did that actually got a reaction from an audience that he could see and feel. All those solitary hours spent with geometrical formulas and hydraulic machines and dissection of corpses provided his brain with the gratification of knowing things no one else did.

But the grateful applause of an audience came only when his mechanical animals and magnificent costumes were paraded past an adoring viewership.

But not all was well with Leonardo da Vinci in this period. In 1517, the artist was plagued by partial paralysis on his right side—fortunately not his writing, his drawing, and his painting hand—after what seems to have been a stroke. Now it's important that we know this, for up until this time—his 65th year—Leonardo had refrained almost entirely from discussing his own health (either physical or emotional) in his notes. And the fact that we have evidence of an affliction suggests that it must have been quite serious—otherwise he would've glossed over it, just like all those colds and cases of the sniffles that he hadn't bothered to mention in his notes and margins. The descent was gradual at first, but then gained speed after the wedding ceremonies for which he designed the ring and the theater set.

In April, 1519, Leonardo acknowledged the contents of his last will and testament, a clear indication in that era that the testator believed he was about to meet his maker. And indeed, on May 2, just two weeks after his birthday, the now 67-year-old Leonardo passed away, presumably joined at his bedside in the Chateau of Cloux by his grieving assistants and confidants, Salai and Francesco Melzi.

Leonardo had seen fit to take care of both of them in his will. Salai was left a vineyard that had been acquired by Leonardo during his Florentine years, along with the great paintings left unfinished at Leonardo's death—the *Mona Lisa*, *Leda and the Swan*, *John the Baptist*, and the *St. Anne Madonna*. Leonardo seems to have recognized the financial needs of low-born Salai, and hoped Salai could fetch good prices for the pictures while living off the income from the vineyard. The aristocratic and well-educated Melzi was left with literally thousands of pages of notes, all of them loose sheets of paper in unbound and un-catalogued stacks. Leonardo knew the intellectual capabilities of the high-born Melzi, and Leonardo obviously felt they'd be the perfect gift for him—but he also surely knew that Melzi would be the better custodian of those vital studies on flight, anatomy, and painting that might one day see the light of day.

Not present at Leonardo's deathbed, however, was Francois I, who was off riding with a hunting party dozens of miles away from Cloux at the time of Leonardo's demise. And this was entirely appropriate for the time, as the monarch was neither expected nor wanted at such a delicate moment. There's a very real possibility that Francois wasn't even aware that Leonardo was on this deathbed that day.

The body was placed in a casket and interred in the cloister of a church next to the Chateau of Amboise called Saint-Florentin, where his tomb was largely forgotten for centuries. During the Napoleonic era, an architect who was appointed to inspect the dilapidated facility, declared that there was nothing salvageable in the church, and he ordered the stones to be removed to repair the adjacent chateau of Amboise. During this reclamation project, the tomb of Leonardo da Vinci was lost.

But—60 years later—the site was explored by archaeologists, who found a tomb, perhaps bearing an inscription containing letters of Leonardo's name. Inside were skeletal remains, including an unusually large skull. And these remains were removed and transported to the nearby chapel of Saint Hubert. It's at Saint Hubert where the remains of Leonardo da Vinci may—or may not—have been moved for veneration by those who visit the French castle today.

Leonardo da Vinci spent the last years of his life beyond the boundaries of his country of origin. But he seems to have done so willingly and with no regrets. It's perhaps a fitting end for a man who transcended classical borders and even the boundaries of language, a man who refused to believe that there was only one idea by which to live, or only one solution to a problem, and a man who resisted the notion that people could be boxed in by geographic or intellectual constraints.

Renaissance Man and Man of the Renaissance
Lecture 34

Both today and during his own lifetime, Leonardo shaped our idea of what it means to be a Renaissance man. His mastery of so many fields—and the effortlessness, or sprezzatura, with which he mastered them—came to define the perfect Renaissance courtier in his day. To us, Leonardo embodies the spirit of relentless curiosity we associate with the Renaissance. But in a very real sense, the Renaissance made Leonardo's achievements possible in a way they would not have been a mere generation before him.

Castiglione and the Perfect Courtier

- **Baldassare Castiglione**'s *Book of the Courtier* recounts a fictitious dialogue that takes place in 1507 among a group at the court of the Duke of Urbino. This quintessential examination of Italian cultural life at the end of the High Renaissance describes the virtues and qualities of the perfect courtier.

- Such a specimen should have physical prowess and beauty, athleticism, and a keen sense of fashion. He should have a sense of elegance of carriage and demeanor. He should be intelligent, wise, and have a classical education. His speech should be colored by wit and a sense of humor.

- Castiglione goes on to say that the courtier not only does many things well but does them with a certain effortlessness and ease that Italians call **sprezzatura**.

- Except for the classical education, Leonardo possessed all these characteristics, and we have good reason to think Castiglione had Leonardo in mind as he wrote his text.

- In 1496, at the age of 16, Castiglione was sent to Milan to begin his humanistic education. He must at least have heard of Leonardo during his three years as student there, which overlapped with the period when Leonardo was painting *The Last Supper*. Leonardo was already a living legend.

- Fifteen years later, Castiglione and Leonardo again shared a city. Both were in Rome from 1513 to 1516, and this time, they also shared a court. Castiglione was Urbino's ambassador to the Vatican. He befriended Raphael and Giuliano de' Medici.

- In a very real sense, Castiglione helped invent the concept of the Renaissance man more than 20 years before Vasari would write about a rebirth, and in a very real sense, Leonardo helped shape Castiglione's conception of the ideal man.

Leonardo's Wealth of Talents

- If there is any doubt that Leonardo was a model Renaissance man, let us consider the fields where we have witnessed his mastery: perspective and optics; mechanical engineering, in every field from flight to weaponry; courtly behavior; hydraulics; architecture; military strategy; the classical painting style; bronze sculpture; and naturalism and environmental science.

- Leonardo excelled in other fields we did not discuss. For example, he undertook botanical studies, usually not for the sake of pure knowledge but in anticipation of a painting. The *Annunciation* relies heavily on the symbolism of the lily and the enclosed garden, so their accurate portrayals were important to Leonardo's message. In *Ginevra de' Benci*, the juniper bush and laurel wreath are important symbols of the sitter's identity and virtues, and a mistake in these areas would have ruined the portrait.

- Due to his inherent inquisitiveness and his dedication to the belief that true knowledge of nature could only come through experience, Leonardo drew plants and flowers with a careful and exacting eye.

- The drawing of multiple types of flowers from the Accademia museum in Venice seems to be more of a scientific drawing than a study for a painting: Different examples have been carefully rendered according to size and shape; identified and distinguished by their formal features, and set apart from their neighbors so as to be more easily inspected.

- The only thing Leonardo was truly trained to do was draw, paint, and sculpt a little on the side. He was not known for doing those things quickly; however, he handled everything that he applied himself to with such apparent ease and grace that we can call it sprezzatura.

What Was the Renaissance?

- Why do we refer to people like Leonardo as Renaissance men, instead of Baroque men or Medieval men? What was it about the period we call the Renaissance that gave rise more frequently to the kind of person who excels at so many diverse and unrelated things?

- The world changed so dramatically during this period that, arguably, it would not have been possible to be a Renaissance man before the Renaissance. These rapid and dramatic changes were caused directly by the inventions and discoveries of the age. Without them, the level of expertise that Leonardo attained would have been impossible to match.

- Leonardo was among the first generation of thinkers who had access to volumes of printed books, which contained a wealth of information on almost any subject that anyone with any curiosity wanted to absorb.

- Leonardo's personal library contained 116 books according to an inventory written while he was in Florence in 1503. These included

    - Vitruvius's architectural treatises

    - Mathematical studies by Euclid and Luca Pacioli

- Theories on art, perspective, and proportion by Leon Battista Alberti and Piero della Francesca

- Scientific essays by Johannes Peckham, Alberto of Saxony, and Claudio Tolomeo

- Three books on the anatomy of horses

- Italian translations of ancient works by Pliny the Elder, Aristotle, and Ovid

- Medieval philosophy by Albertus Magnus, Saint Augustine, and Bernardino da Siena

- The Bible, accounts of Christ's Passion, sermons, and hagiographies

- Aesop's *Fables*

- Anatomical studies by Duns Scotus, Mondino de Liuzzi, and other anonymous authors

- Latin grammars

- Books on civics, political theory, and military principles

- All were printed books—not expensive, hand-written copies—and virtually all of them pertained to the specific projects that Leonardo pursued as a courtier, painter, philosopher, scientist, and an engineer.

- Despite his rather snide comment about the laziness of scholars who depend too heavily on the works of others, Leonardo was familiar with the ideas of generations of thinkers who had come before him.

The Renaissance beyond Europe

- A second crucial part of the Renaissance man phenomenon was a change in the global quality of life. News of the existence of a new continent half way round the world fundamentally changed the way people thought about themselves, the world, and their concepts of the potential of the future.

- The European powers spent a good bit of time and money carving out for themselves colonies in the New World. Just as Europeans were showing greater interest in the world beyond their own shores, so too were people from those distant lands showing greater interest in them.

- In 1500, as Leonardo fled from French forces that had just invaded Milan, the artist received an invitation to join the court of the Sultan Mahmed, the Ottoman ruler, in Istanbul. East and West were on better terms than they had been in centuries, and one of the many results was the spread of Leonardo's fame.

- Leonardo declined the first offer, but a second offer was extended a few months later. In 1502 Leonardo replied to this second summons with a letter that he sent to the son of Mahmed, **Bayezid II**, describing how he might construct a bridge across the Golden Horn. Ultimately Leonardo's proposal for a single-span structure some 720 feet in length was dismissed.

A Rebel among Rebels

- A third reason why Leonardo could have only been a Renaissance man in the Renaissance is that, by the time of his adulthood, these conditions had cultivated a more critical and questioning mentality among Europe's leading thinkers.

- In this era, the people questioning the assumptions of contemporary authorities were not just challenging outmoded traditions and old-fashioned customs; they were challenging cherished concepts of the universal order and the laws and rules that governed life itself.

- The High Renaissance produced more than its fair share of social rebels, and we can understand Leonardo's achievements better if we situate his own work in the context of leading rebels of his time.

  - **Nicolas Copernicus**, the Polish scientist whose groundbreaking astronomical studies determined that the sun, and not the earth, was at the center of the solar system.

Nicolas Copernicus proposed the heliocentric solar system.

  - Niccolò Machiavelli, the courtier whose bold and ambitious political treatise suggested how to govern during times of enormous instability and danger and how the Italian peninsula might be united under a single government.

  - Martin Luther, the Augustinian monk who chafed under the stigma of a corrupt papal institution and whose 95 Theses condemned Pope Leonardo X and the entire hierarchical structure that had brought him to power and kept him there.

- Unlike dissidents driven by a single idea, not everything that Leonardo did or said was borne of a revolutionary mindset. When Leonardo made out his will, he requested that Masses for the Dead be said on his behalf and that he be buried inside the cloister of a monastery. That is not to say that Leonardo was blindly or even actively religious, but questions of spirituality clearly interested him.

- Like all of us, Leonardo was a product his times. But to a larger degree than most of us, Leonardo was also responsible for shaping that world in which he lived, too.

Important Term

sprezzatura: Italian for "ease" or "effortlessness," used by Baldassare Castiglione to praise courtiers who excelled at a variety of activities with a certain grace and elegance.

Names to Know

Bayezid II (1447–1512): Sultan of the Ottoman Empire and son of Mehmed II. Bayezid briefly toyed with the idea of commissioning Leonardo da Vinci to design a bridge to span the Golden Horn of Istanbul.

Castiglione, Baldassare (1478–1529): Diplomat and writer who worked in the courts of Urbino, Mantua, and the Vatican during his successful career. After serving as papal nuncio to Spain, he wrote a widely read and influential description of life at court in Renaissance Italy called *The Book of the Courtier* (1528).

Copernicus, Nicholas (1473–1543): Polish scientist educated in Italian universities whose posthumously published findings posited that the sun, not the Earth, was the center of the solar system.

Luther, Martin (1483–1546): Augustinian friar and professor of theology who was outraged by the excesses of the papal courts of Alexander VI, Julius II, and Leo X. He went public with his protests in 1517, refused to recant in 1520, was excommunicated in 1521, and was hence seen as the founder and leader of the Protestant movement.

Suggested Reading

Morley, "The Plant Illustrations of Leonardo da Vinci."

Reti, "The Two Unpublished Manuscripts of Leonardo da Vinci in the Biblioteca Nacional of Madrid – II."

Renaissance Man and Man of the Renaissance

Lecture 34—Transcript

Just before his death in 1529, the Italian humanist and noted diplomat Baldassare Castiglione published a text called *The Book of the Courtier*. This extremely important study revolves around a fictitious dialogue that takes place in 1507 between a group of men and women placed in the court of the duke of Urbino. In what many today consider to be the quintessential examination of Italian cultural life at the end of the High Renaissance, Castiglione describes the virtues and qualities of the perfect courtier.

Let's keep in mind what we know about Leonardo and see how well he fits the profile. Among characteristics are things like physical prowess and beauty, athleticism, and a keen sense of fashion. The courtier should have a sense of elegance of carriage and demeanor. He should be intelligent, wise, and have a classical education. His speech should be colored by wit and a sense of humor: Except for the classical education, Vasari hints that Leonardo possessed all of these characteristics.

Castiglione goes on to lay out a concept of perfection that revolves around an ability to do many, many, many things very well, and that sounds exactly like Leonardo, but also to do them so well that it seems like you're not even trying. This emphasis on effortlessness and ease is what Italians call sprezzatura. It might remind us a little of Ghirlandaio's boast how easily he could paint all the walls of Florence. Leonardo may not have been the fastest brush in Italy, but he had the ability to move back and forth between different projects—and different fields, even—at the drop of a hat.

So I won't tell you that Castiglione was using as his model Renaissance man the figure of Leonardo da Vinci: But the notion of a single person having the ability to embody so many seemingly different and even unattainable attributes does strike me as Leonardesque. Moreover, Castiglione would've had very good reasons to have had Leonardo in mind as he wrote his text—and here's why.

In 1496, at the age of 16, Castiglione had been sent to Milan to begin his humanistic education—at the very least, he must have heard of Leonardo da Vinci during his three-year career as a student there, which overlapped almost exactly with the period when Leonardo was hard at work painting the mural of *The Last Supper*, layering his oil glazes on top of an egg tempera base. Castiglione might have been one of those people reputed to have come and watch him work. Leonardo had already made his colossal clay horse; he was a famous painter; poems were written about his work; and he collaborated with the architect Bramante, the mathematician, Luca Pacioli, and various engineers and theatrical producers in the Sforza court.

Fifteen years later, Castiglione and Leonardo again shared a city, as both were in Rome from 1513 to 1516—and this time, they also shared a court. Castiglione lived at the Vatican in the capacity of Ambassador to the Papal See from Urbino, where he had gained the favor of the duke Guidobaldo delle Rovere. During that time, Castiglione befriended Raphael, also from Urbino, and had Raphael paint his portrait, which I show here. While in Rome, Castiglione also met and befriended Giuliano de'Medici, and in fact thought very highly enough of him to include him as one of the main characters in *The Book of the Courtier*. Giuliano is the one who praises the virtues of women at court. So Castiglione would very likely have seen and been associated with, the elderly Leonardo da Vinci, who was by then the most famous courtier in all of Rome—and maybe in all of the world.

So the ideal, supremely gifted courtier that Castiglione described matched in many ways, the reputation that Leonardo carried with him for most of his professional life. In a very real sense, Castiglione helped invent the concept of the Renaissance man, over 20 years before Vasari would write about this kind of rebirth, and in a very real sense, Leonardo da Vinci helped shape Castiglione's conception of the ideal man.

If there's any doubt that Leonardo was a model Renaissance man, let's consider his reputation in all of the fields he was thought to lead: His understanding of perspective and optics was unequalled. He was an extraordinarily creative and accurate designer of machines for everything from human flight to weapons of destruction. Few men of common birth knew more princes, dukes, and duchesses than he did. And none had those princes, dukes, and duchesses competing for his services in exactly the same way. He knew more about hydraulics than anyone in Europe.

He was an architectural theorist whose concepts had influenced the single most important Christian edifice constructed in over a millennium. He was a known anatomical researcher who had cut into more bodies than most surgeons. He was a valued military advisor to at least three important and powerful figures. He was the leader of the classical movement in painting that had changed the way artists delivered ideas and the way patrons valued images. He had conceived of the largest sculpture cast in bronze since antiquity. He was Europe's most driven naturalist and environmental scientist. Leonardo could do it all.

In this course we have seen examples of all of these interests, and his eclectic array of specialties amazes us—even more so when we realize that they didn't end with this menu that we've just read.

We know, for example, that Leonardo was interested in botanical studies, although usually his investigations were conducted not for the sake of pure study, but rather in anticipation of a painting that he felt required an accurate rendering of a specific flower or plant.

And his paintings often employed such flora and fauna, either as elements in a foreground to suggest a fertile landscape or as key or central symbol at the very core of his pictures. The *Annunciation of the Virgin*, for example, his very large commission for a public space, revolved primarily around the large white lily held in the hand of the Archangel Gabriel and the fertile *hortus conclusus* that extends out behind this patio: Without these botanical forms, the symbolic force of the painting fades away. We don't see any reference to the cherished virginity that Mary surrenders to God the Father, and we don't see the allusion to the horrible suffering she will endure at the death of her only son. But the fact that Mary accepts the lily, the symbol of her mourning, tells us that she's willing to make the ultimate sacrifice for her unborn baby.

Indeed, sometimes flowers and fauna were central actors on the grand stage of a Leonardo play. In the portrait of *Ginevra de' Benci*, the juniper bush that frames the sitter's head is the identifying feature of the portrait, while his expert handling of the laurel wreath and juniper sprig together remind us of her importance in the world of 15th-century literature in the back.

But because of their central roles in the painting, Leonardo had to make sure that he got these plants right, and that in turn caused him to go outdoors to study them, draw them, and understand them. If he mixed up the appearance of the juniper bush, or confused a laurel branch with an olive branch, the symbolic thrust of his picture would've been completely destroyed, and viewers wouldn't have understood what he was trying to say.

And this meant that Leonardo had to get things right by actually studying the plants he wanted to use in his pictures. This finished brush drawing of a lily was almost unquestionably intended to be featured in an Annunciation picture not unlike the one he painted in Florence in the mid-1470s. We're pretty sure the lily was drawn later than this, probably in the middle of the 1480s, as it turns in the opposite direction of the earlier painting. But because the lines of the drawing have been pricked for transfer through the pouncing method, we're equally sure that this drawing was meant to be copied onto another surface, presumably a painting.

This impressive floral study, dated by some scholars to the mid 1480s and by others to roughly 1505, features a bed of flowers with its stems and tendrils flowing in long arcs from their roots. In this drawing, we see a star of Bethlehem, a wood anemone, and a sun spurge sweep out across the page, indicating that Leonardo was looking at, and copying down, different options that he could include in a painting. It too has been carefully attended to, and the main plant in the upper portion of the drawing has been highly finished—even tinted—in preparation for use.

The painting for which it was drawn may have been the first version of the *Madonna of the Rocks*. We see some vegetation in the middle right section of the picture, just over the outstretched left hand of the Virgin, and plants and flowers extend all the way from the lower left corner in the foreground, back into the middle ground on the left edge of the painting.

Of course, the drawing may also have been the model for Leonardo's painting of *Leda and the Swan* from about 1508, as the foliage that sprouts up next the rock in the preparatory drawing that bears the god Zeus, transformed into the swan, seems based on the plant in the drawing.

Getting the drawings of these plants just right meant studying them in nature; and studying them in nature meant actually getting out there with his pen and his paper to draw these beautiful plants in their natural setting.

And due to his inherent inquisitiveness and his dedication to the belief that true knowledge of nature could come only through experience, Leonardo drew those plants and flowers with a very careful and exacting eye.

The drawing of multiple types of flowers from the Accademia Museum in Venice seems to be more of a scientific drawing than a study for a painting: Different examples have been carefully rendered here according to size and shape. Identified and distinguished by their formal features and placed across the page in areas of the paper that set them apart from their neighbors, they can be more easily inspected by both the artist and the audience. Petals and pistols and stems and leaves all appear here, and even if we're not familiar with the different names of each flower, it's awfully easy to see that each one is a type unto itself.

The only thing Leonardo was truly trained to do was draw and paint (and maybe sculpt a little on the side), and he was not known for doing those things quickly. However, the fact that he handled everything else that he applied himself to—with such apparent ease and grace and effortlessness—does imbue him with that sense of sprezzatura that Castiglione valued so highly.

But I think it might be useful to take just a minute or two to think about that phrase we toss around so frequently when describing someone who knows and can do so many things. Why do we refer to people like Leonardo as Renaissance men, instead of Baroque men or, heaven forbid, Medieval men? What was it about the period we call the Renaissance that gave rise more frequently to the kind of person who excels at so many diverse and unrelated things?

There was something special about the time in which Leonardo lived that actually helps us put his abilities and his skills into the context that, in turn, helps us understand his seemingly relentless pursuit of so many different things. We call Leonardo the Renaissance man, in part, because of the times in which he lived and because of the way the world changed so dramatically while he was alive in it. I don't think it would've been possible to be a Renaissance man before the Renaissance: The rapid and dramatic changes experienced during the period were caused directly by the inventions and discoveries of the age. Without them, the level of expertise that Leonardo attained would've been impossible to match.

Here are a few reasons why. First of all, Leonardo was among the first generation of thinkers who had access to volumes of printed books that contained a wealth of information on almost any subject that anyone with any curiosity might want to absorb. The truly great presses of the 15th and early 16th century printed all sorts of books, from learned works of theology to pornographic poetry written by frustrated friars. Leonardo had access to all sorts of books—on a vast array of subjects that matched his own vast array of interests. This had not been possible, at least not on this level, before Leonardo's birth.

And we know that Leonardo owned books—no fewer than 116 of them are listed in an inventory written while he was in Florence in 1503, before he returned to Milan, lived in Rome, and moved to France.

Among the books listed in the 1503 inventory were architectural treatises by the ancient writer Vitruvius; mathematical studies by Euclid and his friend Luca Pacioli; theories on art, perspective, and proportion by Alberti and Piero della Francesca; scientific essays by Johannes Peckham, Alberto of Saxony, and Claudio Tolomeo. He owned three separate books on the anatomy of horses. He owned Italian translations of ancient works by Pliny the Elder, Aristotle, and Ovid. He owned medieval philosophy by Albertus Magnus, Saint Augustine, and Bernardino da Siena. He owned the Bible, accounts of Christ's Passion, sermons, and hagiographic accounts of saint's lives. He had a copy of *Aesop's Fables*, anatomical studies by Duns Scotus, Mondino de Liuzzi, and other anonymous authors. He also had Latin grammar books that he used in an effort to allow him to expand his library to include more international texts. And he owned other various books on civics, political theory, and military principles.

Now by most standards, this is an eclectic assortment of scholarly texts—maybe *Aesop's Fables* and *The Metamorphoses* by Ovid were for fun, but the rest are pretty highbrow books. Yet all were of the printed variety—as opposed to hand-written manuscripts—which meant they were affordable for a man on a fixed salary. And virtually all of them pertained to the specific scholarly projects and artistic endeavors that Leonardo pursued as a courtier, a painter, a philosopher, a scientist, and an engineer during his career.

And let's remember that this list of books owned by Leonardo was crafted in 1503, just after his 50th birthday in Florence—and at precisely the time he had finally reached superstar status that commanded both the respect and the compensation commensurate with that status. That is to say, the 116 books that he owned in 1503 would almost certainly have been supplemented with many more that he was able to purchase (thanks to increased income and heightened curiosity) by the time he finally passed away in France 16 years later.

And the number of books in this inventory reminds us that, despite his rather snide comment about the laziness of scholars who depend too heavily on the works of others, Leonardo himself was familiar with the ideas and observations and positions of generations of thinkers who had come before him. He had read the ancients, he had read their followers, and he knew his sources.

So one of the reasons why Leonardo could have only been a Renaissance man by living in the Renaissance was that, up until that time, it would've been impossible for him to have owned a private library of specialized books to consult whenever he needed a question answered.

A second crucial part of the Renaissance man phenomenon that could only be realized by somebody living during Leonardo's time was the utter freshness of the global quality of life in that age. News of the existence of a brand new continent half way round the world fundamentally changed the way people thought about themselves, the universe, and their concepts of the potential of the future.

The European powers spent a good bit of time and money carving out for themselves colonies in the New World, with Spain and Portugal taking the approach that the resources they were finding underground needed to be extracted from the earth and brought to the Old World, and then to be hoarded and then spent by their princes. By the time of Leonardo's death in 1519, the stripping of South and Central America's gold supplies was soon to start, with the result that for the remainder of the 16th century, Spain would enjoy enormous prosperity at home and extraordinary success in nearly all of her international ventures.

But the interest in foreign lands was not just one way, and just as Europeans were showing greater interest in the world beyond their own shores, so too were people from those distant lands showing greater interest in them. Although European powers would join forces repeatedly over the next two centuries to defend their borders from Ottoman invaders, elements of Glasnost can be found in the correspondences between East and West right around the year 1500 that simply were not there only 30 years earlier, and one of its many results was the spread of Leonardo's fame, even beyond the borders of Europe, during his own lifetime.

This heightened awareness of people in other land directly touched the career of Leonardo, and not just because his pictures for Ludovico Il Moro had allowed him to encounter foreign emissaries at that court. In 1500 as Leonardo fled from French forces that had just invaded Milan, the artist received an invitation to quit Europe all together and join the court of the Sultan Mahmed, the Ottoman ruler in Instanbul.

Leonardo declined the offer to join the Sultan in Istanbul, but a second offer was extended to him only a few months later which did spark his interest—for the Sultan appears to have had something specific in mind for Leonardo. And in 1502 Leonardo replied to this second summons with a letter that he sent to the son of Mahmed, named Bayezid II.

In a manner not unlike the one he used when pitching his skills to Ludovico Sforza 20 years earlier, Leonardo both promoted his own abilities in general and addressed the particular project that the Sultan sought him for: Leonardo described in this letter an enormous bridge that he proposed to build across the Golden Horn of Istanbul, an enormous span even by today's standards. Here's what Leonardo said in this letter of 1502:

> I, your faithful servant, understand that it has been your intention to erect a bridge from Galata to Stambud, but that this has not been done because there were no experts available. I, your faithful servant, know how to do it. I will erect it as high as an arch, so that no one will wish to contest it, because it will be so high. But I have been thinking about putting up boarding, from which water would be extracted, and placing it on piles. This is how I would do it, so that a ship could sail underneath it.

The idea intrigued Bayezid, but ultimately Leonardo's proposal—a single-span structure, some 750 feet tall, or the length of almost two and half football fields—was dismissed. There was no way, the Sultan thought, that such a bridge could be built, and Leonardo was never invited to join the court in Istanbul.

Some Norwegians, recently, took a look at Leonardo's plan and felt that it actually had some possibilities. In 2001 an architect named Vebjorn Sand built one a little smaller than the one Leonardo described to cross a Norwegian fjord, and in 2006 the Turks themselves finally decided to act on the plan that had been rejected in 1502. In 2011, a Turkish architect began work on the design for the Leonardo bridge, which will soon cross over the Golden Horn in roughly the same place that Leonardo proposed 500 years ago.

Leonardo could only have been a Renaissance man during the Renaissance because it wasn't until then that truly new things—and entirely new worlds—were being discovered with such enthusiasm, and it was really only then that new ways of living were beginning to be studied and valued on their own terms.

A third reason why Leonardo could have only been a Renaissance man in the Renaissance is that, by the time of his adulthood, all those books and all those discoveries and all those new theories about life in the universe had cultivated a more critical and questioning mentality among Europe's leading thinkers.

The intellectual courage shown by dissidents and fantasizers in Leonardo's age was different from what had been present before—for now the people questioning the assumptions of contemporary authorities weren't just challenging outmoded traditions and old-fashioned customs, they were challenging, cherished concepts of the universal order, and the laws and rules that governed life itself.

The High Renaissance produced more than its fair share of social rebels, and we understand Leonardo's achievements better if we remember to situate his own work in the context of leading rebels of that time. Let's consider briefly the leading rebels, or dissidents, in the realms of pure science, politics, and religion.

First, consider Nicolas Copernicus, the Polish scientist whose groundbreaking astronomical study determined that the sun, and not the earth, was at the center of the solar system. Copernicus was educated in Bologna and Rome between 1496 and 1503: In Bologna, in particular, Copernicus the student would have encountered one of the most progressive educational systems in all of Europe, where women had an unusually large number of legal and social rights and could even enroll at the university as students. This kind of environment was conducive to creative intellectual thinking, and it's no coincidence that Copernicus felt liberated enough during his studies to go on to craft his dissident view of the solar system. Although his findings weren't published until just before his death at the age of 70 in 1543, the seeds of his risky—yet scientifically correct—proposals were planted in the fertile soil of the Italian Renaissance that he experienced as a student. We can only wonder what impact Leonardo's scientific work could have had, if he had lived just a few more years to organize and publish the results of his studies.

In politics, Niccolo Machiavelli carved out a name for himself through his bold and ambitious political treatise on how to govern during times of enormous instability and danger, and how the Italian peninsula might be united under a single government to counter the challenges from France, Spain, the Holy Roman Empire, and even England. *The Prince* was written as a private essay in 1513 by Machiavelli while serving a period of exile that had been imposed upon him by the new Medici family, the new rulers of Florence, for his opposition to their destruction of the Republic in 1512. He wrote it a few miles outside of Florence, in a tavern—which still exists and where you can still eat dinner—I have; it's pretty good food. Initially dedicated to Giuliano de'Medici, who was also, at that very moment, the patron of Leonardo da Vinci, and the book was Machiavelli's attempt to return to the good graces of the Medici family, have his ban lifted, and return to his home and his life as a civil servant in Florence.

But it was also an argument about what it would take for Italy to respond to the growing powers on all its borders. Machiavelli's thesis revolved around the central idea that the 16th-century prince had to employ guile, tact, and a detached sense of self-preservation in order to survive in an increasingly hostile world that was now eating Italian dukes alive. Shocking in its cold-hearted view of power, Machiavelli's pamphlet looked beyond old-fashioned traditions of chivalry, honor, and loyalty, to craft an entirely new vision of the modern political animal. We sometimes wonder how differently the Italian Renaissance might have turned out, if the Italian city-states had somehow solved the political problem Machiavelli was trying to address. Might it have lasted longer? Or might it have ended sooner?

In religion, dissident thinking from the period came from those who came to believe that the single greatest impediment to the spirit of personal growth was the ecclesiastical authority in Rome. There were a number of them who voiced their disapproval of the current status quo right at the turn of the 16th century, but perhaps the most outraged dissident of the period was the German Augustinian monk named Martin Luther, whose portrait I show here. Luther taught theology at the University of Wittenberg, but chafed under the stigma of a corrupt papal institution.

Only two years before Leonardo died, Luther defiantly nailed to a church door in Wittenberg a list of 95 accusations, or "Theses," that condemned Pope Leo X and the entire hierarchical structure that had brought him to power and had kept him there. But Luther also began to formulate a deeper, theoretical critique of organized religion as an entity, and he wondered if the tight controls on popular faith that were being held by priests and bishops ought to severed completely.

Luther, Machiavelli, and Copernicus—they were all educated and intellectually nurtured in the great age of the Renaissance that also begat Leonardo da Vinci. And all of them shared a quality that made them distinctly different from those who lived in the previous age: They were innovative, independent, but they were unafraid to challenge old notions if they thought new ones were better suited for the times. But unlike the dissidents driven by a single idea, not everything that Leonardo himself did or said was borne of a revolutionary mindset.

Leonardo made out his will on Easter Sunday in 1519, just days before his death; and when he did, he made sure to request that Masses of the Dead be said on his behalf, and that he be buried not only on consecrated ground, but inside the cloister of the monastery of St. Florentin in Amboise. He wanted a Christian burial that was normally reserved only for the very prosperous or for the very devout.

That's not to say that Leonardo was blindly, or even actively, religious in his daily dealings: Late in life, he famously grumbled in his notes that human beings were good for nothing except filling up toilets. He also felt that the body and soul were inextricably connected to the point where neither could exist without the other. He was unconvinced that human beings should or could live a life after death, for he was unimpressed with their conduct on earth and skeptical of the notion that a dead and decaying corpse had the capacity to be revived with a soul attached to it in the afterlife. Maybe Leonardo had seen too much in his long life as a courtier and a medical researcher.

But these questions clearly interested him. His personal library in 1503 included books he had either bought with his own money or had been given that referred to Christian spirituality. He owned his own Bible—which was unusual, but probably a useful reference for a painter of *The Last Supper*. But he also owned sermons by famously gifted preachers, and he had in his possession books that promoted the sanctity of Christ at the cross—including one in Italian called "On the Immortality of the Soul." He was raised in the Christian tradition, and he died embracing that tradition. While he questioned the motives of his fellow adherents, he also saw value in the faith they professed.

Like all of us, Leonardo was a product his times. But to a larger degree than most of us, Leonardo was also responsible for shaping that world in which he lived, too.

We call Leonardo the Renaissance man not only because he lived in the age of the Renaissance, and not only because in him we see embodied so many of the virtuous things we associate with the period—like intellectual creativity, personal integrity, and a thirst for knowledge. We call him the Renaissance man because he embodied the period even more fully than leading dissidents of the time like Copernicus, Machiavelli, or Martin Luther, dissidents who in various ways, also pointed beyond the Renaissance: Copernicus to a science beyond the visible, Machiavelli to a politics beyond the petty rivalries of city-states, and Martin Luther to a religion beyond an existing Church. The dissidents believed the world of the Renaissance could not last, and they had a vision of what the future held.

Leonardo, too, had a notion of what the future might look like, but he was also pragmatically focused on more immediate issues. Many of his achievements actually embodied, and even made possible, the world of the Italian Renaissance, and Leonardo literally could not have done what he did in any other earlier period in history. And it's perhaps also true that he couldn't have done what he did in any later period of history, either. He was the right man for the right jobs in the right place at the right time. It was a perfect storm.

The End of an Era

Lecture 35

Now and again, a new painting surfaces that art historians wish to attribute to Leonardo. One such painting, called *Salvator Mundi*, bears many of the master's hallmarks, but it also bears problematic differences from his style. Part of the problem in attributing work to Leonardo or his followers lies in how few close followers he had. Shortly after his departure from Italy in 1516, Raphael died suddenly, and Michelangelo's Mannerist approach to art swept the Italian Peninsula, rejecting Leonardo's classical ideals.

A New Leonardo?

- In November 2011, the National Gallery of London opened an exhibition called Leonardo da Vinci: Painter at the Court of Milan. The curators brought together paintings and drawings that Leonardo had produced between 1482 and 1499, including medical drawings, portraits, figure studies, and an assortment of other pictures produced by Leonardo and his small circle of followers.

- The show also included a painting that experts believed is a new, previously unknown work by Leonardo. This was the art-historical equivalent of announcing that a new planet had been discovered in our solar system.

- The painting, called *Salvator Mundi*—or *Savior of the World*—bears all the markings of a Leonardo from his first Milanese period. About 24″ × 18″ and painted in oil on a walnut panel, it shows the figure of Christ, gazing at us stoically and blessing us with his right hand while holding a transparent orb in his left. His blue robe hemmed with gold helps set off the bust-length figure from the dark background. The facial features and body contours seem to float and dissolve, thanks to the sfumato technique.

- *Salvator Mundi* was quickly connected to the *John the Baptist* in the Louvre, which Leonardo largely painted during and after 1510. A more obvious connection was *The Last Supper*, which was the only other figure of the adult Christ that Leonardo had ever been known to paint.

- Some striking similarities connect the two: The eyelids of both figures close just a bit, and long hair is parted in the middle and cascades down the neck and shoulders. There are also significant points of departure, which suggests that *Salvator Mundi* is, in fact, by Leonardo, who was too innovative and ambitious to merely copy himself.

- A technical analysis of the paint, the direction of the brushstrokes, and the undercoat drawings revealed by X-rays also supported an attribution to Leonardo. However, there are still many reasons to doubt the attribution.

The Case against *Salvator Mundi*

- Leonardo had a small following during his own lifetime, but those who imitated him were quite skilled painters. We have a handful of pictures that are close to Leonardo's style but not quite up to par with the great works of the master lumped together under the broad category of School of Leonardo.

- The *Bacchus* found in the Louvre near the *Mona Lisa* was once attributed to Leonardo but now to a follower. It does not have the master's sense of fluidity or grace, and the landscape does not conform to the types of natural settings that he was painting during the 16th century, when this picture was most probably produced.

- A new attribution is made and unmade every few years as a new panel is presented for authentication. It is always small, intimate, and darkened by overcoats of varnish applied by earlier restorers. And every time, a positive analysis is scuttled by the fact that there is no mention of such a picture in Leonardo's notebooks or in the letters and archives of the people and institutions that sought works by him.

- *Salvator Mundi* is first mentioned in 1651 by an engraver who claimed he was copying a Leonardo. It is probably no coincidence that this is the year when Leonardo's *Treatise on Painting* was first released to the wider public, published in French and Italian.

The School of Leonardo

- Unlike most great masters, Leonardo's career moves were not conducive to embracing a traditional arrangement that cultivated a large following of students and partners. He moved around so often that he did not have the opportunity to make those longstanding relationships.

- Leonardo only influenced a small group of immediate disciples. **Giovanni Boltraffio** went on to paint portraits of the Sforza family. **Giovanni de' Predis** worked with Leonardo on both versions of the *Madonna of the Rocks*. Those who carried on Leonardo's approach after his death include **Bernardino Luini**, Francesco Melzi, and Salai.

- We do not know very much about Bernardino Luini, but we can trace his presence in Milan and the surrounding towns in Lombardy from 1500 until about 1520, when he went to Rome to learn from the work of Raphael—too late, for Raphael died that year.

- Luini's *Christ Child with a Lamb*, from about 1515, plucks a number of themes from works by Leonardo: Christ embracing the Lamb was lifted directly from the *Saint Anne Madonna*. Luini mixes Leonardo's two major mature stylistic approaches as well: the tenebristic background and the sfumato contours.

- His *Christ Blessing* also borrows from these sources, and that intimate, personal interaction between the figure and the viewer, in which no authorities are needed to intercede on behalf of the worshiper, reminds us of both Leonardo's *John the Baptist* and the *Salvator Mundi*.

- Salai was a skilled artist, although undisciplined and poorly suited for making it on his own. The few pictures he produced show a heavy dose of Leonardo in nearly every way. His *John the Baptist*, painted in the 1510s, was obviously inspired by Leonardo's, but Salai chose to include more detail in the landscape.

- Salai's approach to the figure of Bacchus—with a more overt attempt to show landscapes and figures than Leonardo had employed—leads one naturally to identify Salai as the author of the other Bacchus in the Louvre.

- The few works attributed to Francesco Melzi suggest a more original take on Leonardo's classicism. His *Portrait of a Woman* adopts the three-quarter pose, the use of flora and fauna as identifiers, and the dramatic spotlighting effects, but it is not a copy or an unoriginal take on a specific picture by Leonardo. He seems to be taking what he learned from the master and applying those lessons in an original way. Melzi did not have the same kind of manual dexterity that Salai did, and the rigid contours of his figure have little in common with the more subtle and gentle feeling of a Leonardo painting.

Michelangelo and the Mannerists

- When Leonardo left Italy in 1516, Italian painters became more willing to experiment with new approaches to figures and scenes. Even Raphael broke free with his highly experimental *Transfiguration*, employing the figure-eight composition.

- Raphael's sudden death in 1520 and dearth of immediate followers cut short the ideal of the High Renaissance that he and Leonardo had worked so hard to create. The one figure who was determined to break it apart was the one figure who survived them both: Michelangelo.

- Michelangelo invented new poses and themes that would allow him to go beyond that which the human eye had already experienced. This hypernaturalism seeks to convey the intensity of a singular emotional sensation through the physicality of gesture. In that sense, Michelangelo had learned this from Leonardo, who, in *The Last Supper* had done this more subtly.

- In 1516, Michelangelo was back in Florence, forced to return to his home town by Pope Leonardo X to design a burial chapel for the Medici in the church of San Lorenzo. For the next 50 years, Michelangelo would hold the field, and the classicial ideals of Leonardo and Raphael would take a distant second place to his vision.

- Michelangelo's sculptural works for the Medici tombs demonstrate his extraordinarily anticlassical, or **Mannerist**, approach. Their bodies twist and turn, coiling and uncoiling in positions that simply cannot be replicated by normal human beings. They are big, bulky, and overly muscled, as though Michelangelo has told us that the laws of nature no longer apply to the works that he wants to produce.

The Politics of Mannerism

- Exacerbating the artistic situation was the chaotic and urgently dangerous political situation in Italy during these crucial years. The rapid ascent of François I and Charles V put two young, ambitious men on the wealthiest thrones in Europe, and they considered each other rivals for the duration of their reigns.

- Charles eventually expelled the French from Italian soil, this time without the interference of papal alliances or outside mercenary troops. However, in 1527, a group of his mutinous troops splintered off from the main force, ransacked the papal city, and humiliated Pope Clement VII.

- This incident served to demonstrate, once and for all, that the concept of Italian unification and glory, with the pope as the Christian Emperor, was pure fantasy. With the destruction of that dream came a reaction amongst artists and thinkers who had worked for so long to celebrate the classical vision that had driven the dream of Renaissance in the first place.

- Within less than a decade, the last true disciples of Raphael and Leonardo had left the field. Those who were left converted to Michelangelo and Mannerism.

- The change of stylistic preferences probably had as much to do with court culture as it did with the presence of foreign soldiers on Italian soil. Instead of a focus on controlling and extending Italian domains, there was an emphasis on manners, figures of speech, and acts of charity.

- By the 1520s, a very different culture, marked by extreme demonstrations of self-awareness and obsequious self-deprecation, had seeped into court life. Italian courts were losing their ambition. Now they just wanted to survive and be recognized by their Spanish overlords as cultural tourist attractions that ought to be preserved.

- The Italian princes who commissioned works of art often insisted that their painters elaborate on eccentricities and expressions of elegance. The sober approach to subject matter that Leonardo had taken was no more than a memory.

- The interest in mannered pictures was exported to wide swaths of European society. Trying to figure out what was going on in a work of art became part of the fun. The logical or natural was considered boring; the fantastic was considered a tour de force.

- This is not to say that Leonardo was forgotten or that those who remembered him dismissed his innovations and ideas. Vasari was one of the great Mannerists of the 16th century, yet he lionized Leonardo in his *Lives of the Artists*.

- Still, by the middle of the 1520s, the dream of the High Renaissance was coming to an end. Maybe the classical style had run its course and had exhausted all its interesting possibilities. Maybe the sway of Michelangelo's fame was too great to ignore. Maybe the deaths of Raphael and Leonardo so close to one another were simply too great to overcome. Maybe there was a collective grieving for the demise of the papacy. Maybe it was due to a realization that life in Italy would never again be the same. Or maybe it was a combination of all of these.

Important Term

Mannerism: An artistic style popularized in the 1520s and 1530s that evolved as an alternative to the classicism of the High Renaissance.

Suggested Reading

Friedlaender, *Mannerism and Anti-Mannerism in Italian Painting.*

Shearman, *Mannerism.*

Syson, ed. *Leonardo da Vinci: Painter at the Court of Milan.*

The End of an Era

Lecture 35—Transcript

In November of 2011, the National Gallery of Art in London opened an exhibition called "Leonardo da Vinci, Painter at the Court of Milan." The curators brought together paintings and drawings that Leonardo had produced from that vital period of personal discovery he enjoyed in the service of Ludovico Sforza between 1482 and 1499. The exhibition included medical drawings, portraits, figure studies, and an assortment of pictures produced in Milan in that period by Leonardo and his small circle of followers.

The one big news coming out of that exhibition was that the show included a painting that experts believed is a new, previously unknown painting by Leonardo da Vinci. This was the art historical equivalent of announcing that a new planet had been discovered in our solar system.

The painting, called the *Salvator Mundi*—or the *Savior of the World*—bears all the markings of a picture by Leonardo da Vinci. It's only about 24 inches by 18 inches and it shows us the figure of the Blessing Christ, gazing at us stoically, and blessing us with his right hand while holding a transparent orb in his left. His blue robe, hemmed with gold helps set off the bust-length figure from the dark background that holds him in place. The features of his face and the contours of his body seem to float and dissolve, thanks to the sfumato technique employed by the artist through his use of oil paints on the walnut panel—the type of wood that Leonardo preferred during his first Milanese period.

It's not hard to see why specialists were so excited about this find when they announced it in 2011. The highly personalized, even intimate relationship forged between figure and viewer was not a common feature in the repertoire of the average painter of the High Renaissance, and the emergence of a holy figure from that kind of setting—and in such a dramatic way—points directly to Leonardo. The *Salvator Mundi* was quickly connected to the bust-length depiction of John the Baptist in the Louvre, which Leonardo had largely painted during and after 1510. Although the picture of the Baptist conveys a livelier sense of movement, the direct gaze of both figures indicated a thematic connection between the two.

A more obvious connection was with the central figure of *The Last Supper*, which was the only other figure of the adult Christ that Leonardo had ever been known to paint. The figure of Christ in *The Last Supper* was examined very closely for similarities, as was the finished preparatory drawing of Christ's head that contains essentially the same features and forms as the figure in Leonardo's mural. And again, some striking similarities connect the two images together: The eyelids of both Christ in the drawing and Christ in the *Salvator Mundi* seem to close just a bit, and his long hair is parted down the middle of his head and cascades down his neck and his shoulders. But the *Salvator Mundi* is not a slavish copy of *The Last Supper*, and there are significant points of departure between the two, which is an important feature suggesting that it is, in fact, by Leonardo—who was too innovative and ambitious to merely copy himself—or even quote himself indirectly. The picture has a lot going for it.

In addition, there was also a technical analysis containing important information about paint samples, the direction of brushstrokes, and the appearance of undercoat drawings revealed by X-rays, and these also supported an attribution to Leonardo. However, even if you have not been privy to all of the technical analysis, you now know enough now to be in a position to consider these claims for yourself. I, for one, have to say that I have my doubts.

This is partly due to the fact that I've seen this movie before, and I know how it ends. Leonardo had only a small following during his own lifetime, for reasons we'll discuss in just a moment, but those who imitated him were actually quite skilled painters who figured out how to make images that looked a lot like his and contained messages similar to those that appeared in works by his own hand. Because of that, we have a very small handful of pictures that are close to Leonardo's style, but are not quite up to par with the great works of the master. They tend to be lumped together under the broad category of "School of Leonardo," although we do know who the painters were for a few of them.

This painting of the *Bacchus* is one such painting. It's located in the Louvre Museum in Paris, and is usually on display in the same room as the *Mona Lisa*—which means it's also usually impossible to see due to the crush of the tour groups that collect around that tiny portrait and literally expel all the other museum-goers who aren't there just necessarily to see *La Gioconda.*

But it's actually quite a nice little picture that features a somewhat ambiguous figure sitting in a landscape, smiling out at us from his perch. Originally, it seems to have represented John the Baptist. But later, recent analysis has shown, the painting was modified to depict the ancient god of wine, Bacchus. Also, the attribution has been taken away from Leonardo and moved to the "School of Leonardo." It doesn't have the master's sense of fluidity or grace, and the landscape does not conform to types of natural settings that he was painting during the 16th century, when this picture was most probably produced.

Now I've said I've seen this movie before? Here's what I mean: This kind of thing happens every few years, as a new panel is presented for authentication. It's always small, intimate, and darkened by overcoats of varnish that had been applied by earlier restorers. And every time this happens, a positive analysis is scuttled by the fact that there's no mention of such a picture in the vast records of Leonardo's notebooks—or in the letters and archives of all those people and institutions that sought works by him.

That's the case here, too. The *Salvator Mundi* is first mentioned only in 1650 by an engraver who claimed that he'd copied a Leonardo—but there's no record of it anywhere before this date. There's no copies of it, no sketches of it, no thoughts or remotely connected precedents for it.

Now it would be convenient if I could tell you that Leonardo's direct circle of followers was extensive and prominent. Raphael had his disciples, and they went on to shape the direction of painting in Italy for several years after he died in 1520. Michelangelo certainly had his admirers to, and he promoted a mini-cult of personality around him, that ensured that his name and his reputation would live on for decades after his death in 1564.

But Leonardo disappoints us in this regard. His career was unlike those of every artist who had come before him and all those of his age who followed him—including Michelangelo and Raphael. His career moves just weren't conducive to the kind of stable life he needed in order to embrace a traditional arrangement in which he could cultivate a large following of fellow painters, former students, and partners. From 1500 onwards, Leonardo was in constant demand—due to his individuality and personal abilities—but he moved around so often that he simply didn't have the opportunity to make those longstanding relationships. His career became largely transient just when he became a superstar, and that made it difficult for him to own property or plant roots toward a genuine legacy that might have continued his vision after he was gone.

Instead, Leonardo influenced only a small group of immediate disciples. There were really only two or three in Milan who worked closely enough with Leonardo to understand his style well enough to implement it: Giovanni Boltraffio was one, and he did a fine job of representing members of the Sforza family that captured likenesses in the tenebristic atmosphere that Leonardo employed. Giovanni de' Predis was another, and the work he did with Leonardo on both versions of the *Madonna of the Rocks* for the Confraternity of the Immaculate Conception, including the angels that flanked the central panel, gave him direct access to the artistic mind of Leonardo da Vinci.

But there weren't many more who carried on Leonardo's approach after his death—Bernardino Luini, Francesco Melzi, and Salai were the most notable ones we know about. But thank goodness for them. It was through their efforts that Leonardo's ideas were disseminated, that paintings that are now lost or severely damaged were copied, and that his disciplined approach to art and science was embraced by future generations of scholars and painters. Were it not for these followers, we wouldn't have the *Treatise on Painting*, the copies of the *Leda and the Swan*, the reproductions of the *Battle of Anghiari*, and the prints of *The Last Supper* as it looked before it began to fall apart.

And some of his assistants and followers were actually quite talented artists. Among the most gifted was a painter named Bernardino Luini, who was born around 1480 in the region around Milan and the Lago Maggiore. We don't know very much about him, as he was not the cause of gossip, legend, or fame during his lifetime. But we can trace his presence in Milan and the surrounding towns in Lombardy from 1500 until about 1520, when he went to Rome to learn from the work of Raphael—too late, as it turns out, for Raphael died in that year.

Luini's paintings reveal a deep and abiding admiration for Leonardo's works and beliefs, even though he doesn't seem to have worked closely with or even near his idol for most of his career.

The image of the *Christ Child with the Lamb*, from about 1515, sees Luini plucking a number of themes from works by Leonardo, who was still alive when this painting was produced. The theme of Christ embracing the Lamb was lifted directly from the *St. Anne Madonna*, although now the focus is on Jesus rather than his mother's extended reach. Luini mixes Leonardo's two major mature stylistic approaches in this picture. His selection of the tenebristic background enshrouding the pair harkens back to Leonardo's portraits from the 1480s and 1490s, during his Milanese period, but his blurring of the contours of his figures refers to that heavily sfumatesque style that Leonardo preferred during the last two decades of his life.

The image of *Christ Blessing* also borrows from these sources, and that intimate, personal interaction between the figure and the viewer—in which no authorities are needed to intercede on behalf of the worshiper—*John the Baptist* from about 1510 and, ironically, the *Salvator Mundi* have that same appearance.

As we might expect, Leonardo's closest associates were the most likely to try their hand at producing pictures that employed his interests and impulses. Gian Caprotti was one of these painters—but we know him better by the nickname that Leonardo gave him: This is Salai.

Salai appears to have been a skilled artist, although undisciplined and poorly suited for making it on his own as an independent artist. The few pictures that he produced, though, show a heavy dose of Leonardo in nearly every way.

This version of *John the Baptist* was painted during the 15-teens and was obviously inspired by the original in his master's possession. The identical positions of the two figures are too obvious to spend much time on, but I do think it's interesting that Salai chose to include more detail in the landscape of his half-length figure: He didn't take the shortcut of enshrouding his figure, and he gave the green meadow and blue mountains a good, honest try. And his approach to the figure of *Bacchus*—with a more overt attempt to show landscapes and figures than Leonardo had employed—leads one naturally to identify Salai as the author of this.

The few works attributed to Francesco Melzi, the noble-born assistant who joined Leonardo late in his career, suggest a more classical, original take on this brand of classicism that was invented by his master. In this *Portrait of a Woman*, Melzi uses the same kind of features that Leonardo employed in the paintings of female sitters: the three-quarter pose, the use of flora and fauna as identifiers, and the dramatic spotlighting effects that illuminate the sitter's body are all here. But it's not a copy or an unoriginal take on a specific picture by Leonardo. He seems to be taking what he learned from the master and applying those lessons in an original way. That said, Melzi did not have the same kind of manual dexterity that Salai did, and the rigid contours of this figure have little in common with the more subtle and gentle feeling of a painting by Salai, or of course by Leonardo, their master. But really, that was about it.

When Leonardo left Italy in 1516 for France, his fellow artists in Rome almost immediately recognized that an opportunity had presented itself to them. With Leonardo gone, there seems to have been a greater willingness to experiment with new approaches to figures and scenes. Raphael now broke free with his highly experimental image of the Transfiguration, employing the figure-eight composition that, on the one hand, acknowledged the importance of a compositional core, but on the other hand, broke it apart by multiplying that core in an effort to encourage an active viewing experience. I don't think it's a coincidence that the Transfiguration was essentially designed and largely painted in the year that Leonardo left Rome.

But where exactly Raphael was going to go with this new approach to art is anyone's guess. For in 1520 the refined and eloquent painter grew sick and died suddenly in Rome. He was buried in the Pantheon. It was a death that caught most of his colleagues and admirers completely off-guard, in part, because even the great Raphael—who was only 37 at the time of his death—

hadn't really thought about ordaining any of his students or followers as a successor. The early admirer of Leonardo and the torchbearer of classicism in Rome during the 15-teens was now gone, and there was no one there to carry on for him.

Just as Leonardo's intense privacy and relatively transitory life had reduced the opportunity for followers to carry on his legacy, so too did Raphael's sudden death and dearth of immediate followers cut short the ideal of the High Renaissance that both of them had worked so hard to create.

And the one figure who was determined to break it apart was the one figure who survived them both. Michelangelo was never afraid of Leonardo, essentially ignored Raphael, and he went ahead with his own projects as he saw fit with no cares for what the two classicists thought about him.

But when Leonardo left Rome in 1516 and died in 1519, and then when Raphael died in 1520, there was truly a vacuum in the world of High Renaissance art, for the only other major giant left in central Italy who could've carried the torch in their absence was adamant that it was time to change the way things had been done in the visual arts for the previous 40 years.

It was a theme that Michelangelo would explore for the rest of his career. In the sculptures for the ill-fated tomb of Julius II that he was able to rough out into even a semifinal form, Michelangelo, shows his inventions of new poses and themes that would allow him to go beyond that which the human eye had already experienced. In these two sculptures of slaves, produced just as Michelangelo was leaving Rome to go to Florence in 1516, we can see how his desire to present for us exaggerated bodies that go beyond the realities of this world were being made manifest in his works. They struggle with their own bodies, and they writhe in ways that seem to invent new contortions never before struck by mortal humans. It's a hyper-naturalism that seeks to convey to viewers the intensity of a singular emotional sensation through the physicality of gesture. In that sense, it's something that Michelangelo had learned from Leonardo, who, in *The Last Supper*, had done just this kind of thing, only in much more subtle fashion.

Now in 1516, as Leonardo rode off to France, Michelangelo was back in Florence, albeit unhappily. He'd been forced to return to his home town on orders from Pope Leonardo X to work for the Medici family, for whom he was to design a burial chapel in the Church of San Lorenzo and sculpt a massive monument to the Pope's two nephews, Lorenzo and Giuliano. It was a bitter moment for Michelangelo, as he knew this massive project—both architectural and sculptural—would sidetrack him indefinitely from the one project he genuinely yearned to complete—the tomb of Julius II. And he was right: It did.

But the work that Michelangelo produced turned out to be the only things left for artists to latch onto for inspiration: For the next 50 years, Michelangelo would hold the field, and the classical ideals of Leonardo and Raphael would take a distant second place to his vision.

Michelangelo's sculptural works for the Medici tombs in the New Sacristy of San Lorenzo reveal the intent of the artist as he worked in Florence for patrons he neither liked nor respected. We still debate about the symbolic meaning of the enormous figures that perch on and above the tombs of Lorenzo and Giulliano de' Medici, the 16th-century nephews of the pope Leonardo X; but we don't debate the extraordinarily anti-classical approach that Michelangelo took when carving these giants. Their bodies twist and turn, coiling and uncoiling in positions that simply cannot be replicated by normal human beings without risking serious back injuries. They're big and bulky and overly muscled, and it's as though Michelangelo has told us that the laws of nature no longer apply to the works that he wants to produce.

Exacerbating this entire artistic situation, of course, was the chaotic and urgently dangerous political situation in Italy during these crucial years. The rapid ascent of Francois I and Charles V to the thrones of France and Spain in 1515 and 1516 meant that Europe's two wealthiest monarchs attained control of their states at equally youthful ages, and thus considered each other rivals for control of Europe throughout the duration of their reigns, which lasted for over 50 years.

This was intensified in 1519. Charles also took on the title of Holy Roman Emperor in 1519, which means he gained control of the German and Dutch principalities that now helped encircle Francois's more centralized and unified French nation-state. And Italy became a major battleground for these two potentates.

Charles eventually expelled the French entirely from Italian soil, this time without the interference of papal alliances or outside mercenary troops. After the Battle of Pavia in 1525, in which the forces of the Holy Roman Emperor routed those of the French King, Charles V was in total control of all of Italy. This tapestry commemorates Charles's victory, and if you look closely you can see in the background the great monastery of the Certosa of Pavia—the place that Ludovico Sforza had used as a retreat, and where Leonardo da Vinci had spent many of his days as a courtier working alongside some of Italy's greatest minds.

The one military force in Italy that Charles V seems to have had trouble controlling, actually, was his own. In 1527, a group of Charles's mutinous troops splintered off from the main force in the north, made their way south through Tuscany and Umbria, and on May 6, 1527, they stormed through the barricades set up by a token force of militiamen in Rome. For six days, rapacious German and Swiss soldiers ransacked the papal city and humiliated the pope, who had to lock himself inside the Castel Sant'Angelo for his own protection. This drawing by Maarten Van Hermskeerk from 1554 recalls that moment, with imperial troops aiming their harquebuses and small cannons at the castle, while Clement VII shouts at them angrily from a balcony on the top floor. This little adventure served to demonstrate, once and for all, that the concept of Italian unification and glory, with the pope as the Christian Emperor, was pure fantasy. A dream that had motivated the Italian Renaissance was dead.

With the destruction of that dream, came a certain cultural reaction amongst those artists and thinkers who had worked for so long to celebrate the classical vision that had driven the dream of Renaissance in the first place.

At first the disciples of Raphael and Leonardo were able to hold to the principles of the previous generation. In Giulio Romano's *Deesis* from 1522, a balanced, hierarchical picture employs some of Raphael's old tricks—it combines the quasi-pyramidal composition of the *Sistine Madonna* with the figure-eight arm-extension of the Transfiguration. Ludovico Mazzolino's *St. Anne Madonna*, also from 1522, returns to Leonardo's old compositional typology of Christ sitting in the lap of Mary, who sits in the lap of Anne. Mazzolino centers his figures well, and his use of rich crimson and gold colors unifies the surface brilliantly. It's truly a beautiful picture.

But these followers were not able to hold off the Michelangelo faction, which was gaining steam in the major artistic centers of Italy. Giulio Romano left Rome to work for the Gonzaga court in Mantua in 1524, and his colleagues, Mazzolino and Gianfresco Penni, both died in 1528; within less than a decade of his death, the last true disciples of Raphael and Leonardo had already left the field. Those who were left converted over to the side of Michelangelo.

Look at these pictures by Jacopo Pontormo, a Florentine who had spent part of his apprentice under Leonardo. It's not that these pictures are not natural, or that we simply cannot believe that we could be a part of them. But they subtly (and sometimes overtly) break the barriers of naturalism to include twists, turns, expressions, positions, and even subjects that we can't always identify (or identify with).

In the *Descent from the Cross*, Christ's body has been twisted horribly by two figures who, somehow, manage to support his weighty body on their shoulders, even they themselves are balancing on their own tiptoes. There's no recognizable background whatsoever, and the brilliant colors seem entirely out of place in what should be a somber and even depressing scene of defeat. It just doesn't make sense.

Some have argued, with some persuasion, that the collapse of a recognizable authority within Italy was in part responsible for this decision by painters to distance themselves from a style intimately connected with a notion that was clearly no longer viable. The dream of the Renaissance was over, and with it went the whole purpose of the High Renaissance artistic style.

But the change of stylistic preferences—called "Anti-classicism" by some and "Mannerism" by others—probably had just as much to do with an evolution of court culture in Italy during the 1520s, 1530s. and 1540s as it did with the presence of foreign soldiers on Italian soil. Instead of a focus on controlling and extending their domains, there was a much more inward-looking emphasis on manners, figures of speech, acts of charity large and small, and even the way in which aristocrats held their hands and fingers while speaking.

Now there were customs and traditions that guided 15th-century princes, and Ludovico Sforza and Cesare Borgia certainly had their expectations of courtiers who were in their service. But those expectations had much more to do with ambitions to expand territory. By the time we get into the 1520s, a very different culture, marked by extreme demonstrations of self-awareness and obsequious self-deprecation had seeped into the way people lived their lives. And it's this Mannerist notion of the courtier, not the High Renaissance courtier exemplified here by Leonardo, that has shaped the way people today see courtiers in general.

The city-states of Italy had lost out to the nation-states of France and Spain, and this transformed what it meant to be at court in Italy. The various courts in there were losing their ambition and were no longer competing with each other as power-brokers. They were no longer restlessly promoting and searching for genuine innovations to expand their power. Now they just wanted to survive and be recognized by their Spanish overlords as cultural tourist attractions that ought to be preserved.

The Italian princes who commissioned works of art from people like Giulio Romano, Raphael's most gifted student, often insisted that their painters elaborate on eccentricities and expressions of elegance in an effort to entertain their guests and bring glory to their courts. When Giulio Romano designed the so-called Palazzo del Te in the city of Mantua for the Gonzaga family, he filled the buildings with paintings of classical giants fictively destroying the very building he'd constructed. The sober approach to subject matter that Leonardo da Vinci had taken to all his works—including the playful *John the Baptist* and the eroticized *Leda and the Swan*—they were no more than faint memories in the minds of artists and patrons alike.

And erudite audiences who had grown up with classical art in their churches and offices and homes ate it up. They loved looking at strange pictures that they couldn't quite recognize, with figures doing things and striking poses that openly flaunted the laws of nature that Leonardo had vehemently considered central to art.

And this interest in mannered pictures that entered into the world of the fantastical was exported to wide swaths of European society, including some you wouldn't expect. The grand duke of Tuscany, Cosimo I de'Medici in 1540 had Agnolo Bronzino paint his own portrait as Orpheus, playing a lute, in the nude—this is the duke of Tuscany. King Francois I of France, the last patron of Leonardo da Vinci, received as a gift from Duke Cosimo this utterly bizarre and still-indecipherable Allegory in 1548. Trying to figure out what was going on in a work of art now became part of the fun of owning and displaying it to one's friends. They became conversation pieces. The logical or natural was considered boring: The fantastic was considered a tour de force.

This is not to say that Leonardo was forgotten, or that those who remembered him irreverently dismissed his innovations and his ideas. Even those Mannerists thumbing their noses at naturalism respected Leonardo for his contributions. Let's not forget that it was Giorgio Vasari, one of the great Mannerists of the 16th century, who in 1550 lionized Leonardo in his Lives of the Artists, calling him the first truly modern artist in history and the father of contemporary art in Italy.

And the very existence of posthumous portraits of Leonardo that sprang up decades after his death indicate an enduring admiration for the groundbreaking work that he did during his life. These two 16th-century pictures seem based on a similar model or template, and remind us of his popularity immediately after his death, even during the height of the Mannerist period.

But still, by the middle of the 1520s the dream of the High Renaissance was already coming to an end. Maybe the classical style had run its course and had exhausted all the interesting possibilities available to new generations of artists looking to make their own mark. Maybe the sway of Michelangelo's fame was too great to ignore. Maybe the deaths of Raphael and Leonardo so close to one another was simply too great to overcome. Maybe there was a collective grieving for the demise of the papacy as a centralizing force and the failed ambitions of cities like Milan and Florence. Maybe it was due to a realization that life in Italy would never again be the same, and that foreign powers would govern them for a very long time. Or maybe it was combination of all of them. Whatever had changed, we can be quite sure that the laws of classicism died—and with them died the High Renaissance itself. It was time to move on.

All good things must come to an end.

The Legacies of Leonardo da Vinci

Lecture 36

Leonardo's legacies are almost too many to count. Whether championing his cause or rebelling against his rules, artists and scientists in the five centuries since his death have all been working in his shadow, thanks to the handful of paintings and treasure trove of sketches and notes he left behind. It is hard to imagine our modern world without Leonardo to help lay its foundations.

The Period

- We have noted three things about the so-called Italian High Renaissance: First, it was not merely a rebirth of antiquity: it was an age of innovation and originality. Much of Leonardo's best work, for example, showed no particular reliance on ancient sources at all.

- Second, the period was not entirely a high point: Much of Leonardo's career took place when Italian city-states were falling underneath the power of France, Spain, or whoever was paying the Swiss mercenaries.

- Third, the Renaissance was never exclusively Italian, not even within Italy. Even the word "Renaissance" was coined by a 19th-century French historian. The fact that we use Renaissance rather than Vasari's term—Rinascita—reminds us that France, among other powers, did a lot to shape the context for what we think of as the High Renaissance.

The Genre

- The paintings Leonardo produced are among the easiest things to discuss, both because they are the most readily available and because in almost every painting he produced, he experimented with some aspect of traditional modes of representation.

- Any great work of art—whether a painting or a poem, a symphony or a sculpture—speaks to us. *The Last Supper* moves us with its dramatic power, with its fleeting references to both the depths of human depravity and the hope for redemption. If any single image from Leonardo's repertoire captures the essence of the man, the artist, and the scientist, it is *The Last Supper*—that failed experiment in mural painting that has been one of the greatest success stories in the entire history of narrative art.

- Leonardo was such a gifted artist at such an early age that most of the things we are told he painted have survived. People who owned a Leonardo usually held onto it, knowing they had something special.

- Of the paintings he left to Salai—*Leda and the Swan*, the *Saint Anne Madonna*, *John the Baptist*, and the *Mona Lisa*—all but the first passed into the hands of the French monarchy and, after the French Revolution, became part of the national collection at the Louvre. Because they became public at such an early date, they became representative of Leonardo's innovative spirit as an artist.

- *Mona Lisa*, the most famous work of art in the world, reminds us of Leonardo's masterful invention of the new genre of portraiture in the High Renaissance. His innovations tie directly to the convictions he held about the importance of human beings as individuals, with brains and ideas and character traits that deserved to be celebrated, no matter who they were, where they came from, or what sex they were.

- We sometimes forget the great distance that portraiture traveled with Leonardo at the helm from the staid and formulaic approach that had been taken by Leonardo's predecessors. When we see his lively, enigmatic, and deeply dramatic representation of Cecilia Gallerani, we remember the power of his observational skills.

- Leonardo's portraiture is also a testament to his scientific innovation. He used his oil paints to hone the appearance of his sitter's heads and faces based on his anatomical studies of the human head and created ways to help viewers identify his sitters and see them as real, living breathing people.

- *John the Baptist* reminds us of the unusually powerful dramatic flair Leonardo had. Tenebrism allowed him to make his sitters and figures leap from the surface, imbuing them with a liveliness that surprised those who saw his pictures for the first time.

- Future generations of artists would recognize the value of these approaches. When art historians consider the greatest age of painted portraiture—the 17th century—and review the work of the Dutch and Flemish artists who made it so great, the kinds of portraits they see all have the trademark qualities of a Leonardo portrait.

- The *Saint Anne Madonna* painting contained important features that continued the artistic interests of Leonardo into the last years of his career. Leonardo invented the theme of the human relationship between his Madonna figures, and his contemporaries who understood this quickly copied the theme in their own works.

- His other great *Saint Anne Madonna*, the cartoon in the British Museum, contains the swimming Christ figure, who squirms from Mary's grasp on his way to greet John the Baptist and his future. This signaled a brand new approach to Madonna paintings in the 16th century.

- In the background of the *Saint Anne Madonna*, we see the vast landscape that has its roots in the drawing that Leonardo did in the Tuscan hills on August 5, 1473, and speaks to his scientific interest in how the atmosphere affects the way that we see objects both near and far away.

- Leonardo's willingness to go outdoors and draw the things he saw with his own eye, to capture the natural world just as it appears to the naked eye, came to inform the great movements of 19th- and 20th-century art, including the Impressionists and the technique of plein aire painting.

- Leonardo was not afraid to paint the nude form, and he was not afraid to speak frankly about the desires of human beings in his notebooks. The Venetians quickly followed this lead, and its trajectory through the 17th, 18th, and 19th centuries leads us through some of history's greatest and most important paintings.

- Probably the longest-lasting and most important painterly contribution Leonardo made to the history of art was his creation of, and insistence on, true classical composition. The triangular format resonated with generations of artists.

- When Leonardo's *Treatise on Painting* was published in 1651, a whole series of his 17th-century admirers and imitators who had looked closely at Leonardo's lessons through his paintings now could do so through his writings. Their adherence to Leonardo's laws resulted in the creation of the Royal Academy of Art in France and the triumph of classical painting in Europe for roughly 200 years.

- Leonardo was a complicated person, who sought to unite within himself what others might have regarded as opposites. On the one hand, Leonardo was adamant that the natural world be his guide in all things. But at the same time, he was interested in perfection and sought to place the elements of this world into order.

- Leonardo was both an Aristotelian and a Platonist. He also looked at Nature as something that unifies all people as members of the human race, while also celebrating the details and specific features that make each of us individuals.

The Academies

- Leonardo, more than anyone else before him, confirmed in the minds of his peers and his followers that practitioners of the visual arts had every right to be considered as intellectuals, on par with poets and philosophers and scientists.

- The notion that artists had to be educated in ancient literature, mathematics, and philosophy had come from Alberti in the middle of the 15th century. Alberti insisted that painters needed to understand how the world looked and worked to draw and paint successfully. Leonardo added that artists could expand on the body of knowledge in each of these subjects and add to our understanding of the natural world.

- Leonardo's determination to add artists to the list of intellectuals was met with general approval soon after his death. Art academies sprang up in Florence, Rome, Paris, and London in the late 16th and 17th centuries. Today, colleges and universities all around the world have fine arts and art history as core components of their academic programs.

The Notebooks

- Yet another important legacy are Leonardo's 7,000 or so pages of notes, drawings, and essays. Only about a third of that survived the 16th century, but this probably is not as big a loss as it sounds. Melzi seems to have thrown out duplicates and pages Leonardo himself believed were useless. The fact that Melzi retained thousands of pages—some of them puzzling and only barely legible—indicates that he erred on the side of caution and preservation.

- After making his choices, Melzi arranged the notes into different categories and had them bound into manuscripts or boxed together as sets. He held onto them for the duration of his life but allowed selected others to study them.

- When he died in 1579, Melzi's descendants inherited the notebooks and sold them off to different collectors. In 1630 Pompeo Leoni, a sculptor in the Spanish court of Philip IV, hunted them down, reassembled, and reorganized them by category.

- Over time, the manuscripts have been sold off to museums and collectors, and today most of them are in European collections. The largest of these is the Codex Atlanticus, 12 volumes containing more than 1,000 pages of inventions, experiments, and scientific observations.

- The legacy of Leonardo that survives in his notebooks is, in some ways, even more relevant today than his paintings are. It would take centuries for science and technology to catch up with Leonardo's visions.

- The development of the combustion engine in the 19th century was the key ingredient that he had lacked. With it, Leonardo's most imaginative inventions changed the course of modern warfare and modern history.

- Of all the inventions that emerge from Leonardo's manuscripts, the one that has probably had the greatest impact on modern society was the airplane. Even into the late 18th century, aviators like Sir George Cayley were designing their flying machines as extensions of Leonardo's, and the questions they were asking about speed, power, and weight were almost identical to the ones Leonardo asked.

- It was in these manuscripts that Leonardo's work as a scientist came to be known, respected, and imitated. He thought everything was fair game for study, and he thought we should care. He wrote, "The acquisition of any knowledge whatever is always useful to the intellect, for nothing can be either loved or hated unless it is first known."

- He urged himself, and anyone who came into contact with his notes, to study, study, study—no matter the subject—for everything was worth review, but nothing could be improved on until it had been studied firsthand.

- His extraordinary talents as a draftsman were matched by his curiosity and courage. As a result, Leonardo was able, for the very first time in human history, to draw with precision human organs, bones, and muscle tissue. His work inspired the first illustrated anatomical textbook in history, produced by the great physician Vesalius in 1543, which became the standard work in Europe for over a century.

The Followers

- The world of the visual arts changed forever because of Leonardo. His approach to the depiction of nature is the standard about which all artists—every single one—have taken a stance, either for or against, ever since.

- The great Mannerists, like Michelangelo, intentionally turned their backs on the classical style and took Leonardo's adages as their point of departure. The Neoclassicism of the 17th century, found in the paintings of Rubens, Poussin, and Caravaggio, was grounded in a conscious return to Leonardo's rules. The Impressionists, rebelling against the academies and their classical rules, simultaneously challenged the assertions of Leonardo and celebrated his legacy, casting him as Romantic hero who had gone beyond the conventions of his own day.

- It is nearly impossible to calculate with any accuracy the magnitude of Leonardo's achievements or the debt we owe him today. What is more, those debts might accrue even more in the coming years. New nuggets of insight and inspiration may be waiting for us, just around the corner.

- Leonardo remains relevant today, and not merely because tourists line up to see his works in museums or because he paved the way for our modern approach to scientific inquiry. Leonardo is relevant because he speaks to us from the grave: in his paintings, which remind us of our human frailty and celebrate the beauty of our potential; in his scientific achievements that impact the lives of millions of people every day; and in his belief that we should never be satisfied with what we already have before us.

Suggested Reading

Cropper, "Poussin and Leonardo: Evidence from the Zaccolini MSS."

The Diaries of Leonardo da Vinci.

Goffen, *Renaissance Rivals*, pt. III.

Klein, *Leonardo's Legacy*, epilogue.

Richter, *Leonardo da Vinci: Notebooks*, pt I.

Robison, "Leonardo's *Trattato della Pittura*."

Zöllner and Nathan, *Leonardo da Vinci: The Complete Paintings and Drawings*.

The Legacies of Leonardo da Vinci
Lecture 36—Transcript

Leonardo da Vinci is one of those rare historical figures whose memory can be invoked across an extraordinarily wide range of topics and concerns. His many roles in the Italian High Renaissance offer legacies and lessons for us in virtually all the areas we've discussed in this course.

But first, let's clarify for ourselves, just briefly, three things we've been learning about the so-called Italian High Renaissance. First, it was not merely a rebirth of antiquity: It was an age of innovation and originality. In fact, apart from a few exceptions like the *Vitruvian Man* and *Leda and the Swan*, much of Leonardo's best work showed no particular reliance on ancient sources at all.

Second, the period was not entirely a "High" point: Much of Leonardo's career took place precisely when Italian city-states from Florence, to Milan, to Rome were falling under the sway of the power of France, or Spain, or whoever was paying the Swiss mercenaries. The presence of foreign powers may have motivated some innovations we admire, but the period coincided with what was, in significant ways, a very low point in Italian history.

Third, the High Renaissance was never exclusively Italian, not even within Italy. Even that word "Renaissance" is worth considering more closely. It's a French word, of course, coined by a 19th-century French historian, named Jules Michelet. Just the fact that we say "Renaissance" rather than the Italian word "rinascita" as used by Vasari, inadvertently reminds us that France, and other powers, did a lot to shape the context for what we think of as the High Renaissance. Remember Leonardo worked for two French kings and died in France.

With that context in mind let's explore the legacies of Leonardo da Vinci, and see what lessons we can draw. The paintings Leonardo produced are among the easiest things to discuss, both because they are the most readily available to us as pieces of evidence and because in almost literally every single one he did, Leonardo was experimenting with some aspect of traditional modes of representation.

Any great work of art—whether a painting or a poem, a symphony or a sculpture—speaks to us. It tells us something about us that maybe we didn't know, or that maybe we'd always known, but had never been able to articulate completely. *The Last Supper* moves us with its dramatic power, with its fleeting references to both the depths of human depravity, and the hope for redemption that is invested in all of us, regardless of our faith or our outlook on life. The artist who created it meant for it to move us this way, and he labored for three years to make sure every detail, every gesture, every glance might speak to the totality of who we are as members of a civilized society.

If any one single image from the vast repertoire of Leonardo da Vinci captures the essence of the man, the artist, and the scientist, it is *The Last Supper*—that failed experiment in mural painting that has been one of the great success stories in the entire history of narrative art.

Leonardo was such a gifted artist at such an early age that most of the things we're told he painted have survived. A few have not—like the important pictures of *Leda and the Swan* and the *Battle of Anghiari*—but as a rule of thumb, those people who owned a Leonardo usually held onto it, knowing they had something special. And Leonardo knew they were special, too: He left the *Leda*, the *St. Anne Madonna*, *John the Baptist*, and *Mona Lisa* to his assistant Salai because he believed that they, along with the vineyard he left him, would generate enough revenue to keep his longest-serving aide solvent for the rest of his life. Salai, however, could not part with the pictures that Leonardo gave him, and he kept them until the day he died. It was only then, when they passed into his sister's hands, that they were finally sold to King Francois I, Leonardo's last patron. They stayed in the French royal collection until the fall of the monarchy at the end of the 18th century, at which time they passed into the national collection and became mainstays of the Louvre.

And that group of pictures, perhaps because they came into public awareness during the French Revolution, has come to form the core group of pictures that are representative of Leonardo's innovative spirit as an artist. Each one, in its own way, reminds us of that innovative approach to painting that he took, and the vast influence that he had on generations of artists that followed him.

The painting of the *Mona Lisa*, the most famous work of art in the world, reminds us of Leonardo's masterful invention of the new genre of portraiture in the High Renaissance. His slow and meticulous handling of oil pigments, which he helped popularize in Italy, allowed him to employ the sfumatic technique to perfection—to work up colors gradually in ways that added an energy, no matter how minute, to figures that are, in fact, frozen paintings.

And this was due, no doubt, to the convictions he held about the importance of human beings as individuals. Leonardo's picture of *Ginevra de' Benci* revolutionized female portraiture by showing his sitter as someone with brains and ideas and character traits that deserved to be celebrated, no matter who she was or what her sex was. His *Mona Lisa* is famous, not only because of her beguiling smile, and not only because of the questions about the sitter's identity and Leonardo's motives for painting her, but also because of his ability to combine character traits, wealth, status, and power in a single likeness.

We sometimes forget the great distance that portraiture traveled with Leonardo at the helm. Looking at the *Portrait of a Woman* by Antonio Pollaiuolo, we remember that staid and formulaic approach that had been taken by Leonardo's predecessors. But then, when we see his lively, enigmatic, and deeply dramatic representation of Cecilia Gallerani, we remember the power of his observational skills. No longer satisfied with conventional modes of representation, Leonardo used his oil paints to hone the appearance of his sitter's heads and faces (that, in turn, were based on his anatomical studies of the human head), and he created ways to help viewers identify his sitters and see them as real, living breathing people.

The painting of *John the Baptist* reminds us of the unusually powerful dramatic flair that Leonardo had, and his desire to employ it in pictures of single figures in his pictures. Leonardo's use of tenebrism—that stark juxtaposition of lights and darks, one against the other—allowed him to make his sitters and figures leap from the surface of his pictures toward the unsuspecting viewer, and imbued his figures with a liveliness that surprised those who saw his pictures for the first time. Bellincione's verses about Leonardo's extraordinary gifts as a painter tell us that the portrait of Cecilia was highly regarded for precisely this reason, and the fact that Leonardo repeated the technique in his figure of *John the Baptist* indicates that Leonardo knew it was an effective device.

Future generations of artists would recognize the value of these approaches. When art historians today consider the greatest age of painted portraiture—the 17th century—and review the work of the Dutch and Flemish artists who were responsible for making it so great, the kinds of portraits they see all have those trademark qualities of a Leonardo portrait. Rembrandt's portrait of his beloved wife, Saskia, shows her emerging out of a deeply blackened background, and when Anthony van Dyck did this very early self-portrait in 1614, it was Leonardo's tenebristic and sfumatesque technique that he employed.

The painting of the *St. Anne Madonna* that Salai inherited contained in its foreground and its background important features that continued the artistic interests of Leonardo into the last years of his career. The interplay between Mary and Christ was a carryover from earlier Madonna pictures, like the *Benois Madonna*, in which Leonardo featured a truly human interaction between a young mother and her only child—in stark contrast to the stilted depictions of Madonna paintings that had dominated the more traditionally rigid art market of the generation immediately preceding Leonardo's—like Domenico Ghirlandaio's version from about 1480 or so.

Leonardo basically invented the theme of the human relationship between his figures, and his contemporaries who saw them and understood them quickly copied them in their own works. Raphael was careful to emphasize this kind of relationship between Mary and Christ in his Madonna paintings of the early 16th century, and his ability to do so effectively resulted in his invitation to Rome to work for the pope as Julius II initiated his grand plan to revive the city as a new imperial center.

But the painting of *St. Anne* also calls to mind Leonardo's other great image of the *St. Anne Madonna* that survives today. The cartoon in the British Museum reminds us of Leonardo's unusual gifts as a draftsman and his ability to render in a monochromatic style the richness of figures in three dimensions. But it also contains that image of the swimming Christ, who squirms his way through the grasp of Mary on his way to greet his little cousin, John the Baptist. This kind of movement and energy in a figure that had traditionally been placed rather rigidly on the lap of his equally rigid mother signaled a brand new approach to the theme of Madonna paintings in the 16th century.

And in the background of the *St. Anne Madonna*, we see the vast landscape that Leonardo painted from his imaginary vantage point at the top of a hill. The expansive mountain range in the deep distance, with snow-capped peaks dissolving into nothingness, has its roots in the drawing that Leonardo did in the Tuscan hills on August 5, 1473, and speaks to his scientific interest in creating an atmospheric quality to his pictures that demonstrates his belief that the air surrounding us was filled with water, that in turn affected the way that we see objects both near and far away.

And that, in turn, reminds us of his experimental drawings of storms and weather events, in which things as transient as rain and as invisible as wind were captured by his pen.

And Leonardo's willingness to go outdoors and draw the things he saw with his own eye, to capture the natural world just as it appeared to the naked eye, came to inform the great movements of 19th and 20th centuries. As Impressionists like Claude Monet strove to break free from the hold of traditions that he felt were binding and restrictive, their one true source of inspiration came from the natural world around them. Their dedication to the process of "plein eire painting," or applying pigments directly onto their canvases while sitting outdoors, was precisely the kind of thing that had inspired Leonardo to do his drawing that afternoon in 1473 when he sat on a hillside and drew the valley below him.

And just as important for the history of art as his portraits and landscapes and deeply dramatic tenebristic handling of painting, was Leonardo's interest in the human figure and in the new genre of erotic painting. Leonardo wasn't afraid to paint the nude form, and he wasn't afraid to speak frankly about the desires of human beings—both as living, breathing creatures who have carnal needs, but also as art viewers who, secretly perhaps, have a deep-seeded interest in seeing the nude form in all its beauty, its glory, and its sensuality. The Venetians immediately understood that Leonardo had put his finger on an enticing subject, and they quickly followed his lead. Within only a few years, pictures like Titian's *Venus of Urbino* would be the object of bidding wars between potential buyers who competed to own erotically charged pictures that they could show off to their friends.

The long history of the nude, and of erotic art, really gets a jump start with the work of Leonardo, and its trajectory through the 17th, 18th, and 19th centuries leads us through some of history's greatest and most important paintings. Francois Boucher's portrait from 1750 of Louise O'Murphy, the mistress of King Louis XV, and Eduard Manet's *Olympia* from 1865 both scandalized Parisian society when they were displayed—and both pictures cemented their respective artists as true leaders in their field.

But probably the longest lasting and most important painterly contribution that Leonardo made to the history of art was his creation of, and insistence on, the true classical composition.

The triangular format that Leonardo employed repeatedly in his works, great and small, resonated with generations of artists. The ebb and flow of the interest in naturalism in art didn't always result in a strict adherence to his rules of painting. But when they were published in 1651, the French painter, Nicolas Poussin, was hired to make drawings to illustrate Leonardo's points—and Poussin was an excellent choice for this project, for he was one of the great champions of Leonardo's classical style. His easel paintings, like the *Judgment of Solomon* from the middle decades of the 17th century, were beacons of light to his contemporaries, for they saw in Poussin a disciple of Leonardo, in the way he both emphasized balance, clarity, emotional believability, and above all, the importance of the central core of the composition.

Poussin was just one of a whole series of 17th-century admirers and imitators who looked very closely at the lessons that Leonardo taught them through his paintings and through his writings. It was their adherence to Leonardo's laws that resulted in the creation of the Royal Academy of Art in France and the triumph of classical painting in Europe for the next 200 years. From middle of the 1600s until the middle of the 1800s, the rules of Leonardo da Vinci governed the appearance of art in Western Europe.

Leonardo was a complicated person, who sought to unite within himself what others might have regarded as opposites. On one hand, Leonardo was adamant that the natural world be his guide in all things. In painting, this meant that he was constantly trying to apply to his pictures details that he had observed in his environment: Showing the actual contours of the human skull behind the veil of skin was his way of using nature as his guide, and that in turn helped him create paintings of great power.

But on the other hand, Leonardo was also interested in the concept of perfection. He sought to place the elements of this world into a kind of order that he could then represent in a way that demonstrated perfection. In terms of the classical sources so important to the Renaissance, he was both an Aristotelian and a Platonist. But more than that, he also looked at the big world of Mother Nature as an idea that brings us all together and unifies us as members of the human race, while also focusing on details that celebrate the specific features that make each of us individuals at the same time.

And this brings us to another one of Leonardo's important legacies, and one which I think he'd be pleased to know has been able to contribute. For Leonardo, more than anyone else before him, confirmed in the minds of his peers and his followers that practitioners of the visual arts had every right to be considered as intellectuals, on par with poets and philosophers and scientists.

The notion that artists had to be educated in ancient literature, mathematics, and philosophy had come from Alberti in the middle of the 15th century. Alberti had made it clear that painters needed to understand how the world looked and how the world worked in order to draw and paint successfully. But it was Leonardo who insisted that artists could expand upon the body of knowledge of each of these subjects and add to our understanding of the natural world at large. He argued and demonstrated how only someone trained in the mathematics of perspective and geometry could see and interpret the visible and clearly reveal the mysteries of God's creations; He argued that the mere use of words was necessarily doomed to failure in this regard. For only artists could make visible the things worthy of study.

Now Leonardo's determination to add artists to the list of intellectuals has been met with general approval and acceptance in our world today, just as it did soon after his death in 1519. The old guild and apprentice system began to be replaced by Art Academies, which sprang up in Florence, Rome, Paris, and London in the late 16th and 17th centuries. Artists like Pieter Paul Rubens, Anthony van Dyck, and Diego Velasquez were respected by kings and courtiers not only for their gifts as painters, but for their erudition in a variety of intellectual subjects and for their administrative skills in diplomatic affairs. And today, colleges and universities all around the world have as core components of their academic programs vibrant departments of art and art history. I'm not convinced that Leonardo succeeded in persuading us that the skills of painters put them in a category superior to everyone else. But his message that the visual arts deserve to be considered in the same breath as mathematics, philosophy, and poetry? That's endured.

And this leads us to yet another important legacy of Leonardo da Vinci. For while Leonardo only left only 20 or so paintings (depending on which are accepted and what are not), he also left behind somewhere around 7000 pages of notes, drawings, and essays.

Only about a third of that survived the 16th century, but this probably isn't quite as big a loss as it sounds. Francesco Melzi, his aristocratic assistant, had these pages in his possession for 50 years, and he treated them like "religious relics" according to Vasari. But during that time, Melzi seems to have thrown out duplicate papers, and pages on subjects that Leonardo himself believed were useless. In any case, the fact that Melzi retained literally thousands of these pages—some of them puzzling and only barely legible—indicates that he erred on the side of caution and preservation.

After making his choices, Melzi arranged the notes that he kept into different categories—scientific drawings of inventions and studies were collated into one set of piles, figure drawings for artistic projects into another, theoretical statements about art into yet another—and then he had them bound into manuscripts or boxed together as sets.

Melzi held onto these drawings for the duration of his life, but clearly allowed others to study them—Leonardo's Theory of Art made the rounds in the mid-16th century, and the artist Carlo Urbino even made a series of drawings based on the text that Melzi provided for him. When he died in 1579, Melzi's descendants inherited the notebooks, but they went about the process of selling them off to different collectors—and Leonardo's notes were widely dispersed.

But in 1630 Pompeo Leoni, a sculptor in the Spanish court of Philip III Hapsburg, tirelessly hunted them down and purchased most of them for his patron. He cut some of them out of old bindings and trimmed others down to make them more manageable, and then he bound them into different manuscripts, and organized them by category. Over time they have been sold off to museums and collectors, and today most of them are in European collections. The largest of these is the Codex Atlanticus, in Milan, which is really a collection of 12 different volumes that covers more than 1000 pages of inventions, experiments, and scientific observations.

The legacy of Leonardo that survives in his notebooks is, in some ways, even more relevant today than his paintings are. For in them, Leonardo didn't just write down a *Treatise on Painting* that would form the foundation for the study of art for two centuries. He used his powers of draftsmanship and his remarkably astute sense of observation to study the world around him; and he managed to notice things that just about everyone who had ever lived before him had somehow missed. He conceived of great buildings, new ways to sanitize cities, and machines to take the danger out of some tasks that put laborers at risk everyday; he observed how mist changes our environment, how wind circulates, and the powers that make birds fly; and when he looked at the world around him, he had the truly unique ability to see ways to improve on current practices and to envision brand new things that no one had ever dreamed of before.

Despite his misgivings about the love of warfare that drove his patrons in nearly every court he worked, Leonardo was frequently engaged in finding ways to give his employers an edge on the battlefield. The vicious war machines he imagined were intended to wipe out huge swaths of humans beings in a single swipe, to run them over, to shoot them with multiple cannon shots. For reasons of cost and complexity, these tremendous weapons of death were never built to his specifications—but if they had been, there's no telling how they would have affected the great military campaigns that ravaged his homeland from 1494 until his departure in 1516.

It would take centuries for science and technology to catch up with Leonardo's visions of an aggressive military force armed with machines to enhance the efficiency of killing one's enemies. The development of the combustion engine in the 19th century was the key ingredient that he had lacked when conceiving of his death machines; but once that ingredient was perfected, Leonardo's most imaginative inventions changed the course of modern warfare and modern history forever.

Many would point to the tank as the key instrument of land warfare in the 20th century, although its introduction on the battlefields of France in 1916 did not immediately alter the stalemate of World War I. Others might argue that the machine gun that Leonardo envisioned had a greater impact, at least until World War II, when the tank was re-outfitted and employed in a more successful way by the German army.

Neither of his designs look much like the 20th century versions of these extremely important and effective weapons: But the Renaissance inventor obviously had a pretty good idea of what these things could look like on the battlefield of the 15th century.

Of all the inventions that emerge from Leonardo's manuscripts, the one that's probably had the greatest impact on modern society was the airplane. His concepts were primitive in many ways, and they revolved around the idea of wings that could take a single person through the air for as long as his legs could pedal. But even into the late 18th-century aviators (like Sir George Cayley) were designing their flying machines as extensions of Leonardo's, and the questions they were asking about speed, power, and weight were almost identical to the ones Leonardo asked.

I honestly think that, of all the things he imagined as a machine that could be used to improve the human condition, the one thing he'd be proudest of today would be his commitment to the concept of human flight. Leonardo would want us to read his studies and observations carefully, and he would be overjoyed to know that we have solved the problem of weight, power, and speed to create flying machines that today carry millions of people to destinations all over the world within a matter of hours. I'm guessing here, but I think Leonardo might want us to consider this his very greatest victory—for it was, by his own reckoning, the most outrageous, most fantastical vision of them all: and it's one that ultimately worked.

Of course, Leonardo thought of parachutes and diving suits and submarines, too. He recognized the potential of high-powered mortars and long-range artillery. He imagined an age when soldiers could come streaming across the Italian countryside in droves, and would have to be cut down in equal numbers in order to defend the homeland. Leonardo imagined modern warfare some 200 years before military strategists did. And it's all right there, in his notebooks.

It was in these manuscripts that Leonardo's work as a scientist came to be known, respected, and even imitated. He thought everything was fair game for study, and he thought we should care. He not only wrote that "The acquisition of any knowledge whatever is always useful to the intellect." He also continued by saying, "For nothing can be either loved or hated unless it is first known." Knowledge is power, certainly, but knowledge also drives our perceptions of virtue, of justice, and of righteousness.

He urged himself, and anyone who came into contact with his notes, to study, study, study—no matter the subject—for everything was worth review, but nothing could be improved upon until it had been studied and even measured first hand. He invented not only the speedometer and odometer, but also the so-called hodometer—to measure distances while surveying—and the anemometer for wind speed, and a hygrometer for humidity.

I'd argue that his most important contributions to the scientific world came in the work he produced in the field of anatomical research. His genuinely extraordinary talents as a draftsman were matched with his curiosity and his courage, with the result that Leonardo was able, for the very first time in human history, to draw with precision human organs, bones, and muscle tissue. It was his inspiration that led to the publication of the first illustrated anatomical textbook in history, produced by the great physician Vesalius in 1543, which became the standard work in Europe for over a century.

To this day, medical students learn about the human body and a variety of medical conditions through dissections—plus a close study of anatomical drawings that sometimes do a better job conveying the various parts of the human body than photographs or written descriptions. The dissections and drawings Leonardo pioneered during his lifetime made possible an improved educational curriculum for doctors, and this has benefited anyone and everyone who has ever been a patient.

And the world of the visual arts changed forever because of him. Leonardo's very special approach to the replication of the natural form through the accurate depiction of things seen with the naked eye served as the standard by which all artists—every single one—have taken a stance, either for or against, for ever after. The great Mannerists, like Michelangelo and Vasari and Giulio Romano, who intentionally turned their backs on the classical style in the 16th century, took as their point of departure a rejection of Leonardo's adages.

The renewed popularity of classicism during the 17th century, found in the paintings of Rubens and Poussin and even Caravaggio, was grounded in a conscious return to Leonardo's rules, which were published, illustrated, and then used as the standard curriculum in art academies all across Europe in the 18th and 19th centuries. And the great reactions of rebellious artists like Manet and Monet and their Impressionist colleagues against those academies, and their classical rules, simultaneously challenged the assertions of Leonardo and celebrated his legacy, which was reformulated to cast him as Romantic hero who had gone beyond the conventions of his own day. One way or another, the idea that nature could be the artist's guide has influenced the history of painting for the last 500 years.

In the end, and this is the end, I think it's nearly impossible to calculate with any accuracy the magnitude of his achievements, or the debt we owe him today. And what's more, those debts might accrue even more in the coming years. Someday, Leonardo's original painting of *Leda and the Swan* may appear. Someday restorers may develop a technique to recover areas of the *Battle of Anghiari* that Vasari painted over in the Palazzo della Signoria in 1565. And someday we may recover the vast collection of documents that mysteriously disappeared from a royal collection in England at the beginning of the 19th century. New nuggets of insights and inspirations may be waiting for us, just around the corner.

And so where does this leave us?

I think Leonardo da Vinci remains relevant today, and not merely because tourists line up to see his works in museums or because he paved the way for our modern approach to scientific inquiry. Leonardo is relevant because he speaks to us from the grave: in his paintings, which remind us of our human frailty and which celebrate the beauty of our potential; in specific scientific achievements, such as medical anatomy, that impact the lives of millions of people every day in the 21st century; and in his belief that we can never be satisfied with what we already have before us.

There are new fields of study just waiting for our attention, he tells us. The many different fields of human endeavor we tend to focus on in isolation, are far more deeply connected than we might believe. And he encourages us to imagine new ways to educate each other, about who we are, and what our lives mean, and what matters in our world, whether today or in the future.

Perhaps our understanding of these basic principles stands as Leonardo da Vinci's greatest legacy.

Kenneth Clarke once famously called Leonardo da Vinci "the most relentlessly curious man in history." I hope that the example set by Leonardo da Vinci, flaws and all, in the face of so many difficulties, may be a source of inspiration in whatever you do today.

Leonardo's Notebooks and the Main Codex Collections

Leonardo da Vinci crafted thousands of pages of notes, drawings, and thought pieces, none of which were published during his lifetime and only a few of which were known to anyone outside his inner circle of assistants and admirers. The range of subject matter astounds us today; his writings cover topics from human anatomy to the examination of clock mechanisms to the development of locks and canals to compositions for paintings large and small. The exact number of pages at his death was never tabulated; some scholars have estimated that there were as many as 13,000 sheets of notes and sketches in Leonardo's possession in 1519, while others believe there were approximately half that number.

Most of those thousands of pages were loose sheets of paper, unbound and unedited, although some were collected in small notebooks. All were bequeathed by Leonardo to his aristocratic assistant, Francesco Melzi. Melzi preserved those that he believed held merit or represented his master's thoughts accurately, but he may also have thrown away a vast number of others that did not meet his criteria for preservation. He then organized some of what he had saved by theme, creating a series of manuscripts. Melzi then acted as an unofficial archivist: He granted access to Leonardo's notes to those who could demonstrate a need to know, and some of Leonardo's ideas—particularly those pertaining to his theory of painting—circulated among a small group of artists and intellectuals.

Melzi died in 1570, and his will stipulated that Leonardo's notes be passed on to his son, Orazio, who soon began to disperse the notes to various collectors in Europe. By the end of the 16th century, the collection was in disarray. Identifying the need to reassemble and centralize Leonardo's output, a sculptor named Pompeo Leoni (1537–1608), then a member of the Spanish royal court, tirelessly hunted them down and purchased most of them for his patrons. Leoni cut some of them out of old bindings, trimmed down others to make them more manageable, and then bound them into different manuscripts, again organized by category. Some of these notes and drawings are quite modest in scale: the so-called Manuscript M in the Bibliothèque de l'Institut de France, Paris, contains pages that measure only 4 × 2¾″ (10 × 7 cm). Other drawings are much larger, like those in the Codex Atlanticus in the Biblioteca Ambrosiana in Milan, some of which measure 25⅝ × 17⅜″ (65 × 44 cm).

With a few notable artistic exceptions from his first period in Florence, the notes and papers bound into discrete books span the period from Leonardo's arrival in Milan in 1482 until about 1517, when a stroke severely hindered his ability to control a stylus. As was common in the period, he usually used both sides of a sheet of paper—known as the **recto** and **verso**—and often crammed onto a surface a variety of ideas that might or might not be related. Annotations accompanied some of his drawings, particularly when he believed he had made an important observation or breakthrough that might not be evident from the sketch (and it appears that Leonardo often, but not always, drew first and wrote later). He commonly used a pen or stylus—a slender writing utensil—that he dipped into an inkwell, but he also applied black and red chalk to some of his drawings, as well as a light wash of translucent inks, to accentuate forms or highlight specific areas of interest.

Leonardo's notebooks and manuscripts are mostly scattered among various European collections. The largest number may be found at the Biblioteca Ambrosiana in Milan, where a 12-volume set of scientific drawings is collectively known as the Codex Atlanticus. ("Codex" is simply a Latin word for book and is used especially to refer to a manuscript book.) Most of the codex's 1,119 separate sheets were bound together by Pompeo Leoni and were later donated to the Biblioteca Ambrosiana in 1636. Napoleon's troops removed the collection and shipped it to Paris, but the Codex Atlanticus was repatriated to Milan in 1815 and has remained there ever since. The drawings were rebound into their current 12 discrete units between 1968 and 1972. The Codex Atlanticus has been scheduled for public exhibition during Expo 2015 in Milan.

The Institut de France in Paris owns 12 smaller manuscripts dedicated to architecture, flight, optics, and engineering. Like the Codex Atlanticus, the so-called Paris Manuscripts were brought to Paris in 1796 by French troops during their occupation of Milan, but this set was never returned to their former home. J. B. Venturi gave each book its own letter name: Manuscripts A (c. 1492), B (1488–1490), C (1490–1491), D (1508–1509), E (1513–1514), F (1508–1513), G (1510–1515), H (1493–1594), I (1497–1505), K (1503–1508), L (1497–1502), and M (1490s–1500). The Paris Manuscripts originally included the Codex Ashburnham I and II (c. 1492), which were separated from Manuscript A and stolen in the 19th century, bound in cardboard, sold by the thieves to the Earl of Ashburnum in 1875, and then returned to the Institut de France in 1890.

The Codex Arundel (1490s–c. 1518) is in the British Library in London. The contents of its 283 sheets spans the period from 1478 to 1518. Pompeo Leoni brought these drawings to the Habsburg court in Spain, where they were seen and purchased by the British art collector Thomas Howard, Earl of Arundel (d. 1646). His family then passed them to the British Royal Society in 1667. A digitized version of this book may be consulted online at http://www.armadillosystems.com/ttp_commercial/case.html.

The Biblioteca Nacional in Madrid has two volumes of notes: Madrid Codex I contains works from the 1490s, and Madrid Codex II features drawings from 1503 to 1504. The 700 pages that comprise these two manuscripts were only discovered in 1966, when long-forgotten boxes were examined in library storage. Codex I features a written text about machines, while Codex II contains geometrical studies and tinted maps of Tuscany and the Arno River.

The **folios** of the Royal Collection at Windsor Castle in England are dedicated primarily to Leonardo's anatomical drawings and his figural studies for artistic projects. Most of these drawings were purchased in the late 17th century but were either ignored or forgotten for more than 100 years.

The Codex Leicester (c. 1508–1512) is dedicated primarily to the study of hydraulics and is comprised of 18 folio sheets that have been folded into 72 pages. Leonardo personally bound these sheets but detached them later. The book was in the possession of the Earl of Leicester in 1717 and was retained by his descendants until 1980, when it was sold to Armand Hammer. The book was sold at auction to Bill and Melinda Gates in 1994 and has since been exhibited in different cities around the world.

Leonardo's observations on aviation are contained in the Codex on the Flight of Birds (1490–1505) in the Biblioteca Reale, Turin. This manuscript is comprised of 18 recto and verso sheets and was originally located in Milan; it was looted by French soldiers in 1796 and attached to what became known as Paris Manuscript B, but it was stolen during the 19th century and sold to a Russian collector, who then donated it to King Umberto I of Savoy in 1893.

The Codex Urbinas in the Biblioteca Vaticana contains Leonardo's manuscript of the *Treatise on Painting*, organized and edited posthumously by Melzi.

The Codex Trivulzianus (c. 1487–1490) in the Archivio de Stato, Milan, features architectural and military drawings, along with Leonardo's attempts to learn Latin.

The three-volume set called the Codex Forster in the Victoria & Albert Museum in London (1487 and 1490–1505; 1495-1497; and 1490–1496) focuses on geometry, weights, and hydraulic machines. The first volume measures 5½ × 4″ (14 × 10 cm), the second 4 × 2¾″ (10 × 7 cm), and the third only 3½ × 2¾″ (9 × 7 cm). They are the smallest of all the Leonardo manuscripts.

In addition, noteworthy collections of Leonardo drawings never bound into a codex can also be found in other museums, including the Gabinetto dei Disegni e delle Stampe of the Uffizi in Florence; the National Gallery in London; the Gallerie dell'Accademia in Venice; and the Louvre in Paris.

Important Terms

folio: A single sheet of paper or parchment. Scholars refer to Leonardo's papers using folio numbers (abbreviated as *fol.*) instead of page numbers.

recto: The front side of a piece of parchment or paper, always the right-hand page of an open book.

verso: The back side of a piece of parchment or paper, always the left-hand page of an open book.

Suggested Reading

Keele and Roberts, *Leonardo da Vinci: Anatomical Drawings from the Royal Library, Windsor Castle.*

Kemp, *Leonardo da Vinci: The Marvellous Works of Nature and Man.*

Pedretti, *The Codex Atlanticus of Leonardo da Vinci.*

Works Discussed

Note: Renaissance paintings, including those by Leonardo da Vinci, were almost never given a title by the artist. The descriptive phrases used to refer to drawings are even less standardized; the most reliable way to identify a given drawing is with codex information.

Lectures where a specific work is discussed are generally indicated in square brackets at the end of each entry.

Works by Leonardo da Vinci

The Paintings and Major Works

Adoration of the Magi. c. 1481. Oil on wood, 7′11⅝″ × 8′⅞″ (2.43 × 2.46 m). Galleria degli Uffizi, Florence. [1, 9, 15, 18, 23, 36]

Annunciation. c. 1473–1474. Oil and tempera on wood, 3′2⅝″ × 7′1⅜″ (98 × 217 cm). Galleria degli Uffizi, Florence. [1, 5, 7, 8, 15, 32]

Benois Madonna (*Madonna with a Flower*). 1478–1481 Oil on panel transferred to canvas in the 19th century, 19½ × 13″ (49.5 × 33 cm). The State Hermitage Museum, St. Petersburg. [1, 7, 8, 36]

Ceiling Fresco with Trellis and Coat of Arms at Center. c. 1488–1498. Sala delle Asse, Castello Sforzesco, Milan. [11]

Ginevra de' Benci [obverse]. c. 1474/1478. Oil on wood, 15 × 14 9/16″ (38.1 × 37 cm). National Gallery of Art, Washington, DC. [1, 6, 7, 26, 36]

Ginevra de' Benci [reverse]. c. 1474/1478. Tempera on panel, 15 × $14^{9}/_{16}$″ (38.1 × 37 cm). National Gallery of Art, Washington, DC. [6]

Isabella d'Este. 1499–1500. Red and ochre chalks, heightened with white on prepared white paper and pricked for transfer, 24 × 18⅜″ (61 × 46.5 cm). Musée du Louvre, Paris. [2, 12, 22, 23, 26]

La belle ferronnière (*Portrait of a Lady*—Lucrezia Crivelli). c. 1496. Oil on wood, 24⅞ × 17¾″ (63 × 45 cm). Musée du Louvre, Paris. [1, 12, 28, 36]

Lady with an Ermine (Cecilia Gallerani; Dama z Gronostajem). c. 1490–1491. Oil on wood, 21⅝ × 15⅞″ (54.8 × 40.3 cm). Czartoryski Museum, National Museum, Kraców, Poland. [1, 12, 26, 36]

Litta Madonna (Madonna Litta). c. 1482–1490. Tempera on canvas transferred from wood, 16½ × 13″ (42 × 33 cm). The State Hermitage Museum, St. Petersburg. [11]

Madonna of the Carnation (*Madonna mit der Nelke*). 1473–1476. Oil on wood, 24½ × 18¾″ (62 × 47.5 cm). Alte Pinakothek, Munich. [1, 7, 8, 11]

Madonna of the Rocks (*Virgin of the Rocks*; *La Vierge aux rochers).* 1483–1489. Oil on canvas, 6′6⅜″ × 4′ (1.99 × 1.22 m). Musée du Louvre, Paris. [1, 10, 11, 23, 28, 34, 36]

Madonna of the Rocks (London). c. 1491–1508. Oil on wood, 6′2⅜″ × 4′ (1.89 × 1.20 m). The National Gallery, London. [10, 28]

Madonna of the Yarnwinder (The Lansdowne Madonna). c. 1501–1507. Oil on wood, 19¾ × 14⅜″ (50.2 × 36.4 cm). Private collection. [1, 23]

Madonna of the Yarnwinder (*Madonna with a Yarnwinder*). c. 1501. Oil on wood. 19½ × 14″ (48.3 × 36.9 cm). The Trustees of the 9th Duke of Buccleuch's Chattels Fund, Bowhill, Selkirk, Scotland. [1, 23]

Mona Lisa (*La Gioconda; La Joconde; Portrait de Lisa Gherardini).* 1503–1506 and/or 1516–1519. Oil on wood, 30⅜ × 20⅞" (77 × 53 cm). Musée du Louvre, Paris. [1, 2, 26, 31, 33, 36]

Portrait of a Musician (*Il ritratto di musico*). 1485–1490. Oil on wood, 17 × 12¼" (43 × 31 cm). Pinacoteca Ambrosiana, Milan. [11]

Saint Anne Madonna (*Virgin and Child with Saint Anne and a Lamb; La Vierge à l'Enfant avec Sainte Anne*). c. 1510. Oil on wood, 5'6¼" × 4'3¼" (1.68 × 1.30 m). Musée du Louvre, Paris. [1, 7, 18, 31, 32, 33, 36]

Saint Anne Madonna (*Virgin and Child with Saint Anne and Saint John the Baptist*). c. 1505–1508. Black chalk and touches of white chalk on brownish paper, mounted on canvas, 4'7¾" × 3'5¼" (1.41 × 1.05 m). The National Gallery, London. [1, 23, 25, 27, 31, 36]

Saint Jerome (*Saint Girolamo*). c. 1480. Tempera and oil on wood, 40½ × 29½" (103 × 75 cm). Pinacoteca, Vatican Museums. [8, 21, 23, 29]

Saint John the Baptist (*Saint Jean Baptiste*). 1508–1516. Oil on wood, 27⅛ × 22½" (69 × 57 cm). Musée du Louvre, Paris. [28, 36]

Salvator Mundi. c. 1500. Oil on wood, 25¾ × 17¾"(65.5 × 45.1 cm). Private collection. Attributed to Leonardo in 2011. [35]

The Last Supper (*Il Cenacolo*; also *L'Ultima Cena*). c. 1495–1498. Oil and tempera on plaster, 15'2" × 28'10" (4.6 × 8.8 m). Santa Maria delle Grazie Refectory, Milan. [1, 2, 20, 21, 36]

Vitruvian Man. c. 1487–1490. Pen and ink, brush and some brown wash over metalpoint on paper, 13 9/16 × 9⅝" (34.44 × 24.45 cm). Gallerie dell'Accademia, Venice. [1, 2, 15]

Preparatory Drawings for Known Paintings

Adoration of the Magi (background and architecture). c. 1480–1481. Pen and ink on paper, 6½ × 11½″ (16.3 × 29 cm). Gabinetto dei Disegni e delle Stampe, Galleria degli Uffizi, Florence. [9, 15, 18, 20, 30]

Adoration of the Magi (Joseph and two shepherds and sketches for the Christ child). c. 1481. Pen and ink on paper, 6¾ × 4⅜″ (17.2 × 11.0 cm). Hamburger Kunsthalle, Hamburg, Germany. [18]

Adoration of the Magi (six figures study). 1481. Pen and ink with silverpoint on paper, 11 × 10½″ (27.8 × 26.8 cm). Musée du Louvre, Paris. [18]

Adoration of the Magi (study). 1481. Pen and ink over black chalk on paper, 11¼ × 8⅜″ (28.5 × 21.2 cm). Musée du Louvre, Paris. [9]

Adoration of the Magi (Virgin Mary). c. 1481. Metalpoint on paper, 7 × 6⅝″ (17.9 × 16.8 cm). Musée du Louvre, Paris. [11]

Battle of Anghiari (skirmish of horses and footsoldiers). c. 1503–1505. Pen and ink on paper. Gallerie dell'Accademia, Venice. [25, 30]

Battle of Anghiari (studies of horsemen, including one charging with a spear at top left). c. 1503–1505. Pen and ink on paper, 3¼ × 4¾″ (8.2 × 12 cm). British Museum, London. [18, 25]

Battle of Anghiari (study for the heads of two warriors). c. 1505. Charcoal and traces of red chalk on paper, 7½ × 7⅜″ (19.1 × 18.8 cm). Esterhazy Collection, Museum of Fine Arts (Szepmuveszeti Muzeum), Budapest. [25]

Battle of Anghiari (study of a warrior's head). c. 1505. Red pencil on paper, 8⅞ × 7⅜″ (22.6 × 18.6 cm). Esterhazy Collection, Museum of Fine Arts (Szepmuveszeti Muzeum), Budapest. [25]

Battle of Anghiari (warrior on horseback). c. 1503–1505. Pen and ink on paper. Gabinetto dei Disegni e delle Stampe, Galleria degli Uffizi, Florence. [25]

Leda and the Swan. c. 1505. Pen and brown ink over black chalk on paper, 6¼ × 5½" (16 × 13.7 cm). Chatsworth House, Bakewell, Derbyshire, UK. [27]

Nativity or Adoration of the Christ Child; Perspectival Projection (recto); Slight Doodles (verso). 1480–1485. Metalpoint partly reworked with pen and ink on pink prepared paper; lines ruled with metalpoint (recto); pen and ink (verso), 7⅝ × 6⅜" (19.3 × 16.2 cm). The Metropolitan Museum of Art, New York. [18]

Saint Anne Madonna (*Madonna and Child with Saint Anne and a Lamb*), first study. 1501. Pen and ink on paper, 4¾ × 4" (12.1 × 10 cm). Gallerie dell'Accademia, Venice. [22, 23]

Saint John the Baptist. c. 1485. Metalpoint with white heightening on paper. The Royal Collection, Windsor. [8]

The Last Supper, Christ. 1495–1497. Pen and brush on paper, 15¼ × 12⅝" (40 × 32 cm). Pinacoteca di Brera, Milan. [20, 35]

The Last Supper, figure studies. c. 1495–1497. Pen and brown ink over metalpoint on paper, 11 × 8¼" (27.8 × 20.8 cm). Musée du Louvre, Paris. [18, 20]

The Last Supper, head of Saint James and architectural sketches. c. 1495. Red chalk, pen and ink on paper, 9 15/16 × 6¾" (25.2 × 17.2 cm). The Royal Collection, Windsor. [20]

The Last Supper, Saint Peter. c. 1495–1497. Pen and ink on paper, 5¾ × 4½" (14.5 × 11.3 cm). Graphische Sammlung Albertina, Vienna. [20]

The Last Supper, study. 1495–1497. Red chalk on paper, 10¼ × 15½" (26 × 39.2 cm). Gallerie dell'Accademia, Venice. [20, 21]

Preparatory Drawings for Known Sculptures

Casting hood for a horse's head. c. 1511. Red chalk on paper, 8⅜ × 11⅞″ (21 × 30 cm). Codex Madrid II, fol. 157 recto. Biblioteca Nacional, Madrid. [1, 19, 30]

Casting pit for the Sforza horse seen from above and the side. c. 1493. Pen and ink on paper, 9⅞ × 14½″ (25 × 37 cm). Codex Madrid I, fol. 149 recto. Biblioteca Nacional, Madrid. [1, 19]

Sforza Monument, horse in profile and from the front. c. 1490. Silverpoint on paper. The Royal Collection (1232), Windsor. [19]

Trivulzio Monument, c. 1509–1510. Pen and ink on paper, 11 × 7⅞″ (28.0 × 19.8). The Royal Collection, Windsor. [30]

Studies for an equestrian monument. c. 1508–1511. Pen and ink over black chalk on paper, 8⅞ × 6⅜″ (22.4 × 16 cm). The Royal Collection, Windsor. [30]

Study for *Sforza Monument*, no. 19 (facsimile). c. 1493. Pen and ink on paper. Gabinetto dei Disegni e delle Stampe, Galleria degli Uffizi, Florence. [19, 30]

Studies of Anatomy

Coitus. c.1490–1493. Pen and ink on paper, 10⅞ × 8⅛″ (27.6 × 20.4 cm). The Royal Collection, Windsor. [29]

Foetus in the womb and the external genitalia, c. 1507. Pen and ink with wash over black and red chalk on paper, 12 × 8⅜″ (30.4 × 21.3 cm). The Royal Collection, Windsor. [29, 31]

Heart and pulmonary vessels of an ox. c. 1511–1513. Pen and ink over black chalk on blue paper, 11⅜ × 8″ (28.8 × 20.3 cm). The Royal Collection, Windsor. [29]

Lungs, bladder, and male genitalia, with notes. c. 1508–1510. Pen and ink over chalk on paper, 10¾ × 7⅝″ (27.2 × 19.2 cm). The Royal Collection, Windsor. [29]

Male anatomical figure showing the viscera and principal vessels. c. 1490–1493. Pen and ink with wash over black chalk on paper, 11⅛ × 7⅞″ (28.0 × 19.8 cm). The Royal Collection, Windsor. [29]

Male musculature. c. 1508. Pen and ink on paper. The Royal Collection, Windsor. [29]

Man's face and study of human skull. c. 1488–1492. Pen and ink on paper. Codex Atlanticus, fol. 118 verso. Biblioteca Ambrosiana, Milan. [34]

Mesentery of the bowel and its blood supply, with notes. c. 1508. Pen and ink over black chalk on paper, 7⅝ × 5⅝″ (19.3 × 14.3 cm). The Royal Collection, Windsor. [29]

Muscles of the shoulder. c. 1510. Pen and ink with wash over black chalk on paper, 11½ × 7⅞″ (29.2 × 19.8 cm). The Royal Collection, Windsor. [29, 36]

Neck. c. 1512–1513. Pen and ink on blue paper, 10⅞ × 8¼″ (27.6 × 20.7 cm). The Royal Collection, Windsor. [29]

Principal organs and vessels of a woman. c. 1510. Pen and ink with chalk and wash on paper, 18¾ × 13⅛″ (47.6 × 33.2 cm). The Royal Collection, Windsor. [1, 29, 31, 36]

Skull, sectioned (frontal view). c. 1489. Pen and ink over black chalk on paper, 7½ × 5½″ (19.0 × 13.7 cm). The Royal Collection, Windsor. [29]

Skull, sectioned (side view). c. 1489. Pen and ink over black chalk on paper, 7⅜ × 5⅜″ (18.8 × 13.4 cm). The Royal Collection, Windsor. [29]

Stomach and intestines. c.1508–1509. Pen and ink over black chalk on paper, 7⅝ × 5½″ (19.2 × 13.8 cm). The Royal Collection, Windsor. [14]

Surface anatomy of the shoulder and arm. c. 1510. Pen and ink with black chalk on paper, 11¼ × 7⅞″ (28.6 × 20.0 cm). The Royal Collection, Windsor. [29]

Figure Drawings

Bust and head of a man seen in profile with schematic proportions of the human head. c. 1497. Pen and ink on paper, 11 × 8⅞″ (27.9 × 22.3 cm). Gallerie dell'Accademia, Venice. [18]

Bust of a young man with wild hair. c. 1495. Pen and ink over red chalk on paper. Gallerie dell'Accademia, Venice. [18]

Child with cat (from facsimile). c. 1478. Pen and ink on paper, 8⅛ × 5⅝″ (20.6 × 14.3 cm). Gabinetto dei Disegni e delle Stampe, Galleria degli Uffizi, Florence, Italy. [7, 18]

Drapery for a seated figure. c. 1475. Distemper with white highlights on paper, 10½ × 10″ (26.5 × 25.3 cm). Musée du Louvre, Paris. [18]

Drapery study for a kneeling figure, c. 1472–1475. Brush and grey tempera with white on canvas, 7⅛ × 9¼″ (18.1 × 23.4 cm). Galleria degli Uffizi, Florence. [5]

Fall of light on a face. c. 1488. Pen and ink over black chalk on paper, 8 × 5⅝″ (20.3 × 14.3 cm). The Royal Collection, Windsor. [30]

Five studies of grotesque faces. c. 1490. Red chalk on paper. Gallerie dell'Accademia, Venice. [18]

Folds of the dress of a female figure. c. 1472–1478. Silverpoint and wash drawing heightened with white on red paper, 10 × 7.5″ (25.7 × 19 cm). Galleria Nazionale d'Arte Antica di Palazzo Corsini, Rome. [5, 20]

Hand and notations. c. 1490. Pen and ink on paper. Codex Atlanticus, fol. 146 recto. Biblioteca Ambrosiana, Milan. [14]

Hanged man. 1479. Pen and ink on paper, 7½ × 2⅞″ (19.2 × 7.3 cm). Musée Bonnat, Bayonne, France. [9]

Head of a child three-quarter view. c. 1483. Metalpoint with white highlights on grey paper, 5⅜ × 3⅜″ (13.5 × 8.5 cm). Musée du Louvre, Paris. [18]

Heads of horses, a lion, and a man. c.1503–1504. Pen and ink with wash and red chalk on paper, 7¾ × 12⅛″ (19.6 × 30.8 cm). The Royal Collection, Windsor. [30]

Human physiognomy and horseback riders. Gallerie dell'Accademia, Venice. [21]

Infant Christ. c.1501–1510. Red chalk on paper, 11⅛ × 7¾″ (28.4 × 19.6 cm). Gallerie dell'Accademia, Venice. [18]

Madonna and Child with a cat. c. 1479. Pen and ink on beige paper, 9⅛ × 6⅞″ (23.2 × 17.5 cm). Musée Bonnat, Bayonne, France. [18]

Madonna offering a bowl of fruit to the Child. Pen and ink on paper. Facsimile. Gabinetto dei Disegni e delle Stampe, Galleria degli Uffizi, Florence. [4, 5]

Man blowing a trumpet into the ear of a nude man, and two seated men, c. 1480–1481. Pen and ink over stylus sketch on paper, 10⅛ × 7⅝″ (25.8 × 19.3 cm). Malcolm Collection, British Museum, London. [18]

Man tricked by gypsies. c. 1493. Pen and ink on paper, 10¼ × 8″ (26 × 20.5 cm). The Royal Collection, Windsor. [18]

Nude man, standing with right hand on hip, holding a staff with his left hand, looking to right. c. 1504. Pen and ink over black chalk on paper, 4¼ × 2⅛″ (10.8 × 5.4 cm). British Museum, London. [25]

Old man (self-portrait?). c. 1512. Red chalk on paper, 13⅛ × 8⅜″ (33.3 × 21.3 cm). Biblioteca Reale, Turin, Italy. [1, 34, 36]

Profile, three-quarter and frontal study of a male head, possibly a portrait of Cesare Borgia. 1502. Sanguine on yellowed white paper. Biblioteca Reale, Turin, Italy. [24]

Seven studies of grotesque faces. Red chalk on paper. Gallerie dell'Accademia, Venice. [18, 36]

Standing figure, draped; view of profile from right. c. 1475. Distemper with point of brush on canvas, heightened with white, on paper. $12\frac{3}{8} \times 6\frac{5}{8}''$ (31.5 × 16.8 cm). Musée du Louvre, Paris. [4]

Studies of hands. c. 1480. Metalpoint, much faded, on pink prepared paper, $11 \times 7\frac{3}{8}''$ (27.8 × 18.5 cm). Photographed under ultraviolet light. The Royal Collection, Windsor. [4]

Study for a Madonna's head. c. 1481. Silverpoint on prepared paper. $7 \times 6\frac{5}{8}''$. Musée du Louvre, Paris. [11]

Study of a "nutcracker" man and beautiful youth. c. 1500. Red chalk on paper, $8\frac{1}{4} \times 5\frac{7}{8}''$ (20.8 × 15.0 cm). Galleria degli Uffizi, Florence. [18]

Three female figures dancing and a head. c. 1515. Pen and ink on paper, $3\frac{7}{8} \times 5\frac{7}{8}''$ (9.8 × 14.9 cm). Gallerie dell'Accademia, Venice. [15, 31]

Three studies of the Virgin and Child, seated. c. 1478. Metalpoint with pen and ink on prepared paper. $8 \times 6\frac{1}{8}''$ (20.3 × 15.6 cm). British Museum, London. [7]

Two studies of the Virgin and Child with a cat and three studies of the Child with a cat. Late 1470s or early 1480s. Pen and ink over stylus on paper, $11 \times 7\frac{3}{4}''$ (28 × 19.7 cm). British Museum, London. [7]

Virgin and Child with cat (verso) and Virgin and Child with cat (recto). c. 1478–1481. Pen and ink with brown wash on paper, $5\frac{1}{4} \times 3\frac{3}{4}''$ (13.0 × 9.4 cm). British Museum, London. [7, 18, 23]

The Physical Sciences and Technology, General

Draft of a letter to Ludovico il Moro. c. 1485. Codex Atlanticus, fol. 1082 recto. Biblioteca Ambrosiana, Milan, Italy. [10, 16]

Architecture

Architectural study of Castello Sforzesco (with detail for a helical staircase). c. 1485–1490. Pen and ink on paper, 5¾ × 8⅝″ (14.5 × 22.0 cm). Musée du Louvre, Paris. [11, 22, 33]

Bridge designs. c. 1487–1488. Pen and ink on paper. Manuscript B, fol. 23 recto. Bibliotheque de l'Institut de France, Paris. [14, 15]

Colosseum on a plaza. 1485–1488. Chalk and ink, 9⅛ × 6½″ (23.2 × 16.5 cm). Manuscript B, Ms. 2173, fol. 11 verso. Bibliotheque de l'Institut de France, Paris. [15]

Elevation and plan of a church. Imitation ship. 1485–1488. Pen and ink on paper, 9⅛ × 6½″ (23.2 × 16.5 cm). Manuscript B. Ms. 2173, fol. 23/24. Bibliotheque de l'Institut de France, Paris. [15, 28]

Geometrical drawings about transformation from curved to rectilinear surfaces and vice versa; in left center, planimetry of a building. Codex Atlanticus, fol. 429, recto. Biblioteca Ambrosiana, Milan. [15]

Istanbul Bridge. 1497–1502. Manuscript L, fol. 65/66. Bibliotheque de l'Institut de France, Paris. [34]

Octagonal plan (and elevation of a church); plan of two levels of the Basilica of the Holy Sepulchre in Milan. 1485–1488. Pen and ink on paper, 9⅛ × 6½″ (23.2 × 16.5 cm). Manuscript B, Ms. 2173, fol. 56 verso and fol. 57 recto. Bibliotheque de l'Institut de France, Paris. [15]

Plan and elevation of a church (fol. 93 verso); plan and elevation of a church (fol. 94 recto). Pen and ink on paper, 8½ × 5¾″ (21.4 × 14.6 cm). 1487–1490. Codex Ashburnham, Manuscript B, Ms. 2184, fol. 93 verso and fol. 94 recto. Bibliotheque de l'Institut de France, Paris. [15, 20]

Plan of a church and device for pearl fishing (underwater breathing). c. 1488. Pen and ink over chalk on paper, 9⅛ × 6½″ (23.2 × 16.5 cm). Manuscript B, Ms. 2173, fol. 17 verso. Bibliotheque de l'Institut de France, Paris. [15, 28]

Stage set, Orpheus. 1508–1516. Pen and ink on paper. Codex Arundel 263, fol. 224 recto. British Library, London. [15]

Aviation

Birds in flight. 1505. Pen and ink on paper, 8⅜ × 6″ (21 × 15 cm). Page from the Codex on the Flight of Birds. Biblioteca Reale, Turin, Italy. [17]

Birds in flight. c. 1507. Pen and ink on paper. Codex Atlanticus, fol. 214 verso. Biblioteca Ambrosiana, Milan. [17, 33]

Experiment on lifting power of wings. c. 1488. Pen and ink on paper. Manuscript B, Ms. 2173, fol. 88 verso. Bibliotheque de l'Institut de France, Paris. [17]

Flight of birds. 1513–1515. Pen and ink on paper, 6 × 4″ (15.1 × 10.2 cm). Manuscript E, Ms. 2176, fol. 42/43. Bibliotheque de l'Institut de France, Paris. [17]

Flying machine (man in ornithopter). c. 1487. Pen and ink on paper. Codex Atlanticus, fol. 276 recto. Biblioteca Ambrosiana, Milan. [1, 17]

Flying machine, mechanical wings. Flying machine, structure of the wings. 1485–1488. Pen and ink on paper, 9⅛ × 6½″ (23.2 × 16.5 cm). Manuscript B, Ms. 2173, fol. 74 recto. Bibliotheque de l'Institut de France, Paris. [1, 17, 21, 36]

Flying machine, propelling devices. c. 1490. Pen and ink on paper. Codex Atlanticus, fol. 897 recto. Biblioteca Ambrosiana, Milan. [17]

Flying machine with operator in lower parts (ornithopter). c. 1487–1490. Pen and ink on paper. Manuscript B, Ms. 2173, fol. 80 recto. Bibliotheque de l'Institut de France, Paris. [17]

Flying machine with pulleys. Pulley system. Detail of a wooden arch. Method of framework for a festival platform. 1485–1488. Pencil and ink. 9⅛ × 6½″ (23.2 × 16.5 cm). Manuscript B, Ms. 2173, fol. 78 verso and fol. 79 recto. Bibliotheque de l'Institut de France, Paris. [17]

Helicopter: propeller (aerial screw) of a flying machine; propulsion system for a flying machine. c. 1487–1490. Pen and ink over chalk on paper, 9⅛ × 6½″ (23.2 × 16.5 cm). Manuscript B. Ms. 2173, fol. 83 verso and fol. 88 recto. Bibliotheque de l'Institut de France, Paris. [17]

Human figure with wings on his back. Pen and ink on paper. Codex Atlanticus, fol. 166 recto. Biblioteca Ambrosiana, Milan. [17]

Machine for artificial flight, with caption. c. 1487–1490. Pen and ink on paper. Codex Atlanticus, fol. 824 verso. Biblioteca Ambrosiana, Milan. [17, 34]

Man in an ornithopter. c. 1485–1487. Pen and ink on paper. Manuscript B, Ms. 2173, fol. 77 verso, detail. Bibliotheque de l'Institut de France, Paris. [1, 17, 21, 36]

Methods and devices to obtain the alternate motion of wings, having in common a screw with inverse threads. c. 1487–1490. Pen and ink on paper. Codex Atlanticus, fol. 755 recto. Biblioteca Ambrosiana, Milan. [17]

Machines and Engineering

Assault chariot with scythes. c. 1485. Silverpoint, pen and ink on paper, 8¼ × 11½″ (21.0 × 29.2 cm). Biblioteca Reale, Turin, Italy. [16, 21, 22, 24]

Bridge crane (that can be lifted by a big screw). c. 1485–1490. Pen and ink on paper. Codex Atlanticus, fol. 1083 verso. Biblioteca Ambrosiana, Milan. [14]

Canal digging machine (with its measures); below, devices for the automatic dumping of the soil from a box with bottom that can be opened (the power for lifting the box is given by an ox or two men). Pen and ink on paper. Codex Atlanticus, fol. 1012 recto. Biblioteca Ambrosiana, Milan. [24]

Carriage-mounted bombard made of several barrels fitted to a rotating drum. c. 1481–1485. Pen and ink on paper. Codex Atlanticus, fol. 16 recto. Biblioteca Ambrosiana, Milan. [16]

Catapult. c. 1485–1490. Pen and ink on paper, 8½ × 11 ¾″ (21.7 × 29.7 cm). Codex Atlanticus, fol. 181 recto. Biblioteca Ambrosiana, Milan. [16]

Clock. c. 1497. Pen and ink on paper. Codex Madrid, Ms. 8937, fol. 27. Biblioteca Nacional, Madrid. [14]

Covered drawbridge provided with ladders for crossing moats and climbing walls; three-wheeled carriage for carrying bombards. c. 1485. Pen and ink on paper. Codex Atlanticus, fol. 49 recto. Biblioteca Ambrosiana, Milan. [16]

Double water pump (machine to lift water with a double pump). Pen and ink on paper. Codex Atlanticus, fol. 20 recto. Biblioteca Ambrosiana, Milan. [14]

Dredges: device to dredge and wipe the bottom of harbor; barrage to stop access to sea; systems of dredges; tool for discharging sea water after pumps have lowered harbor level. c. 1485–1490. Pen and ink on paper. Codex Atlanticus, fol. 904 recto. Biblioteca Ambrosiana, Milan. [14]

Giant crossbow (below); spontoon with iron spikes to use against enemies; two models of a crossbow on stand; bombard mounted on a boat with shield; mechanical machine to align and to screw the elements of a bombard (above). c. 1485. Pen and ink over chalk on paper, 8⅛ × 10⅞″ (20.5 × 27.5 cm). Codex Atlanticus, fol. 149 recto. Biblioteca Ambrosiana, Milan. [16]

Machines for lifting and pumping water, towers, and buildings on top of which water is lifted by Archimedean spirals. c. 1485–1490. Pen and ink on paper. Codex Atlanticus, fol. 1069 verso. Biblioteca Ambrosiana, Milan. [1, 14]

Machine to draw rods; up left, details of the same machine. c. 1500. Pen and ink on paper. Codex Atlanticus, fol. 10 recto. Biblioteca Ambrosiana, Milan. [1, 14]

Machines to lift water. On the left, machine to lift water; on the right, machine to draw water from a well and bring it into the houses. c. 1480. Pen and ink on paper. Codex Atlanticus, fol. 26 verso. Biblioteca Ambrosiana, Milan. [1, 14, 24]

Machine to study velocity composed of 24 rotating axes, each fitted with a gearwheel with 100 teeth and a spool with ten spindles at the opposite side. c. 1487–1490. Pen and ink on paper. Codex Atlanticus, fol. 83 verso. Biblioteca Ambrosiana, Milan. [14, 15]

Mechanism for repelling ladders. c. 1481. Pen and ink on paper, 10⅛ × 7¾″ (25.6 × 19.6 cm). Codex Atlanticus, fol. 139 recto. Biblioteca Ambrosiana, Milan. [1, 14]

Military machines (human scythe; human-powered covered cart). c. 1487. Pen and ink with brown wash on paper, 6⅞ × 9⅝″ (17.3 × 24.5 cm). British Museum, London. [1, 16, 36]

Mortar machine. c. 1485–1490. Pen and ink on paper, 25⅝ × 17⅜″ (65 × 44 cm). Codex Atlanticus, fol. 31 recto. Biblioteca Ambrosiana, Milan. [16]

Motion device. c. 1485–1490. Pen and ink on paper, 25⅝ × 17⅜″ (65 × 44 cm). Codex Madrid, Ms. 8937, fol. 30 recto. Biblioteca Nacional, Madrid. [14]

Needle-grinding machine. c. 1487–1490. Pen and ink on paper. Codex Atlanticus, fol. 74 recto. Biblioteca Ambrosiana, Milan. [14]

Notes and diving suit. c. 1500. Pen and ink on paper. Codex Arundel 263, fol. 24 verso. British Library, London. [22]

Odometer. c. 1500–1505. Pen and ink on paper. Codex Atlanticus, fol. 1 recto. Biblioteca Ambrosiana, Milan. [14]

Screw-threading machine (machine to thread female screw and screw; in the center, boat; above and below, machine to raise and to collect water). c. 1485–1490. Pen and ink on paper. Codex Atlanticus, fol. 156 recto. Biblioteca Ambrosiana, Milan. [14]

Self-propelled cart (automotive wagon, moved by system of springs and equipped with differential transmission). c. 1478–1482. Metalpoint, pen, and brush on paper, 10⅝ × 7⅞″ (27 × 20 cm). Codex Atlanticus, fol. 296 verso. Biblioteca Ambrosiana, Milan. [1, 14]

Seven types of machines to lift and collect water with gears, wheels, bellows, levers, pumps, Archimedean screw; on the left, at the border, instruments to walk on water and to breathe underwater. c. 1480. Pen and ink on paper. Codex Atlanticus, fol. 26 recto. Biblioteca Ambrosiana, Milan. [14]

Shearing machine with detailed captions explaining its working. 1496. Pen and ink on paper. Codex Atlanticus, fol. 1105 recto. Biblioteca Ambrosiana, Milan. [14]

Siege machine with horizontal bridge (for crossing the walls of the enemy fortress). c. 1483. Pen and ink on paper, 10⅝ × 7¾″ (27 × 19.5 cm). Codex Atlanticus, fol. 1084 recto. Biblioteca Ambrosiana, Milan. [16]

Siege machine with horizontal bridge for crossing the walls of the enemy fortress (preparatory drawing for fol. 1084 verso); above, small round dome-shaped cage, containing an animal head; below, sketches of bombard. c. 1483. Pen and ink on paper. Codex Atlanticus, fol. 1087 recto. Biblioteca Ambrosiana, Milan. [16, 36]

Sixteen guns mounted on a rotating platform; on the right, wheelbarrow equipped with an instrument to measure miles and a wheelbarrow equipped to count steps. c. 1500–1505. Pen and ink on paper. Codex Atlanticus, fol. 1 recto. Biblioteca Ambrosiana, Milan. [16, 36]

Teaselling machine to manufacture plush fabric. c. 1495. Pen and ink on paper. Codex Atlanticus, fol. 106 recto. Biblioteca Ambrosiana, Milan. [1, 14, 36]

Three machines to raise columns (above, the first drawn in pencil; in the center, the second in a triangular scaffolding drawn in ink, on the right, the third). c. 1495. Pen and ink on paper. Codex Atlanticus, fol. 138 recto. Biblioteca Ambrosiana, Milan. [14]

Unsinkable ships (right) and "submarine" (top left). 1485–1488. Pen and ink on paper, Manuscript B, Ms. 2173, fol. 11 recto. Bibliotheque de l'Institut de France, Paris. [16]

War machine composed of a big wheel with 44 steps, set in motion by the weight of 10 men mounting on a ladder and by a soldier sitting on a seat hung from the fixed pin; 1485–1488. Pen and ink on paper. Codex Atlanticus, fol. 1070 recto. Biblioteca Ambrosiana, Milan. [16]

Nature, Landscapes, and Maps

Canal to bypass the Arno. c. 1503. Brush and ink over black chalk on paper, 13¼ × 19″ (33.5 × 48.2 cm). The Royal Collection, Windsor. [24, 26]

Deluge. c. 1515. Pen and ink with wash on paper, 6⅜ × 8″ (16.2 × 20.3) cm. The Royal Collection, Windsor. [33, 36]

Flowers. c. 1485. Black chalk and ink on paper, 9⅛ × 6½″ (23.2 × 16.5 cm). Manuscript B, Ms. 2173; fol. 14 recto. Bibliotheque de l'Institut de France, Paris. [34]

Landscape. 1473. Pen and ink on paper, 7.5 × 11″ (19 × 28.5 cm). Gabinetto dei Disegni e delle Stampe, Galleria degli Uffizi, Florence. [5, 33, 36]

Lily (Madonna lily; *Lilium candidium*). c. 1485. Pen and ink, wash, chalk, and white heightening on paper. The Royal Collection, Windsor. [1, 34]

Plan of Imola. 1502. Pen and ink, wash and chalk on paper, 17⅜ × 23¾″ (44 × 60.2 cm). The Royal Collection, Windsor. [1, 24]

Star of Bethlehem, wood anemone and sun spurge. c. 1485–1505. Pen and ink with red chalk on paper. The Royal Collection, Windsor. [1, 34]

Studies of flowers. c. 1481–1483. Pen and ink on paper, 7¼ × 8″ (18.3 × 20.1 cm). Gallerie dell'Accademia, Venice. [34]

Physics and Math

Calculating diameter of sun and moon. Pen and ink on paper. Codex Atlanticus, fol. 662 recto. Biblioteca Ambrosiana, Milan. [2, 14, 15]

Illustrated scientific manuscript (optics). Codex Ashburnham, Manuscript A, fol. 14. Pen and ink on paper. Bibliotheque de l'Institut de France, Paris. [22, 29]

Perspectograph (optical instrument) with a man that is examining inside. c. 1480–1482. Pen and ink on paper. Codex Atlanticus, fol. 5 recto. Biblioteca Ambrosiana, Milan. [15]

Study of perspective and calculation of distances. c. 1490–1493. Pen and ink on paper. Codex Atlanticus, fol. 119 recto. Biblioteca Ambrosiana, Milan. [15]

Models of Leonardo's Designs

Aerial screw. Model after a drawing in Manuscript B, fol. 83 verso. c. 1487–1490. Museo Ideale Leonardo da Vinci, Vinci, Italy. [17]

Akamu, Nina. Leonardo da Vinci's Horse, outside the Milan Hippodrome. 1999. Bronze, 24′ (7.3 m). Milan. [19]

———. Leonardo da Vinci's Horse. 1999. Bronze, 24′ (7.3 m). The Frederik Meijer Gardens and Sculpture Park, Grand Rapids, Michigan. [19]

Ginevra de' Benci. 2001. Digital reconstruction. National Gallery of Art, Washington, DC. [6]

Mechanism for a clock. Model after a drawing in the Codex Madrid I, fol. 14 recto. Collection Niccolai, Florence. [14]

Model for an articulated wing. Model after a drawing in the Codex Atlanticus, fol. 308 recto. Museo Ideale Leonardo da Vinci, Vinci, Italy. [17]

Model of a machine with flapping wings. Museo della Scienza e della Tecnica, Milan. [17]

Model of an inclined flying machine (ornithopter). Model (detail) after a drawing in the Codex Atlanticus, fol. 302 verso. Museo Ideale Leonardo da Vinci, Vinci, Italy. [17]

Mileage meter (odometer). Model after a drawing in the Codex Atlanticus, fol. 1 recto. Collection Niccolai, Florence. [14]

Model of the first automobile, designed by Leonardo da Vinci. Castle of Clos Luce, Amboise, France. [14]

War machine: chariot with scythes, detail. Model after a drawing in the Codex Turin. Collection Niccolai, Florence, Italy. [16]

War machine, detail. Model after a drawing in the British Museum, London. Museo Ideale Leonardo da Vinci, Vinci, Italy. [16]

Wreath of laurel, palm, and juniper with a scroll inscribed "Virtutem Forum Decorat" [reverse of *Ginevra de' Benci*]. 2001. Digital reconstruction. National Gallery of Art, Washington, DC. [6]

Works by Other Artists

Agnese, Gian Battista. Map of Central Europe. Mid-16th century. Museo Correr, Venice. [13]

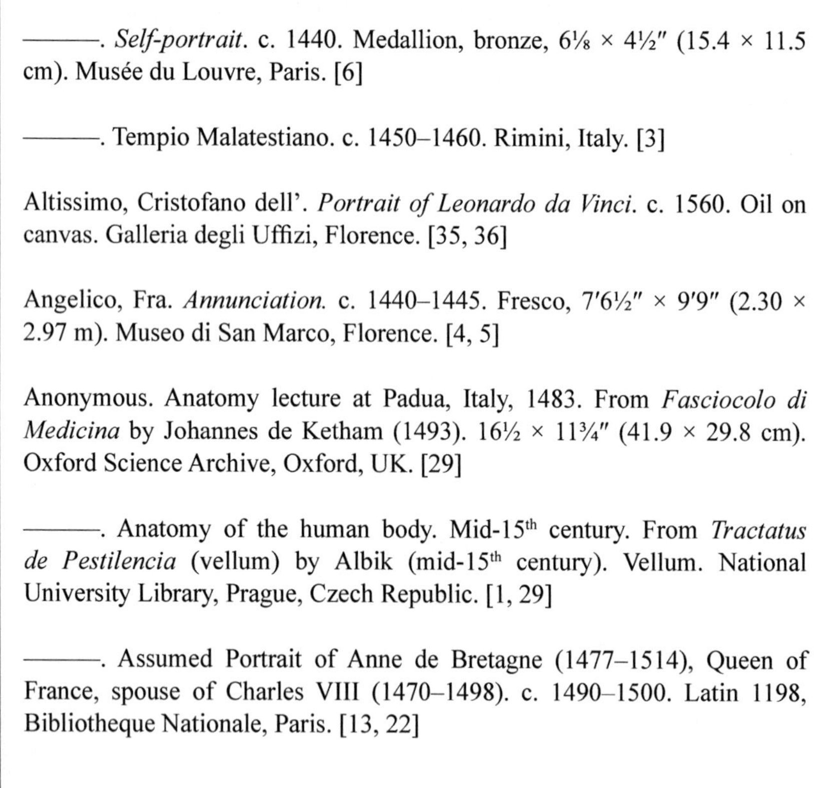

Alberti, Leon Battista. Facade of the Palazzo. Begun c. 1453. Palazzo Rucellai, Florence. [3, 5]

———. Santa Maria Novella. c. 1458–1470. Florence. [3]

———. *Self-portrait*. c. 1440. Medallion, bronze, 6⅛ × 4½″ (15.4 × 11.5 cm). Musée du Louvre, Paris. [6]

———. Tempio Malatestiano. c. 1450–1460. Rimini, Italy. [3]

Altissimo, Cristofano dell'. *Portrait of Leonardo da Vinci*. c. 1560. Oil on canvas. Galleria degli Uffizi, Florence. [35, 36]

Angelico, Fra. *Annunciation*. c. 1440–1445. Fresco, 7′6½″ × 9′9″ (2.30 × 2.97 m). Museo di San Marco, Florence. [4, 5]

Anonymous. Anatomy lecture at Padua, Italy, 1483. From *Fasciocolo di Medicina* by Johannes de Ketham (1493). 16½ × 11¾″ (41.9 × 29.8 cm). Oxford Science Archive, Oxford, UK. [29]

———. Anatomy of the human body. Mid-15th century. From *Tractatus de Pestilencia* (vellum) by Albik (mid-15th century). Vellum. National University Library, Prague, Czech Republic. [1, 29]

———. Assumed Portrait of Anne de Bretagne (1477–1514), Queen of France, spouse of Charles VIII (1470–1498). c. 1490–1500. Latin 1198, Bibliotheque Nationale, Paris. [13, 22]

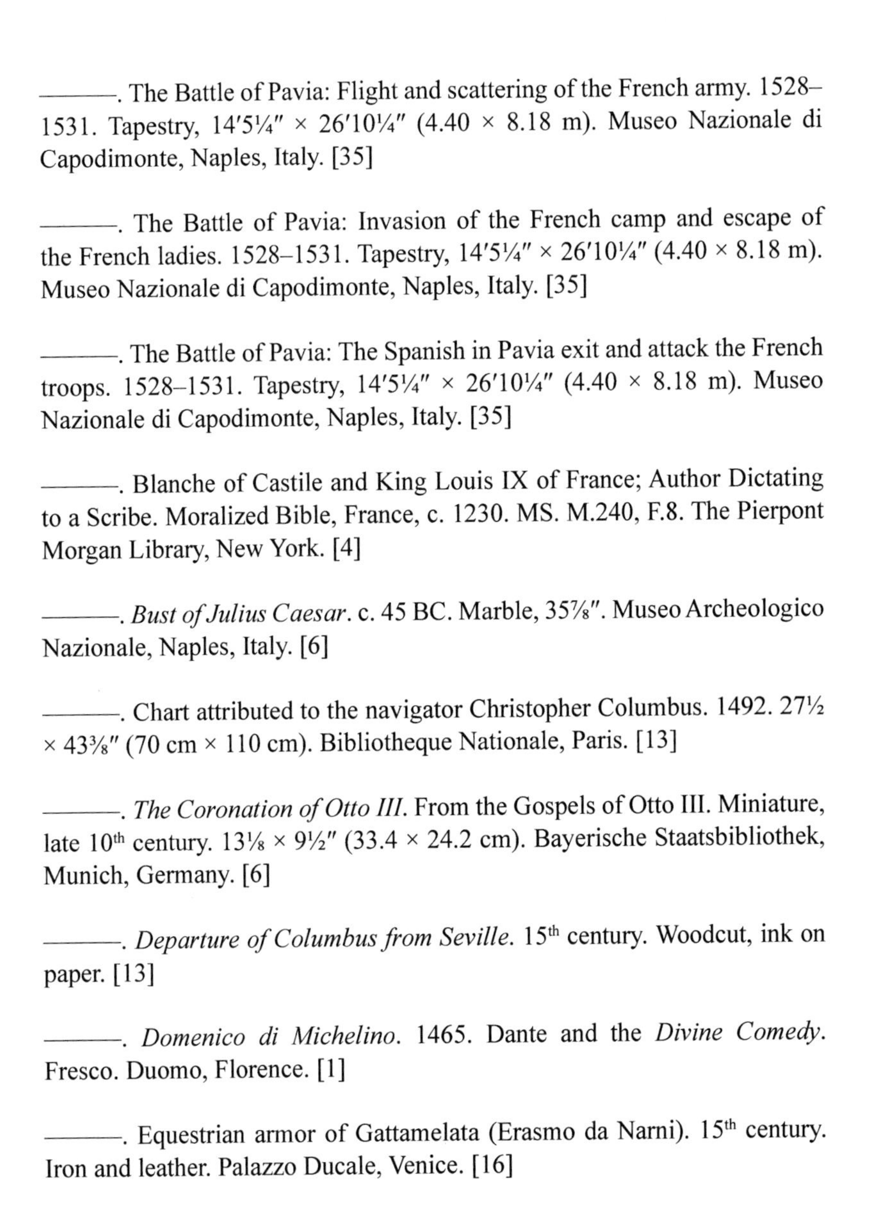

———. The Battle of Pavia: Flight and scattering of the French army. 1528–1531. Tapestry, 14′5¼″ × 26′10¼″ (4.40 × 8.18 m). Museo Nazionale di Capodimonte, Naples, Italy. [35]

———. The Battle of Pavia: Invasion of the French camp and escape of the French ladies. 1528–1531. Tapestry, 14′5¼″ × 26′10¼″ (4.40 × 8.18 m). Museo Nazionale di Capodimonte, Naples, Italy. [35]

———. The Battle of Pavia: The Spanish in Pavia exit and attack the French troops. 1528–1531. Tapestry, 14′5¼″ × 26′10¼″ (4.40 × 8.18 m). Museo Nazionale di Capodimonte, Naples, Italy. [35]

———. Blanche of Castile and King Louis IX of France; Author Dictating to a Scribe. Moralized Bible, France, c. 1230. MS. M.240, F.8. The Pierpont Morgan Library, New York. [4]

———. *Bust of Julius Caesar*. c. 45 BC. Marble, 35⅞″. Museo Archeologico Nazionale, Naples, Italy. [6]

———. Chart attributed to the navigator Christopher Columbus. 1492. 27½ × 43⅜″ (70 cm × 110 cm). Bibliotheque Nationale, Paris. [13]

———. *The Coronation of Otto III*. From the Gospels of Otto III. Miniature, late 10th century. 13⅛ × 9½″ (33.4 × 24.2 cm). Bayerische Staatsbibliothek, Munich, Germany. [6]

———. *Departure of Columbus from Seville*. 15th century. Woodcut, ink on paper. [13]

———. *Domenico di Michelino*. 1465. Dante and the *Divine Comedy*. Fresco. Duomo, Florence. [1]

———. Equestrian armor of Gattamelata (Erasmo da Narni). 15th century. Iron and leather. Palazzo Ducale, Venice. [16]

———. Firing a blunderbuss. From the Bellifortis Manuscript. 15th century. Illuminated manuscript, 13⅜ × 10¼″ (33.8 × 25.8 cm). Universitaetsbibliothek, Goettingen, Germany. [16]

———. Florence in c. 1470–1480. Detail from the Catena Map, showing the Duomo, Piazza della Signoria, and Palazzo Vecchio. Museo di Firenze com'era, Florence. [1, 24]

———. Great bronze gun, Turkish. 1464. Bronze, 37,630 pounds (17,069 kg); 17′ (5.18 m); caliber 25″ (63.5 cm). The Board of Trustees of the Armouries, Leeds, UK. [16]

———. Harquebusier aiming, wounded knights. Illustration from *Theuerdank*, an epic tale by Emperor Maximilian I (1449–1519). Augsburg, 1517. Colored woodcut, 8⅞ × 6″ (22.5 × 15 cm). Dillingen Library, Dillingen, Germany. [16]

———. *Head of Pompey the Great*. c. 50 B.C. Marble. Ny Carlsberg Glyptotek, Copenhagen, Denmark. [6]

———. Illuminated page from the Bible of Charles the Bald. 9th century. Ms. Lat. 1, fol. 423. Bibliotheque Nationale, Paris. [6]

———. Intarsia door showing armor. 1476. 7′3⅜″ × 11′ (2.22 × 3.35 m). Studiolo, Palazzo Ducale, Urbino, Italy. [16]

———. Jerusalem besieged by Anthiocus. From *Chronique Universelle*, by Jean de Courcy. Bruges, c. 1470. 17 × 12⅝″ (43 × 32 cm). MS. M.224, fol. 117 verso. The Pierpont Morgan Library, New York. [16]

———. *Jocasta's Embassy to Adrastus*. The siege of Thebes; King Adrastus receives Jocasta and her ladies. c. 1525. 15⅝ × 11⅛″ (39.5 × 28 cm). From the *Troy Book* and the *Story of Thebes*, by John Lydgate. Roy D II fol. 158 verso. British Library, London. [16]

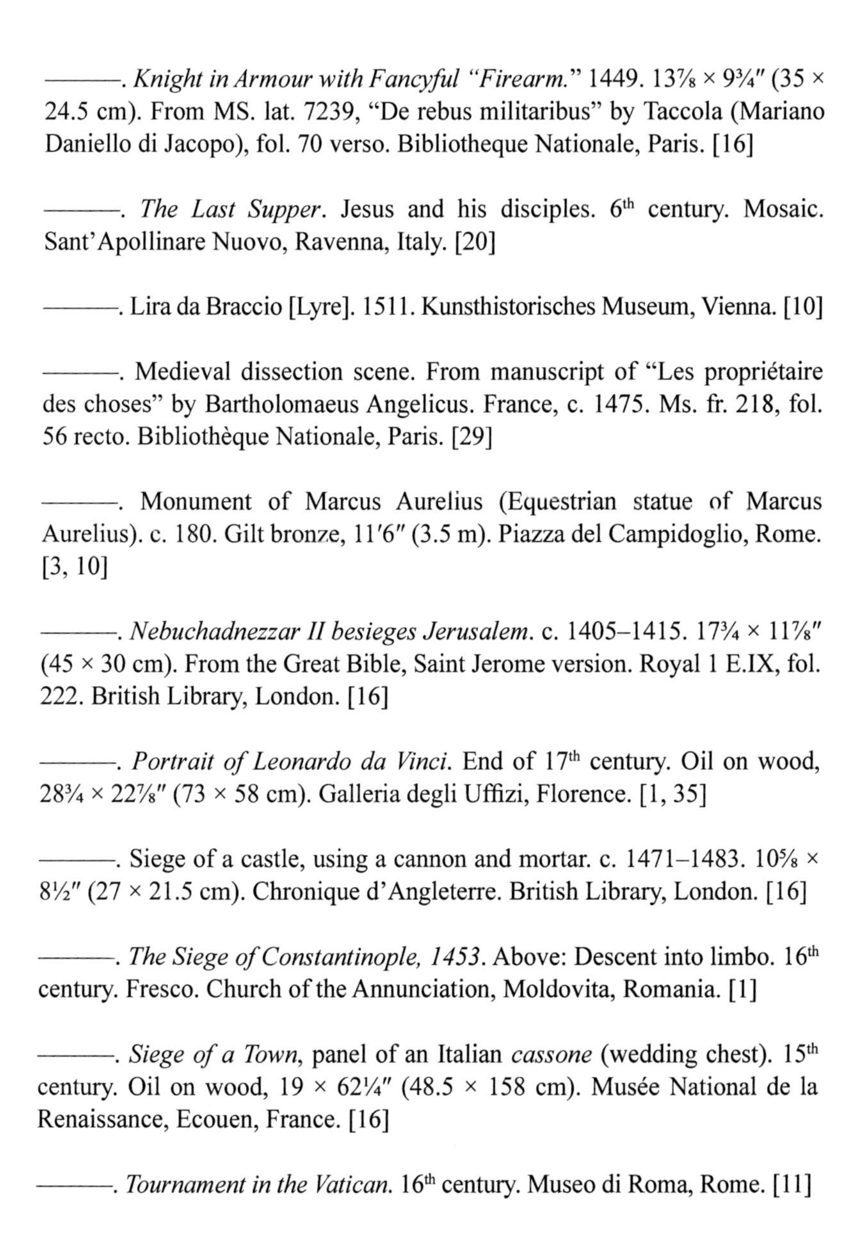
———. *Knight in Armour with Fancyful "Firearm."* 1449. 13⅞ × 9¾″ (35 × 24.5 cm). From MS. lat. 7239, "De rebus militaribus" by Taccola (Mariano Daniello di Jacopo), fol. 70 verso. Bibliotheque Nationale, Paris. [16]

———. *The Last Supper*. Jesus and his disciples. 6th century. Mosaic. Sant'Apollinare Nuovo, Ravenna, Italy. [20]

———. Lira da Braccio [Lyre]. 1511. Kunsthistorisches Museum, Vienna. [10]

———. Medieval dissection scene. From manuscript of "Les propriétaire des choses" by Bartholomaeus Angelicus. France, c. 1475. Ms. fr. 218, fol. 56 recto. Bibliothèque Nationale, Paris. [29]

———. Monument of Marcus Aurelius (Equestrian statue of Marcus Aurelius). c. 180. Gilt bronze, 11′6″ (3.5 m). Piazza del Campidoglio, Rome. [3, 10]

———. *Nebuchadnezzar II besieges Jerusalem*. c. 1405–1415. 17¾ × 11⅞″ (45 × 30 cm). From the Great Bible, Saint Jerome version. Royal 1 E.IX, fol. 222. British Library, London. [16]

———. *Portrait of Leonardo da Vinci*. End of 17th century. Oil on wood, 28¾ × 22⅞″ (73 × 58 cm). Galleria degli Uffizi, Florence. [1, 35]

———. Siege of a castle, using a cannon and mortar. c. 1471–1483. 10⅝ × 8½″ (27 × 21.5 cm). Chronique d'Angleterre. British Library, London. [16]

———. *The Siege of Constantinople, 1453*. Above: Descent into limbo. 16th century. Fresco. Church of the Annunciation, Moldovita, Romania. [1]

———. *Siege of a Town*, panel of an Italian *cassone* (wedding chest). 15th century. Oil on wood, 19 × 62¼″ (48.5 × 158 cm). Musée National de la Renaissance, Ecouen, France. [16]

———. *Tournament in the Vatican*. 16th century. Museo di Roma, Rome. [11]

Anonymous. *Upright Shields*, illustration from the Bellifortis Manuscript. 15th century. 13⅜ × 10¼″ (33.8 × 25.8 cm). Universitaetsbibliothek, Goettingen, Germany. [16]

———. View of the Certosa in Pavia. 16th century. Certosa di Pavia, Pavia, Italy. [11]

———. Wilton Diptych. c. 1396–1399. Tempera on wood, 20⅞ × 14⅝″ (53 × 37 cm). The National Gallery, London. [6]

Anonymous, after Leonardo da Vinci. A horseman wearing helmet and armour and riding to left. Pen and ink, with brown wash, heightened with white, on pink prepared paper. 10⅝ × 9⅜″ (27 × 23.9 cm). Malcolm Collection, British Museum, London. [25]

———. *Bacchus.* Oil on wood, transferred to canvas, 5′10″ × 3′9″ (177 × 115 cm). Musée du Louvre, Paris. [1, 35]

———. *The Battle of Anghiari*. c. 1560. Oil on canvas. Palazzo Vecchio, Florence. [25]

———. *Bust-Length Female Nude*. Early 16th century, Lombard School. Oil on canvas, 22¼ × 16⅝″ (56 × 42 cm). Musée du Louvre, Paris. [32]

———. Grotesque caricature heads of five men and two women. Pen and ink on paper, 6¾ × 4¾″ (17.2 × 12.0 cm). British Museum, London. [18, 21]

———. *Leda and the Swan*. c. 1515. Tempera on wood, 44⅛ × 33⅞″ (112 × 86 cm). Galleria Borghese, Rome. [1, 27]

———. *Leda and the Swan*. Red chalk on paper, 10⅞ × 6¾″ (27.5 × 17.0 cm). Musée du Louvre, Paris. [27, 32, 36]

———. *Mounted Warrior (formerly attributed to Giovan Francesco Rustici)*. 1516–1519. Bronze with artificial verdigris, 9½″ (24 cm). The Museum of Fine Arts, Budapest. [30]

———. *The Virgin and Child.* After 1510. Oil on wood, 23½ × 17¼″ (59.7 × 43.8 cm). The National Gallery, London. [32]

———. Three caricature heads with grotesque features. Pen and ink on paper, 7⅜ × 5¼″ (18.5 × 13.3 cm). British Museum, London. [18]

Anonymous, after Raphael. *Giuliano de' Medici.* c. 1515. Tempera and oil on canvas, 32¾ × 26″ (83.2 × 66 cm). The Jules Bache Collection. The Metropolitan Museum of Art, New York. [31]

Anonymous Dutch painter. *King Ferdinand II of Aragon.* c. 1490–1500. Kunsthistorisches Museum, Vienna. [13]

Anonymous (Ferrarese School). *Portrait of a Man in Red.* c. 1450–1475. Oil on wood, 15½ × 10⅛″ (39.5 × 25.7 cm). The Wallace Collection, London. [6]

Anonymous (Spanish School). *Portrait of Alexander VI.* c. 1492. Pinacoteca, Vatican Museums. [13, 21]

Antonio, di. *The Siege of Troy: The Death of Hector.* c. 1490. Tempera on wood, 18½ × 63⅜″ (47 × 161 cm). Fitzwilliam Museum, Cambridge, UK. [16]

Bartolommeo, Fra (Baccio della Porta). *Portrait of Girolamo Savonarola.* c. 1499–1500. Oil on wood, 18⅜ × 12⅞″ (46.5 × 32.5 cm). Museo di San Marco, Florence. [25]

Bellini, Giovanni. *Madonna and Child with Saints*, from the *Saint Giobbe Altarpiece.* c. 1487. Oil on wood, 15′5½″ × 8′5¾″ (4.71 × 2.58 m). Gallerie dell'Accademia, Venice. [32]

———. *Madonna and Child.* c. 1475–1485. Oil on canvas, 18½ × 13½″ (47 × 34 cm). Accademia Carrara, Bergamo, Italy. [32]

———. *Madonna of the Meadow.* c. 1500. Oil and egg on synthetic panel, transferred from wood, 26½ × 34″ (67.3 × 86.4 cm). The National Gallery, London. [32]

Bembo, Bonifacio. *Francesco Sforza*. c. 1460. Tempera on wood, 15¾ × 12¼″ (40 × 31 cm). Pinacoteca di Brera, Milan. [10, 19]

Bergen, Claus. *German Submarine Sinks a British Fishing Steamer*. 1917. Watercolor. Collection of Claus Bergen, Germany. [36]

Birago, Giovanni Pietro da. *The Last Supper, with a Spaniel, after Leonardo da Vinci*. c. 1500. Engraving on paper, 8⅜ × 17⁵⁄₁₆″ (21.3 × 44.0 cm). The Metropolitan Museum of Art, New York. [20, 21]

Boltraffio, Giovannio Antonio. *Portrait of Ludovico il Moro*. 1490s. Private collection. [10, 22]

Bonfigli, Benedetto. *Siege of Perugia by Totila and Decapitation of Saint Ercolano*. 1461–1477. Fresco. Galleria Nazionale dell'Umbria, Perugia, Italy. [16]

Botticelli, Sandro. *Adoration of the Magi*. c. 1475. Tempera on wood, 43¾ × 52¾″ (111 × 134 cm). Galleria degli Uffizi, Florence. [9]

———. *The Annunciation*. 1489–1490. Tempera on wood, 59¼ × 61½″ (150 × 156 cm). Galleria degli Uffizi, Florence. [5]

———. *Birth of Venus*. c. 1484–1486. Tempera on canvas, 5′8″ × 9′1⅝″ (1.72 × 2.78 m). Galleria degli Uffizi, Florence. [3, 27, 32]

———. *Calumny of Apelles*. 1490s. Tempera on wood, 24½ × 35⅞″ (62 × 91 cm). Galleria degli Uffizi, Florence. [32]

———. *Portrait of a Man with a Medal of Cosimo the Elder*. 1474. Tempera on wood, 22⅝ × 17⅜″ (57.5 × 44 cm). Galleria degli Uffizi, Florence. [10]

———. *Primavera (Spring)*. c. 1481. Tempera on wood. 6′7⅞″ × 10′3⅝″ (203 × 314 cm). Galleria degli Uffizi, Florence. [31]

———. *Virgin and Child*. 1464–1470. Oil on wood, 28⅜ × 20⅛″ (72 × 51 cm). Musée du Petit Palais, Avignon, France. [7]

Boucher, François. *Reclining Girl (portrait of Louise O'Murphy, mistress of Louis XV)*. 1750. Oil on canvas, 23¼ × 28¾″ (59 × 73 cm). Alte Pinakothek, Bayerische Staatsgemaeldesammlungen, Munich, Germany. [36]

Bourdichon, Jean. *King Louis XII enters Genova.* 1507. Miniature. Manuscript illustration in *La Conquête de Gênes* by Jean Marot. Bibliotheque Nationale, Paris. [13, 22]

Bramante, Donato. Church of Santa Maria delle Grazie. Milan. [14, 15]

———. Cloister, Santa Maria della Pace. Façade designed by Bramante in 1500–04. [28]

———. Plan for the new St. Peter's Basilica. 1506. No. 20A. Pen and ink on paper. Gabinetto dei Disegni e delle Stampe, Galleria degli Uffizi, Florence. [15, 28]

———. Santa Maria delle Grazie. Exterior of apse (1492–1497); interior facing the altar. 15th century. Milan. [15, 20]

———. Santa Maria presso San Satiro. 1477–1491. Milan, Italy. [15]

———. Tempietto. 1502–1511. San Pietro in Montorio, Rome. [15, 28]

Bronzino, Agnolo. *An Allegory with Venus and Cupid.* c. 1540–1550. Oil on wood, 57½ × 45¾″ (146.1 × 116.2 cm). The National Gallery, London. [35]

Bronzino, Agnolo. *Portrait of Cosimo I de' Medici as Orpheus*. c. 1538–1540. Oil on wood, unframed: 36⅞ × 30 1/16″ (93.7 × 76.4 cm). Philadelphia Museum of Art. [35]

Brunelleschi, Filippo. Baptistry. 1420–1436. Duomo, Florence. [1, 3]

———. Dome lantern. 1446–1470. Duomo, Florence. [3]

———. Facade. 1419–1460s. Church of San Lorenzo, Florence. [3]

———. Old Sacristy. 1428. Church of San Lorenzo, Florence. [5]

Campin, Robert. *Portrait of a Man.* Undated. Oil on wood, 11¼ × 7″ (28.5 × 17.7 cm). Gemäldegalerie, Staatliche Museen zu Berlin. [6, 9]

Caprotti, Gian Giacomo (Salai). *Saint John the Baptist.* 1510–1520. Tempera and oil on wood, 28¾ × 20⅛″ (73 × 51 cm). Pinacoteca Ambrosiana, Milan. [35]

Caravaggio, Michelangelo Merisi da (1571–1610). *Young Bacchus.* 1596–1598. Oil on canvas, 37⅜ × 33½″ (95 × 85 cm). Galleria degli Uffizi, Florence. [8]

Castagno, Andrea del. *The Last Supper.* 15th century. Fresco, 15′5″ × 32′ (4.70 × 9.75 m). Convent of Sant'Apollonia, Florence. [20]

Christus, Petrus. *Portrait of a Carthusian.* 1446. Oil on wood, overall 11½ × 8½″ (29.2 × 21.6 cm); painted surface 11½ × 7⅜″ (29.2 × 18.7 cm). The Metropolitan Museum of Art, New York. [6, 9]

Cione, Andrea di (Andrea Orcagna). *Cenacolo di Santo Spirito.* Early 1360s. Santo Spirito, Florence. [20]

Claesz, Pieter. *The Last Supper.* Copy of work by Peter Paul Rubens after Leonardo da Vinci. c. 1620. Etching, 11¾ × 19⅘″ (29.8 × 50.3 cm). Herzog Anton Ulrich-Museum, Braunschweig, Germany. [20, 21]

Clouet, Jean. *François I.* c. 1525–1530. Oil and tempera on wood, 37¾ × 29¼″ (95.9 × 74 cm). Musée du Louvre, Paris. [33]

Clouet, Jean, workshop of. *François I.* c. 1525–1530. Oil on wood, 8⅜ × 6¾″ (21 × 17 cm). Musée du Louvre, Paris. [33]

Danti, Ignazio. *The Duchy of Milan, including a map of the city of Milan.* 1580–1582. Fresco, 10′6″ × 13′11″ (320 × 425 cm). Galleria delle Carte Geografiche, Vatican Museums. [10]

De Predis, Cristoforo (attributed). *The Professions*. From *De Sphaera*. c. 1475. Vellum. Ms. Lat 209 fol. 11 recto. Biblioteca Estense, Modena, Italy. [11]

Donatello. *David*. c. 1455–1459. Bronze, 5′2¼″ (1.58 m). Museo Nazionale del Bargello, Florence. [2, 3, 8, 19, 22]

———. *Equestrian statue of Gattamelata*. 1447–1453. Bronze on marble and stone base, 11′2″ (3.4 m). Piazza del Santo, Padua, Italy. [3, 10, 19, 30]

———. *Feast of Herod (Detail from the Baptistery Font)*. 1423–1425. Gilt bronze relief. Baptistery, Siena Cathedral, Siena, Italy. [1]

Flandes, Juan de. *Isabella the Catholic*. c. 1500. Oil on wood, 8¾ × 5⅛″ (21 × 13 cm). Museo del Prado, Madrid. [13]

Francesca, Piero della. *The Baptism of Christ*. Late 1440s. Tempera on wood, 5′6″ × 3′9⅝″ (1.67 × 1.16 m). The National Gallery, London. [4]

———. *Portraits of Federico da Montefeltro, Duke of Urbino, and his wife Battista Sforza*. c. 1465–66. Tempera on wood, 18½ × 13″ (47 × 33 cm) each. Galleria degli Uffizi, Florence. [26]

———. *Sigismondo Pandolfo Malatesta*. c. 1451. Oil on wood, 17⅜ × 13⅜″ (44 × 34 cm). Musée du Louvre, Paris. [6]

Gaddi, Taddeo. Wall with frescoes of the *Tree of the Cross* and other scenes. c. 1355. Fresco, 36′9″ × 38′4⅝″ (11.2 × 11.7 m). Museo dell'Opera, Santa Croce, Florence. [20]

Gagliardi, Filippo. *Fresco depicting the interior of Old St. Peter's, Rome*. San Martino ai Monti, Rome. [28]

Ghiberti, Lorenzo. *East Doors of the Florence Baptistry (Gates of Paradise)*. 1425–1452. Gilded bronze, 15′ (4.57 m). Baptistery of San Giovanni, Florence. [3]

———. *Flagellation*. North Door. 1407–1424. Baptistery, Florence. [1]

———. *Sacrifice of Isaac*. c. 1401. Bronze, partly gilded, 18⅜ × $15^{3}/_{5}$″ (4.65 × 4.0 cm) including frame. Museo Nazionale del Bargello, Florence. [1]

Ghirlandaio, Domenico. *Adoration of the Shepherds.* From the *Sassetti Altarpiece*. 1485. Tempera on wood, 5′6″ × 5′6″ (1.67 × 1.67 m). Santa Trinita, Florence. [9, 32]

———. *Calling of Saints Peter and Andrew*. 1480–1482. Fresco. Sistine Chapel, Vatican Palace. [9]

———. *Last Supper*. 1480. Fresco, 13′1½″ × 28′10½″ (4.0 × 8.8 m). Museo di San Marco, Florence. [20]

———. *Old Man with a Young Boy.* c. 1490. Tempera on wood, $24^{2}/_{5}$ × 18 $^{1}/_{10}$″ (62 × 46 cm). Musée du Louvre, Paris. [6]

———. *Virgin and Child.* Oil on wood, 31 × 21⅝″ (78.7 × 55 cm). Musée du Louvre, Paris. [3, 36]

Giambologna. *The Rape of Sabine*. 1583. Marble, 13′5½″ (4.1 m). Loggia dei Lanzi, Florence. [35]

Giorgione (Giorgio da Castelfranco). *Portrait of Laura*. 1506. Oil on canvas on wood, 16¼ × 13¼″ (41 × 33.6 cm). Kunsthistorisches Museum, Vienna. [32]

———. *The Sleeping Venus* (*The Dresden Venus*). 1508–1510. Oil on canvas, 42½ × 69″ (1.08 × 1.75 m). Gemäldegalerie Alte Meister, Staatliche Kunstsammlungen, Dresden, Germany. [27, 32]

———. *Old Woman*. c. 1508. Oil on canvas, 26¾ × 23¼″ (68 × 59 cm). Gallerie dell'Accademia, Venice. [32]

Giotto di Bondone. *The Last Supper.* c. 1305. Fresco, 16′1″ × 15′5⅞″ (4.90 × 4.72 m). Scrovegni (Arena) Chapel, Padua, Italy. [2, 20]

———. *Ognissanti Madonna.* 1306–1310. Tempera on wood, 10′8″ × 6′8⅜″ (3.25 × 2.04 m). Galleria degli Uffizi, Florence. [3, 7, 22]

———. *Stefaneschi Altarpiece* (recto). c. 1330. Tempera on wood, 5′10⅛″ × 8′4½″ (1.78 × 2.55 m). Pinacoteca, Vatican Museums. [6]

———. *Stigmatization of Saint Francis.* c. 1320. Fresco, 9′2¼″ × 14′9¼″ (2.8 × 4.5 m). Bardi Chapel, Santa Croce, Florence. [1]

Gozzoli, Benozzo. *Adoration of the Magi.* 1459. Fresco. Palazzo Medici Riccardi, Florence [3]

Gutenberg, Johannes. *Gutenberg Bible.* Biblia Latina. Mainz: Johann Gutenberg & Johann Fust, c. 1455. PML 818, Volume II, fol. 131 verso–132 recto. The Pierpont Morgan Library, New York. [18]

Guy of Pavia. *Dissection of the Thorax of a Corpse.* From *Liber notabilium Philippi septimi, Francorum regis, a libri Galieni extratus*, written by Guy of Pavia. 1345. 12⅝ × 8¾″ (32 × 22 cm). Ms. 334, fol. 264. Musée Condé, Chantilly, France. [29]

Heemskerck, Maarten van. Pillar of the crossing of New St. Peter's Basilica and remnants of the northern wing of Old St. Peter's. c. 1532–1536. From the Roman Sketchbook I. Pen and ink on paper, 5⅜ × 8⅜″ (13.5 × 21 cm). Kupferstichkabinett, Staatliche Museen, Berlin. [15]

———. Pope Clement VII during the siege of the Castel Sant'Angelo near the Vatican in 1527 (Sack of Rome). 1554. Pen and ink over black chalk on paper, 5⅞ × 9¼″ (14.8 × 23.4 cm). Hamburger Kunsthalle, Hamburg, Germany. [35]

Hogenbergh, Franz. Plan of Milan. 1572. Engraving on paper. [10]

Illustration from the *Hypnerotomachia Poliphili* by Francesco Colonna. Manutius: Venice, 1499. [27]

Ingres, Jean Auguste Dominique. *François I of France at Leonardo da Vinci's Deathbed.* 1818. Oil on canvas, 15¾″ × 19⅞″ (40 × 50.5 cm). Musée du Petit Palais, Paris. [2, 36]

Koelderer, Joerg. *Arquebuses*. From the Zeugbucher, the Books of Arms of Emperor Maximilian I. c. 1512. Kunsthistorisches Museum, Vienna. [16]

———. *Guns*. From the Zeugbucher, the Books of Arms of Emperor Maximilian I. c. 1512. Kunsthistorisches Museum, Vienna. [16]

Lippi, Filippino. *The Adoration of the Magi*. 1496. Tempera on wood, 6′6″ × 6′10½″ (2.0 × 2.1 cm). Galleria degli Uffizi, Florence. [9, 23]

Lippi, Fra Filippo. *Madonna and Child.* c. 1440. Tempera on wood, 31⅛ × 20⅛″ (79 × 51.1 cm) National Gallery of Art, Washington, DC. [7]

———. *Portrait of a Woman and a Man at a Casement*. c. 1440. Tempera on wood, 25¼ × 16½″ (64.1 × 41.9 cm). Marquand Collection. The Metropolitan Museum of Art, New York. [6]

———. *Virgin and Child with Two Angels*. 1455. Tempera on wood, 37⅜ × 24⅜″ (95 × 62 cm). Galleria degli Uffizi, Florence. [3, 7, 26]

Lorenzo di Credi. *The Annunciation*. c. 1478–1480. Oil on wood, 6⅜ × 23⅝″ (16 × 60 cm). Musée du Louvre, Paris. [8, 32]

———. *Madonna and Child with a Pomegranate*. Oil on wood, 6½ × 5¼″ (16.5 × 13.4 cm). National Gallery of Art, Washington, DC. [8]

———. *Madonna and Child with Saint John the Baptist*. c. 1480–1485. Oil on wood, 14½ × 10⅝″ (37 × 27 cm). Gemäldegalerie Alte Meister, Dresden. [8]

Luini, Bernardino. *Christ Blessing*. c. 1520. Tempera and oil on wood, 17 × 14⅝″ (43 × 37 cm). Pinacoteca Ambrosiana, Milan. [35]

———. *The Holy Family*. Oil on wood, 20⅛ × 17″ (51 × 43 cm). Musée du Louvre, Paris. [35]

———. *Infant Jesus with a Lamb.* 1500–1524. Tempera and oil on wood, 11⅛ × 9⅞″ (28 × 25 cm). Pinacoteca Ambrosiana, Milan. [35]

———. *The Virgin and Child in a Landscape.* c. 1520. Oil on wood, 28⅞ × 21½″ (73.2 × 54.4 cm). Wallace Collection, London. [35]

Manet, Edouard. *Olympia.* 1863. Oil on canvas, 4′3¼″ × 6′2⅞″ (1.3 × 1.9 m). Musée d'Orsay, Paris, France. [36]

Mantegna, Andrea. *Decoration of the Camera degli Sposi (Camera Picta).* 1465–1474. Fresco and dry tempera, 26′3″ × 26′3″ (8 × 8 m). Palazzo Ducale, Mantua, Italy. [11, 22]

Martini, Simone. *Annunciation with Saints Ansano and Margaret.* Four medallions: Prophets Jeremiah, Ezechiel, Isaiah, and Daniel. 1333. Tempera on wood. 6′½″ × 6′10¾″ (1.84 × 2.10 m). Galleria degli Uffizi, Florence. [5]

Masaccio (Tommaso di Giovanni di Simone Cassai). *Expulsion from Paradise.* c. 1427. Fresco, 84½ × 35½″ (214 × 90 cm). Brancacci Chapel, Santa Maria del Carmine, Florence. [3]

———. *Tribute Money.* c. 1425. Fresco, 7′6½″ × 19′7″ (2.3 × 6 m). Brancacci Chapel, Santa Maria del Carmine, Florence. [3, 5]

———. *Trinity.* 1427. Fresco, 21′ × 10′4⅞″ (6.40 × 3.17 m). Santa Maria Novella, Florence. [2, 3, 10]

Masaccio (Tommaso di Giovanni di Simone Cassai), perhaps with Tommaso Masolino da Panicale. *Saint Anne Madonna* (*Madonna and Child with Saint Anne*). 1424–1425. Tempera on wood, 5′8⅞″ × 3′4½″ (1.75 × 1.03 m). Galleria degli Uffizi, Florence. [3, 7, 27]

Masolino da Panicale, Tommaso. *Temptation of Adam and Eve.* 1425. Fresco, 81⅞ × 34¾″ (208 × 88 cm). Brancacci Chapel, Santa Maria del Carmine, Florence. [27]

Master of the Pala Sforzesca. *The Sforza Altarpiece (Madonna and Child Enthroned with the Doctors of the Church and the Family of Ludovico il Moro; Includes Detail of Duchess Beatrice d'Este)*. c. 1495. Tempera on wood, 7′6½″ × 5′5″ (2.30 × 1.65 m). Pinacoteca di Brera, Milan. [12, 20, 22]

Mazzolino, Ludovico. *Madonna and Child, Saint Anne, Saint Joachim, and Saint John the Baptist*. 1522–1523. 11⅝ × 9″ (29.5 × 22.8 cm). Galleria degli Uffizi, Florence. [35]

Melozzo da Forli. *Sixtus IV Founding the Vatican Library*. 1477. Fresco transferred to canvas, 12′1¾″ × 10′4″ (3.70 × 3.15 m). Pinacoteca, Vatican Museums. [13, 28]

Melzi, Francesco. *Portrait of a Woman*. 1510–1515. Oil on canvas, 30 × 24⅞″ (76 × 63 cm). The State Hermitage Museum, St. Petersburg. [35]

———. *Vertumns and Pomona*. c. 1518–1522. Oil on wood, 6′1¼″ × 4′5¼″ (1.86 × 1.35 cm). Gemäldegalerie, Staatliche Museen zu Berlin. [35]

Messina, Antonello da. *Portrait of a Man (in Red Cap)*. c. 1475. Oil on wood, 14 × 10″ (35.6 × 25.4 cm). The National Gallery, London. [4, 6, 11]

———. *Portrait of a Man*. c. 1475. Oil on wood, 11⅞ × 9½″ (30 × 24 cm). Galleria Borghese, Rome. [6, 26]

———. *Portrait of a Man (Gian Giacomo Trivulzio?)*. c. 1474. Oil on wood, 14½ × 11″ (37 × 28 cm). Museo Civico D'Arte Antica, Turin, Italy. [6]

———. *Virgin Annunciate*. 1473–1474. Oil on wood, 16¾ × 13″ (42.5 × 32.8 cm). Alte Pinakothek, Munich. [28, 32]

Michelangelo Buonarroti. *Atlas Slave*. 1519–1536. Marble, 9′1½″ (2.78 m). Galleria dell'Accademia, Florence. [35]

———. *Creation of Adam*. 1508–1512. Fresco, 9′2¼″ × 18′8½″ (2.8 × 5.7 m). Sistine Chapel, Vatican. [1, 28]

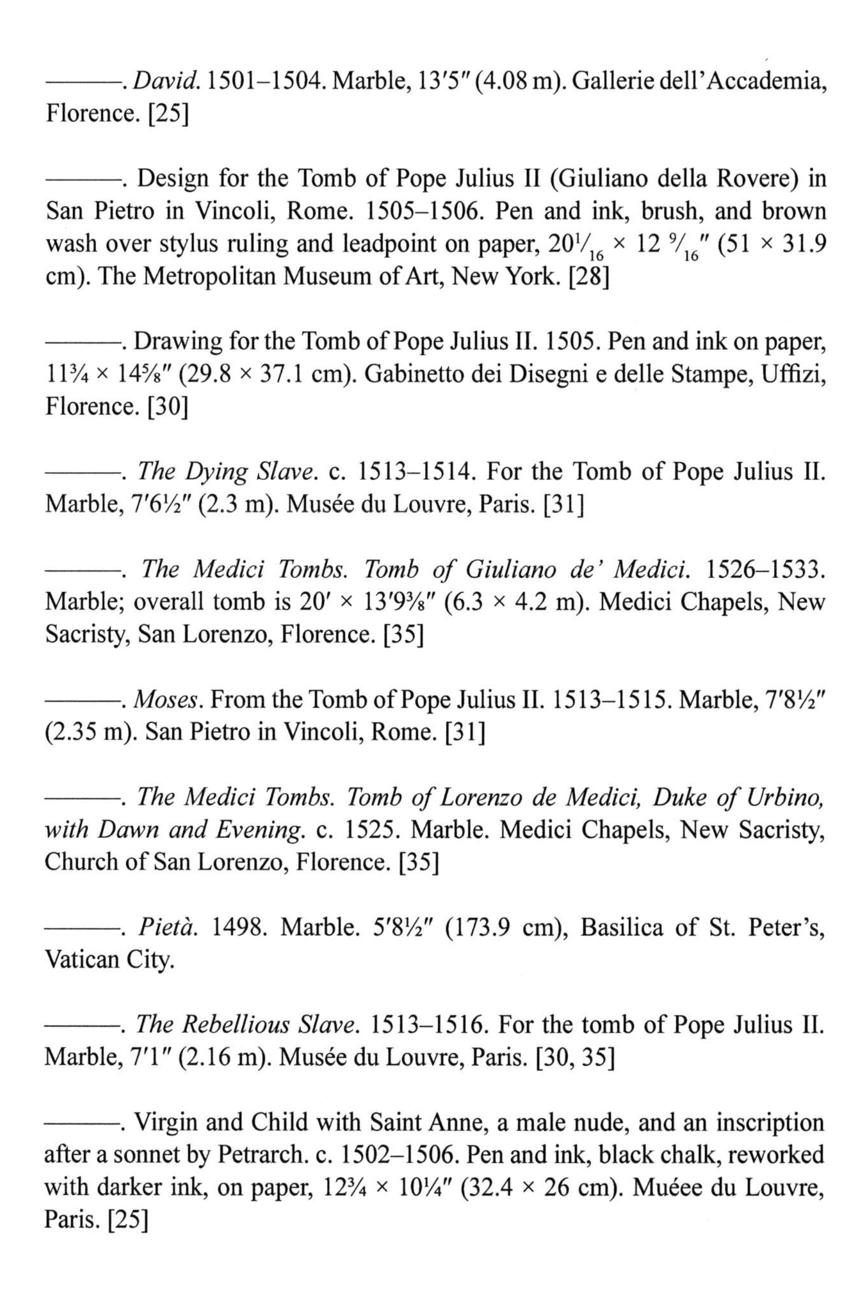

———. *David.* 1501–1504. Marble, 13′5″ (4.08 m). Gallerie dell'Accademia, Florence. [25]

———. Design for the Tomb of Pope Julius II (Giuliano della Rovere) in San Pietro in Vincoli, Rome. 1505–1506. Pen and ink, brush, and brown wash over stylus ruling and leadpoint on paper, $20\frac{1}{16} \times 12\frac{9}{16}$″ (51 × 31.9 cm). The Metropolitan Museum of Art, New York. [28]

———. Drawing for the Tomb of Pope Julius II. 1505. Pen and ink on paper, 11¾ × 14⅝″ (29.8 × 37.1 cm). Gabinetto dei Disegni e delle Stampe, Uffizi, Florence. [30]

———. *The Dying Slave.* c. 1513–1514. For the Tomb of Pope Julius II. Marble, 7′6½″ (2.3 m). Musée du Louvre, Paris. [31]

———. *The Medici Tombs. Tomb of Giuliano de' Medici.* 1526–1533. Marble; overall tomb is 20′ × 13′9⅜″ (6.3 × 4.2 m). Medici Chapels, New Sacristy, San Lorenzo, Florence. [35]

———. *Moses*. From the Tomb of Pope Julius II. 1513–1515. Marble, 7′8½″ (2.35 m). San Pietro in Vincoli, Rome. [31]

———. *The Medici Tombs. Tomb of Lorenzo de Medici, Duke of Urbino, with Dawn and Evening.* c. 1525. Marble. Medici Chapels, New Sacristy, Church of San Lorenzo, Florence. [35]

———. *Pietà.* 1498. Marble. 5′8½″ (173.9 cm), Basilica of St. Peter's, Vatican City.

———. *The Rebellious Slave.* 1513–1516. For the tomb of Pope Julius II. Marble, 7′1″ (2.16 m). Musée du Louvre, Paris. [30, 35]

———. Virgin and Child with Saint Anne, a male nude, and an inscription after a sonnet by Petrarch. c. 1502–1506. Pen and ink, black chalk, reworked with darker ink, on paper, 12¾ × 10¼″ (32.4 × 26 cm). Muéee du Louvre, Paris. [25]

Michelozzo di Bartolomeo. Palazzo Medici Riccardi. 1444–1459. Florence. [3]

Monaco, Lorenzo. *The Man of Sorrows (Christ in Pietà) and the Symbols of the Passion.* 1404. Tempera on wood, 8′9⅛″ × 5′7⅜″ (2.67 × 1.71 m). Gallerie dell'Accademia, Florence, Italy. [20, 21]

Monet, Claude. *The Basin of Argenteuil.* c. 1872. Oil on canvas, 23⅝ × 31¾″ (60 × 80.5 cm). Musée d'Orsay, Paris. [36]

Oggiono, Marco da. *Last Supper, after Leonardo da Vinci.* c. 1515. Oil on canvas, 8′6⅜″ × 18′ (2.60 × 5.49 m). Musée national de la Renaissance, Ecouen, France. [21]

Parmigianino (Girolamo Francesco Maria Mazzola). *Madonna and Child with Angels* (*Madonna of the Long Neck*). 1534–1540. Oil on wood. 7′2¼″ × 4′5⅛″ (2.19 × 1.35 m). Galleria degli Uffizi, Florence. [35]

———. *Madonna and Child with Saints John the Baptist and Jerome.* 1526–1527. Oil on wood, 11′3″ × 4′10¾″ (3.43 × 1.49 m). The National Gallery, London. [35]

Perugino, Pietro. Study of a kneeling youth and of the head of another. 1500. Metalpoint on pale pink-beige prepared paper, 8 11/16 × 4½″ (22 × 11.5 cm). The Metropolitan Museum of Art, New York. [18]

Perugino, Pietro (attributed to). Head of the virgin, view of the face. Musée du Louvre, Paris. [4, 7, 18, 27]

Pisanello, Antonio. *Portrait of Filippo Maria Visconti.* Pen and black ink, black chalk on paper, 11⅜ × 7⅜″ (28.9 × 18.6 cm). Musée du Louvre, Paris. [10]

Pollaiuolo, Antonio del. *Galeazzo Maria Sforza.* c. 1471. Tempera on wood, 25⅝ × 16½″ (65 × 42 cm). Galleria degli Uffizi, Florence. [10, 19]

———. *Monument of Sixtus IV.* 1484–1493. Bronze, 14′7¼″ (4.45 m). Museo Petriano, St. Peter's Basilica, Vatican City. [19]

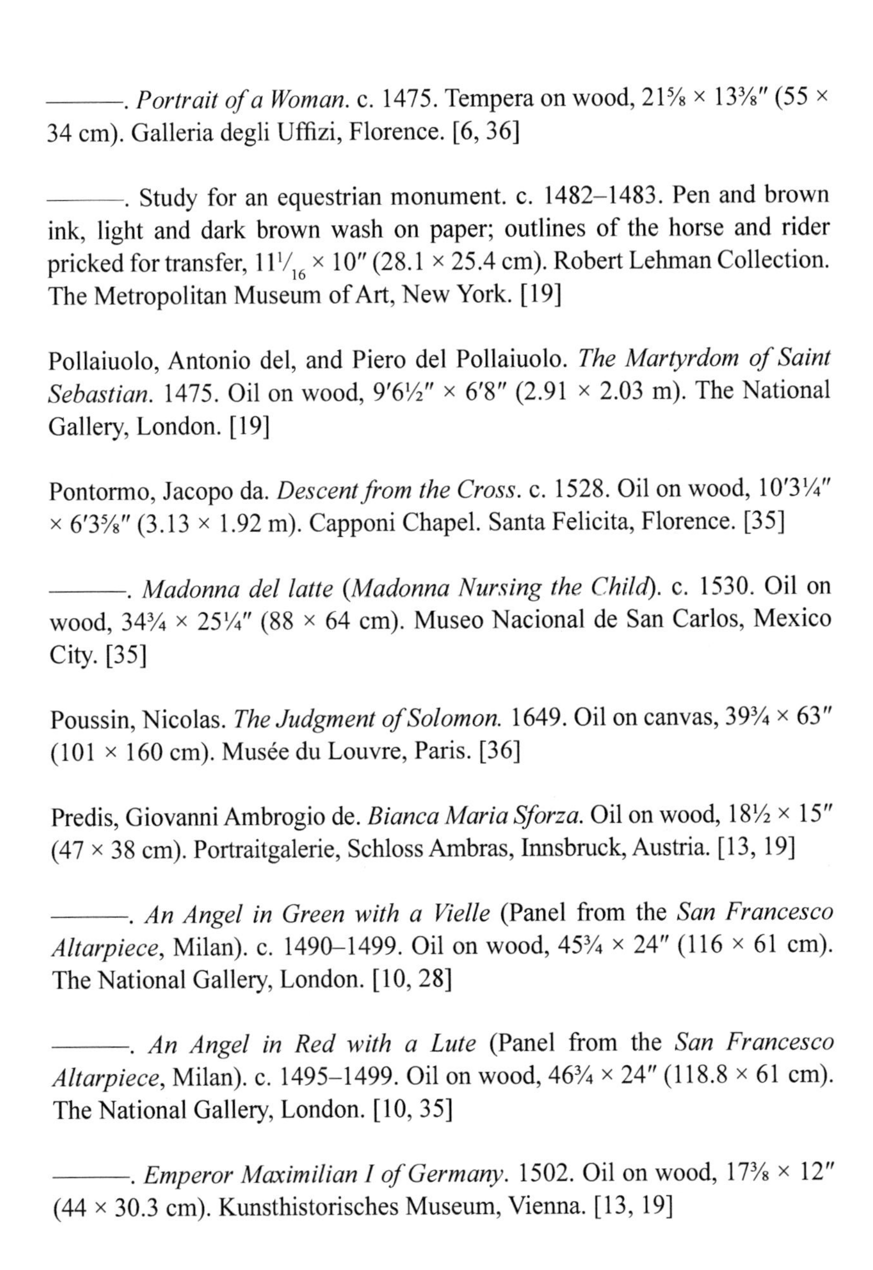

———. *Portrait of a Woman.* c. 1475. Tempera on wood, 21⅝ × 13⅜″ (55 × 34 cm). Galleria degli Uffizi, Florence. [6, 36]

———. Study for an equestrian monument. c. 1482–1483. Pen and brown ink, light and dark brown wash on paper; outlines of the horse and rider pricked for transfer, $11^{1}/_{16}$ × 10″ (28.1 × 25.4 cm). Robert Lehman Collection. The Metropolitan Museum of Art, New York. [19]

Pollaiuolo, Antonio del, and Piero del Pollaiuolo. *The Martyrdom of Saint Sebastian.* 1475. Oil on wood, 9′6½″ × 6′8″ (2.91 × 2.03 m). The National Gallery, London. [19]

Pontormo, Jacopo da. *Descent from the Cross.* c. 1528. Oil on wood, 10′3¼″ × 6′3⅝″ (3.13 × 1.92 m). Capponi Chapel. Santa Felicita, Florence. [35]

———. *Madonna del latte* (*Madonna Nursing the Child*). c. 1530. Oil on wood, 34¾ × 25¼″ (88 × 64 cm). Museo Nacional de San Carlos, Mexico City. [35]

Poussin, Nicolas. *The Judgment of Solomon.* 1649. Oil on canvas, 39¾ × 63″ (101 × 160 cm). Musée du Louvre, Paris. [36]

Predis, Giovanni Ambrogio de. *Bianca Maria Sforza.* Oil on wood, 18½ × 15″ (47 × 38 cm). Portraitgalerie, Schloss Ambras, Innsbruck, Austria. [13, 19]

———. *An Angel in Green with a Vielle* (Panel from the *San Francesco Altarpiece*, Milan). c. 1490–1499. Oil on wood, 45¾ × 24″ (116 × 61 cm). The National Gallery, London. [10, 28]

———. *An Angel in Red with a Lute* (Panel from the *San Francesco Altarpiece*, Milan). c. 1495–1499. Oil on wood, 46¾ × 24″ (118.8 × 61 cm). The National Gallery, London. [10, 35]

———. *Emperor Maximilian I of Germany*. 1502. Oil on wood, 17⅜ × 12″ (44 × 30.3 cm). Kunsthistorisches Museum, Vienna. [13, 19]

———. *Portrait of a Woman (Beatrice d'Este)*. 1495–1500. Tempera and oil on wood, 20 × 13⅜″ (51 × 34 cm). Pinacoteca Ambrosiana, Milan. [12, 14, 15]

Raphael. *Baldassare Castiglione*. c. 1514–1515. Oil on canvas, 32⅜ × 26⅜″ (82 × 67 cm). Musée du Louvre, Paris. [33, 34]

———. Bust of a woman, three-quarters to the left, arms crossed. Pen and brown ink, black chalk, on paper, 8¾ × 6¼″ (22.2 × 15.8 cm). Musée du Louvre, Paris. [27]

———. *La Velata*. c. 1516. Oil on wood, 33½ × 25¼″ (85 × 64 cm). Galleria Palatina, Palazzo Pitti, Florence. [32]

———. *Lady with a Unicorn*. c. 1505–1507. Oil on wood (transferred to canvas), 26⅝ × 21″ (67.7 × 53.2 cm). Galleria Borghese, Rome. [27]

———. *Leda and the Swan*. c. 1507. Pen and ink over black chalk on paper, 12¼ × 7⅝″ (31 × 19.2 cm). The Royal Collection, Windsor. [27]

———. *Madonna of the Goldfinch (Madonna del Cardellino)*. 1506. Oil on wood, 42⅛ × 30⅜″ (107 × 77 cm). Galleria degli Uffizi, Florence. [23, 27]

———. *Madonna of the Meadow*. 1505. Oil on wood, 44 × 35″ (113 × 88 cm). Kunsthistorisches Museum, Vienna. [27, 36]

———. *Parnassus*. 1510–1511. Fresco, 19 × 22′ (5.8 × 6.7 m). Stanza della Segnatura, Stanze di Raffaello, Vatican Palace. [31]

———. *Pope Leo X with Cardinals Giulio de' Medici and Luigi de' Rossi*. c. 1517. Oil on wood, 5′1¼″ × 3′11″ (1.55 × 1.19 m). Galleria degli Uffizi, Florence. [32]

———. *Portrait of Agnolo Doni*. c. 1506. Oil on wood, 24⅞ × 17¾″ (63 × 45 cm). Galleria Palatina, Palazzo Pitti, Florence. [27]

———. *Portrait of Maddalena Strozzi Doni*. c. 1506. Oil on wood, 24⅞ × 17¾″ (63 × 45 cm). Galleria Palatina, Palazzo Pitti, Florence, Italy. [27]

———. *Portrait of Pope Julius II.* 1511–1512. Oil on wood, 42¾ × 31⅞″ (108.7 × 81 cm). The National Gallery, London. [28, 31]

———. *The School of Athens.*1512. Fresco, width at base 25′3⅛″ (7.7 m). Stanza della Segnatura, Stanze di Raffaello, Vatican. [1, 28, 31]

———. *Self-Portrait.* 1506. Oil on wood, 26 × 20½″ (66 × 52 cm). Galleria Palatina, Palazzo Pitti, Florence. [23, 35]

———. *Sistine Madonna.* c. 1513. Oil on canvas, 8′10¼″ × 6′7″ (2.70 × 2.01 m). Gemäldegalerie Alte Meister, Staatliche Kunstsammlungen, Dresden, Germany. [32]

———. *The Transfiguration.* 1516–1520. Oil on wood, 13′5½ × 9′1⅞″ (4.10 × 2.79 m). Pinacoteca, Vatican Museums. [32, 35]

———. *The Virgin and Child with the Young Saint John the Baptist (La belle jardiniere).* 1507. Oil on canvas, 48 × 31½″ (122 × 80 cm). Musée du Louvre, Paris. [27]

Reiser, Niclas. *Mary of Burgundy.* 15th century. Oil on wood, 29¾ × 21½″ (75.5 × 54.5 cm). Portraitgalerie, Schloss Ambras, Innsbruck, Austria. [13]

Rembrandt van Rijn. *Saskia van Uylenburgh as a Girl.* 1633. Oil on wood, 20¾ × 17⅜″ (52.5 × 44 cm). Gemäldegalerie Alte Meister, Staatliche Kunstsammlungen, Dresden, Germany. [36]

Romano, Gian (Giovanni) Cristoforo. *Francesco Gonzaga, Margrave of Mantua and Condottiere.* 1498. Terracotta, 24¼″ (69 cm). Palazzo Ducale, Mantua, Italy. [23]

———. *Gian Galeazzo Visconti* (1351–1402), 1st Duke of Milan. Mid-1490s. Marble. Certosa di Pavia, Pavia, Italy. [10, 30]

Romano, Giulio. *Deesis (Christ between Saint Mary and John the Baptist) with Saints Paul and Catherine of Alexandria.* 1520–1522. Oil on wood, 48⅞ × 38⅝″ (124 × 98 cm). Galleria Nazionale, Parma, Italy. [35]

———. *Olympus*. c. 1530–1532. Fresco. Palazzo del Te, Mantua, Italy. [35]

Rubens, Peter Paul. *Battle of Anghiari* (also called the *Battle for the Standard*). c. 1603. Black chalk, pen and brown ink, heightened with gray white, on paper, 17⅞ × 25⅛″ (45.2 × 63.7 cm). Musée du Louvre, Paris. [25]

———. *Felicity of the Regency*. 1623–1625. Oil on canvas, 12′11⅛″ × 9′8¼″ (3.94 × 2.95 m). Musée du Louvre, Paris. [36]

———. *Self-Portrait with Hat.* 1639. Oil on canvas, 43⅛ × 33½″ (109.5 × 85 cm). Kunsthistorisches Museum, Vienna. [36]

———. *The Philosophers (Self-Portrait with the Artist's brother Philip, Justus Lipsius, and Jan van der Wouwere)*. 1611–1612. Oil on wood, 64⅝ × 54¾″ (164 × 139 cm). Galleria Palatina, Palazzo Pitti, Florence. [36]

Sand, Vebjorn. Leonardo Bridge Project. 2001. Oslo, Norway. [34]

Sangallo, Aristotile da. *Copy of the Drawing of the Cartoon for Michelangelo's "Battle of Cascina."* 1542. Oil on wood, 30⅛ × 50$\frac{7}{9}$″ (76.5 × 129 cm). Collection Leicester, Holkham Hall, Norfolk, UK. [25, 27]

Sano di Pietro. *Saint Jerome Penitent*. From *The Life of Saint Jerome*, predella of an altar for a Monastery in Siena. c. 1444. Tempera on wood, 9 × 14″ (23.5 × 36 cm). Musée du Louvre, Paris. [8]

Sarto, Andrea del. *The Last Supper*. 1520–1525. Fresco, 17′2¾″ × 28′7″ (5.25 × 8.71 m). San Salvi, Florence. [32]

———. *Madonna of the Harpies*. 1515–1517. Oil on wood, 6′9½ × 5′10″ (2.07 × 1.78 m). Galleria degli Uffizi, Florence. [32]

Sebastiano del Piombo. *Portrait of a Man, said to be Christopher Columbus*. 1519. Oil on canvas, 42 × 34¾″ (106.7 × 88.3 cm). The Metropolitan Museum of Art, New York. [13]

Solario, Andrea. *Portrait of Charles II d'Amboise*. Oil on wood, 29⅝ × 20½″ (75 × 52 cm). Musée du Louvre, Paris. [28]

Student of Leonardo da Vinci. Horses, machinery, and an angel, c. 1503–1504. Black chalk and pen and ink, 7⅞ × 11¼″ (20.0 × 28.3 cm). The Royal Collection, Windsor. [28]

Titian (Tiziano Vecellio). *Assumption of the Virgin*. 1516–1518. Oil on wood, 22′7½″ × 11′9¾″ (6.9 × 3.6 m). Santa Maria Gloriosa dei Frari, Venice. [32]

———. *Isabella d'Este*. 1534. Oil on canvas, 40¼ × 25¼″ (102 × 64 cm). Kunsthistorisches Museum, Vienna. [22]

———. *Sacred and Profane Love* (*Amor sacro e Amor profano*). c. 1514. Oil on canvas, 3′10½″ × 9′1⅞″ (1.18 × 2.79 m). Galleria Borghese, Rome. [32]

———. *Venus of Urbino*. 1538. Oil on canvas. 46⅞ × 65″ (119 × 165 cm). Uffizi, Florence, Italy. [32, 36]

Titian (Tiziano Vecellio) or Giorgione (da Castelfranco). *Concert in the Open Air*. c. 1510. Oil on canvas, 43⅜ × 54⅜″ (110 × 138 cm). Musée du Louvre, Paris. [32]

Tito, Santi di. *Portrait of Niccolò Machiavelli*. c. 1575. Oil on wood, 41 × 33 ½″ (104 × 85 cm). Palazzo Vecchio, Florence. [34]

Uccello, Paolo (1397–1475). *Battle of San Romano*. c. 1438–1440. Egg tempera and oil on wood, 5′11⅝″ × 10′6″ (1.82 × 3.20 m). The National Gallery, London. [16]

———. *The Battle of San Romano in 1432 (The Counterattack of Micheletto da Cotignola)*. 1450–1456. Oil on wood, 5′10⅞″ × 10′4⅜″ (1.80 × 3.16 m). Musée du Louvre, Paris. [11, 16]

Urbino, Carlo. *Treatise on Art Theory, after Leonardo da Vinci*. Pen and ink on paper. Codex Huygens, M.A. 1139, fol. 10. [30]

Van der Goes, Hugo. *Portinari Altarpiece*. 1475–1476. Tempera on wood, 8′3½ × 9′11⅝″ (2.53 × 3.04 m). Galleria degli Uffizi, Florence. [9]

Van der Weyden, Rogier. *Entombment of Christ*. 1450. Oil on wood, 43⅝ × 37¾″ (110 × 96 cm). Galleria degli Uffizi, Florence. [9]

———. *Virgin with the Child and Four Saints* (*The Medici Madonna*). 1450–1451. Oil on wood, 24⅜ × 18⅛″ (61.7 × 46.1 cm). Staedelsches Kunstinstitut, Frankfurt am Main, Germany. [9]

Van Dyck, Anthony. *Self-Portrait*. 1614. Oil on wood, 10¼ × 7⅞″ (26 × 20 cm). Akademie der Bildenden Kuenste, Vienna. [36]

Van Eyck, Jan. *Portrait of a Man (Man in Red Turban)*. 1433. Oil on wood, 10¼ × 7½″ (26 × 19 cm). The National Gallery, London. [4, 11]

Van Orley, Bernaert. *Charles V jeune*. 1515. Oil on wood, 14⅜ × 10½″ (36.5 × 26.5 cm). Musée du Louvre, Paris. [35]

Vasari, Giorgio, and assistants. *Battle of Scannagallo in Valdichiana*. c. 1565–1571. Fresco. Salone dei Cinquecento, Palazzo Vecchio, Florence. [25]

———. *Saint Luke Painting a Portrait of the Madonna (Self-Portrait)*. 1565. Fresco. Santissima Annunziata, Florence. [4]

———. *Self-Portrait*. c. 1550–1566/68. Oil on canvas, 39½ × 31½″ (100.5 × 80 cm). Galleria degli Uffizi, Florence. [1, 2, 21]

Velazquez, Diego Rodriguez. *Las Meninas (The Family of Philip IV)*. 1656. Oil on canvas, 9′ × 10′5¼″ (2.76 × 3.18 m). Museo del Prado, Madrid, Spain. [36]

Veneziano, Domenico. *Madonna and Child*. c. 1445/50. Tempera (and oil?) on wood. 32 11/16 × 22 7/16″ (83 × 57 cm). National Gallery of Art, Washington, DC. [7]

———. *The Annunciation.* From *The Saint Lucy Altarpiece.* c. 1445. Tempera on wood, 10¾″ × 21¼″ (27.3 × 54.0 cm). Fitzwilliam Museum, Cambridge, UK. [5]

Vernet, Horace. *Raphael at the Vatican.* 1832. Oil on canvas, 12′10⅜″ × 9′10⅛″ (3.92 × 3.00 m). Musée du Louvre, Paris. [36]

Verrocchio, Andrea del. *Baptism of Christ.* 1472–1480s. Tempera and oil on wood, 5′10⅞ × 4′11⅞″ (1.80 × 1.52 m). Galleria degli Uffizi, Florence. [1, 4, 5]

———. *David.* c. 1468–1472. Bronze, 4′1½″ (1.26 m). Museo Nazionale del Bargello, Florence. [4, 5]

———. *Equestrian statue of the Condottiere Bartolomeo Colleoni.* c. 1479–1492. Bronze, 13′ (3.95 m). Campo Santissimi Giovanni e Paolo, Venice. [10, 19, 22, 30]

———. *Giuliano de' Medici.* c. 1475/78. Teracotta, 24 × 26 × 11⅛″ (61 × 66 × 28.3 cm). National Gallery of Art, Washington, DC. [9]

———. *Head of an Angel.* c. 1475. Black chalk on paper, Gabinetto dei Disegni e delle Stampe. Galleria degli Uffizi, Florence. [4, 18]

———. *The Incredulity (Doubting) of Saint Thomas.* 1466–1483. Bronze, H 7′6⅝″ (2.30 m). Museo di Orsanmichele, Florence. [4]

———. *Lorenzo de' Medici.* c. 1478/1521. Painted terracotta, 25⅞ × 23¼ × 12⅞″ (65.8 × 59.1 × 32.7 cm). National Gallery of Art, Washington, D.C. [9]

———. *Madonna and Child.* c. 1470. Oil on wood, 26½ × 19½″ (67.3 × 49.4 cm). Gemäldegalerie, Staatliche Museen zu Berlin. [4, 7]

———. *Madonna and Child.* c. 1470. Tempera and gold on wood, 26 × 19″ (66 × 48.3 cm). The Metropolitan Museum of Art, New York. [7]

———. *Putto Holding a Dolphin.* c. 1470. Bronze, 49¼″ (125 cm). Palazzo Vecchio, Florence. [3, 22, 23]

———. *The Virgin and Child with Two Angels*. c. 1470–1480. Tempera on wood, 38 × 27¾″ (96.5 × 70.5 cm). The National Gallery, London. [4]

———. *Tomb of Piero and Giovanni de' Medici*. 1469–1472. Marble, porphyry, serpentine, bronze, and pietra serena, 17′8⅝″ (5.40 m). Church of San Lorenzo, Florence. [5]

———. *Woman Holding Flowers*. 1475–1480. Marble, 24″ (61 cm). Museo Nazionale del Bargello, Florence. [6]

Verrocchio, Andrea del, workshop of. *Tobias and the Angel*. 1470–1480. Tempera on wood, 33 × 26″ (83.6 × 66 cm). The National Gallery, London. [4]

Verrocchio, Andrea del, and Lorenzo di Credi. *Madonna and Child*. 1480–1500. Oil and tempera on wood, 28 × 19.5″ (71.1 × 49.5 cm). The National Gallery, London. [3, 4]

Vivarini, Alvise (1442/53–1503/05). *Assumption of the Virgin*. 1480. Commissioned for the church of Santa Maria dell'Incoronata at Martinengo near Bergamo. Oil on wood, 7′4⅝″ × 3′8⅞″ (2.25 × 1.14 m). Pinacoteca di Brera, Milan. [11]

Volterra, Daniele da. Portrait bust of Michelangelo. 1564–1570. Bronze, 23¼″ (59 cm). Casa Buonarroti, Florence. [25, 35]

Waldseemuller, Martin. *World Map; Ptolemy with His System and Amerigo Vespucci with His Discoveries*. 1507. Woodcut print made with 12 blocks. Originally published in Saint-Dié, Lorraine. Map Division, Staatsbibliothek zu Berlin, Stiftung Preussischer Kulturbesitz, Berlin, Germany. [13]

Timeline

Leonardo da Vinci's Life

1452.. Born in Vinci, about 22 miles west of Florence, to Ser Piero da Vinci and Caterina, a maid.

1457.. Listed as a dependent of his grandfather, Antonio di Ser Piero.

1464.. Deaths of grandfather and stepmother, Albiera degli Amadori.

1465–1469.................................. Begins apprenticeship in Florence with Andrea del Verrocchio.

1472.. Participates in production of *Baptism of Christ*; joins confraternity of San Luca, Florence.

1473–1476 .... Paints *Annunciation* for San Bartolomeo in Monte Oliveto; paints *Madonna of the Carnation* (a.k.a. *Munich Madonna*).

1474–1475.................................. Paints *Ginevra de' Benci.*

1478.. Receives commission for *The Virgin and Child with Saints.*

1478–1479.................................. Paints *Benois Madonna* (unfinished, perhaps continuing until 1481); designs the self-propelled cart for a Medicean theatrical production.

1479 .... Receives commission for *Adoration of the Magi* from the Augustinians at San Donato a Scopeto; draws *Bernardo di Bandino Baroncelli hanging*.

1480 .... Paints *Saint Jerome*.

1481 .... *Adoration of the Magi* begun for San Donato a Scopeto (unfinished; project completed with a different image by Filippino Lippi, c. 1496); sent on diplomatic mission to Milan on behalf of Lorenzo de' Medici.

1482 .... Meets Donato Bramante (Ludovico Sforza's official architect).

c. 1482–1490 .... *Madonna Litta*.

1483 .... Commission of *Madonna of the Rocks* for the Oratory of the Immaculate Conception, Milan.

1484–1485 .... Draws *New City*—designs for model urban center, precipitated by plague in Milan; goes to Pavia with the Sforza court, meets Fazio Cardano, university mathematician; begins intensive study of Euclidian geometry, optics, perspective, and astrology.

1485 .... Sees a total eclipse of the sun; paints *Portrait of a Musician* (portrait of Franchino Gaffurio or Atalante Migliorotti).

1485–1499.. Milan notebooks: flying machines and experiments with winged contraptions.

1487... Begins work on the examination of the senses; earliest anatomical drawings.

1488... Work commences on *Colossus*.

1489... Begins book on the human figure, including proportional drawings of the human skull.

1490... Teams with Francesco di Giorgio Martini to repair Cathedral of Pavia; paints *Portrait of Cecilia Gallerani* (*Lady with the Ermine*); writes earliest outlines for *Treatise on Painting*; designs stage sets for Bellincioni's *Feast of Paradise*, Castello Sforzesco, and a musical play celebrating the marriage of Giangaleazzo Sforza and Isabella of Aragon.

c. 1492... Draws *Vitruvian Man*.

1493... Clay model of *Colossus* is installed in Milan Cathedral for marriage of Emperor Maximilian I to Bianca Maria Sforza, niece of Ludovico Sforza.

1494... Bronze allocated for *Colossus* (c. 75 tons) is diverted to Ercole d'Este to cast cannons for defense against French invaders; Leonardo plans a test-flight of a flying machine or glider.

1495–1498.. Paints *The Last Supper*, Santa Maria delle Grazie.

1496.. Collaborates with Fra Luca Pacioli on studies of geometry, proportion, and mathematics; paints *La belle ferronnière* (*Portrait of Lucrezia Crivelli*); creates stage set for Taccone's *Jupiter and Danae.*

1499.. Leaves Milan.

February 1500 .... Arrives in Mantua; draws *Isabella d'Este*, a preparatory sketch for portrait never completed.

March 1500 .... Arrives in Venice; produces drawings for military machines for defense of Venice from the Turkish threat (diving equipment, flying machines, ship hulls, catapults, crossbows, and cannon).

April 1500 .... Moves to Florence and sets up his home and workshop near Santissima Annunziata.

1501.. Exhibits cartoon of *Virgin and Child with Saint Anne and Lamb*; paints *Madonna of the Yarnwinder*.

1502.. Named family architect and general engineer in Marches and Romagna by Cesare Borgia.

1503.. Leaves Borgia family, returns to Florence; receives commission to assist Florence in siege against Pisa; embarks on the canal project with Machiavelli; receives commission for *Battle of Anghiari*, Sala dei Cinquecento, Palazzo della Signoria; begins *Mona Lisa*.

1504.. Becomes member of the committee to determine location of Michelangelo's *David*; death of father, Ser Piero; goes to Piombino to work on fortifications.

1504–1506................................ Works on *Battle of Anghiari* (unfinished) in encaustic; paints *Leda and the Swan*.

1505.. Writes *Treatise on Flying*.

1506.. Called to Milan by its French governor, Charles d'Amboise, to complete commission for *Madonna of the Rocks* for the Oratory of the Immaculate Conception.

1507.. Receives rights to water in the canal of San Cristoforo, Milan; begins cartoon of *Saint Anne Madonna*; meets and befriends Francesco Melzi, who becomes his pupil and companion; anatomical drawings intensify.

1508.. Begins formal work on *Treatise on Anatomy*; draws entire human pulmonary system; dissects a 100-year-old man in the hospital of Santa Maria Nuova, Florence.

1509 .... Creates artificial heart model, demonstrating blood flow to and from the aorta.

1509–1510 .... Produces designs for *Trivulzio Monument.*

1510 .... Works with Marcantonio della Torre, professor of anatomy at the University of Pavia, to hone anatomical drawing techniques; begins production of 56 detailed drawings of the cardiovascular system; draws a human fetus in the womb.

1513 .... Swiss invade Milan; Leonardo flees to Melzi villa in Vaprio d'Adda; joins the court of Giuliano de' Medici, brother of Pope Leonardo X in Rome (December) in Bramante's Palazzo Belvedere.

1513–1516 .... Works alternately on mechanical lion, anatomical studies, *Treatise on Painting*, maps, architectural designs, and burning mirrors; draws *The Deluge*; sculpts lightweight wax animals that fly short distances, using internal sacks of compressed air; designs huge concave mirrors to direct concentrated sun rays at enemy ship riggings.

1515 .... Produces mechanical lion as gift for François I; designs plans for new facade of old Medici Palace in Florence; paid to participate in grand papal procession from Rome to Bologna, via Florence.

1516.. Giuliano de' Medici dies in March; Leonardo writes, "The Medici made me, and the Medici destroyed me"; invited to France by François I to become "peintre du Roi"; goes to French court at Amboise; works on *Saint Anne Madonna* and *John the Baptist*.

1517.. Partially paralyzed on right side by a possible stroke; draws plans for Chateau at Romorantin, near Blois.

1518.. Royal fountain at Amboise; possible advisor for double helix staircase at Chambord; designs wedding ring for Maddalena de la Tour d'Auvergne, niece of François I; designs stage set for Bellincioni's *Feast of Paradise*.

1519.. Acknowledges will in April; dies on May 2 at Chateau de Cloux; buried in the cloister of church of Saint-Florentin in Amboise (later destroyed).

Leonardo's Artistic Predecessors and Contemporaries

1305.. Giotto, *Arena Chapel*, Padua.

1417.. Donatello, *St. George*, Orsanmichele.

1420s.. Brunelleschi designs dome of Florentine Cathedral.

1425.. Masaccio and Masolino, *Brancacci Chapel*.

1427 .... Masaccio, *Trinity.*

1432 .... Jan van Eyck, *Arnolfini Double Portrait, Ghent Altarpiece.*

1435–1436 .... Leon Battista Alberti, *On Painting.*

1436 .... Van Eyck, *Van der Paele Madonna, Madonna of Chancellor Rolin.*

1440–1455 .... Fra Filippo Lippi active in Florence: portraits of women.

1440 .... Fra Angelico, *San Marco Altarpiece*; Donatello, *Cantoria*, Florence Cathedral.

1445 .... Domenico Veneziano, *Saint Lucy Altarpiece.*

1450 .... Alberti, *Tempio Malatestiano*, Rimini and *Palazzo Rucellai*, Florence; Michelozzo, *Palazzo Medici*, Florence; Rogier van der Weyden in Florence.

1452 .... Ghiberti, *Gates of Paradise*; *I Commentarii.*

1453 .... Donatello, *Gattamelata.*

1455–1459 .... Donatello, *David.*

1457 .... Andrea Mantegna, *San Zeno Altarpiece*, Verona.

1459 .... Mantegna court artist in Mantua.

1461 .... Andrea del Verrocchio working independently in Florence.

1465 .... Piero della Francesca joins court of Federigo de Montefeltro in Urbino.

1465 .... Mantegna, *Camera Picta*, Ducal Palace, Mantua.

1466–1483 .... Verrocchio, *Doubting Thomas*, Orsanmichele.

1471 .... Verrocchio, *Orb*, Florentine Cathedral.

1472 .... Verrocchio, *Baptism of Christ*.

1475–1481 .... Hugo van der Goes active in Flanders.

1475 .... Birth of Michelangelo, Settignano; birth of Albrecht Durer, Nuremburg; Giovanni Bellini active in Venice.

1476 .... Antonello da Messina in northern Italy.

1477–1491 .... Bramante, *Santa Maria presso San Satiro*, Milan.

1479–1483 .... Construction and decoration, Sistine Chapel.

1480 .... Ghirlandaio, *Last Supper*, Florence.

1481–1496 .... Verrocchio and assistants in Venice, *Bartolommeo Colleoni*.

1482–1492.. Botticelli, *Primavera, Birth of Venus, Venus and Mars.*

1483.. Birth of Raphael, Urbino; Arrival of *Portinari Altarpiece* in Florence.

1494.. Durer in Venice.

1498.. Michelangelo, *Pieta,* Chapel of the French, Old St. Peter's.

1500–1505.. Giorgione at work in Venice; *Dresden Venus, Fete Champetre*; Signorelli, *Last Judgment*, Orvieto Cathedral.

1500.. Durer, *Self-Portrait.*

1501–1504.. Michelangelo in Florence, *David*; Bramante, *Tempietto*, Rome.

1504.. Michelangelo commissioned to paint *Battle of Cascina.*

1505.. Michelangelo, cartoon of *Battle of Cascina*; Raphael in Florence, *Madonna of the Goldfinch.*

1505–1516.. Michelangelo in Rome.

1505.. Old St. Peter's dismantled.

1506.. Michelangelo, first designs of *Tomb of Julius II*; Bramante, designs for New St. Peter's.

1508–1520.. Raphael in Rome.

1508–1512.. Michelangelo, *Sistine Ceiling.*

1509... Raphael, *Disputa.*

1511... Raphael, *Parnassus.*

1512... Raphael, *School of Athens*, *Julius II.*

1513... Raphael, *Sistine Madonna.*

1514... Titian, *Sacred Allegory.*

1515... Death of Bramante.

1516... Michelangelo in Florence; New Sacristy; Raphael, *Leo X.*

1516–1518.. Raphael, *Transfiguration.*

1517... Andrea del Sarto, *Madonna of the Harpies.*

1518... Titian, *Assumption of the Virgin*, Venice.

1520... Death of Raphael.

Politics in Leonardo's Lifetime

1450... Francesco Sforza establishes the Duchy of Milan and dynastic lineage in Lombardy.

1453 .... Constantinople falls.

1454 .... Peace of Lodi, enforced by Sforza, protects territories in Lombardy, Marches, Emilia-Romagna from Venice.

1469 .... Death of Piero de' Medici; government of Lorenzo and Giuliano de' Medici in Florence.

1476 .... Assassination of Duke Galeazzo Maria Sforza; Milan governed by his widow, Bona Sforza, as regent for the infant Giangaleazzo Sforza; Ludovico Sforza (Galeazzo's brother) exiled by Bona Sforza.

1478 .... Pazzi Conspiracy: assassination of Giuliano de' Medici.

1478-1479 .... War between Florence and the papacy.

1479 .... Return of Ludovico Sforza as new regent of Milan for still-minor Giangaleazzo Sforza.

1483–1484 .... Milan at war with Venice.

1484–1485 .... Plague in Milan; Sforza court relocates to Pavia.

1492 .... Columbus lands on islands in the Caribbean Sea; Death of Lorenzo de' Medici; election of Rodrigo Borgia as Pope Alexander VI.

1494 .... Invasion of Milan by French under King Charles VIII; rise to power of Fra Savonarola in Florence; birth of François I, future king of France; death of Giangaleazzo Sforza; Ludovico Sforza named duke of Milan by Holy Roman Emperor Maximilian I; Alexander VI partitions the New World among European powers.

1494–1512 .... Medici expelled from Florence.

1495 .... French depart Italian soil.

1498 .... Fra Savonarola arrested and executed; Niccolò Machiavelli named chancellor of Florence; Cesare Borgia, son of Pope Alexander VI, assumes command of Papal Armies in Italy; Amerigo Vespucci charts eastern coast of the New World.

1499 .... French under King Louis XII invade Milan; Ludovico Sforza exiled.

1500 .... Ludovico Sforza briefly retakes Milan with German mercenaries, then is captured and imprisoned in France.

1503 .... Death of Alexander VI; election and quick death of Pius III; election of Giuliano della Rovere as Pope Julius II; Cesare Borgia relinquishes to Julius II territories claimed in name of his father, Alexander VI.

1508... Death of Cesare Borgia; death of Ludovico Sforza, in exile.

1509... Venetians defeated by papal armies.

1512... Battle of Ravenna: French driven from Italy; Swiss restore Duchy of Milan to Maximilian Sforza; death of Julius II; Medici return to Florence.

1513... Election of Giovanni dei Medici as Pope Leonardo X; Machiavelli writes *The Prince*.

1515... Death of Louis XII of France; coronation of François I.

1517... Martin Luther nails the 95 Theses to church door in Wittenburg.

1527... Sack of Rome; Medici expelled from Florence.

Glossary

altarpiece: An image—usually a painting or a sculpture—placed on an altar facing the priest and congregation. Often covered by curtains or shutters and revealed during the Mass.

atmospheric perspective: The effect of deep space in a landscape painting, created by diminution of scale and softened contour line and by giving a bluish-green tint to distant objects. This technique imitates what our eyes perceive when looking at a landscape, which results from water and dust particles suspended in the atmosphere. Also called aerial perspective.

Archimedean screw: A large screw that, when turned, pulls both liquids and solids up and out of the ground.

armature: A wooden model of a sculpture that an artist covers in clay.

basilica: Any church that has a longitudinal nave flanked by side aisles and terminating in a domed area called an apse. Originally the name for an ancient Roman public building with the same ground plan.

blunderbuss: A small cannon derived from the harquebus.

caravel: A sailing vessel used by navigators and explorers in the 15th century.

caricature: An exaggerated facial study, often comical in intent.

cartoon: From the Italian *cartone* ("cardboard"), a full-size preparatory drawing from which a design is transferred to a surface for painting.

cathedral: From the Latin *cathedra* ("throne"), a church where a bishop has his diocese and official seat.

chiaroscuro: Italian word meaning "light-dark"; refers to the dramatic or theatrical contrast of light and dark in painting.

Cinquecento: The century of the 1500s.

cire perdue: In French, literally "lost wax"; a technique used to cast figures in bronze. A clay mold is covered with wax, which is in turn encased in a shell. Molten bronze is poured between the shell and the mold, replacing the wax, which melts and drips out from between the two surfaces. The shell is then chipped away and the mold dug out from the hardened bronze encasement.

classical composition: A triangular or pyramidal approach to artistic compositional design that emphasizes balance.

condottiere: A mercenary general.

contrapposto: From the Italian for "set against"; the method of introducing movement into the human form in sculpture or painting by placing the weight principally on one leg with the other leg relaxed, which causes the body to assume an asymmetrical posture with a modified S-curve.

courtier: A member of a noble or royal court, often employed as an advisor, entertainer, or thinker paid to publish scholarly works while in the service of an enlightened patron.

crossing: The juncture in a church where the nave meets the transept.

cruciform: An architectural term used to describe a church designed in the shape of a cross, formed by a long nave and a shorter, perpendicular transept.

cupola: A dome.

diptych: A religious image consisting of two paintings of the same size side-by-side, usually on panels, often hinged to be opened and closed.

dowry: A fixed gift—usually property, cash holdings, and/or textiles—that accompanied brides as they left their parents' homes and entered into the marital union with their husbands.

duomo: The Italian word for a cathedral; when capitalized, refers to the cathedral of Florence.

egg tempera: Water-based painting medium in which ground colors are suspended in egg yolk. It is characterized by a gleaming surface, decorative flatness, and durability. The principal paint medium before the Cinquecento.

encaustic: A painterly process whereby pigments are mixed with melted wax and applied to a dry surface.

equestrian monument: A large-scale sculpture of a horse and rider.

Eucharist: The sacrament of the Lord's Supper, celebrated in the Mass.

figure eight composition: Created simultaneously by Raphael and Titian, a compositional pattern that causes the eye to move in a circular interweave across a picture's design.

folio: A single sheet of paper or parchment. Scholars refer to Leonardo's papers using folio numbers (abbreviated as *fol.*) instead of page numbers. *See also* **recto** and **verso**.

fresco: Italian for "fresh," the technique of painting in wet plaster on a wall. If the color becomes part of the plaster wall, the painting is a true fresco (*buon fresco*).

gesso: A thick, glue-like white pigment used as the base coat for Renaissance paintings.

golden ratio: The theoretically perfect proportion for art, equal to approximately 1.618:1, whereby the dimensions of a rectangular appendix to a square are equal to the dimensions of the new rectangle formed by the square and the appendix.

Greek cross: An architectural term for a church plan where each of the four arms of the building is of the same length and width.

harquebus: A firearm used by infantrymen standing in a fixed position.

High Renaissance: A historical and cultural era that extended from the middle of the 15th century through the first quarter of the 16th century. This period of innovation and exploration combined references to the lessons of ancient writers and the independent discoveries of contemporary thinkers and artists.

hodometer: A device used to measure distances traveled by foot. Leonardo's design for one resembled a wheelbarrow.

Holy Roman Empire: A collection of states under the domain of a single ruler that originally comprised the Germanic principalities of Central Europe. Various emperors added to this core, so that by the time of Charles V (r. 1519–1559), the empire also included Flanders, the Netherlands, Spain, and most of Italy.

linear perspective: The system of creating the illusion of three-dimensional space on a flat surface that was first known in ancient Rome and was redeveloped in the early 15th century in Florence. The architect Filippo Brunelleschi is generally credited with its reinvention.

Mannerism: An artistic style popularized in the 1520s and 1530s that evolved as an alternative to the classicism of the High Renaissance.

maquette: A small-scale preparatory sculpture for a larger monument, usually created to garner a patron's approval before moving ahead with a project.

metal point: An instrument used by Renaissance artists when drawing. A metal stick (often made of silver) is dragged across a surface to create lines.

mural: A generic term for a painting on a wall. The term often used to distinguish the image from a true fresco painting.

nave: The central aisle of a basilican church, extending from the entrance to the chancel.

Neoplatonism: A system that attempted to reconcile the ancient philosophy of Plato and Plotinus with the teachings of Christianity. Developed in Alexandria and other Greek centers in the 3rd century A.D. and revived during the Italian Renaissance.

notary: A member of the legal profession during the Renaissance, usually educated in Latin, primarily called on to negotiate and write contracts.

oil: A medium, such as linseed oil or walnut oil, in which pigments are suspended while they dry. Because pigments in oil do not dry rapidly, they can be applied freely over a wide area, and because they are translucent rather than opaque, they create effects of depth and luminosity. When dry, they are solid films. The Renaissance development of oil paint as a medium can be traced to the Netherlands in the early 15th century, and it became the dominant medium from the 16th century onward.

ornithopter: Literally "bird vehicle," the name given by Leonardo to his earliest flying machines.

orthogonal lines: Diagonal lines drawn or painted on a two-dimensional surface that illusionistically extend into space, appearing to converge at a single point (the vanishing point) and giving the effect of a measurable three-dimensional space in linear perspective. Also used in relief sculpture.

palazzo: Italian for "big building," usually referring to a structure occupied by government workers or bureaucrats (e.g., Palazzo della Signoria), although it can also be used to describe a large home of a wealthy family (e.g., Palazzo Medici).

paragone: An Italian word meaning "debate" or "discourse"; a popular form of intellectual inquiry in the Renaissance, in which the author or speaker demonstrated the virtues of one particular theme or concept by comparing it favorably to another.

parchment: A writing surface made from dried and treated animal skins. Also known as vellum.

pattern book: A bound book of drawn compositions and figures that could be reused whenever patrons sought particular images. Apprentices and assistants were taught to copy them, and those who could replicate the master's style were the most celebrated members of the workshop. Pattern books gradually went out of style near the end of the 15th century.

piazza: Italian word for a city square, usually bracketed by public buildings.

pittura infamante: Italian term for pictures of the executed painted on the sides of prisons and government buildings. These images were part of the punishment meted out for particularly heinous crimes of high treason and murder.

polyptych: A multi-panel altarpiece or other devotional picture or relief sculpture. Typically, the central panel is flanked by wings and surmounted by gables or other forms and sometimes placed on a base, called a predella.

porphyry: A rare and expensive colored stone used for special sculptural or architectural projects.

pouncing: A process whereby chalk dust is placed inside a cheesecloth sack and lightly patted against a drawing that has been pinpricked along its contours and laid on top of the surface to be painted. The dust pushes through the pinpricks, forming an exact copy of the original drawing on the new surface.

putto (pl. **putti**): Small nude boys, sometimes winged, seen in both religious and secular Renaissance painting and sculpture.

Quattrocento: The century of the 1400s.

recto: The front side of a piece of parchment or paper, always the right-hand page of an open book.

refectory: The dining hall in a convent or monastery.

Renaissance: The period of Western history loosely bracketed by the 13th and 16th centuries and characterized by an overt and intentional appropriation of ideas, themes, and images from the ancient cultures of Greece and Rome. The age featured gradual and then rapid shifts in political systems, manufacturing, social hierarchies, literature, scientific inquiry, and artistic production.

Renaissance man: A phrase coined after the Renaissance, used to describe a person who demonstrates superior skill and talent in a number of different and unrelated fields. Frequently used to reference Leonardo da Vinci's mastery of the areas of engineering, hydraulics, aerodynamics, anatomy, painting, music, and sculpture. During the Renaissance itself, the expression used by writers such as Leon Battista Alberti and influential for Leonardo da Vinci was "universal man" (*uomo universale*).

sfumato: An Italian word meaning "smoky"; the method of painting subtle gradations of light and dark, especially in modeling the human figure, developed by Leonardo da Vinci.

simony: The practice of selling church offices for money. This method of raising revenue was popular during the pontificates of Alexander VI, Julius II, and particularly Leonardo X.

sprezzatura: Italian for "ease" or "effortlessness," used by Baldassare Castiglione to praise courtiers who excelled at a variety of activities with a certain grace and elegance.

Stanze: From the Italian word for "rooms," the rooms built in the Vatican Palace during the pontificate of Alexander VI and decorated by Raphael and his followers between 1509 and 1524.

tenebrism: An intense and dramatic juxtaposition of light and dark colors on a painted surface.

terminus post quem: Latin term meaning "completed after this date."

transept: The short axis, or cross arm, of a basilican church. It intersects the nave just before the chancel. The ground plan of such a church is cross-shaped.

triptych: An altarpiece or other devotional image made up of three painted or carved panels. The wings are usually smaller than the center panel and are sometimes hinged for closing.

triglyph: A block that forms part of a Doric frieze.

Ufficiali di Notte: The Guardians of the Night, Renaissance Florence's vice squad, charged with prosecuting cases of sexual misconduct—usually defined as acts of prostitution or sodomy.

underdrawing: A charcoal or chalk sketch on the penultimate coat of plaster laid on a wall before the final fresco coat was placed over it.

vanishing point: The place where orthogonal lines converge on the visual field of a two-dimensional surface when linear perspective is employed by an artist.

verso: The back side of a piece of parchment or paper, always the left-hand page of an open book.

Biographical Notes

Alberti, Leon Battista (1404–1472): Humanist writer, architect, and social commentator. Alberti became interested in the visual arts during a visit to Florence. His subsequent writings—*On Painting, On Sculpture,* and *Ten Books on Architecture*—codified new rules that came to represent a new style of artistic production that we now refer to as Renaissance.

Alexander VI (a.k.a. **Rodrigo Borgia**; 1431–1503): Pope and son of Spanish nobility. Alexander was the nephew of Pope Calixtus III and rose through the ecclesiastical hierarchy as a cleric and administrator in Rome. Notoriously ambitious and prone to prodigious (and lecherous) vices, Rodrigo bribed and bullied his way to the papal throne in 1492. He extorted and embezzled funds to support his insatiable appetites, funded his children's rapacious military exploits in eastern Italy during the late 1490s and early 1500s, and shortsightedly invited both French and Spanish troops onto Italian soil to undermine his political enemies. To this day, Alexander VI is considered among the most corrupt figures in modern European history.

Alighieri, Dante (1265–1322): Florentine thinker, poet, politician, and social critic. Dante wrote theologically driven love poetry and treatises on modern government but found himself on the wrong side of a civil war in Florence and was exiled from his homeland in 1301. During his itinerant years as persona non grata, Dante penned the most important work of literature of the early modern period, *The Divine Comedy*, which was the very first work of literature written in Italian.

Bayezid II (1447–1512): Sultan of the Ottoman Empire and son of Mehmed II. Bayezid briefly toyed with the idea of commissioning Leonardo da Vinci to design a bridge to span the Golden Horn of Istanbul.

Bellincioni, Bernardo (1452–1492): Poet and humanist favored by both Lorenzo de' Medici and Ludovico Sforza. Bellincioni wrote plays and sonnets for the entertainment and edification of the Milanese court. Leonardo designed stage sets for his theatrical pieces, and Bellincioni mentioned Leonardo by name in his poems.

Bellini, Giovanni (c. 1430–1516): Painter and son of another important artist, Jacopo Bellini, Giovanni pioneered the oil technique in Venice through his depictions of Madonnas and landscapes. He was the master of Titian and influenced Giorgione with his subtle forms and balanced compositions.

Bembo, Bernardo (1433–1519): Venetian aristocrat and diplomat who travelled to Florence in 1475 and witnessed the famous tournament in which Giuliano de' Medici conquered the field. He is also reputed to have met Ginevra de' Benci there and initiated a platonic relationship that was recognized in Leonardo's portrait of her.

Benci, Ginevra de' (c. 1458–1520): The wife of Luigi di Bernardo Niccolini and the presumptive muse of the Venetian diplomat Bernardo Bembo, she was the subject of humanistic poems and a painting by Leonardo da Vinci in the 1470s.

Boltraffio, Giovanni (c. 1466–1516): Painter of distinction in the Milanese court of Ludovico Sforza and a colleague and follower of Leonardo da Vinci during the 1490s. He specialized in portraits of Ludovico's courtiers and mistresses and may have assisted Leonardo on the *Madonna Litta*.

Borgia, Cesare (1475–1507): Known during his lifetime as "the wickedest man in Italy," Cesare Borgia was made a cardinal by his father, Rodrigo Borgia (Pope Alexander VI), when he was only 18 years old. He resigned that office in 1498 to pursue political and military ventures and, with his father's blessing and assistance, attempted to conquer lands in eastern Italy and create a duchy for himself. His reputation for duplicity, brutality, and murder earned him the fear and respect of his contemporaries, including Machiavelli and Leonardo da Vinci. He was expelled from Italy by his father's successor, Pope Julius II, and died on the battlefield outside Viana, Spain, in 1507.

Borgia, Lucrezia (1480–1519): Daughter of Rodrigo Borgia (Pope Alexander VI), Lucrezia carried a reputation for wantonness and promiscuity that has lasted to this day. She was married to a string of Italian princes and was the mistress of Francesco Gonzaga, who was the duke of Mantua and the husband of Isabella d'Este. She is known to have given birth to at least eight children, although a number of others born out of wedlock have also been assigned to her.

Rodrigo Borgia: *See* **Alexander VI**.

Botticelli, Sandro (1445–1510): Popular painter of religious pictures in Florence during the 1470s who caught the attention of the Medici family. During the 1480s, he worked for Pope Sixtus IV in Rome and for Lorenzo de' Medici in Florence, the latter of whom encouraged Botticelli's exploration of pagan and allegorical subjects. With the rise of Fra Savonarola during the 1490s, Botticelli rejected his own allegiance to the Medici and their humanistic court.

Bramante, Donato (1444–1514): Painter who made his mark as an architect. Born near Urbino, he worked in Milan during the 1470s, 1480s, and 1490s, where he met and collaborated with Leonardo da Vinci, and then worked in Rome for Pope Julius II, who hired him to design the new cathedral of Saint Peter. Bramante was responsible for the Tempietto and Palazzo Belvedere in Rome.

Brunelleschi, Filippo (1377–1446): Goldsmith who achieved fame as an architect, sculptor, and artistic theoretician. His design of the cupola of the Florentine cathedral was considered the pinnacle of early modern architectural design during the latter half of the 15th century, and he has been widely credited with perfecting the use of linear perspective in the painterly arts.

Buonarroti, Michelangelo (1475–1564): One of the most prolific artists of all time, who revolutionized the world of the visual arts through his drawings, paintings, sculptures, and architectural works—primarily in Florence and Rome. Among Michelangelo's most famous and influential projects were the frescoes for the Sistine Chapel, the sculptures for the Tomb of Julius II, and his designs for the New Sacristy in the Church of San Lorenzo, Florence.

Campin, Robert (1375–1444): Perhaps the first great master of Northern Renaissance painting, Campin produced paintings for French and Flemish patrons during the 15th century. His portraits of anonymous men and women reveal his acute interest in light and shadows, but his best-known work—the *Merode Triptych* in the Cloisters Museum in New York—is an explosion of mystical color.

Castagno, Andrea del (c. 1419–1457): Florentine fresco painter who worked for a variety of patrons, including the nuns in the convent of Sant'Apollonia, where his *Last Supper* demonstrated how linear perspective could be employed on a horizontal surface to great effect.

Castiglione, Baldassare (1478–1529): Diplomat and writer who worked in the courts of Urbino, Mantua, and the Vatican during his successful career. After serving as papal nuncio to Spain, he wrote a widely read and influential description of life at court in Renaissance Italy called *The Book of the Courtier* (1528).

Charles VIII (1470–1498): French king of the Valois dynasty who led a military campaign into Italy in 1494 to dislodge Naples from Spanish hands. He succeeded briefly but was forced to retreat back across the Alps by an alliance of European powers that feared the balance of power had tilted too heavily in France's favor.

Christus, Petrus (c. 1420–1476): Northern painter active in Bruges who was deeply influenced by the works of Robert Campin and Jan van Eyck. His *Portrait of a Carthusian* (1446) in New York's Metropolitan Museum of Art displays his understanding of oil paint and his interest in tenebrism.

Colleoni, Bartolomeo (1400–1475): Knight, mercenary soldier, and military leader who fought alternately for the Milanese and the Venetians. Colleoni's will stipulated that a monument to him be erected in the city of Venice. Andrea del Verrocchio was commissioned to produce the equestrian statue in his honor, and the finished product was installed in 1496.

Columbus, Christopher (1451–1506): Genoese navigator who sought the support of a variety of European powers as he considered a new route to India. He found favor in the Spanish court of Ferdinand and Isabella, and in 1492 he led the first of four voyages that resulted in his accidental landing on islands in the Caribbean Sea.

Copernicus, Nicholas (1473–1543): Polish scientist educated in Italian universities whose posthumously published findings posited that the sun, not the Earth, was the center of the solar system.

d'Amboise, Charles (1473–1511): Military leader and skilled diplomat who served in the French royal court and was appointed governor of Milan after the occupation of Northern Italy by the forces of Louis XII in 1499. As head of state, Charles acted as patron and protector of Leonardo da Vinci from 1506 to 1511.

da Messina, Antonello (c. 1430–1479): Sicilian painter who traveled widely during his professional career. Active in Naples, Venice, and probably France or Flanders, Antonello perfected the use of oil pigments in his paintings and helped teach artists in Italy how to employ them.

da Vinci, Leonardo (1452–1519): The quintessential Renaissance man, Leonardo's innovations in painting, architecture, engineering, anatomy, and aerodynamics revolutionized the fields of art and science during and after his lifetime. His travels and professional missions took him from Florence to Milan, Rome, and France, during which time he was able to influence a host of artists, patrons, and thinkers. Among his most famous works are *The Last Supper*, *Mona Lisa*, and *Vitruvian Man.*

della Francesca, Piero (c. 1420–1492): One of the most dedicated and skillful practitioners of linear perspective in all of Renaissance Italy. Born in the city of Arezzo, he was brought to the court of Federigo da Montfeltro in 1465, where he served faithfully as the duke's painter and courtier until his death. Among his most celebrated works are the frescoes of *The Legend of the True Cross* in the Church of San Francesco in Arezzo and the *Portrait of Federigo da Montelfetro and Battista Sforza* in the Uffizi Gallery, Florence.

d'Este, Beatrice (1475–1497): Beatrice was the daughter of Ercole d'Este, the duke of Ferrara, and the sister of Isabella d'Este. In 1491 she was married to Ludovico Sforza and spent the rest of her short life learning the ways of courtly life in Milan.

d'Este, Isabella (1474–1539): One of the day's greatest art connoisseurs and collectors, Isabella d'Este was the daughter of the prince of Ferrara and the wife of Francesco Gonzaga, the duke of Mantua. She was noted for her literary eloquence and her avid love of painting, and she went to great lengths to procure works from the day's most important artists. Well-educated and articulate, she also went on diplomatic missions of great sensitivity and counted as friends and confidants some of Europe's most important political and intellectual figures.

di Cione, Andrea (a.k.a. **Orcagna**; c. 1308–1368): Popular and prolific painter and sculptor in Florence during the middle decades of the 14th century. Among his best-known works are the monumental marble tabernacle in the Florentine church of Orsanmichele and his *Strozzi Altarpiece* for Santa Maria Novella.

di Credi, Lorenzo (1459–1537): Florentine painter and colleague of Leonardo da Vinci from the workshop of Andrea del Verrocchio who was noted for his intimate depictions of the Madonna.

di Giorgio Martini, Francesco (1439–1501/2): Architect and theoretician who experimented with the idea that designs of buildings could correspond to the proportions of the human figure.

Donatello (1386–1466): Perhaps the most inventive and influential artist of the early Renaissance, Donatello's sculptures repeatedly redefined the medium. Active in Florence and Padua, his bronze equestrian monument of *Gattamelata* was the first of its kind since antiquity. His marble relief *St. George and the Dragon* and his bronze relief *The Banquet of Herod* are among the earliest surviving examples of linear perspective on a two-dimensional surface. His appropriation of ancient motifs and subtle naturalistic elements helped create the standard by which all sculptures would be judged until the time of Michelangelo Buonarroti.

Eyck, Jan van (c. 1395–1441): Flemish painter and courtier who is largely considered the finest painter of the Northern European 15th century, a reputation he held even within his own lifetime. His best-known works are the *Ghent Altarpiece* (1432) and the *Arnolfini Double Portrait* (1434), now in London. His *Man in the Red Turban* (1433) is widely believed to be a self-portrait.

Francis of Assisi (1182–1226): Merchant's son who denounced his inheritance and initiated a spiritual movement that called on his followers to preach stories from the Gospels in public and in vernacular tongues. At his death in 1226, his Order of Friars Minor was known across Western Christendom as a key player in the popularization of religion among lay worshippers.

François I (1494–1547): French king of the Valois dynasty and distant relative of Louis XII, who preceded him on the throne. François ascended to power in 1515 and gradually enjoyed a political and military career that made him one of the most important and successful figures in early modern history. He was well educated and politically savvy. One of François's early acts as head of state was to invite Leonardo da Vinci to serve as his courtier. Leonardo accepted the invitation in 1516, thus giving François's court instant credibility.

Gaddi, Taddeo (c. 1300–1366): A disciple of Giotto, Taddeo Gaddi painted frescoes and altarpieces primarily in Florence from 1328 until 1360. Among his best-known works are the cycle called *The Life of the Virgin* in the Baroncelli Chapel of Santa Croce (1328–1330) and the *Tree of Life and Last Supper* in the refectory of the same complex (c. 1355).

Gaffurio, Franchino (1451–1522): Musician and composer of the late 15th century who worked in the court of Ludovico Sforza at the same time as Leonardo da Vinci.

Gallerani, Cecilia (1473–1536): The aristocratic mistress of Ludovico Sforza during the late 1480s and early 1490s. The subject of Leonardo's *Woman with the Ermine*, Cecilia was Ludovico's favored consort even after his marriage to Beatrice d'Este in 1491, and she bore him a child in 1491. Under pressure from Beatrice, Cecilia was later married to a local count and left the Sforza court permanently.

Ghiberti, Lorenzo (c. 1378–1455): A contemporary of Filippo Brunelleschi and Donatello, with whom he competed repeatedly, Ghiberti produced two sets of bronze reliefs for the doors of the Florentine Baptistery, the second of which (1430–1452) was later dubbed by Michelangelo *The Gates of Paradise.*

Ghirlandaio, Domenico (1449–1494): Painter who trained with Andrea del Verrocchio in Florence and was a colleague of Leonardo da Vinci during the 1460s and 1470s. He was known for his mastery of Madonna forms and his adherence to traditional modes of painting. He helped teach his student Michelangelo the fresco technique during the production of a series of paintings called *The Life of the Virgin Mary* for the Florentine church of Santa Maria Novella in 1488.

Gioconda, Elisabetta Gherardini (1479–1542/51): Traditionally recognized as the sitter of Leonardo's *Mona Lisa* (known as *La Gioconda* in Italian), she was the wife of a political figure named Francesco and was buried in the Florentine nunnery of Sant'Orsola.

Giorgione (a.k.a. **Giorgio da Castelfranco**; c. 1476/8–1510): The extraordinary career of this talented Venetian artist was mysteriously cut short in 1510, yet his allegorical pictures remain among the period's most innovative and influential paintings, and his employment of oil paint was rivaled only by that of his master, Giovanni Bellini, and his colleague Titian.

Giotto (a.k.a. **Giotto di Bondone**; 1266–1337): Giotto's origins are largely unknown, but it appears that he made his reputation in Rome during the 1290s as a fresco painter. His murals in the Arena Chapel of Padua (1304–1306) and his paintings in Florence (1310–1325), including the *Ognissanti Madonna*, ushered into European painting a naturalistic style that emphasized the careful use of human proportions, figural details, and rational representations of depth.

Goes, Hugo van der (c. 1440–1482): Flemish painter who was commissioned by Tommaso Portinari, the director of a branch office of the Medici bank in Flanders, to paint an enormous triptych now known as *The Portinari Altarpiece* (1476; installed 1483) for the Florentine hospital church of Santa Maria Nuova.

Gutenberg, Johannes (1398–1468): A blacksmith by trade who focused his energies on creating a printing press that could produce multiple copies of texts through the employment of reusable, movable type. His perfection of this process led to the artistic medium of printmaking, provided a communications revolution for thinkers and poets, and caused an increased demand for paper that completely changed the way writers and artists approached their respective subjects.

Julius II (a.k.a. **Giuliano della Rovere**; 1443–1513): Elected pope in 1503, Julius II served in that capacity for a decade. He worked to expel foreign armies from Italian soil and to organize a confederation of states loyal to the pope as a common leader. He also organized one of the most grandiose (and expensive) urban renewal projects in history and brought to Rome three of the day's greatest artists—Bramante, Michelangelo, and Raphael—to rebuild and redecorate the city.

Leonardo X (a.k.a. **Giovanni de' Medici**; 1475–1521): The second son of Lorenzo the Magnificent; he succeeded Julius II to the papal throne in 1513. Whereas Julius II initiated a systematic program of "revenue enhancements" to help pay for the rebuilding of Rome during his pontificate, Leo expanded on these approaches to cover the expenses of his personal art collection and parties.

Lippi, Filippino (1457/8–1504): The son of the mendicant painter Fra Filippo Lippi, Filippino was a successful painter in his own right. Among his best-known works are frescoes in the Brancacci Chapel in the Florentine church of Santa Maria del Carmine, scenes from the *Life of Saint Philip* in Santa Maria Novella, and the altarpiece *Adoration of the Magi*, which ultimately replaced the version that Leonardo had intended to install in the church of San Donato a Scopeto (but then abandoned) in 1481.

Lippi, Fra Filippo (c. 1406–1469): Carmelite friar who continued the early Renaissance explorations and experiments of Masaccio. Among his best known works are *Annunciation of the Virgin* in San Lorenzo and *Madonna and Child with Angels* in the Uffizi Gallery (which, according to tradition, celebrates the birth of Filippino Lippi to Lucrezia Buti, the nun to whom Fra Filippo was married in secret).

Lorenzo Monaco (c. 1372–1424): Monk who left his cloister at Santa Maria degli Angeli in Florence to pursue a career as a lay painter. Among his most important works were panels of *The Coronation of the Virgin* (1414) and *The Man of Sorrows (Vir Dolorum)* (1404)—both in Florence today.

Louis XII (1462–1515): A French king of the Valois-Orleans family and distant cousin of Charles VIII, Louis XII took control of France in 1498 after Charles died from a brain hemorrhage caused by a fall at a tennis match—and after Charles's wife, Anne, agreed to marry Louis in an act of political unification. In 1499, Louis invaded Italy and conquered Milan, which resulted in the expulsion of Ludovico Sforza and the departure of Leonardo da Vinci.

Luini, Bernardino (c. 1480–1532): Lombard painter who was an admirer and follower of Leonardo da Vinci, although direct contact between the two was minimal.

Luther, Martin (1483–1546): Augustinian friar and professor of theology who was outraged by the excesses of the papal courts of Alexander VI, Julius II, and Leo X. He went public with his protests in 1517, refused to recant in 1520, was excommunicated in 1521, and was hence seen as the founder and leader of the Protestant movement.

Machiavelli, Niccolò (1469–1527): Government official and political theorist. Machiavelli took on a number of diplomatic posts as a representative of the new Florentine republic during the early years of the 1500s. During this time he met and collaborated with Leonardo da Vinci on a number of projects. He was arrested when the Medici returned to take control of Florence in 1513 and wrote his political treatise *The Prince* and a number of plays during a self-imposed exile.

Mantegna, Andrea (c. 1430/31–1506): Painter who worked in Padua and Verona but made his most important contributions as a member of the Gonzaga court in Mantua, where he worked from about 1465 until his death in 1506. He is best known for his imaginative mural paintings in one of the bedchambers of the ducal palace there, known as the Camera Picta.

Masaccio (a.k.a. **Tommaso di ser Giovanni**; 1401–1428): The most important and influential painter of the early Renaissance. Masaccio employed the lessons of Giotto and Donatello in his monumental fresco paintings and literally invented early modern painting in Florence. His best known pictures—which were copied repeatedly by generations of artists—are *The Life of Saint Peter* in Santa Maria del Carmine (1425) and *The Trinity* in Santa Maria Novella (1427).

Maximilian I (1459–1519): Holy Roman Emperor of the Hapsburg dynasty, Maximilian was the son of Frederick III and in 1493 inherited his father's title as Holy Roman Emperor. In 1494 he married Bianca Sforza, Ludovico Sforza's niece, which gave Maximilian and his descendants a claim to Milanese territories in later years. Although not known for his accomplishments on the battlefield, Maximilian was a gifted and savvy politician who expanded the territories of the Holy Roman Empire. When he died, his grandson Charles V was able to transform the power and wealth that Maximilian had accumulated into the largest and most potent international force of the early modern period.

Medici, Cosimo de' (1389–1464): Banker by training but politician by inclination, before his exile in 1433, Cosimo opposed the policies of the Florentine government and was punished for his views and tactics. After his return to power in 1434, he became the de facto ruler of the city, manipulating the electoral process and orchestrating public policy from behind the scenes—all to the benefit of the city, which enjoyed an age of peace and prosperity during his reign.

Medici, Giovanni de': *See* **Leonardo X**.

Medici, Giuliano di Lorenzo de' (1479–1516): The third son of Lorenzo di Piero de' Medici (a.k.a. Lorenzo the Magnificent), Giuliano was one of the leaders of the coup d'etat that reinstated his family as the governors of Florence in 1512. One of the characters in Baldassare Castiglione's *Book of the Courtier* and the person to whom Machiavelli's *The Prince* was originally dedicated, Giuliano was both a poet and a diplomat. He spent much of his time in Rome at the side of his brother, Pope Leonardo X, and was the patron of Leonardo da Vinci from 1513 to 1516.

Medici, Giuliano di Piero de' (1453–1478): The second son of Piero de' Medici and the grandson of Cosimo the Elder, Giuliano governed the city of Florence, together with his brother Lorenzo, from 1469 until his assassination in 1478.

Medici, Lorenzo di Piero de' (a.k.a. **Lorenzo the Magnificent**; 1449–1492): The first son of Piero de' Medici and the grandson of Cosimo the Elder, Lorenzo was known just as much for his interest in the arts and letters as he was a political ruler. In addition to governing the city for the duration of his adult life, Lorenzo created around himself one of Italy's most prominent courts of thinkers and writers. Included in his entourage were the philosophers Giovanni Pico della Mirandola and Marsilio Ficino and the artists Sandro Botticelli, Michelangelo Buonarroti, and Leonardo da Vinci.

Medici, Piero de' (1416–1469) The son of Cosimo the Elder and the father of Lorenzo the Magnificent, Piero the Gouty governed Florence for five years after his father's death in 1464.

Melzi, Francesco (c. 1491–1570): A painter of noble birth, Melzi joined the studio of Leonardo as a teenager and became a trusted member of the inner circle for the rest of Leonardo's life. Melzi inherited Leonardo's notes and writings and maintained them carefully until his own death.

Pacioli, Luca (1447–1517): Mathematician from Pavia who befriended Leonardo da Vinci late in the artist's tenure as a courtier in the Sforza court.

Perugino (a.k.a. **Pietro Vanucci**; 1446–1523): A native of the city of Perugia and an accomplished artist who worked in Perugia, Florence, and Rome during his highly successful career. Among his students was the painter Raphael.

Petrarch, Francesco (1304–1374): Bibliophile, poet, and philosopher, and one of the founders of early modern humanism. A keen student of ancient Roman history, Petrarch helped revive the study of antique Latin during the 14th century.

Pollaiuolo, Antonio (1433–1498): Prominent sculptor, painter, draftsman, and printmaker, Pollaiuolo and his brother Piero operated one of Florence's largest artistic workshops. He designed the sculptural tomb monument for Pope Sixtus IV and painted the influential altarpiece of *The Martyrdom of Saint Sebastian*, now in London.

Predis, Ambrogio de' (c. 1455–**c.** 1508): Milanese painter and colleague of Leonardo's in the 1480s who continued to work with and for Leonardo into the 16th century. The two artists collaborated on both versions of *The Madonna of the Rocks* (Paris and London).

Raphael (a.k.a. **Raffaello Sanzio** or **Raffaello Santi**; 1483–1520): Enormously talented painter and deft courtier who earned a reputation for artistic elegance and diplomatic skill during his years in Florence and Rome. A member of Julius II's entourage of artists from 1508 to 1513, Raphael painted frescoes in the Vatican (*The School of Athens*, 1512), portraits of his papal patrons (*Julius II*, 1512; *Leo X*, 1516), and altarpieces for Roman churches (*The Transfiguration of Chrst*, 1518), before his sudden death at the age of 37.

Romano, Giulio (1499–1546): Painter and printmaker of great creativity and ingenuity who trained with Raphael and spent his youth assisting his master on the frescoes painted inside the Vatican Stanze. Romano left Rome after Raphael's death and spent 10 years designing and decorating the Palazzo del Te in Mantua.

Salai (a.k.a. **Gian Giacomo Caprotti da Oreno**; 1480–1524): Salai, or "the little devil," was Leonardo's assistant and colleague for 30 years. In 1519, he inherited from Leonardo *Mona Lisa*, *Saint Anne Madonna*, *John the Baptist,* and the now-lost *Leda and the Swan*, all of which passed into the hands of his sisters on his death. They, in turn, sold the pictures to King François I of France.

Sarto, Andrea del (1486–1530): Follower of Raphael and Leonardo who worked in the classical idiom, primarily in Florence. His best-known work is *The Madonna of the Harpies* (1517).

Savonarola, Fra Girolamo (1452–1498): Fiery preacher who opposed the humanistic interests of Lorenzo de' Medici and led the reactionary movement against the family in the 1490s. He organized bonfires of the vanities, in which common people burned the material possessions they were ashamed to own. He led the Florentine government from 1494 until 1498, when moderates overthrew him and burned him at the stake in the middle of the Piazza della Signoria.

Sforza, Francesco (1401–1466): Italian knight, mercenary soldier, and husband of Biana Maria Visconti. When his brother-in-law—Filippo Maria Visconti, duke of Milan—died without a male heir, Francesco claimed the throne. After a four-year war to determine the rightful ruler, Francesco was installed as the autocrat of Milan. His sons—Galeazzo Maria and Ludovico—forever worried that their father's method of attaining power was illegitimate, thus stained their own regimes.

Sforza, Galeazzo Maria (1444–1476): Known primarily for his cruelty, Galeazzo Maria Sforza inherited the throne of Milan from his father, Francesco, in 1466. His reputation as a bully, extortionist, and rapist helped forge an alliance of his enemies, and he was assassinated by members of his own court in 1476.

Sforza, Giangaleazzo (1469–1494): The legitimate and rightful heir to the throne of Milan after the assassination of his father, Galeazzo Maria, Giangaleazzo was outmaneuvered by his uncle, Ludovico, for control of Milan. He died at the age of 25, perhaps from poison.

Sforza, Ludovico (1452–1508): Leonardo's patron from 1482 to 1499, Ludovico Sforza came to power by wresting control from his sister-in-law, who was acting as regent on behalf of her infant son (who had inherited the throne of Milan after the assassination of Galeazzo Maria Sforza in 1476). Ludovico served—without official title—as the ruler of the city until Maximilian I made him duke of Milan in 1494. Ludovico was chased from Milan by a French army in 1499 and, after a brief return to the city the next year, was captured and imprisoned by them.

Sixtus IV (a.k.a. **Francesco della Rovere**; 1414–1484): A scholar of great intellect and sobriety who was elected pope in 1471 and helped solidify Rome's place as a political and spiritual entity at the beginning of the High Renaissance. A large chapel was built to commemorate his victory over Florence in 1478, and in the early 1480s the artists Botticelli, Perugino, and Ghirlandaio helped decorate the side walls of his so-called Sistine Chapel.

Soderini, Piero (1450–1522): Gifted politician and a favorite of Lorenzo de' Medici, after Lorenzo's death in 1492 and the execution of Fra Savonarola in 1498, Soderini helped organize and then presided over the new republican government of Florence until its fall at the hands of the Medici during the coup d'etat of 1512. Soderini worked with both Leonardo and Michelangelo during the project to paint murals in the Salone dei 500 of the Palazzo della Signoria from 1503 to 1505.

Titian (a.k.a. **Tiziano Vecellio**; c. 1488/90–1576): Along with Giorgione, Titian is widely regarded as the greatest of all Venetian painters. After completing his studies with Giovanni Bellini around 1510, he went on to produce a series of highly influential oil paintings on canvas, including the *Assumption of the Virgin* for the church of the Frari, the *Venus of Urbino* in the Uffizi Gallery, and a series of portraits of Holy Roman Emperor Charles V.

Trivulzio, Giovanni (c. 1440–1518): Aristocrat, mercenary soldier, military commander, and political leader. Eager to establish a legacy for himself, he briefly engaged Leonardo da Vinci to produce designs for an equestrian monument in his honor. The project was dropped when Trivulzio took control of Milan in 1511 and focused his energies on matters of state.

Uccello, Paolo (1397–1475): Early practitioner of linear perspective and the painter of three battle scenes produced in the mid-15th century—each of which illustrates the *Battle of San Romano*—now in Paris, London, and Florence.

Vasari, Giorgio (1511–1574): Prolific painter, architect, and historian who worked for the Medici family in Florence during the 1550s and 1560s. He helped remodel the Palazzo della Signoria for the new duke, Cosimo I de' Medici, and painted a number of pictures for the family, including the *Battle of Scannagallo*, which may have covered over Leonardo's mural of the

Battle of Anghiari. Vasari is best known for his encyclopedic treatment of contemporary art, called *The Lives of the Artists*, which includes some of the earliest biographies of Leonardo, Raphael, and Michelangelo. The first edition appeared in 1550, and the second (corrected) version was published in 1568.

Veneziano, Domenico (c. 1410–1461): Northern Italian painter who came to Florence in search of commissions in the late 1430s. He quickly learned the trade secret of linear perspective and in 1445 produced one of the very best examples of a modern picture with his *Saint Lucy Altarpiece*, now in the Uffizi Gallery.

Verrocchio, Andrea del (c. 1435–1488): Exceptionally gifted sculptor and painter who operated one of Florence's largest and most successful artistic workshops during the 1460s and 1470s. Among his students were Perugino, Botticelli, and Ghirlandaio, and he went into a brief partnership with his most famous protégé—Leonardo da Vinci. Verrocchio is best known for *The Incredulity of Saint Thomas* for the Orsanmichele in Florence, *Putto with Dolphin* in the Palazzo della Signoria, and *The Monument of Bartolommeo Colleoni* that was cast posthumously and installed outside the Venetian church of Santissimi Giovanni e Paolo in 1496.

Vitruvius (c. 75 B.C.E.–c. 15 B.C.E.): Soldier and engineer in the Roman legions best known for his treatise *De architectura* (*On Architecture*), which articulates the building practices and design theories of antiquity. Vitruvius's lessons formed the foundation of architectural study during the 15th century, informed Leon Battista Alberti's approach to Renaissance architecture, and inspired Leonardo's drawing known as the *Vitruvian Man.*

Weyden, Rogier van der (c. 1400–1464): A Flemish painter of enormous skill who trained with Robert Campin and perfected the Northern European approach to early Renaissance painting that employed heavy shadows mixed with rich colors. He traveled to Italy in 1450 and lived for a time in Florence, thus helping introduce the traditions of his homeland to artists and audiences south of the Alps.

Bibliography

The scholarly literature dedicated to the life and career of Leonardo da Vinci is vast. Still, a few sources stand out. The first great monograph on Leonardo's career was by Kenneth Clark, whose *Leonardo da Vinci: An Account of His Development as an Artist* (1939) struck an excellent balance between the artist's life and work as a painter and courtier. Clark continued his examination of Leonardo's drawings for decades thereafter, including *The Drawings of Leonardo da Vinci in the Collection of Her Majesty the Queen at Windsor Castle* (1968). His legacy has been continued by Martin Kemp, whose monograph *Leonardo da Vinci: The Marvellous Works of Nature and Man* (1981) is the most comprehensive and sophisticated treatment of Leonardo's artistic career. David Alan Brown's important contributions include new findings and compelling hypotheses about Leonardo's early work in Florence, especially *Leonardo da Vinci: Origins of a Genius* (1998).

Works especially useful for placing Leonardo in the context of his times are Lauro Martines's *Power and Imagination: City-States in Renaissance Italy*; Peter Burke's *The Italian Renaissance: Culture and Society in Italy*; and *History of Italian Renaissance Art* by Frederick Hartt and David G. Wilkins, now in its 7th edition. Their approaches to politics, culture, and patronage help readers understand why works of art and architecture were so vital to Italian power brokers in the 15th and 16th centuries.

Among the more unorthodox interpretations of the artist's work is *Leonardo's Incessant Last Supper* (2001) by Leo Steinberg, which still stands as the most innovative and interesting interpretation of the mural in Milan. A catalog produced in tandem with an exhibition in London during the fall of 2011 and winter of 2012, edited by Luke Syson and titled *Leonardo da Vinci: Painter at the Court of Milan*, brings together an abundance of paintings, drawings, and documents about the artist and his circle of colleagues during his first Milanese period (1482–1499). The recently restored image of the *Salvator Mundi* is a featured component of the exhibition.

Ahl, Diane Cole. *Leonardo a Vinci's Sforza Monumental Horse: The Art and the Engineering.* Bethlehem, PA: Lehigh University Press, 1995. An extensive examination of Leonardo's project for Ludovico Sforza, Ahl's study includes drawings and interpretations of the monument in the context of late 15th-century art and politics.

Alberti, Leon Battista. *On Painting.* Translated by John R. Spencer. New Haven, CT: Yale University Press, 1956. Alberti wrote his treatise in 1435 but then revised his Latin text into Italian so it could be read by the artists for whom it had been written. Alberti codifies the rules of linear perspective that had been worked out by Donatello and Masaccio between 1415 and 1425. This was one of the textbooks that Leonardo read and digested as an apprentice in the workshop of Andrea del Verrocchio, and the lessons it contains remain essential components of the studio arts curriculum to this day.

Allison, Ann H. "Antique Sources of Leonardo's *Leda.*" *The Art Bulletin* 56, no. 3 (1974): 375–384. Argues that Leonardo either knew or consulted ancient images of Leda as he developed his drawings and painting of the erotic image *Leda and the Swan.* It suggests that Leonardo was more indebted to the classical past than is traditionally claimed.

Barcilon, Pinin Brambilla, and Pietro Marani. *Leonardo: The Last Supper.* Chicago: University of Chicago Press, 2001. Marani and Barcilon collect the drawings and studies made by Leonardo as he prepared his mural for Santa Maria delle Grazie and include a review of the various copies produced since its completion in 1498 (42 paintings, 6 sculptures, and 2 textiles). The final chapter explains the restoration project of the 1970s, 1980s, and 1990s. A discussion of Leonardo's experimental technique describes the secco approach. This book is generally considered to be the best overview of the painting published since its restoration in the late 20th century.

Bell, Janice. "*Sfumato* and Acuity Perspective." In *Leonardo da Vinci and the Ethics of Style*, edited by Claire Farago, 161–188. Manchester, UK: Manchester University Press, 2008. Reviews the concept of *sfumato*.

Brown, David Alan. *Leonardo da Vinci: Origins of a Genius*. New Haven, CT: Yale University Press, 1998. Brown's book covers the early years of Leonardo's career as an apprentice and partner of Andrea del Verrocchio. His chapters on Leonardo's work as a sculptor and his paintings of the angel in the *Baptism of Christ*, the *Annunciation,* and his Florentine Madonnas are the most thorough summations of Leonardo's career up to 1478. Brown reviews the technical and interpretative history of Leonardo's portrait *Ginevra de'Benci* and places the picture in the context of Leonardo's development as a young artist in Florence during the 1470s.

__________. "The Profile of a Youth and Leonardo's *Annunciation*." *Mitteilungen des Kunsthistorischen Institutes in Florenz* 15, no. 3 (1971): 265–272. Brown connects a drawing to the *Annunciation*'s figure of the archangel Gabriel and demonstrates the importance of sketches on paper for the young artist early in his career.

__________. "Raphael, Leonardo, and Perugino: Fame and Fortune." In *Leonardo, Michelangelo, and Raphael in Renaissance Florence from 1500 to 1508*, edited by Serafina Hager, 29–53. Washington, DC: Georgetown University Press, 1992. Reviews the works of these three artists in Florence during the first decade of the 16th century and demonstrates Raphael's rapid turn away from the stylistic impulses of Perugino, his master, and his turn toward those of Leonardo.

Brugnoli, Maria Vittoria. "The Sculptor." In *Leonardo: The Artist*, edited by Ladislao Reti, 96–135. New York: McGraw-Hill, 1980. This short (but well illustrated) chapter details the project to design and cast the enormous equestrian monument for Ludovico Sforza.

Budny, Virginia. "The Sequence of Leonardo's Sketches for *The Virgin and Child with Saint Anne and Saint John the Baptist*." *The Art Bulletin* 65, no. 1 (1983): 34–50. Considers drawings that served as preparatory studies for both the cartoon and painting versions of the *Saint Anne Madonna*. It traces the development of this theme over the course of a decade.

Burke, Peter. *The Italian Renaissance: Culture and Society in Italy.* Princeton, NJ: Princeton University Press, 1986. Burke's study is still the standard overview of the cultural and political traditions that governed life in Italy during the 15th and 16th centuries.

Cennini, Cennino. *The Craftsman's Handbook:* "Il *Libro dell'Arte.*" Translated by Daniel V. Thompson Jr. New York: Dover, 1933. Cennini, a student of a student of a student of Giotto's, wrote this "recipe book" for painters sometime around 1405. Cennini describes how to prepare a panel for painting, how to mix egg tempera paint, how to apply gold leaf, and how to lay down wet plaster for frescoes, among literally scores of other secrets of the trade.

Cianchi, Marco. *Leonardo: Anatomy.* Translated by Christine Cesarini. Florence: Giunti, 1998. A short survey of Leonardo's anatomical drawings, this book is a good introduction to the artist's renderings of dissected bodies.

Cianchi, Marco, Alessancro Vezzosi, and Lisa Goldenberg Stoppato. *Leonardo's Machines.* Translated by Lisa Goldenberg Stoppato. Florence: Becocci Editore, 1988. This short but well-illustrated introduction to some of Leonardo's inventions combines photographs of his drawings with brief descriptions of their intended functions.

Clark, Kenneth. *The Drawings of Leonardo da Vinci in the Collection of Her Majesty the Queen at Windsor Castle*. London: Phaidon, 1968. A large-scale review of drawings that includes the preparatory studies for the *Trivulzio Monument*.

__________. *Leonardo da Vinci: An Account of His Development as an Artist*. Cambridge: Macmillan Co., 1939. The first truly exhaustive and authoritative study of Leonardo's career, Clark's work provides an overview of Leonardo's career with particular attention paid to his artistic output.

Cole, Alison. *Virtue and Magnificence: Art of the Italian Renaissance Courts.* Englewood Cliffs, NJ: Prentice Hall, 1995. A short but thoughtful examination of life at court in northern Italy during the 15th century. Cole argues that artists were of fundamental importance to princes during this period, as the level of prestige that their courts enjoyed abroad often influenced their ability to realize their diplomatic goals.

Cole, Bruce. *The Renaissance Artist at Work.* New York: Harper & Row, 1983. Cole discusses the business of being an artist during the Italian Renaissance. From the system of training and education received by apprentices to the role of patrons and contracts in the process of forming a commission, Cole describes the multiple concerns that occupied the attention of artists in Leonardo's time.

Colvin, Sidney. "A Note on the *Benois Madonna* of Leonardo da Vinci." *Burlington Magazine* 20, no. 106 (1912): 230–233. A short essay that connects preparatory sketches with the *Benois Madonna*, this is an important early landmark in Leonardo studies.

Cropper, Elizabeth. "Poussin and Leonardo: Evidence from the Zaccolini MSS." *The Art Bulletin* 62, no. 4 (1980): 570–583. Examines the clear debts of Poussin to Leonardo and notes what appears to be a copy of the *Treatise on Painting* in the former's self-portrait from 1649. Poussin's interest in geometrical formula to create perspectival vistas is seen as a particularly classical notion, with its roots grounded in the work of Leonardo.

Dibner, Bern. "Machines and Weaponry." In *Unknown Leonardo*, edited by Ladislao Reti, 166–189. London: McGraw-Hill, 1974. A well-illustrated treatment of Leonardo's various military designs, with special attention paid to his interest in firearms and siege machines.

Duke, Neville. *The Saga of Fight, from Leonardo da Vinci to the Guided Missile.* New York: John Day, 1961. Traces the development of human aviation into the 20th century, with its scientific origins firmly rooted in Leonardo's experimentations.

Farago, Claire, ed. *Leonardo da Vinci: Selected Scholarship.* 5 vols. New York: Garland, 1999. A compendium of articles and essays written by scholars over the course of three centuries about every possible facet of Leonardo's career.

__________. "'Three ducats in Venice.' Connecting Giorgione and Leonardo." In *Leonardo da Vinci and the Ethics of Style*, edited by Claire Farago, 146–159. Manchester, UK: Manchester University Press, 2008. This essay addresses the issue of artistic influences and notes that Leonardo both learned from the images he saw in Venice and encouraged the young Giorgione to borrow from him.

Farago, Claire J. "Leonardo's *Battle of Anghiari*: A Study in the Exchange between Theory and Practice." *The Art Bulletin* 76, no. 2 (1994): 301–330. Considers the entire mural project, from preparatory studies to compositional choices to the encaustic technique. It argues that the painting is an example of an experimental artist applying his art philosophies in an actual commission.

Fletcher, Jennifer. "Bernardo Bembo and Leonardo's Portrait of Ginevra de' Benci." *Burlington Magazine* 131, no. 1041 (1989): 811–816. Argues persuasively that Bernardo Bembo's emblem appears on the back of Ginevra's portrait and that she and Bembo enjoyed a platonic relationship during his stay in Florence in 1475.

Freud, Sigmund. *Leonardo da Vinci and a Memory of His Childhood.* Translated by Alan Tyson. Edited by James Strachey in collaboration with Anna Freud. New York: Norton, 1964. This translation of Freud's early essay (1910) interprets Leonardo's recollection of a childhood dream in which a bird visited him in his crib and touched his lips with its wings. Freud saw this as both proof of and an explanation for Leonardo's homosexuality and was one of his best known forays into the field of art history.

Friedlaender, Walter. *Mannerism and Anti-Mannerism in Italian Painting.* New York: Columbia University Press, 1957. A famous text that describes the stylistic distinctions that marked 16th-century painting at the conclusion of the High Renaissance.

Garrard, Mary D. "Leonardo da Vinci: Female Portraits, Female Nature." In *The Expanding Discourse: Feminism and Art History*, edited by Norma Broude and Mary D. Garrard, 58–85. New York: Icon Editions, 1992. Garrard argues that Leonardo's portrait of Ginevra de' Benci uses elements of the natural world as symbols for the intellectual agency of female sitters.

Goffen, Rona. *Renaissance Rivals: Michelangelo, Leonardo, Raphael, Titian.* New Haven, CT: Yale University Press, 2002. A survey of the four major leaders of the High Renaissance in Italian art, this book moves quickly between them but manages to connect the four together.

Gombrich, Ernst. "Leonardo da Vinci's Method of Analysis and Permutation: The Grotesque Heads." In *The Heritage of Apelles*, edited by Ernst Gombrich, 57–75. London: Phaidon Press, 1976. One of the earliest attempts to consider Leonardo's caricatures as works of art, Gombrich's essay is a rich examination of the artist's interests in expressiveness, humor, and fantasy.

Gould, Cecil. "Leonardo's Great Battle-Piece: A Conjectural Reconstruction." *The Art Bulletin* 36, no. 2 (1954): 117–129. Attempts to imagine the appearance of Leonardo's mural in the Palazzo della Signoria by using preparatory drawings as models. This is an impressive and compelling work of scholarly creativity.

Grabski, Josef, and Janusz Walek, eds. *Leonardo da Vinci (1452–1519): Lady with an Ermine from the Czartoryski Collection, National Museum, Cracow.* Vienna: IRSA, 1991. A detailed analysis of the portrait of Cecilia Gallerani.

Greenstein, Jack. "Leonardo, *Mona Lisa*, and *La Gioconda*. Reviewing the Evidence," *Artibus et Historiae* 25, no. 50 (2004): 17–34. Greenstein reviews the scholarly literature, various interpretations of the facts, and some of the legends surrounding the picture. This is an excellent overview of the historiography of the picture.

Hartt, Frederick, and David Wilkins. *History of Italian Renaissance Art.* 7th edition. Upper Saddle River, NJ: Prentice Hall, 2011. Still the authoritative survey of art and architecture of the period, Hartt's first edition appeared in American college classrooms in the 1960s. Wilkins's thoughtful update includes recent research that has subtly altered some of the specific interpretations of artworks but not the metanarrative that traces the development of early modern art from its origins in the workshop of Cimabue to the fall of mannerism in the late 16th century.

Heydenreich, Ludwig. "Leonardo da Vinci, Architect of Francis I." *Burlington Magazine* 94, no. 595 (1952): 277–285. This essay considers Leonardo's drawings of buildings for the French royal court as well as maps of local canals in the Loire Valley. The author connects the drawings to Leonardo's earlier interests and argues that he produced these plans for Francois I between 1516 and 1519.

__________. *Leonardo: The Last Supper.* London: Allen Lane, 1974. This short but clear study of Leonardo's mural addresses its impact on other Last Suppers painted in the 16th century.

__________. "The Military Architect." In *The Unknown Leonardo,* edited by Ladislao Reti, 136–165. London: McGraw-Hill, 1974. This chapter focuses on Leonardo's architectural work for military projects and describes the project to alter the course of the Arno River.

Hills, Paul. "Leonardo and Flemish Painting." *Burlington Magazine* 122, no. 930 (1980): 608–615. Notes the relationship between Flemish paintings of the third quarter of the 15th century and Leonardo's works of the 1470s and 1480s. Focuses particularly on *The Adoration of the Magi.*

Hochstetler Meyer, Barbara. "Leonardo's Hypothetical Painting of *Leda and the Swan.*" *Mitteilungen des Kunsthistorischen Institutes in Florenz* 34, no. 3 (1990): 279–294. Considers the drawings of Leda by Leonardo and his followers but questions the existence of a painting of the subject by Leonardo.

Hollingsworth, Mary. *Patronage in Renaissance Italy: From 1400 to the Early Sixteenth Century*. London: John Murray, 1994. A survey of different princely patrons at different courts in Italy. The chapter on Pope Julius II provides a particularly useful overview of the man and his motives.

Keele, Kenneth D., and Jane Roberts. *Leonardo da Vinci: Anatomical Drawings from the Royal Library, Windsor Castle.* New York: The Metropolitan Museum of Art, 1983. This exhibition catalog reviews the development of the artist's interest in the human body. Richly illustrated, the book reveals Leonardo's gifts as a draftsman and a close observer of nature.

Kemp, Martin. *Leonardo da Vinci: The Marvellous Works of Nature and Man.* Cambridge, MA: Harvard University Press, 1981. Kemp's biography of Leonardo is particularly useful for the period of Leonardo's employment in Milan, Florence, and Rome from 1482 to 1516. His analysis of the artist's mathematical and scientific work captures Leonardo's interests accurately and thoughtfully.

———, ed. *Leonardo da Vinci. The Mystery of the Madonna of the Yarnwinder.* Edinburgh: National Gallery of Scotland, 1992. In this exhibition catalog, Kemp reviews the condition, appearance, and literature of the titular picture.

———, ed. *Leonardo on Painting: An Anthology of Writings by Leonardo da Vinci, with a Selection of Documents Relating to His Career as an Artist.* Translated by Martin Kemp and Margaret Walker. New Haven, CT: Yale University Press, 1989. A thorough collection of Leonardo's writings about art, poetry, and philosophy, this abridged translation includes comments about sculpture as a base art and the superiority of painting to poetry.

Klein, Stefan. *Leonardo's Legacy: How Da Vinci Reimagined the World.* Cambridge, MA: Da Capo Press, 2010. A study of Leonardo's work as an engineer and technical draftsman, this work includes a chapter on the artist's conceptions of weapons for use on the battlefield, as well as Leonardo's interest in aviation both from a hypothetical perspective and a logistical one.

Ladwein, Michael, *Leonardo da Vinci, The Last Supper: A Cosmic Drama and an Act of Redemption.* Forest Row, UK: Temple Lodge, 2006. A basic introduction to Leonardo's fresco, *The Last Supper.*

Landrus, Matthew. *Leonardo da Vinci: The Genius, His Work, and the Renaissance.* London: Andre Deutsch, 2009. This concise review of Leonardo's career contains facsimiles of his drawings, writings, and designs. What it lacks in length it makes up for in clarity.

Letze, Otto, and Thomas Buchsteiner. *Leonardo da Vinci: Scientist, Inventor, Artist.* New York: Distribution Art, 1997. This exhibition catalog includes brief texts and essays about Leonardo's scientific and artistic drawings.

Most of the material chronicles his work as an inventor, and the material on aviation is most useful.

Maiorino, Giancarlo. *Leonardo da Vinci: The Daedalian Mythmaker.* University Park, PA: The Pennsylvania State University Press, 1992. Maiorino's book addresses Leonardo's philosophical nature and his use of drawings and paintings to express his beliefs, particularly Leonardo's drawings and designs of war machines, the *Vitruvian Man*, and the caricatures.

Mariotti, Josephine Rogers. *Monna Lisa: La 'Gioconda' del Magnifico Giuliano.* Florence: Polistampa, 2009. A thorough review of documentation surrounding the Giocondo family. Mariotti focuses on its affiliation with Giuliano de' Medici and the governors of Florence during the 16th century and argues that Giuliano saw Elisabetta as his muse of poetry, which inspired his commission of the portrait from Leonardo da Vinci.

Martines, Lauro. *Power and Imagination: City-States in Renaissance Italy*. New York: Knopf, 1979. Martines's broad survey of Italian political systems also addresses issues of art, education, economics, and philosophy. A brilliant blend of varying themes, his chapters on "The Princely Courts," "Art: An Alliance with Power," and "Invasion: City-States in Lightning and Twilight" are most pertinent for this course.

Masters, Roger. *Fortune is a River: Leonardo da Vinci and Niccolò Machiavelli's Magnificent Dream to Change the Course of Florentine History.* New York: The Free Press, 1998. An examination of the project to alter the course of the Arno River, this study also reviews the careers of Leonardo and Machiavelli before and after their work for the Florentine state.

Morley, Brian. "The Plant Illustrations of Leonardo da Vinci." *Burlington Magazine* 121, no. 918 (1979): 553–562. Examines a set of botanical drawings by Leonardo and identifies the flowers illustrated. Morley demonstrates that Leonardo's examination of plants was detailed and specific and merges the painter's interests in art and science nicely.

Nathan, Johannes. "Some Drawing Practices of Leonardo da Vinci: New Light on the *St. Anne.*" *Mitteilungen des Kunsthistorischen Institutes in Florenz* 36, nos. 1/2 (1992): 85–102. Considers a number of studies that led to the completion of the cartoon of 1501, followed by the cartoon now in the British Museum. Nathan demonstrates the evolution of the theme in Leonardo's career.

Nicholl, Charles. *Leonardo da Vinci: Flights of the Mind.* New York: Viking Press, 2004. This lengthy summary of the artist's career includes a discussion of his work with Verrocchio as an apprentice and his work on his arrival at Ludovico Sforza's court in 1482. Among the projects examined here is the *Madonna of the Rocks,* which is considered from the perspective of both the artist and the institutional patron that rejected it.

O'Malley, Charles Donald, ed. *Leonardo's Legacy: An International Symposium.* Berkeley: University of California Press, 1969. A collection of essays examining Leonardo's interests in physiology, architecture, engineering, and philosophy.

Pallanti, Giuseppe. *Mona Lisa Revealed: The True Identity of Leonardo's Model.* London: Thames and Hudson, 2006. Pallanti's short review of the documentation pertaining to the Giocondo family of Florence summarizes conventional interpretations of the painting and the circumstances of its commission. The author also presents observations about the career of Leonardo and argues that there was a personal relationship between the artist and the sitter that influenced his representation of Elisabetta.

Partridge, Loren. *Renaissance Rome*. Upper Saddle River, NJ: Prentice Hall, 1996. A review of the court of Pope Julius II and the contextual circumstances that motivated papal patronage at the turn of the 16th century. Short and focused, this book is an excellent introduction to the period and its main characters.

Pedretti, Carlo. *The Codex Atlanticus of Leonardo da Vinci: A Catalogue of Its Newly Restored Sheets.* 2 vols. New York: Johnson Reprint, 1978–1979. A thorough and exhaustive study of the largest collection of notes and drawings by Leonardo da Vinci. Pedretti examines the technical designs of the artist and considers them in the context of his work for Ludovico Sforza.

__________. *Leonardo Architect*. Translated by Sue Brill. New York: Rizzoli, 1981. An exhaustive survey of Leonardo's architectural, engineering, and sculptural drawings. Includes an examination of Leonardo's town planning for Pavia and Milan, his vision for the church of Santa Maria delle Grazie, and his conceptual drawings for structures conceived in collaboration with Donato Bramante.

__________. *Leonardo da Vinci: The Royal Palace at Romorantin.* Cambridge, MA: Harvard University Press, 1972. Pedretti argues that the designs for the French palace at Romorantin reflect Leonardo's earlier architectural conceptions.

Phillips, William D., Jr. and Carla Rahn Phillips. *The Worlds of Christopher Columbus.* New York: Cambridge University Press, 1992. An excellent survey of the life of the Genoese explorer. William and Carla Phillips describe the traditions that shaped his formative years and the results of his exploration of the Caribbean Sea in the 1490s.

Radke, Gary. *Leonardo da Vinci and the Art of Sculpture.* New Haven: Yale University Press, 2009. An exhibition catalogue dedicated to Leonardo's preliminary work for the Colossus of Milan, this book examines in detail various components of the project, including the complicated method of casting the bronze horse. Also addresses the problems faced (and the solutions found) by Leonardo during his work on the project for the *Trivulzio Monument.* An excellent treatment of one of Leonardo's least studied mediums.

Reti, Ladislao. "The Two Unpublished Manuscripts of Leonardo da Vinci in the Biblioteca Nacional of Madrid – II," *Burlington Magazine* 110, no. 779 (1968): 81–91. Motivated by the discovery of a new manuscript by Leonardo da Vinci in Spain, Reti published the inventory of Leonardo's library holdings in 1503, with comments on the books he owned and read. This article was an important contribution to Leonardo studies in that it alerted scholars to the artist's interests and personal education.

Richner, Jean Paul, trans. *The Diaries of Leonardo da Vinci.* New Orleans: Cornerstone Books, 2007. An exhaustive translation of hundreds of pages of notes by Leonardo da Vinci.

Richter, Irma. *Leonardo da Vinci: Notebooks*. 3rd edition. Thereza Wells, ed. and trans. New York: Oxford University Press, 2008. This selective compilation of notes and drawings includes his observations on flight, mechanics, physics, the arts, and philosophy.

Robison, Pauline Maguire. "Leonardo's *Trattato della Pittura*, Nicolas Poussin, and the Pursuit of Eloquence in Seventeenth-Century France." In *Leonardo da Vinci and the Ethics of Style*, edited by Claire Farago, 189–236. Manchester, UK: Manchester University Press, 2008. Robison examines the project undertaken by Nicolas Poussin to illustrate the first published version of Leonardo's *Treatise on Painting*. The French painter's debts to Leonardo, Raphael, and Italian classicism are considered in the context of ancient literature and the ideal of intellectual eloquence.

Rocke, Michael. *Forbidden Friendships: Homosexuality and Male Culture in Renaissance Florence.* New York: Oxford University Press, 1996. The first—and best—examination of homosexuality in 15th-century Florence, Rocke's important study reviews the laws against sodomy, the punishments meted out to the guilty, and the standards and expectations of society at large. Rocke's work helps us put Leonardo's indiscretion of 1476 squarely in the context of normative behavioral patterns of the age.

Rosand, David. *Painting in Cinquecento Venice.* New Haven, CT: Yale University Press, 1982. Through case studies, Rosand makes the point that Venetian painting of the 16th century was fundamentally different from its Florentine and Roman rivals in both technique and execution.

Schapiro, Meyer. "Leonardo and Freud: An Art-Historical Study," *Journal of the History of Ideas* 17, no. 2 (1956): 147–178. Schapiro reviewed Freud's essay from 1910 (see above) but offered an alternative interpretation, arguing that Leonardo's recollection invoked a medieval legend that promoted the theory that genius was passed along to human beings by the touch of a kite's tail to their lips.

Shearman, John. "Leonardo's Colour and Chiaroscuro," *Zeitschrift für Kunstgeschichte* 25, no. 1 (1962): 13–47. A lengthy discussion of the use of color and light in Leonardo's paintings. Shearman argues that the *Madonna of the Rocks* serves as an early illustration of Leonardo's theory of painting, which includes a tonal unity within paintings and depends on the use of light as a dramatic effect.

_________. *Mannerism.* New York: Penguin Books, 1967. The best description and definition of the cultural period that evolved out of Leonardo's classical age. Shearman's interest in fountains, gardens, and theatrical performances places sculptures and paintings into an important context.

Simons, Patricia. "Women in Frames: The Gaze, the Eyes, the Profile in Renaissance Portraiture." In *The Expanding Discourse: Feminism and Art History*, edited by Norma Broude and Mary D. Garrard, 39–57. New York: Icon Editions, 1992. This essay notes the custom of painting women in profile during the 15th century and argues that this artistic choice was tied to the social and cultural status of women at the time. An extremely important and influential essay in the history of Italian Renaissance studies.

Steinberg, Leo. *Leonardo's Incessant Last Supper.* New York: Zone Books, 2001. Steinberg's inventive (and unconventional) reading of *The Last Supper* argues that the painting was not a static image but rather touched on a variety of themes and subjects all at once. Still the most interesting approach to the mural in scholarly literature.

Stites, Raymond S. *The Sublimations of Leonardo da Vinci.* Washington, DC: Smithsonian Institution, 1970. Along with a translation of the Codex Trivulzianus, Stites connects the artistic and technical drawings of Leonardo to his painterly projects, including *The Adoration of the Magi*, *The Madonna of the Rocks*, and the other paintings produced by Leonardo during the early years of his tenure at the court of Ludovico Sforza.

Strathern, Paul. *The Artist, the Philosopher, and the Warrior: The Intersecting Lives of Da Vinci, Machiavelli, and Borgia and the World They Shaped.* New York: Bantam Books, 2009. Mostly a study of the patron and his interests. Strathern recounts the works and interests of Cesare Borgia in 1502, with an emphasis on his use of Leonardo and Machiavelli to further them.

Suh, H. Anna, ed. *Leonardo's Notebooks.* New York: Black Dog and Leventhal, 2005. This book is divided into sections according to the categories of Leonardo's interests. Unlike other collections of designs, this book includes translations of Leonardo's backwards notes that describe how his inventions were supposed to work.

Syson, Luke, ed. *Leonardo da Vinci: Painter at the Court of Milan.* London: Yale University Press, 2011. This exhibition catalog from the National Gallery's show of Leonardo's drawings and paintings produced in Milan during the 1480s and 1490s reviews the artist's work for Ludovico Sforza. Images and arguments work together nicely here, and the catalog of works—including the *Salvator Mundi* (attributed to Leonardo in 2011)—defines the School of Leonardo thoroughly.

Syson, Luke, and Rachel Billinge. "Leonardo da Vinci's Use of Underdrawing in the 'Virgin of the Rocks' in the National Gallery and 'St. Jerome' in the Vatican," *Burlington Magazine* 147, no. 1228 (2005): 450–463. Considers the preparatory studies and the iconographic features of these two paintings from the early mature phase of Leonardo's career.

Travers Newton, H., and John Spencer. "On the Location of Leonardo's *Battle of Anghiari.*" *The Art Bulletin* 64, no. 1 (1982): 45–52. Reports on an ultrasonic examination of the Salone dei Cinquecento, which indicates that the *Battle of Anghiari* is located on the west wall of the room and that enough of the mural survives to warrant a temporary removal of Vasari's painting that covers it today.

Turner, Richard. *Inventing Leonardo.* New York: Alfred A. Knopf, 1993. Turner addresses the myths, legends, and misconceptions about Leonardo da Vinci and argues that many of them were born of the period in which they were promulgated.

Vasari, Giorgio. *The Lives of the Artists.* Translated by Julia Conaway Bondanella and Peter Bondanella. New York: Oxford University Press, 1991. The first modern book of art history, Vasari's *Lives* contains the first attempt to piece together a biography of Leonardo da Vinci. It used a mixture of factual information, personal observation, gossip, legend, and hypothesis.

Verdon, Timothy. "Pagans in the Church: The *School of Athens* in Religious Context." In *Raphael's School of Athens,* edited by Marcia Hall, 114–130. New York: Cambridge University Press, 1997. A thoughtful interpretation of Raphael's famous fresco, which identifies the various scholars depicted there as well as some of the contemporary portraits that Raphael included.

Wallace, William. "Michelangelo In and Out of Florence Between 1500 and 1508." In *Leonardo, Michelangelo, and Raphael in Renaissance Florence from 1500 to 1508*, edited by Serafina Hager, 55–88. Washington, DC: Georgetown University Press, 1992. A brief account of Michelangelo's works during his Florentine period, Wallace's essay includes commentary on the cartoon of the *Battle of Cascina.*

Wasserman, Jack. "The Dating and Patronage of Leonardo's Burlington House Cartoon," *Art Bulletin* 53, no. 3 (1971): 312–325. Addresses the stylistic similarities between the London cartoon of the *St. Anne Madonna* and the *Madonna of the Yarnwinder*. Wasserman suggests that the patron for the cartoon was Louis XII of France.

Wittkower, Richard. *Architectural Principles in the Age of Humanism.* New York: W. W. Norton, 1971. A brilliant iconographic reading of Renaissance buildings, Wittkower's analysis includes an examination of Neoplatonic themes and the use of harmonic proportions in architecture of the period.

Zammattio, Carlo. "The Mechanics of Water and Stone." In *The Unknown Leonardo*, edited by Ladislao Reti, 190–215. London: McGraw-Hill, 1974. This chapter in a book of Leonardo's private notes and drawings features the engineer's interest in hydraulics and his experimental attempts to harness water power.

Zöllner, Frank, and Johannes Nathan. *Leonardo da Vinci: The Complete Paintings and Drawings*, 2 vols. London: Taschen, 2003. An overview of Leonardo's artistic career, with excellent color reproductions of his painterly works.

Zwijnenberg, Robert. "*St. John the Baptist* and the Essence of Painting." In *Leonardo da Vinci and the Ethics of Style*, edited by Claire Farago, 96–118. Manchester, UK: Manchester University Press, 2008. Zwijnenberg argues that *John the Baptist* is an experimental picture in which Leonardo tested his theories on painting, sfumato, light, and gesture.

Notes

Notes

Notes